The Develc

of the

Feeling for

In the Middle Ages and
Modern Times

BY

ALFRED BIESE

Burt Franklin Research and Source Works Series # 61

BURT FRANKLIN
NEW YORK

Published by
BURT FRANKLIN
514 West 113th Street
New York 25, N. Y.

ORIGINALLY PUBLISHED
LONDON - 1905

PN

B513

PRINTED IN THE U.S.A.

ISBN 978-1-331-54815-7
PIBN 10204394

1 MONTH OF
FREE
READING

at

www.ForgottenBooks.com

By purchasing this book you are eligible for one month membership to ForgottenBooks.com, giving you unlimited access to our entire collection of over 700,000 titles via our web site and mobile apps.

To claim your free month visit:

www.forgottenbooks.com/free204394

English
Français
Deutsche
Italiano
Español
Português

www.forgottenbooks.com

Mythology Photography **Fiction**
Fishing Christianity **Art** Cooking
Essays Buddhism Freemasonry
Medicine **Biology** Music **Ancient
Egypt** Evolution Carpentry Physics
Dance Geology **Mathematics** Fitness
Shakespeare **Folklore** Yoga Marketing
Confidence Immortality Biographies
Poetry **Psychology** Witchcraft
Electronics Chemistry History **Law**
Accounting **Philosophy** Anthropology
Alchemy Drama Quantum Mechanics
Atheism Sexual Health **Ancient History**
Entrepreneurship Languages Sport
Paleontology Needlework Islam
Metaphysics Investment Archaeology
Parenting Statistics Criminology
Motivational

AUTHOR'S PREFACE

THE encouraging reception of my " Development of the Feeling for Nature among the Greeks and Romans " gradually decided me, after some years, to carry the subject on to modern times. Enticing as it was, I did not shut my eyes to the great difficulties of a task whose dimensions have daunted many a savant since the days of Humboldt's clever, terse sketches of the feeling for Nature in different times and peoples. But the subject, once approached, would not let me go. Its solution seemed only possible from the side of historical development, not from that of *a priori* synthesis. The almost inexhaustible amount of material, especially towards modern times, has often obliged me to limit myself to typical forerunners of the various epochs, although, at the same time, I have tried not to lose the thread of general development. By the addition of the chief phases of landscape, painting, and garden craft, I have aimed at giving completeness to the historical picture ; but I hold that literature, especially poetry, as the most intimate medium of a nation's feelings, is the chief source of information in an enquiry which may form a contribution, not only to the history of taste, but also to the comparative history of literature. At a time too when the natural sciences are so highly developed, and the cult of Nature is so widespread, a book of this kind may perhaps claim the interest of that wide circle of educated readers to whom the modern delight in Nature on its many sides makes appeal. And this the more, since books are rare which seek to embrace the whole mental development of the Middle Ages and modern times, and are, at the same time, intended for and intelligible to all people of cultivation.

The book has been a work of love, and I hope it will be read with pleasure, not only by those whose special domain it touches, but by all who care for the eternal beauties of Nature. To those who know my earlier papers in the *Preussische Jahrbücher*, the *Zeitschrift für Vergleichende Litteraturgeschichte*, and the *Litteraturbeilage des Hamburgischen Correspondents*, I trust this fuller and more connected treatment of the theme will prove welcome.

ALFRED BIESE.

Published Translations of the following Authors have been used.

SANSCRIT.—Jones, Wilson, Arnold, anonymous translator in a publication of the Society for Resuscitation of Ancient Literature.

LATIN AND GREEK.—Lightfoot, Jowett, Farrar, Lodge, Dalrymple, Bigg, Pilkington, Hodgkin, De Montalembert, Cary, Lok, Murray, Gibb, a translator in Bohn's Classics.

ITALIAN.—Cary, Longfellow, Cayley, Robinson, Kelly, Bent, Hoole, Roscoe, Leigh Hunt, Lofft, Astley, Oliphant.

GERMAN.—Horton and Bell, Middlemore, Lytton, Swanwick, Dwight, Boylau, Bowring, Bell, Aytoun, Martin, Oxenford, Morrison, M'Cullum, Winkworth, Howorth, Taylor, Nind, Brooks, Lloyd, Frothingham, Ewing, Noel, Austin, Carlyle, Storr, Weston, Phillips.

SPANISH.—Markham, Major, Bowring, Hasell, M'Carthy, French.

FRENCH.—Anonymous translator of Rousseau.

PORTUGUESE.—Aubertin.

The Translator's thanks are also due to the author for a few alterations in and additions to the text, and to Miss Edgehill, Miss Tomlinson, and Dr B. Scheifers for translations from Greek and Latin, Italian, and Middle German respectively.

INTRODUCTION

NATURE in her ever-constant, ever-changing phases is indispensable to man, his whole existence depends upon her, and she influences him in manifold ways, in mind as well as body.

The physical character of a country is reflected in its inhabitants; the one factor of climate alone gives a very different outlook to northerner and southerner. But whereas primitive man, to whom the darkness of night meant anxiety, either feared Nature or worshipped her with awe, civilised man tries to lift her veil, and through science and art to understand her inner and outer beauty—the scientist in her laws, the man of religion in her relation to his Creator, the artist in reproducing the impressions she makes upon him.

Probably it has always been common to healthy minds to take some pleasure in her; but it needs no slight culture of heart and mind to grasp her meaning and make it clear to others. Her book lies open before us, but the interpretations have been many and dissimilar. A fine statue or a richly-coloured picture appeals to all, but only knowledge can appreciate it at its true value and discover the full meaning of the artist. And as with Art, so with Nature.

For Nature is the greatest artist, though dumb until man, with his inexplicable power of putting himself in her place, transferring to her his bodily and mental self, gives her speech.

Goethe said 'man never understands how anthropomorphic he is.' No study, however comprehensive, enables him to overstep human limits, or conceive a concrete being, even the highest, from a wholly impersonal point of view. His own self always remains an encumbering factor. In a real sense he only understands himself, and his measure for all things is man. To understand the world outside him, he must needs ascribe his own attributes to it, must lend his own being to find it again.

This unexplained faculty, or rather inherent necessity, which implies at once a power and a limit, extends to persons as well as things. The significant word sympathy expresses it. To feel a friend's grief is to put oneself in his place, think from his standpoint and in his mood—that is, suffer with him. The fear and sympathy which condition the action of tragedy depend upon the same mental process; one's own point of view is shifted to that of another, and when the two are in harmony, and only then, the claim of beauty is satisfied, and æsthetic pleasure results.

By the well-known expression of Greek philosophy, 'like is only understood by like,' the Pythagoreans meant that the mathematically trained mind is the organ by which the mathematically constructed cosmos is understood. The expression may also serve as an æsthetic aphorism. The charm of the simplest lyrical song depends upon the hearer's power to put himself in the mood or situation described by the poet, on an interplay between subject and object.

Everything in mental life depends upon this faculty. We observe, ponder, feel, because a kindred vibration in the object sets our own fibres in motion.

'You resemble the mind which you understand.'

It is a magic bridge from our own mind, making

access possible to a work of art, an electric current conveying the artist's ideas into our souls.

We know how a drama or a song can thrill us when our feeling vibrates with it; and that thrill, Faust tells us, is the best part of man.

If inventive work in whatever art or science gives the purest kind of pleasure, Nature herself seeming to work through the artist, rousing those impulses which come to him as revelations, there is pleasure also in the passive reception of beauty, especially when we are not content to remain passive, but trace out and rethink the artist's thoughts, remaking his work.

'To invent for oneself is beautiful; but to recognise gladly and treasure up the happy inventions of others is that less thine?' said Goethe in his *Jahreszeiten*; and in the *Aphorisms*, confirming what has just been said: 'We know of no world except in relation to man, we desire no art but that which is the expression of this relation.' And, further, 'Look into yourselves and you will find everything, and rejoice if outside yourselves, as you may say, lies a Nature which says yea and amen to all that you have found there.'

Certainly Nature only bestows on man in proportion to his own inner wealth. As Rückert says, 'the charm of a landscape lies in this, that it seems to reflect back that part of one's inner life, of mind, mood, and feeling, which we have given it.' And Ebers, 'Lay down your best of heart and mind before eternal Nature; she will repay you a thousand-fold, with full hands.'

And Vischer remarks, 'Nature at her greatest is not so great that she can work without man's mind.' Every landscape can be beautiful and stimulating if human feeling colours it, and it will be most so to him who brings the richest endowment of heart and mind to bear: Nature only discloses her whole self to a whole man.

But it is under the poet's wand above all, that, like the marble at Pygmalion's breast, she grows warm and breathes and answers to his charm ; as in that symbolic saga, the listening woods and waters and the creatures followed Orpheus with his lute. Scientific knowledge, optical, acoustical, meteorological, geological, only widens and deepens love for her and increases and refines the sense of her beauty. In short, deep feeling for Nature always proves considerable culture of heart and mind.

There is a constant analogy between the growth of this feeling and that of general culture.

As each nation and time has its own mode of thought, which is constantly changing, so each period has its 'landscape eye.' The same rule applies to individuals. Nature, as Jean Paul said, is made intelligible to man in being for ever made flesh. We cannot look at her impersonally, we must needs give her form and soul, in order to grasp and describe her.

Vischer says [1] ' it is simply by an act of comparison that we think we see our own life in inanimate objects.' We say that Nature's clearness is like clearness of mind, that her darkness and gloom are like a dark and gloomy mood ; then, omitting ' like,' we go on to ascribe our qualities directly to her, and say, this neighbourhood, this air, this general tone of colour, is cheerful, melancholy, and so forth. Here we are prompted by an undeveloped dormant consciousness which really only compares, while it seems to take one thing for another. In this way we come to say that a rock projects boldly, that fire rages furiously over a building, that a summer evening with flocks going home at sunset is peaceful and idyllic ; that autumn, dripping with rain, its willows sighing in the wind, is elegiac and melancholy and so forth.

Perhaps Nature would not prove to be this ready symbol of man's inner life were there no secret rapport between the two. It is as if, in some mysterious way, we meet in her another mind, which speaks a language we know, wakening a foretaste of kinship; and whether the soul she expresses is one we have lent her, or her own which we have divined, the relationship is still one of give and take.

Let us take a rapid survey of the course of this feeling in antiquity. Pantheism has always been the home of a special tenderness for Nature, and the poetry of India is full of intimate dealings between man and plants and animals.

They are found in the loftiest flights of religious enthusiasm in the Vedas, where, be it only in reference to the splendour of dawn or the ' golden-handed sun,' Nature is always assumed to be closely connected with man's inner and outer life. Later on, as Brahminism appeared, deepening the contemplative side of Hindoo character, and the drama and historical plays came in, generalities gave way to definite localizing, and in the Epics ornate descriptions of actual landscape took independent place. Nature's sympathy with human joys and griefs was taken for granted, and she played a part of her own in drama.

In the *Mahábhárata*, when Damajanti is wandering in search of her lost Nala and sees the great mountain top, she asks it for her prince.

> Oh mountain lord !
> Far seen and celebrated hill, that cleav'st
> The blue o' the sky, refuge of living things,
> Most noble eminence, I worship thee ! . . .
> O Mount, whose double ridge stamps on the sky
> Yon line, by five-score splendid pinnacles
> Indented ; tell me, in this gloomy wood
> Hast thou seen Nala ? Nala, wise and bold !
> Ah mountain ! why consolest thou me not,
> Answering one word to sorrowful, distressed,
> Lonely, lost Damajanti ?

And when she comes to the tree Asoka, she implores :

Ah, lovely tree ! that wavest here
Thy crown of countless shining clustering blooms
As thou wert woodland king ! Asoka tree !
Tree called the sorrow-ender, heart's-ease tree !
Be what thy name saith ; end my sorrow now,
Saying, ah, bright Asoka, thou hast seen
My Prince, my dauntless Nala—seen that lord
Whom Damajanti loves and his foes fear.

In Maghas' epic, *The Death of Sisupala*, plants and animals lead the same voluptuous life as the ' deep-bosomed, wide-hipped ' girls with the ardent men.

' The mountain Raivataka touches the ether with a thousand heads, earth with a thousand feet, the sun and moon are his eyes. When the birds are tired and tremble with delight from the caresses of their mates, he grants them shade from lotos leaves. Who in the world is not astonished when he has climbed, to see the prince of mountains who over-shadows the ether and far-reaching regions of earth, standing there with his great projecting crags, while the moon's sickle trembles on his summit ? '

In Kalidasa's *Urwasi*, the deserted King who is searching for his wife asks the peacock :

Oh tell,
If, free on the wing as you soar,
You have seen the loved nymph I deplore—
You will know her, the fairest of damsels fair,
By her large soft eye and her graceful air ;
Bird of the dark blue throat and eye of jet,
Oh tell me, have you seen the lovely face
Of my fair bride—lost in this dreary wilderness ?

and the mountain :

Say mountain, whose expansive slope confines
The forest verge, oh, tell me hast thou seen
A nymph as beauteous as the bride of love
Mounting with slender frame thy steep ascent,
Or wearied, resting in thy crowning woods ?

As he sits by the side of the stream, he asks whence comes its charm :

Whilst gazing on the stream, whose new swollen waters
Yet turbid flow, what strange imaginings
Possess my soul and fill it with delight.
The rippling wave is like her aching brow ;
The fluttering line of storks, her timid tongue ;
The foaming spray, her white loose floating vest ;
And this meandering course the current tracks
Her undulating gait.

Then he sees a creeper without flowers, and a strange attraction impels him to embrace it, for its likeness to his lost love :

Vine of the wilderness, behold
A lone heartbroken wretch in me,
Who dreams in his embrace to fold
His love, as wild he clings to thee.

Thereupon the creeper transforms itself into Urwasi.

In Kalidasa's *Sakuntala*, too, when the pretty girls are watering the flowers in the garden, Sakuntala says : ' It is not only in obedience to our father that I thus employ myself. I really feel the affection of a sister for these young plants.' Taking it for granted that the mango tree has the same feeling for herself, she cries : ' Yon Amra tree, my friends, points with the fingers of its leaves, which the gale gently agitates, and seems inclined to whisper some secret '; and with maiden shyness, attributing her own thoughts about love to the plants, one of her comrades says : ' See, my Sakuntala, how yon fresh Mallica which you have surnamed Vanadosini or Delight of the Grove, has chosen the sweet Amra for her bridegroom. . . .'

' How charming is the season, when the nuptials even of plants are thus publicly celebrated ! '—and elsewhere :

' Here is a plant, Sakuntala, which you have forgotten.' Sakuntala : ' Then I shall forget myself.'

Birds, clouds,[2] and waves are messengers of love ; all Nature grieves at the separation of lovers. When

Sakuntala is leaving her forest, one of her friends says: 'Mark the affliction of the forest itself when the time of your departure approaches!

'The female antelope browses no more on the collected Cusa grass, and the pea-hen ceases to dance on the lawn; the very plants of the grove, whose pale leaves fall on the ground, lose their strength and their beauty.'

The poems of India, especially those devoted to descriptions of Nature, abound in such bold, picturesque personifications, which are touching, despite their extravagance, through their intense sympathy with Nature. They shew the Hindoo attitude toward Nature in general, as well as his boundless fancy. I select one example from 'The Gathering of the Seasons' in Kalidasa's *Ritusanhare* : a description of the Rains.

'Pouring rain in torrents at the request of the thirst-stricken Chatakas, and emitting slow mutterings pleasing to the ears, clouds, bent down by the weight of their watery contents, are slowly moving on. . . .

'The rivers being filled up with the muddy water of the rivers, their force is increased. Therefore, felling down the trees on both the banks, they, like unchaste women, are going quickly towards the ocean. . . .

'The heat of the forest has been removed by the sprinkling of new water, and the Ketaka flowers have blossomed. On the branches of trees being shaken by the wind, it appears that the entire forest is dancing in delight. On the blossoming of Ketaka flowers it appears that the forest is smiling. Thinking, "he is our refuge when we are bent down by the weight of water, the clouds are enlivening with torrents the mount Vindhya assailed with fierce heat (of the summer)."'

Charming pictures and comparisons are numerous, though they have the exaggeration common to oriental imagination. 'Love was the cause of my distemper, and love has healed it ; as a summer's day, grown black with clouds, relieves all animals from the heat which itself had caused.'

'Should you be removed to the ends of the world, you will be fixed in this heart, as the shade of a lofty tree remains with it even when the day is departed.'

'The tree of my hope which had risen so luxuriantly is broken down.'

'Removed from the bosom of my father, like a young sandal tree rent from the hill of Malaja, how shall I exist in a strange soil ? '

This familiar intercourse with Nature stood far as the poles asunder from the monotheistic attitude of the Hebrew. The individual, it is true, was nothing in comparison with Brahma, the All-One ; but the divine pervaded and sanctified all things, and so gave them a certain value ; whilst before Jehovah, throned above the world, the whole universe was but dust and ashes. The Hindoo, wrapt in the contemplation of Nature, described her at great length and for her own sake, the Hebrew only for the sake of his Creator. She had no independent significance for him ; he looked at her only ' sub specie eterni Dei,' in the mirror of the eternal God. Hence he took interest in her phases only as revelations of his God, noting one after another only to group them synthetically under the idea of Godhead. Hence too, despite his profound inwardness—' The heart is deceitful above all things and desperately wicked, who can know it ? ' (*Jeremiah*)—human individuality was only expressed in its relation to Jehovah.

'The heavens declare the glory of God ; and the firmament sheweth his handiwork. Day unto day uttereth speech, and night unto night sheweth knowledge.'—*Psalm* 19.

'Let the heavens rejoice and let the earth be glad ; let the sea roar, and the fulness thereof.

' Let the field be joyful, and all that is therein ; then shall all the trees of the wood rejoice.'—*Psalm* 96.

' Let the floods clap their hands : let the hills be joyful together.'—*Psalm* 98.

' The floods have lifted up, O Lord, the floods have lifted up their voice; the floods lift up their waves. The Lord on high is mightier than the noise of many waters, yea, than the mighty waves of the sea.'—*Psalm* 93.

' The sea saw it, and fled : Jordan was driven back. The mountains skipped like rams, and the little hills like lambs.'—*Psalm* 114.

' The waters saw thee, O God, the waters saw thee ; they were afraid : the depths also were troubled.'—*Psalm* 77.

All these lofty personifications of inanimate Nature only characterise her in her relation to another, and that not man but God. Nothing had significance by itself, Nature was but a book in which to read of Jehovah ; and for this reason the Hebrew could not be wrapt in her, could not seek her for her own sake, she was only a revelation of the Deity.

' Lord, how great are thy works, in wisdom hast thou made them all : the earth is full of thy goodness.'

Yet there is a fiery glow of enthusiasm in the songs in praise of Jehovah's wonders in creation.

' O Lord my God, thou art very great ; thou art clothed with honour and majesty.

' Who coverest thyself with light as with a garment ; who stretchest out the heavens like a curtain.

' Who layeth the beams of his chambers in the waters ; who maketh the clouds his chariot ; who walketh upon the wings of the wind.

' Who maketh his angels spirits ; his ministers a flaming fire ; who laid the foundations of the earth, that it should not be removed for ever.

' Thou coveredst the deep as with a garment ; the waters stood above the mountains.

'At thy rebuke they fled; at the voice of thy thunder they hasted away.

'They go up by the mountains; they go down by the valleys unto the place which thou hast founded for them.

'Thou hast set a bound that they may not pass over; that they turn not again to cover the earth.

'He sendeth the springs into the valleys, which run among the hills.

'They give drink to every beast of the field: the wild asses quench their thirst.

'By them shall the fowls of the heaven have their habitation, which sing among the branches. . .

'He causeth the grass to grow for the cattle, and herb for the service of man : that he may bring forth food out of the earth.

'And wine that maketh glad the heart of man. . .

'The trees of the Lord are full of sap ; the cedars of Lebanon, which he hath planted.

'Where the birds make their nests : as for the stork, the fir trees are her house.

'The high hills are a refuge for the wild goats, and the rocks for the conies.

'He appointed the moon for seasons: the sun knoweth his going down.

'Thou makest darkness, and it is night : wherein all the beasts of the forest do creep forth.

'The young lions roar after their prey, and seek their meat from God.

'The sun ariseth, they gather themselves together, and lay them down in their dens.

'Man goeth forth to his work and to his labour until the evening. . . .

'This great and wide sea, wherein are creeping things innumerable, both small and great beasts. . . .

'He looketh on the earth, and it trembleth ; he toucheth the hills, and they smoke.

'I will sing unto the Lord as long as I live; I will

sing praise to my God as long as I have my being.' —*Psalm* 104.

And what a lofty point of view is shewn by the overpowering words which Job puts into the mouth of Jehovah: 'Where wast thou when I laid the foundations of the earth? Declare, if thou hast understanding. Who hath laid the measures thereof if thou knowest, or who hath stretched the line upon it?

' Whereupon are the foundations thereof fastened? or who laid the corner stone thereof?

' When the morning stars sang together, and all the sons of God shouted for joy? . . .

' Hast thou commanded the morning since thy days; and caused the dayspring to know his place?

' That it might take hold of the ends of the earth, that the wicked might be shaken out of it? . . .

' Hast thou entered into the springs of the sea, or hast thou walked in the search of the deep? . . .

' Declare, if thou knowest it all! . . .

' Where is the way where light dwelleth, and as for darkness, where is the place thereof?' etc.

Compare with this *Isaiah* xl. verse 12, etc.

Metaphors too, though poetic and fine, are not individualized.

' Deep calleth unto deep at the noise of thy waterspouts: all thy waves and thy billows are gone over me.'—*Psalm* 42.

' Save me, O God; for the waters are come in unto my soul. I sink in deep mire, where there is no standing; I am come into deep waters, where the floods overflow me.'—*Psalm* 69.

There are many pictures from the animal world; and these are more elaborate in Job than elsewhere (see *Job* xl. and xli.). Personifications, as we have seen, are many, but Nature is only called upon to sympathise with man in isolated cases, as, for instance, in 2 *Samuel* i.:

' Ye mountains of Gilboa, let there be no dew,

neither let there be rain upon you, nor fields of offerings: for there the shield of the mighty is vilely cast away, the shield of Saul, as if he had not been anointed with oil.'

The Cosmos unfolded itself to the Hebrew[3] as one great whole, and the glance fixed upon a distant horizon missed the nearer lying detail of phenomena. His imagination ranged the universe with the wings of the wind, and took vivid note of air, sky, sea, and land, but only, so to speak, in passing; it never rested there, but hurried past the boundaries of earth to Jehovah's throne, and from that height looked down upon creation.

The attitude of the Greek was very different. Standing firmly rooted in the world of sense, his open mind and his marvellous eye for beauty appreciated the glorious external world around him down to its finest detail. His was the race of the beautiful, the first in history to train all its powers into harmony to produce a culture of beauty equal in form and contents, and his unique achievement in art and science enriched all after times with lasting standards of the great and beautiful.

The influence of classic literature upon the Middle Ages and modern times has not only endured, but has gone on increasing with the centuries; so that we must know the position reached by Greece and Rome as to feeling for Nature, in order to discover whether the line of advance in the Middle Ages led directly forward or began by a backward movement— a zigzag.

The terms ancient and modern, naive and sentimental, classic and romantic, have been shibboleths of culture from Jean Paul, Schiller, and Hegel, to Vischer. Jean Paul, in his *Vorschule zur Aesthetik*, compares the ideally simple Greek poetry, with its objectivity, serenity, and moral grace, with the musical poetry of the romantic period, and speaks of one as the sunlight that pervades our waking

hours, the other as the moonlight that gleams fitfully
on our dreaming ones. Schiller's epoch-making
essay *On Naive and Sentimental Poetry*, with its
rough division into the classic-naive depending on
a harmony between nature and mind, and the
modern-sentimental depending on a longing for a
lost paradise, is constantly quoted to shew that the
Greeks took no pleasure in Nature. This is mis-
leading. Schiller's Greek was very limited ; in the
very year (1795) in which the essay appeared in
The Hours, he was asking Humboldt's advice as to
learning Greek, with special reference to Homer and
Xenophon.

To him Homer was the Greek *par excellence*, and
who would not agree with him to-day ?

As in Greek mythology, that naive poem of
Nature, the product of the artistic impulse of the
race to stamp its impressions in a beautiful and
harmonious form, so in the clear-cut comparisons in
Homer, the feeling for Nature is profound ; but the
Homeric hero had no personal relations with her,
no conscious leaning towards her ; the descriptions
only served to frame human action, in time or
space.

But that cheerful, unreflecting youth of mankind,
that naive Homeric time, was short in spite of
Schiller, who, in the very essay referred to, included
Euripides, Virgil, and Horace among the sentimental,
and Shakespeare among the naive, poets—a fact often
overlooked.

In line with the general development of culture,
Greek feeling for Nature passed through various
stages. These can be clearly traced from objective
similes and naive, homely comparisons to poetic
personifications, and so on to more extended descrip-
tions, in which scenery was brought into harmony
or contrast with man's inner life ; until finally, in
Hellenism, Nature was treated for her own sake,
and man reduced to the position of supernumerary

both in poetry and also — so approaching the modern—in landscape-painting.

Greece had her sentimental epoch ; she did not, as we have said, long remain naïve. From Sophist days a steady process of decomposition went on— in other words, a movement towards what we call modern, a movement which to the classic mind led backward ; but from the wider standpoint of general development meant advance. For the path of culture is always the same in the nations ; it leads first upward and then downward, and all ripening knowledge, while it enriches the mind, brings with it some unforeseen loss. Mankind pays heavily for each new gain ; it paid for increased subjectivity and inwardness by a loss in public spirit and patriotism which, once the most valued of national possessions, fell away before the increasing indi- viduality, the germ of the modern spirit. For what is the modern spirit but limitless individuality ?

The greater the knowledge of self, the richer the inner life. Man becomes his own chief problem— he begins to watch the lightest flutter of his own feelings, to grasp and reflect upon them, to look upon himself in fact as in a mirror ; and it is in this doubling of the ego, so to speak, that sentimentality in the modern sense consists. It leads to love of solitude, the fittest state for the growth of a conscious love of Nature, for, as Rousseau said ' all noble passions are formed in solitude,' 'tis there that one recognizes one's own heart as ' the rarest and most valuable of all possessions.' ' Oh, what a fatal gift of Heaven is a feeling heart ! ' and elsewhere he said : ' Hearts that are warmed by a divine fire find a pure delight in their own feelings which is independent of fate and of the whole world.' Euripides, too, loved solitude, and avoided the noise of town life by retiring to a grotto at Salamis which he had arranged for himself with a view of the sea ; for which reason, his biographer tells us, most of his similes are drawn from the sea.   He, rather than Petrarch or Rousseau, was the father of sentimentality. His morbidly sensitive Hippolytos cries 'Alas! would it were possible that I should see myself standing face to face, in which case I should have wept for the sorrows that we suffer'; and in the chorus of *The Suppliants* we have : 'This insatiate joy of mourning leads me on like as the liquid drop flowing from the sun - trodden rock, ever increasing of groans.' In Euripides we have the first loosening of that ingenuous bond between Nature and the human spirit, as the Sophists laid the axe to the root of the old Hellenic ideas and beliefs. Subjectivity had already gained in strength from the birth of the lyric, that most individual of all expressions of feeling; and since the lyric cannot dispense with the external world, classic song now shewed the tender subjective feeling for Nature which we see in Sappho, Pindar, and Simonides.   Yet Euripides (and Aristophanes, whose painful mad laugh, as Doysen says, expresses the same distraction and despair as the deep melancholy of Euripides) only paved the way for that sentimental, idyllic feeling for Nature which dwelt on her quiet charms for their own sake, as in Theocritus, and, like the modern, rose to greater intensity in the presence of the amorous passion, as we see in Kallimachos and the Anthology.   It was the outcome of Hellenism, of which sentimental introspection, the freeing of the ego from the bonds of race and position, and the discovery of the individual in all directions of human existence, were marks.   And this feeling developing from Homer to Longos, from unreflecting to conscious and then to sentimental pleasure in Nature, was expressed not only in poetry but in painting, although the latter never fully mastered technique.

The common thoughtless statement, so often supported by quotations from Schiller, Gervinus, and others, that Greek antiquity was not alive to the beauty of Nature and her responsiveness to human moods, and neither painted scenery nor felt the melancholy poetic charm of ruins and tombs, is therefore a perversion of the truth ; but it must be conceded that the feeling which existed then was but the germ of our modern one. It was fettered by the specific national beliefs concerning the world and deities, by the undeveloped state of the natural sciences, which, except botany, still lay in swaddling-clothes, by the new influence of Christendom, and by that strict feeling for style which, very much to its advantage, imposed a moderation that would have excluded much of our senseless modern rhapsody.

It was not unnatural that Schiller, in distaste for the weak riot of feeling and the passion for describing Nature which obtained in his day, was led to overpraise the Homeric naïvete and overblame the sentimentality which he wrongly identified with it.

In all that is called art, the Romans were pupils of the Greek, and their achievements in the region of beauty cannot be compared with his. But they advanced the course of general culture, and their feeling — always more subjective, abstract, self-conscious, and reflective — has a comparatively familiar, because modern, ring in the great poets.

The preference for the practical and social-economic is traceable in their feeling for Nature. Their mythology also lay too much within the bounds of the intelligible ; shewed itself too much in forms and ceremonies, in a cult ; but it had not lost the sense of awe—it still heard the voices of mysterious powers in the depths of the forest.

The dramatists wove effective metaphors and descriptions of Nature into their plays.

Lucretius laid the foundations of a knowledge of her which refined both his enjoyment and his descriptions ; and the elegiac sentimental style, which we see developed in Tibullus, Propertius, Ovid, Virgil.

and Horace, first came to light in the great lyrist Catullus. In Imperial times feeling for Nature grew with the growth of culture in general ; men turned to her in times of bad cheer, and found comfort in the great sky spaces, the constant stars, and forests that trembled with awe of the divine Numen.

It was so with Seneca, a pantheist through and through. Pliny the younger was quite modern in his choice of rural solitudes, and his appreciation of the views from his villa. With Hadrian and Apuleius the Roman rococo literature began ; Apuleius was astonishingly modern, and Ausonius was almost German in the depth and tenderness of his feeling for Nature. Garden-culture and landscape-painting shewed the same movement towards the sympathetic and elegiac-sentimental.

Those who deny the Roman feeling for Nature might learn better from a glance at the ruins of their villas. As H. Nissen says in his *Italische Landeskunde* :

'It was more than mere fashion which drew the Roman to the sea-side, and attracted so strongly all those great figures, from the elder Scipio Africanus and his noble daughter, Cornelia, down to Augustus and Tiberius and their successors, whenever their powers flagged in the Forum. There were soft breezes to cool the brow, colour and outline to refresh the eye, and wide views that appealed to a race born to extensive lordship.

'In passing along the desolate, fever-stricken coasts of Latium and Campania to-day, one comes upon many traces of former splendour, and one is reminded that the pleasure which the old Romans took in the sea-side was spoilt for those who came after them by the havoc of the time.'

In many points, Roman feeling for Nature was more developed than Greek. For instance, the Romans appreciated landscape as a whole, and

distance, light and shade in wood and water, reflec-
tions, the charms of hunting and rowing, day-dreams
on a mountain side, and so forth.

That antiquity and the Middle Ages had any
taste for romantic scenery has been energetically
denied; but we can find a trace of it. The land-
scape which the Roman admired was level, graceful,
and gentle; he certainly did not see any beauty in
the Alps. Livy's 'Foeditas Alpinum' and the
dreadful descriptions of Ammian, with others, are
the much - quoted vouchers for this. Nor is it
surprising; for modern appreciation, still in its
youth, is really due to increased knowledge about
Nature, to a change of feeling, and to the conveni-
ences of modern travelling, unknown 2000 years
ago.

The dangers and hardships of those days must
have put enjoyment out of the question; and only
served to heighten the unfavourable contrast be-
tween the wildness of the mountain regions and the
cultivation of Italy.

Lucretius looked at wild scenery with horror,
but later on it became a favourite subject for de-
scription; and Seneca notes, as shewing a morbid
state of mind, in his essay on tranquillity of mind,
that travelling not only attracts men to delightful
places, but that some even exclaim : ' Let us go now
into Campania; now that delicate soil delighteth
us, let us visit the wood countries, let us visit the
forest of Calabria, and let us seek some pleasure
amidst the deserts, in such sort as these wandering
eyes of ours may be relieved in beholding, at our
pleasure, the strange solitude of these savage places.'

We have thus briefly surveyed on the one hand,
in theory, the conditions under which a conscious
feeling for Nature develops, and the forms in which
it expresses itself ; and, on the other, the course this
feeling has followed in antiquity among the Hindoos,
Hebrews, Greeks, and Romans. The movement

toward the modern, toward the subjective and individual, lies clear to view. We will now trace its gradual development along lines which are always strictly analogous to those of culture in general, through the Middle Ages.

Feeling for Nature

CHAPTER I

CHRISTIANITY AND GERMANISM

WHEN the heathen world had outlived its faculties, and its creative power had failed, it sank into the ocean of the past—a sphinx, with her riddle guessed, —and mediæval civilization arose, founded upon Christianity and Germanism. There are times in the world's history when change seems to be abrupt, the old to be swept away and all things made new at a stroke, as if by the world-consuming fire of the old Saga. But, in reality, all change is gradual; the old is for ever failing and passing out of sight, to be taken up as a ferment into the ever emerging new, which changes and remodels as it will. It was so with Christianity. It is easy to imagine that it arose suddenly, like a phœnix, from the ashes of heathendom; but, although dependent at heart upon the sublime personality of its Founder, it was none the less a product of its age, and a result of gradual development—a river with sources partly in Judea, partly in Hellas. And mediæval Christianity never denied the traces of its double origin.

Upon this syncretic soil its literature sprang up, moulded as to matter upon Old Testament and specifically Christian models, as to form upon the great writers of antiquity; but matter and form are only separable in the abstract, and the Middle Ages are woven through and through with both Greco-Roman and Jewish elements.

But these elements were unfavourable to the development of feeling for Nature; Judaism admitted no delight in her for her own sake, and Christianity intensified the Judaic opposition between God and the world, Creator and created.

' Love not the world, neither the things that are in the world; if any man love the world, the love of the Father is not in him ' : by which John meant, raise your eyes to your Heavenly Father, throned above the clouds.

Christianity in its stringent form was transcendental, despising the world and renouncing its pleasures. It held that Creation, through the entrance of sin, had become a caricature, and that earthly existence had only the very limited value of a thoroughfare to the eternal Kingdom.

While joy in existence characterized the Hellenic world until its downfall, and the Greek took life serenely, delighting in its smooth flow; with Christianity, as Jean Paul put it, ' all the present of earth vanished into the future of Heaven, and the Kingdom of the Infinite arose upon the ruins of the finite.'

The beauty of earth was looked upon as an enchantment of the devil; and sin, the worm in the fruit, lurked in its alluring forms.

Classic mythology created a world of its own, dimly veiled by the visible one; every phase of Nature shewed the presence or action of deities with whom man had intimate relations; every form of life, animated by them, held something familiar to him, even sacred—his landscape was absorbed by the gods.

To Judaism and Christianity, Nature was a fallen angel, separated as far as possible from her God. They only recognized one world—that of spirit; and one sphere of the spiritual, religion—the relation between God and man. Material things were a delusion of Satan's ; the heaven on which their eyes were fixed was a very distant one.

The Hellenic belief in deities was pandemonistic and cosmic ; Christianity, in its original tendency, anti-cosmic and hostile to Nature. And Nature, like the world at large, only existed for it in relation to its Creator, and was no longer ' the great mother of all things,' but merely an instrument in the hands of Providence.

The Greek looked at phenomena in detail, in their inexhaustible variety, rarely at things as a whole ; the Christian considered Nature as a work of God, full of wonderful order, in which detail had only the importance of a link in a chain.

As Lotze says, ' The creative artistic impulse could be of no use to a conception of life in which nothing retained independent significance, but everything referred to or symbolized something else.' But yet, the idea of individuality, of the importance of the ego, gained ground as never before through this introspection and merging of material in spiritual, this giving spirit the exclusive sway ; and Christianity, while it broke down the barriers of nation, race, and position, and widened the cleft between Nature and spirit, discovered at the same time the worth of the individual.

And this individuality was one of the chief steps towards an artistic, that is, individual point of view about Nature, for it was not possible to consider her freely and for her own sake alone, until the unlimited independence of mind had been recognized.

But the full development of Christianity was only reached when it blended with the Germanic spirit, with the German Gemüth (for which no other language has a word), and intensified, by so doing, the innately subjective temperament of the race.

The northern climate gives pause for the development of the inner life ; its long bleak winter, with the heavy atmosphere and slow coming of spring, wake a craving for light and warmth, and throw man back on himself. This inward inclination, which made itself felt very early in the German race, by bringing out the contemplative and independent sides of his character, and so disinclining him for combined action with his fellows, forwarded the growth of the over-ripe seeds of classic culture and vital Christianity.

The Romanic nations, with their brilliant, sharply-defined landscape and serene skies, always retained something of the objective delight in life which belonged to antiquity ; they never felt that mysterious impulse towards dreams and enthusiastic longing which the Northerner draws from his lowering skies and dark woods, his mists on level and height, the grey in grey of his atmosphere, and his ever varying landscape. A raw climate drives man indoors in mind as well as body, and prompts that craving for spring and delight in its coming which have been the chief notes in northern feeling for Nature from earliest times.

Vischer has shewn in his *Aesthetik*, that German feeling was early influenced by the different forms of plant life around it. Rigid pine, delicate birch, stalwart oak, each had its effect ; and the wildness and roughness of land, sea, and animal life in the North combined with the cold of the climate to create the taste for domestic comfort, for fireside dreams, and thought-weaving by the hearth.

Nature schooled the race to hard work and scanty pleasure, and yet its relationship to her was deep and heartfelt from the first. Devoutly religious, it gazed at her with mingled love and fear ; and the deposit of its ideas about her was its mythology.

Its gods dwelt in mountain tops, holes in the rocks, and rivers, and especially in dark forests and in the leafy boughs of sacred trees ; and the howling of wind, the rustle of leaves, the soughing in the tree tops, were sounds of their presence. The worship of woods lasted far into Christian times, especially among the Saxons and Frisians.[1]

Wodan was the all-powerful father of gods and men—the highest god, who, as among all the Aryan nations, represented Heaven. Light was his shining helmet, clouds were the dark cap he put on when he spread rain over the earth, or crashed through the air as a wild hunter with his raging pack. His son Donar shewed himself in thunder and lightning, as he rode with swinging axe on his goat-spanned car. Mountains were sacred to both, as plants to Ziu. Freyr and Freya were goddesses of fertility, love, and spring ; a ram was sacred to them, whose golden fleece illuminated night as well as day, and who drew their car with a horse's speed.[2] As with Freya, an image of the goddess Nerthus was drawn through the land in spring, to announce peace and fertility to mortals.

The suggestive myth of Baldur, god of light and spring, killed by blind Hödur, was the expression of general grief at the passing of beauty.

The *Edda* has a touching picture of the sorrow of Nature, of her trees and plants, when the one beloved of all living things fell, pierced by an arrow. Holda was first the mild and gracious goddess, then a divine being, encompassing the earth. She might be seen in morning hours by her favourite haunts of lake and spring, a beautiful white woman, who bathed and vanished. When snow fell, she was making her bed, and the feathers flew. Agriculture and domestic order were under her care.

Ostara was goddess of bright dawn, of rising light, and awakening spring, as Hel of subterranean night, the darkness of the underworld. Frigg, wife of the highest god, knew the story of existence, and protected marriage. She was the Northern Juno or Hera.

Ravines and hollows in the mountains were the dwelling-places of the dwarfs (Erdmännlein), sometimes friendly, sometimes unfriendly to man ; now peaceful and helpful, now impish spirits of mischief in cloud caps and grey coats, thievish and jolly.

They were visible by moonlight, dancing in the fields ; and when their track was found in the dew,[1] a good harvest was expected. Popular belief took the floating autumn cobwebs for the work of elves and fairies. The spirits of mountain and wood were related to the water-spirits, nixies who sat combing their long hair in the sun, or stretched up lovely arms out of the water. The elves belonged to the more spiritual side of Nature, the giants to the grosser. Rocks and stones were the weapons of the giants; they removed mountains and hills, and boulders were pebbles shaken out of their shoes.

Among animals the horse was sacred to many deities, and gods and goddesses readily transformed themselves into birds. Two ravens, Hugin and Munin, whose names signify thought and memory, were Odin's constant companions. The gift of prophecy was ascribed to the cuckoo, as its monotonous voice heralded the spring :

Kukuk vam haven, wo lange sall ik leven ?

There were many legends of men and snakes who exchanged shapes, and whom it was unlucky to kill.[1]

The sun and moon, too, were familiar figures in legends.

Their movement across the sky was a flight from two pursuing wolves, of which one, the Fenris wolf, was fated one day to catch and devour the moon. The German, like the Greek, dreaded nothing more than the eclipse of sun or moon, and connected it with the destruction of all things and the end of the world. In the moon spots he saw a human form carrying a hare or a stick or an axe on his shoulder,

The Solstices impressed him most of all, with their almost constant day in sum ner, almost constant night in winter. Sun, moon, and stars were the eyes of heaven ; there was a pious custom to greet the stars before going to bed. Still earlier, they were sparks of fire from Muspilli, to light the gods home. Night, day, and the sun had their cars— night and day with one horse, the sun with two : sunrise brought sounds sweeter than the song of birds or strings ; the rising sun, it was said, rings for joy, murmuring daybreak laughs.'

Day brought joy, night sorrow ; the first was good and friendly, the second bad and hostile. The birds greeted daytime and summer with songs of delight, but grieved in silence through night and winter : the first swallow and stork were hailed as spring's messengers. May with greening woods led in beloved summer, frost and snow the winter.

So myth, fable, and legend were interlaced in confusion ; who can separate the threads ?

At any rate, the point of view which they indicate remained the common one even far into the Middle Ages, and shewed simple familiar intercourse with Nature. Even legal formulæ were full of pictures from Nature. In the customary oath to render a contract binding, the promise is to hold, so it runs, ' so long as the sun shines and rivers flow, so long as the wind blows and birds sing, so far off as earth is green and fir trees grow, so far as the vault of heaven reaches.' As Schnaase says,' though with some exaggeration, such formulæ, in their summary survey of earth and sky, often give a complete land-scape poem in a few words. He points out that in northern, as opposed to classic mythology, Nature was considered, not in the cursory Hebrew way, that hurried over or missed detail, but as a whole, and in her relation to man's inner life.

' The collective picture of heaven and earth, of cloud movement, of the mute life of plants—that side of Nature which had almost escaped the eye of antiquity—occupied the Northerner most of all.

'The *Edda* even represents all Nature together in one colossal form—the form of the giant Ymir, whom the sons of Boer slew, in order to make the mountains from his bones, the earth from his flesh, the skies from his skull.'

A still grander mythical synthesis was the representation of the whole world under the form of the sacred ash tree Yggdrasil. This was the world tree which united heaven, earth, and hell. Its branches stretched across the world and reached up to the skies, and its roots spread in different directions— one toward the race of Asa in heaven, another toward the Hrimthursen, the third toward the underworld; and on both roots and branches creatures lived and played—eagle, squirrel, stag, and snake; while by the murmuring Urdhar stream, which rippled over one root, the Nones sat in judgment with the race of Asa.

Not less significant was the conception of the end of the world, the twilight of the gods (Götterdämmerung), according to which all the wicked powers broke loose and fought against the gods; the sun and moon were devoured by wolves, the stars fell and earth quaked, the monster world-serpent Joermungande, in giant rage, reared himself out of the water and came to land: Loki led the Hrimthursen and the retinue of hell, and Surt, with his shining hair, rode away from the flaming earth across Bifröst, the rainbow, which broke beneath him.

After the world conflagration a new and better earth arose, with rejuvenated gods.'

German mediæval poetry, as a whole, epic and lyric, was interwoven with a hazy network of suggestive myth and legend; and moral elements, which in mythology were hidden by the prominence of Nature, stood out clear to view in the fate and character of the heroes. The germ of many of our fairy tales is a bit of purest poetry of Nature—a genuine Nature myth transferred to human affairs, which lay nearer to the child-like popular mind, and were therefore more readily understood by it.

So, for instance, from the Maiden of the Shield, Sigrdrifa, who was pierced by Odin's sleep thorn, and who originally represented the earth, frozen in winter, kissed awake by the sun-god, came Brunhild, whose mail Siegfried's sword penetrated as the sun rays penetrate the frost, and lastly the King's daughter, who pricked herself with the fateful spindle, and sank into deep sleep. And as Sigrdrifa was surrounded by walls of flame, so now we have a thorny hedge of wild briar round the beautiful maiden (hence named Dornröschen) when the lucky prince comes to waken her with a kiss.[*]

Not all fairy tales have preserved the myth into Christian times in so poetic and transparent a form as this. Its poetic germ arose from hidden depths of myth and legend, and, like heathen superstitions in the first centuries of Christianity, found its most fruitful soil among the people. It has often been disguised beyond recognition by legends, and by the worship of the Madonna and saints, but it has never been destroyed, and it keeps its magic to the present day.

We see then that the inborn German feeling for Nature, conditioned by climate and landscape, and pronounced in his mythology, found both an obstacle and a support in Christianity—an obstacle in its transcendentalism, and a support in its inwardness.

CHAPTER II

THE THEOLOGICAL CHRISTIAN AND THE SYMPATHETIC HEATHEN FEELING OF THE FIRST TEN CENTURIES A.D.

THE Middle Ages employed its best intellectual power in solving the problems of man's relation to God and the Redeemer, his moral vocation, and his claim to the Kingdom of the blessed. Mind and heart were almost entirely engrossed by the dogmas of the new faith, such as the incarnation, original sin, and free-will, and by doubts which the Old Testament had raised and not solved. Life was looked upon as a test-place, a thoroughfare to the heavenly Kingdom; earth, with its beauty and its appeal to the senses, as a temptress.

To flee the world and to lack artistic feeling were therefore marks of the period. We have no trace of scientific knowledge applied to Nature, and she was treated with increasing contempt, as the influence of antiquity died out. In spite of this, the attitude of the Apostolic Fathers was very far from hostile. Their fundamental idea was the Psalmist's 'Lord, how great are Thy works; in wisdom hast Thou made them all!' and yet they turned to Nature—at any rate, the noblest Grecians among them—not only for proof of divine wisdom and goodness, but with a degree of personal inclination, an enthusiasm, to which antiquity was a stranger.

Clement of Rome wrote to the Corinthians:

'Let us note how free from anger He is towards all His creatures. The heavens are moved by His direction and obey Him in peace. Day and night accomplish the course assigned to them by Him, without hindrance one to another. The sun and the moon and the dancing stars, according to His appointment, circle in harmony within the bounds assigned to them, without any swerving aside. The earth, bearing fruit in fulfilment of His will at her proper seasons, putteth forth the food that sup-plieth abundantly both men and beasts and all living things which are thereupon, making no dis-sension, neither altering anything which He hath decreed. Moreover, the inscrutable depths of the abysses and unutterable statutes of the nether regions are constrained by the same ordinances. The basin of the boundless sea, gathered together by His workmanship into its reservoirs, passeth not the barriers wherewith it is surrounded ; but even as He ordered it, so it doeth. For He said, " so far shalt thou come, and thy waves shall be broken within thee." The ocean which is impassable for men, and the worlds beyond it, are directed by the same ordinances of the Master. The seasons of spring and summer and autumn and winter give way in succession one to another in peace. The winds in their several quarters at their proper seasons fulfil their ministry without disturbance, and the overflowing fountains, created for enjoy-ment and health, without fail give their breasts which sustain the life for men. Yea, the smallest of living things come together in concord and peace.'

The three great Cappadocians, the most represen-tative of the Greek Fathers and leaders of the fourth century, wrote about the scenery round them in a tone of sentimentality not less astonishing, in view of the prejudice which denies all feeling for Nature to the Middle Ages, than their broad humanity and free handling of dogma.

It was no ascetic renouncing the world and solitude[1]; but rather a sensitive man, thoughtful and dreamy at once, who wrote as follows (Basil the Great to Gregory Nazianzen):

It is a lofty mountain overshadowed with a deep wood, irrigated on the north by cold and transparent streams. At its foot is spread a low plain, enriched perpetually with the streams from the mountains. The wood, a virgin forest of trees of various kinds and foliage which grows around it, almost serves it as a rampart; so that even the Isle of Calypso, which Homer evidently admired as a paragon of loveliness, is nothing in comparison with this. For indeed it is very nearly an island, from its being enclosed on all sides with rocky boundaries. On two sides of it are deep and precipitous ravines, and on another side the river flowing from the steep is itself a continuous and almost impassable barrier. The mountain range, with its moon-shaped windings, walls off the accessible parts of the plain. There is but one entrance, of which we are the masters. My hut is built on another point, which uplifts a lofty pinnacle on the summit, so that this plain is outspread before the gaze, and from the height I can catch a glimpse of the river flowing round, which to my fancy affords no less delight than the view of the Strymore as you look from Amphipolis. For the Strymore broadens into lakes with its more tranquil stream, and is so sluggish as almost to forfeit the character of a river. The Iris, on the other hand, flowing with a swifter course than any river I know, for a short space billows along the adjacent rock, and then, plunging over it, rolls into a deep whirlpool, affording a most delightful view to me and to every spectator, and abundantly supplying the needs of the inhabitants, for it nurtures an incredible number of fishes in its eddies.

Why need I tell you of the sweet exhalations from the earth or the breezes from the river? Other persons might admire the multitude of the flowers, or of the lyric birds, but I have no time to attend to them. But my highest eulogy of the spot is, that, prolific as it is of all kinds of fruits from its happy situation, it bears for me the sweetest of all fruits, tranquillity; not only because it is free from the noises of cities, but because it is not traversed by a single visitor except the hunters, who occasionally join us. For,

besides its other advantages, it also produces animals
—not bears and wolves, like yours—heaven forbid !
But it feeds herds of stags, and of wild goats and hares,
and creatures of that kind. Do you not then observe
what a narrow risk I ran, fool that I was, to change
such a spot for Tiberine, the depth of the habitable
world ? I am now hastening to it, pardon me. For
even Alcmæon, when he discovered the Echinades, no
longer endured his wanderings.[3]

This highly-cultured prince of the Church clearly
valued the place quite as much for its repose, its
idyllic solitude, for what we moderns would call its
romantic surroundings, sylvan and rugged at once,
as for its fertility and practical uses. But it is too
much to say, with Humboldt[4] :

> In this simple description of scenery and forest life,
> feelings are expressed which are more intimately in
> unison with those of modern times, than anything which
> has been transmitted to us from Greek or Roman
> antiquity. From the lonely Alpine hut to which Basil
> withdrew, the eye wanders over the humid and leafy
> roof of the forest below. . . . The poetic and mythical
> allusion at the close of the letter falls on the Christian
> ear like an echo from another and earlier world.

The Hellenic poets of the Anthology, and the
younger Pliny in Imperial days, held the same tone,
elegiac and idyllic[5] ; as Villemain says, ' These
pleasant pictures, these poetic allusions, do not shew
the austerity of the cloister.'[6] The specifically
Christian and monastic was hidden by the purely
human.

Other writings of Basil's express still more
strongly the mild dejection which longs for solitude.
For instance, when Gregory had been dwelling upon
the emptiness of all earthly things, he said in reply,
that peace of soul must be man's chief aim, and could
only be attained by separation from the world, by
solitude ; ' for the contemplation of Nature abates
the fever of the soul, and banishes all insincerity
and presumption.' Therefore he loved the quiet

corner where he was undisturbed by human inter-
course.

He drew melancholy comparisons from Nature :
men were compared to wandering clouds that
dissolve into nothing, to wavering shadows, and
shipwrecked beings, etc.

His homilies on the Hexameron, too, shew thought
of Nature.   There is a fine sense for the play of colour
on the sea here : ' A pleasant sight is the glistening
sea when a settled calm doth hold it ; but pleasant
too it is to behold its surface ruffled by gentle breezes,
and its colour now purple, now white, now dark ;
when it dasheth not with violence against the
neighbouring coast, but holdeth it in tranquil
embrace.'[7]

There is enthusiastic admiration for Nature
mixed with his profound religious feeling in the
whole description of the stars, the seasons, etc.
The expression of Ptolymäos, that when he gazed at
the stars he felt himself raised to the table of Zeus,
is weak in comparison with Basil's words, ' If, on
a clear night, you have fixed your gaze upon the
beauty of the stars, and then suddenly turned to
thoughts of the artist of the universe, whoever he be,
who has adorned the sky so wonderfully with these
undying flowers, and has so planned it that the
beauty of the spectacle is not less than its con-
formity to law . . . . if the finite and perishable
world is so beautiful, what must the infinite and
invisible be ? '[8]

For him, as for modern minds, starlight brought
thoughts of eternity : ' If the greatness of the sky is
beyond human comprehension, what mind, what
understanding could fathom eternal things ? '

Gregory Nazianzen's feeling for Nature was
intensely melancholy.   His poem *On Human
Nature* says :

For yesterday, worn out with my grief alone, I sat
apart in a shady grove, gnawing my heart out.   For

somehow I love this remedy in time of grief, to talk with mine own heart in silence.   And the breezes whispered to the note of the songster birds, and from the branches brought to me sweet slumber, though my heart was well-nigh broken.   And the cicadas, friends of the sun, chirped with the shrill note that issues from their breasts, and filled the whole grove with sound.   A cold spring hard by bedewed my feet as it flowed gently through the glen ; but I was held in the strong grip of grief, nor did I seek aught of these things, for the mind, when it is burdened with sorrow, is not fain to take part in pleasure.

The classic writers had also contrasted Nature with mind, as, for example, Ibykos in his famous *Spring Song* '; but not with Gregory's brooding melancholy and self-tormenting introspection.   The poem goes on to compare him to a cloud that wanders hither and thither in darkness, without even a visible outline of that for which he longed ; without peace :

> I am a stream of troubled water : ever onward I move, nor hath any part of me rest ; thou wilt not a second time pass over that stream thou didst before pass over, nor wilt thou see a second time the man thou sawest before.

In his dreamy enthusiasm he likes nothing better than solitude : 'Happy he who leads a lonely life, happy he who with the mighty force of a pure mind seeth the glory of the lights of heaven.'

The same tone constantly recurs in his writings. Human life is but dust, blown by the wind; a stormy voyage, faded grass ; kingdoms and powers are waves of the sea, which suck under and drown ; a charming girl is a rose with thorns, etc.

Gregory of Nyssa again praises the order and splendour of Nature and her Creator in Old Testament style : 'Seeing the harmony of the whole, of wonders in heaven and in earth, and how the elements of things, though mutually opposed, are all by Nature welded together, and make for one aim through a certain indefinable intercommunion.'

With the pathos of Job he cries:

> Who has spread out the ground at my feet?
> Who has made the sky firm over me as a dome?
> Who carries the sun as a torch before me?
> Who sends springs into the ravines?
> Who prepares the path of the waters?
> And who gives my spirit the wing for that high flight in which I leave earth behind and hasten through the wide ocean of air, know the beauty of the ether, and lift myself to the stars and observe all their splendour, and, not staying there, but passing beyond the limits of mutable things, comprehend unchangeable Nature—the immutable Power which is based upon itself, and leads and supports all that exists?

This, with its markedly poetic swing, is surprisingly like the passage in Plato's *Phædo*, where Socrates says: 'If any man could arrive at the exterior limit or take the wings of a bird and come to the top, then, like a fish who puts his head out of the water and sees this world, he would see a world beyond; and if the nature of man could sustain the sight, he would acknowledge that this other world was the place of the true heaven and the true light and the true earth.' But even the thought, that the order and splendour of Nature witnessed to the eternal powers which had created her, was not strange to the Greek, as Aristotle proves in the remarks which Cicero preserved to us in his treatise *On the Nature of the Gods.*

Well then did Aristotle observe: 'If there were men whose habitations had been always underground, in great and commodious houses, adorned with statues and pictures, finished with everything which they who are reputed happy abound with, and if, without stirring from thence, they should be informed of a certain divine power and majesty, and after some time the earth should open, and they should quit their dark abode to come to us, where they should immediately behold the earth, the seas, the heavens, should consider the vast extent of the clouds and force of the winds, should see the sun, and observe his grandeur and beauty, and also his generative power, inasmuch as day is occasioned by the diffusion of his light through the sky, and when night has obscured the earth, they should contemplate the heavens bespangled and adorned with stars, the surprising variety of the moon in her increase and wane, the rising and setting of all the stars and the inviolable regularity of all their courses ; when,' says he, 'they should see these things, they would undoubtedly conclude that there are gods, and that these are their mighty works.'

Thus unconsciously the Greek Fathers of the Church took over the thoughts of the great classic philosophers, only substituting a unity for a plurality of godhead.   To soar upon the wings of bird, wind, or cloud, a *motif* which we find here in Gregory of Nyssa, and which reached its finest expression in Ganymede and the evening scene in Faust, had reached a very modern degree of development in antiquity.[10]

Gregory of Nyssa was still more sentimental and plaintive than Basil and Gregory Nazianzen :

> When I see every ledge of rock, every valley and plain, covered with new-born verdure, the varied beauty of the trees, and the lilies at my feet decked by Nature with the double charms of perfume and of colour, when in the distance I see the ocean, towards which the clouds are onward borne, my spirit is overpowered by a sadness not wholly devoid of enjoyment.   When in autumn the fruits have passed away, the leaves have fallen, and the branches of the trees, dried and shrivelled, are robbed of their leafy adornments, we are instinctively led, amid the everlasting and regular change in Nature, to feel the harmony of the wondrous powers pervading all things.   He who contemplates them with the eye of the soul, feels the littleness of man amid the greatness of the universe.

Are not these thoughts, which Humboldt rightly strings together, highly significant and modern ?

Especially in view of the opinion which Du Bois Reymond, for example, expresses : 'In antiquity, mediæval times, and in later literature up to the last century, one seeks in vain for the expression of what we call a feeling for Nature.'[11]

Might not Werther have written them ? They have all his sentimental melancholy, coupled with that 'delight of sorrow' which owes its name (Wonne der Wehmuth) to Goethe, although its meaning was known to Euripides.

Yet it was only in rare cases, such as Seneca and Aristotle, that classic writers combined such appreciation of Nature's individual traits with that lofty view of the universe which elevates and humbles at once.

Gregory shewed the blending of Christian with classic feeling; and the deepening of the inner life through the new faith is quite as clear in patristic writings as their close relationship to the classic.

But the thinkers and poets of the Middle Ages did not always see Nature under the brilliant light of Hellenic influence ; there were wide spaces of time in which monkish asceticism held sway, and she was treated with most unscientific contempt. For the development of feeling did not proceed in one unswerving line, but was subject to backward movements. The rosy afterglow of the classic world was upon these Greek Fathers; but at the same time they suffered from the sorrowfulness of the new religion, which held so many sad and pessimistic elements.

The classic spirit seemed to shudder before the eternity of the individual, before the unfathomable depths which opened up for mankind with this religion of the soul, which can find no rest in itself, no peace in the world, unless it be at one with God in self-forgetting devotion and surrender.

Solitude, to which all the deeper minds at this time paid homage, became the mother of new and great thoughts, and of a view of the world little behind the modern in sentimentality.

What Villemain says of the quotation from Gregory Nazianzen just given, applies with equal force to the others :

> No doubt there is a singular charm in this mixture of abstract thoughts and emotions, this contrast between the beauties of Nature and the unrest of a heart tormented by the enigma of existence and seeking to find rest in faith. . . . It was not the poetry of Homer, it was another poetry. . . . It was in the new form of contemplative poetry, in this sadness of man about himself, in these impulses towards God and the future, in this idealism so little known by the poets of antiquity, that the Christian imagination could compete without disadvantage. It was there that that poetry arose which modern satiety seeks for, the poetry of reverie and reflection, which penetrates man's heart and deciphers his most intimate thoughts and vaguest wishes.

Contempt for art was a characteristic of the Fathers of the Church, and to that end they extolled Nature ; man's handiwork, however dazzling, was but vanity in their eyes, whereas Nature was the handiwork of the Creator. Culture and Nature were purposely set in opposition to each other.[1] St Chrysostom wrote :

> If the aspect of the colonnades of sumptuous buildings would lead thy spirit astray, look upwards to the vault of heaven, and around thee on the open fields, in which herds graze by the water's side. Who does not despise all the creations of art, when in the stillness of his soul he watches with admiration the rising of the sun, as it pours its golden light over the face of the earth ; when resting on the thick grass beside the murmuring spring, or beneath the sombre shade of a thick and leafy tree, the eye rests on the far receding and hazy distance ?

The visible to them was but a mirror of the invisible; as Paul says (13th of the 1st Corinthians): ' Here we see in a glass darkly,' and Goethe: ' Everything transitory is but a similitude.'

God (says St Chrysostom again) has placed man in the world as in a royal palace gleaming with gold and precious stones ; but the wonderful thing about this palace is, that it is not made of stone, but of far costlier material ; he has not lighted up a golden candelabra, but given lights their fixed course in the roof of the palace, where they are not only useful to us, but an object of great delight.[13]

The Roman secular writers of the first Christian centuries had not this depth of thought and sadness ; but from them too we have notable descriptions of Nature in which personal pleasure and sympathy are evident motives as well as religious feeling.

In the little *Octavius* of Minucius Felix, a writing full of genuine human feeling of the time of Commodus, the mixture of the heathen culture and opinions of antiquity with the Christian way of thinking has a very modern ring.   The scenery is finely sketched.

The heats of summer being over, autumn began to be temperate . . . . we (two friends, a heathen and a Christian) agreed to go to the delightful city of Ostia. . . . As, at break of day, we were proceeding along the banks of the Tiber towards the sea, that the soft breeze might invigorate our limbs, and that we might enjoy the pleasure of feeling the beach gently subside under our footsteps, Cæcilius observed an image of Serapis, and having raised his hands to his lips, after the wont of the superstitious vulgar, he kissed it. . . . Then Octavius said : ' It is not the part of a good man, brother Marcus, thus to leave an intimate companion and friend amidst blind popular ignorance, and to suffer him, in such open daylight, to stumble against stones,' etc. . . . Discoursing after this sort, we traversed the space between Ostia and the sea, and arrived at the open coast.   There the gentle surges had smoothed the outermost sands like a pleasure walk, and as the sea, although the winds blow not, is ever unquiet, it came forward to the shore, not hoary and foaming, but with waves gently swelling and curled.   On this occasion we were agreeably amused by the varieties of its appearance, for, as we stood on the margin and dipped the soles of our feet in the water, the wave alternately struck at us, and then receding, and sliding away, seemed to swallow up itself. We saw some boys eagerly engaged in the game of throwing shells in the sea. . . . Cæcilius said: ' All things ebb into the fountain from which they spring, and return back to their original without contriver, author, or supreme arbiter . . . . showers fall, winds blow, thunder bellows, and lightnings flash . . . . but they have no aim.' Octavius answers: ' Behold the heaven itself, how wide it is stretched out, and with what rapidity its revolutions are performed, whether in the night when studded with stars, or in the day-time when the sun ranges over it, and then you will learn with what a wonderful and divine hand the balance is held by the Supreme Moderator of all things ; see how the circuit made by the sun produces the year, and how the moon, in her increase, wanes and changes, drives the months around. . . . Observe the sea, it is bound by a law that the shore imposes ; the variety of trees, how each of them is enlivened from the bowels of the earth ! Behold the ocean, it ebbs and flows alternately. Look at the springs, they trickle with a perpetual flow ; at rivers, they hold on their course in quick and continued motion. Why should I speak of the ridges of mountains, aptly disposed ? of the gentle slope of hills, or of plains widely extended ? . . . . In this mansion of the world, when you fully consider the heaven and the earth, and that providence, order, and government visible in them, assure yourself that there is indeed a Lord and Parent of the whole . . . . do not enquire for the name of God—God is his name. . . . If I should call Him Father, you would imagine Him earthly ; if King, carnal ; and if Lord, mortal. Remove all epithets, and then you will be sensible of His glory. . . .'

How like Faust's confession of faith to Gretchen :

Him who dare name
And yet proclaim,
Yes ! I believe . . . .
The All-embracer,
All-sustainer,
Doth he not embrace, sustain,
Thee, me, Himself ?
Lifts not the Heaven its dome above ?
Doth not the firm-set earth beneath us rise ? . . .
And beaming tenderly with looks of love
Climb not the everlasting stars on high ? . . .
Fill thence thy heart, how large so e'er it be,

And in the feeling when thou'rt wholly blest,
Then call it what thou wilt—Bliss ! Heart ! Love ! God !
I have no name for it—'tis feeling all
Name is but sound and smoke
Shrouding the glow of Heaven.

Such statements of belief were not rare in the
Apologists ; but Nature at this time was losing
independent importance in men's minds, like life
itself, which after Cyprian was counted as nothing
but a fight with the devil.[14]

There is deep reverence for Nature in the lyrics,
the hymns of the first centuries A.D., as a work of God
and an emblem of moral ideas. Ebert observes[15] :

> In comparison with the old Roman, one can easily
> see the peculiarities and perfect originality of these
> Christian lyrics. I do not mean merely in that domin-
> ance of the soul life in which man appeared to be
> quite merged, and which makes them such profound
> expressions of feeling ; but in man's relationship to
> Nature, which, one might say, supplies the colour to
> the painter's brush.[16] Nature appears here in the
> service of ideal moral powers and robbed of her inde-
> pendence[17] ; the servant of her Creator, whose direct
> command she obeys. She is his instrument for man's
> welfare, and also at times, under the temporary mastery
> of the devil, for his destruction. Thus Nature easily
> symbolizes the moral world.

'Bountiful Giver of light, through whose calm
brightness, when the time of night is past and gone,
the daylight is suffused abroad, Thou, the world's
true morning star, clearer than the full glorious sun,
Thou very dayspring, very light in all its fulness,
that dost illumine the innermost recesses of the
heart,' sings St Hilary in his Morning Hymn ; and in
another hymn, declaring himself unworthy to lift
his sinful eyes to the clear stars, he urges all the
creatures, and heaven, earth, sea and river, hill and
wood, rose, lily, and star to weep with him and
lament the sinfulness of man.

In the Morning Hymn of St Ambrose dawn is

used symbolically ; dark night pales, the light of the world is born again, and the new birth of the soul raises to new energy ; Christ is called the true sun, the source of light ; 'let modesty be as the dawn, faith as the noonday, let the mind know no twilight.'

And Prudentius sings in a Morning Hymn [18] : 'Night and mist and darkness fade, light dawns, the globe brightens, Christ is coming ! ' and again : ' The herald bird of dawn announces day, Christ the awaker calls us to life.'   And in the ninth hymn : ' Let flowing rivers, waves, the seashore's thundering, showers, heat, snow, frost, forest and breeze, night, day, praise Thee throughout the ages.' [19]

He speaks of Christ as the sun that never sets, never is obscured by clouds, the flower of David, of the root of Jesse ; of the eternal Fatherland where the whole ground is fragrant with beds of purple roses, violets, and crocuses, and slender twigs drop balsam.

St Jerome united Christian genius, as Ebert says, with classic culture to such a degree that his writings, especially his letters, often shew a distinctly modern tone,[20] and go to prove that asceticism so deepened and intensified character that even literary style took individual stamp.[21] But the most perfect representative, the most modern man, of his day was Augustine.

As Rousseau's *Confessions* revealed the revolutionary genius of the eighteenth century, Augustine's opened out a powerful character, fully conscious of its own importance, striving with the problems of the time, and throwing search-lights into every corner of its own passionate heart.   He had attained, after much struggling, to a glowing faith, and he described the process in characteristic and drastic similes from Nature, which are scarcely suitable for translation. He said on one occasion :

> For I burned at times in my youth to satiate myself with deeds of hell, and dared to run wild in many

> a dark love passage. . . . In the time of my youth
> I took my fill passionately among the wild beasts, and
> I dared to roam the woods and pursue my vagrant
> loves beneath the shade ; and my beauty consumed
> away and I was loathsome in Thy sight, pleasing
> myself and desiring to please the eyes of men. . . .
> The seething waves of my youth flowed up to the
> shores of matrimony. . . .

Comfortless at the death of his friend :

> I burned, I sighed, I wept, I was distraught, for
> I bore within me a soul rent and bloodstained, that
> would no longer brook my carrying ; yet I found no
> place where I could lay it down, neither in pleasant
> groves nor in sport was it at rest. All things, even the
> light itself, were filled with shuddering.

Augustine, like Rousseau, understood ' que c'est
un fatal présent du ciel qu'une ame sensible.'
He looked upon his own heart as a sick child, and
sought healing for it in Nature and solitude, though
in vain.

The pantheistic belief of the Manicheans that all
things, fire, air, water, etc., were alive, that figs
wept when they were picked and the mother tree
shed milky tears for the loss of them, that everything
in heaven and earth was a part of godhead, gave
him no comfort ; it was rather the personal God of
the Psalms whom he saw in the ordering of Nature.

The cosmological element in theism has never
been more beautifully expressed than in his words :

> I asked the earth, and she said : ' I am not He,' and all
> things that are in her did confess the same. I asked
> the sea and the depths and creeping things, and they
> answered : ' We are not thy God, seek higher.' I asked
> the blowing breezes, and the whole expanse of air with
> its inhabitants made anwer : ' Anaxagoras was at
> fault, I am not God.' I asked the sky, the sun, the
> moon, the stars, and with a loud voice did they exclaim :
> ' He made us.' My question was the enquiry of my
> spirit, their answer was the beauty of their form.

In another place :

> Not with uncertain but with sure consciousness,
> Lord, I love Thee. But behold, sea and sky and all

things in them from all sides tell me that I must love
Thee, nor do they cease to give all men this message,
so that they are without excuse.   Sky and earth speak
to the deaf Thy praises : when I love Thee, I love not
beauty of form, nor radiancy of light ; but when I
love my God, I love the light, the voice, the sweetness,
the food, the embrace of my innermost soul.   That is
what I love when I love my God.

Augustine's interest in Nature was thus religious.
At the same time, the soothing influence of quiet
woods was not unknown to him.

The likeness and unlikeness between the Christian
and heathen points of view are very clear in the
correspondence between Ausonius, the poet of the
Moselle, and Paulinus, Bishop of Nola; and the deep
friendship expressed in it raises their dilettante
verses to the level of true poetry.

Ausonius, thoroughly heathen as he was, carries
us far forward into Christian-Germanic times by his
sentimentality and his artistic descriptions of the
scenery of the Moselle.[22]

It is characteristic of the decline of heathendom,
that the lack of original national material to serve
as inspiration, as the Æneas Saga had once served,
led the best men of the time to muse on Nature, and
describe scenery and travels.   Nothing in classic
Roman poetry attests such an acute grasp of Nature's
little secret charms as the small poem about the
sunny banks of the Moselle, vine-clad and crowned
by villas, and reflected in the crystal water below.
It seemed as if the Roman, with the German climate,
had imbibed the German love of Nature ; as if its
scenery had bewitched him like the German maiden
whom he compared to roses and lilies in his song.

Many parts of his poetical epistles are in the same
tone, and we learn incidentally from them that a
lengthy preamble about weather and place belonged
to letter-writing even then.[23]

Feeling for Nature and love of his friend are inter-
woven into a truly poetic appeal in No. 64, in which

Ausonius complains that Paulinus does not answer his letters :

> Rocks give answer to the speech of man, and his words striking against the caves resound, and from the groves cometh the echo of his voice. The cliffs of the coast cry out, the rivers murmur, the hedge hums with the bees that feed upon it, the reedy banks have their own harmonious notes, the foliage of the pine talks in trembling whispers to the winds : what time the light south-east falls on the pointed leaves, songs of Dindymus give answer in the Gargaric grove. Nature has made nothing dumb ; the birds of the air and the beasts of the earth are not silent, the snake has its hiss, the fishes of the sea as they breathe give forth their note. . . . Have the Basque mountains and the snowy haunts of the Pyrenees taken away thy urbanity ? . . . May he, who advises thee to keep silence, never enjoy the singing of sweet songs nor the voices of Nature . . . . sad and in need may he live in desolate regions, and wander silent in the rounded heights of the Alpine range.

The sounds of Nature are detailed with great delicacy in this appeal, and we see that the Alps are referred to as desolate regions.

In another letter (25) he reminded his friend of their mutual love, their home at Burdigala, his country-house with its vine-slopes, fields, woods, etc., and went on :

> Yet without thee no year advanceth with grateful change of season ; the rainy spring passeth without flower, the dog-star burns with blazing heat, Pomona bringeth not the changing scents of autumn, Aquarius pours forth his waters and saddens winter. Pontius, dear heart, seest thou what thou hast done ?

Closing in the same tender strain with a picture of his hope fulfilled :

> Now he leaves the snowy towns of the Iberians, now he holds the fields of the Tarbellians, now passeth he beneath the halls of Ebromagus, now he is gliding down the stream, and now he knocketh at thy door ! Can we believe it ? Or do they who love, fashion themselves dreams ?

The greater inwardness of feeling here, as contrasted with classic times, is undeniable; the tone verges on the sentimentality of the correspondences between 'beautiful souls' in the eighteenth century.

Paulinus was touchingly devoted to his former teacher Ausonius, and in every way a man of fine and tender feeling. He gave himself with zeal to Christianity, and became an ascetic and bishop.

It was a bitter grief to him that his Ausonius remained a heathen when he himself had sworn allegiance to Christ and said adieu to Apollo. There is a fine urbanity and humanity in his writings, but he did not, like Ausonius, love Nature for her own sake. The one took the Christian ascetic point of view, the other the classic heathen, with sympathy and sentiment in addition.

Paulinus recognized the difference, and contrasted their ideas of solitude. 'They are not crazed, nor is it their savage fierceness that makes men choose to live in lonely spots; rather, turning their eyes to the lofty stars, they contemplate God, and set the leisure that is free from empty cares, to fathom the depths of truth they love.'

In answer to his friend's praise of home, he praised Spain, in which he was living, and many copious descriptions of time and place run through his other writings[24]; but while he yielded nothing to Ausonius in the matter of friendship, 'sooner shall life disappear from my body than thy image from my heart,' he was without his quiet musing delight in Nature. For her the heathen had the clearer eye and warmer heart; the Christian bishop only acknowledged her existence in relation to his Creator, declaring with pride that no power had been given to us over the elements, nor to them over us, and that not from the stars but from our own hearts come the hindrances to virtue.

Lives of the saints and paraphrases of the story of creation were the principal themes of the Christian poets of the fourth and fifth centuries. In some of these the hermit was extolled with a dash of Robinson Crusoe romance, and the descriptions of natural phenomena in connection with Genesis often showed a feeling for the beauty of Nature in poetic language. Dracontius drew a detailed picture of Paradise with much self-satisfaction.

> Then in flight the joyous feathered throng passed through the heavens, beating the air with sounding wings, various notes do they pour forth in soothing harmony, and, methinks, together praise for that they were accounted worthy to be created.[26]

For the charming legend of Paradise was to many Christian minds of this time what the long-lost bliss of Elysium and the Golden Age had been to the Hellenic poets and the Roman elegist—the theme of much vivid imagery and highly-coloured word-painting.

> Eternal spring softens the air, a healing flame floods the world with light, all the elements glow in healing warmth ; as the shades of night fade, day rises. . . . Then the feathered flocks fly joyfully through the air, beating it with their wings in the rush of their passage, and with flattering satisfaction their voices are heard, and I think they praise God that they were found worthy to be created ; some shine in snowy white, some in purple, some in saffron, some in yellow gold ; others have white feathers round the eyes, while neck and breast are of the bright tint of the hyacinth . . . . and upon the branches, the birds are moved to and fro with them by the wind.

This shews careful observation of detail ; but, for the most part, such idyllic feeling was checked by lofty religious thoughts.

'Man,' he cries, 'should rule over Nature, over all that it contains, over all earth offers in fruit, flowers, and verdure that tree and vine, sea and spring, can give.' He summons all creation to praise the Creator—stars and seasons, hail-storm and lightning, earth, sea, river and spring, cloud and night, plants, animals, and light ; and he describes the flood in bold flights of fancy.

In the three books of Avitus [27] we have 'a complete poem of the lost Paradise, far removed from a mere paraphrase or versification of the Bible,' [28] which shews artistic leanings and sympathetic feeling here and there. As Catullus [29] pictures the stars looking down upon the quiet love of mortals by night, and Theocritus [30] makes the cypresses their only witnesses, the Christian poet surrounds the marriage of our first parents with the sympathy of Nature :

> And angel voices joined in harmony and sang to the chaste and pure ; Paradise was their wedding-chamber, earth their dowry, and the stars of heaven rejoiced with gladsome radiance. . . .   The kindness of heaven maintains eternal spring there ; the tumultuous south wind does not penetrate, the clouds forsake an air which is always pure. . . .   The soil has no need of rains to refresh it, and the plants prosper by virtue of their own dew. The earth is always verdant, and its surface animated by a sweet warmth resplendent with beauty. Herbs never abandon the hills, the trees never lose their leaves, etc.

And when Adam and Eve leave it, they find all the rest of the beautiful world ugly and narrow in comparison. 'Day is dark to their eyes, and under the clear sun they complain that the light has disappeared.'

It was the reflection of their own condition in Nature. Among heathen writers who were influenced, without being entirely swayed, by Christian teaching, and imitated the rhetorical Roman style in describing Nature, Apollonius Sidonius takes a prominent place. In spite of many empty phrases and a stilted style, difficult to understand as well as to translate, his poems, and still more his letters, give many interesting pictures of the culture of his part of the fifth century. In Carm. 2 he draws a highly-coloured picture of the home of Pontius Leontas,[31] a fine country property, and paints the charms of the villa with all the art of his rhetoric and some real appreciation. The meeting of the two rivers, the Garonne and the Dordogne, in the introduction is poetically rendered, and he goes on to describe the cool hall and grottos, state-rooms, pillars—above all, the splendid view : ' There on the top of the fortress I sit down and lean back and gaze at the mountains covered by olives, so dear to the Muse and the goats. I shall wander in their shade, and believe that coward Daphne grants me her love.' He delighted in unspoilt Nature, and describes :

> My fountain, which, as it flows from the mountain-side, is overshadowed by a many-covered grotto with its wide circle. It needs not Art; Nature has given it grace. That no artist's hand has touched it is its charm ; it is no masterpiece of skill, no hammer with resounding blow will adorn the rocks, nor marble fill up the place where the tufa is worn away.

He lays stress upon the contrast between culture and Nature, town luxury and country solitude, in his second letter to Domidius, and describes the beauties of his own modest estate with sentimental delight :

> You reproach me for loitering in the country ; I might complain with more reason that you stay in the town when the earth shines in the light of spring, the ice is melting from the Alps, and the soil is marked by the dry fissures of tortuous furrows . . . . the stones in the stream, and the mud on the banks are dried up . . . . here neither nude statues, comic actors, nor Hippo-drome are to be found . . . . the noise of the waters is so great that it drowns conversation. From the dining-room, if you have time to spare at meals, you can occupy it with the delight of looking at the scenery, and watch the fishing . . . . here you can find a hidden recess, cool even in summer heat, a place to sleep in. Here what joy it is to listen to the cicadas chirping at noonday, and to the frogs croaking when the twilight is coming on, and to the swans and geese giving note at the early hours of the night, and at midnight to the cocks crowing together, and to the boding crows with three-

fold note greeting the ruddy torch of the rising dawn ; and in the half light of the morning to hear the nightingale warbling in the bushes, and the swallow twittering among the beams. . . . Between whiles, the shepherds play in their rustic fashion. Not far off is a wood where the branches of two huge limes interlace, though their trunks are apart (in their shade we play ball), and a lake that rises to such fury in a storm that the trees that border it are wetted by the spray.

In another letter to Domidius he described a visit to the country-seat of two of his friends :

We were torn from one pleasure to another—games, feastings, chatting, rowing, bathing, fishing.

As a true adherent even as a bishop of classic culture and humanity, Sidonius is thus an interesting figure in these wild times, with his Pliny-like enthusiasm for country rather than city, and his susceptibility to woodland and pastoral life. The limit of extravagance in the bombastic rhetoric of the period was reached in the travels of Ennodius,[32] who was scarcely more than a fantastic prattler. The purest, noblest, and most important figure of the sixth century was undoubtedly Bœtius ; but it is Cassiodorus, a statesman of the first rank under Theodoric, who in his *Variorium libris* gives the most interesting view of the attitude of his day towards Nature. He revelled in her and in describing her. After praising Baja for its beauty[33] and Lactarius for its healthiness, he said of Scyllacium :

The city of Scyllacium hangs upon the hills like a cluster of grapes, not that it may pride itself upon their difficult ascent, but that it may voluptuously gaze on verdant plains and the blue back of the sea. The city beholds the rising sun from its very cradle, when the day that is about to be born sends forward no heralding Aurora ; but as soon as it begins to rise, the quivering brightness displays its torch. It beholds Phœbus in his joy ; it is bathed in the brightness of that luminary so that it might be thought to be itself the native land of the sun, the claims of Rhodes to that honour being outdone. . . . It enjoys a translucent air, but withal so temperate, that its winters are sunny and its summers cool, and life passes there without sorrow, since hostile seasons are feared by none. Hence, too, man himself is here freer of soul than elsewhere, for this temperateness of the climate prevails in all things. . . . Assuredly for the body to imbibe muddy waters is a different thing from sucking in the transparency of a sweet fountain. Even so the vigour of the mind is repressed when it is clogged by a heavy atmosphere. Nature itself hath made us subject to these influences . . . . clouds make us feel sad, and again a bright day fills us with joy. . . . At the foot of the Moscian Mount we hollowed out the bowels of the rock, and tastefully introduced therein the eddying waves of Nereus. Here a troop of fishes sporting in free captivity refreshes all minds with delight, and charms all eyes with admiration. They run greedily to the hand of man, and, before they become his food, seek dainties from him.

He described the town as rich in vineyards and olive woods, cornfields and villas.

He awarded the palm of beauty to Como and its lake, and although he wrote in the clumsy language of a decaying literature, this sixth-century sketch still strikes us as surprisingly complete and artistic in feeling :

Como, with its precipitous mountains and its vast expanse of lake, seems placed there for the defence of the Province of Liguria ; and yet again, it is so beautiful, that one would think it was created for pleasure only.

To the south lies a fertile plain with easy roads for the transport of provisions ; on the north, a lake sixty miles long abounding in fish, soothing the mind with delicious recreation. . . . Rightly is it called Como, because it is adorned with such gifts. The lake lies in a shell-like valley with white margins. Above rises a diadem of lofty mountains, their slopes studded with bright villas ; a girdle of olives below, vineyards above, while a crest of thick chestnut woods adorns the very summit of the hills. Streams of snowy clearness dash from the hill-sides into the lake. On the eastern side these unite to form the river Addua, so called because it contains the added volume of two streams. . . . So delightful a region makes men delicate and averse to labour. . . . Therefore the inhabitants deserve special consideration, and for this reason we wish them to enjoy perpetually the royal bounty.

This shews, beyond dispute, that the taste for the beauty of Nature, even at that wild time, was not dead, and that the writer's attitude was not mainly utilitarian. He noted the fertility of the land in wine and grain, and of the sea in fish, but he laid far greater stress upon its charms and their influence upon the inhabitants.

On *a priori* grounds (so misleading in questions of this kind) one would scarcely expect the most disturbed period in the history of the European people to have produced a Venantius Fortunatus, the greatest and most celebrated poet of the sixth century. His whole personality, as well as his poetry, shewed the blending of heathenism and Christianity, of Germanism and Romanism, and it is only now and then among the Roman elegists and later epic poets that we meet a feeling for Nature which can be compared to his. Like all the poets of this late period, his verse lacks form, is rugged and pompous, moving upon the stilts of classic reminiscences, and coining monstrous new expressions for itself ; but its feeling is always sincere. It was the last gleam of a setting sun of literature that fell upon this one beneficent figure. He was born in the district of Treviso near Venice, and crossed the Alps a little before the great Lombard invasion, while the Merovingians, following in the steps of Chlodwig, were outdoing each other in bloodshed and cruelty. In the midst of this hard time Fortunatus stood out alone among the poets by virtue of his talent and purity of character. His poems are often disfigured by bombast, prolixity, and misplaced learning ; but his keen eye for men and things is undeniable, and his feeling for Nature shews not only in dealing with scenery, but in linking it with the inner life.

The lover's wish in *On Virginity*,[34] one of his longer poems, suggests the Volkslieder :

O that I too might go, if my hurrying foot could poise amid the lights of heaven and hold on its starry course. But now, without thee, night comes drearily with its dark wings, and the day itself and the glittering sunshine is darkness to me. Lily, narcissus, violet, rose, nard, amomum, bring me no joy—nay, no flower delights my heart. That I may see thee, I pass hovering through each cloud, and my love teaches my wandering eyes to pierce the mist, and lo! in dread fear I ask the stormy winds what they have to tell me of my lord. Before thy feet I long to wash the pavement, and with my hair to sweep thy temples. Whatever it be, I will bear it; all hard things are sweet; if only I see thee, this penalty is my joy. But be thou mindful, for thy vows do I yearn; I have thee in my heart, have me in thy heart too.

This is more tender in feeling than any poem by Catullus or Tibullus. We can only explain it by two facts—the deepening of the inner life through Christianity (we almost hear Christ's words about the 'great sinner'), and the intimate friendship which Fortunatus enjoyed with a German lady, who may justly be called the noblest and purest figure of her time in Franconia.

This was Radegunde, the unhappy daughter of a Thuringian king, who first saw her father's kingdom lost, and then, fleeing from the cruelty of her husband, the bloodstained Chlotaire, took the veil in Poitiers and founded a convent, of which she made Agnes, a noble Franconian lady, the abbess. When Fortunatus visited the place, these ladies became his devoted friends, and he remained there as a priest until the death of Radegunde. His poems to them, which were often letters and notes written off-hand, are full of affection and gratitude (he was, by the way, a gourmet, and the ladies made allowance for this weakness in dainty gifts), and form an enduring witness of a pure and most touching friendship. They contain many pretty sketches of Nature and delicate offerings of flowers. In one he said: 'If the season brought white lilies or blossomed in red roses,

I would send them to you, but now you must be content with purple violets for a greeting'; and in another, because gold and purple are not allowable, he sends her flowers, that she may have 'her gold in crocuses, her purple in violets, and they may adorn her hair with even greater delight than she draws from their fragrance.' Once, when following pious custom, she had withdrawn into her cell, his 'straying thoughts go in search of her':

> How quickly dost thou hide the light from mine eyes! for without thee I am o'erweighted by the clouds that bear me down, and though thou flee and hide thyself here but for a few short days, that month is longer than the whole hurrying year. Prithee, let the joys of Easter bring thee back in safety, and so may a twofold light return to us at once.

And when she comes out, he cries:

> Thou hadst robbed me of my happiness; now it returns to me with thee, thou makest me doubly celebrate this solemn festival. . . . Though the seedlings are only just beginning to shoot up from the furrows, yet I to-day will reap my harvest in seeing thee once more. To-day do I gather in the fruit and lay the peaceful sheaves together. Though the field is bare, nor decked with ears of corn, yet all, through thy return, is radiant fulness.

The comparison is tedious and spun out; but the idea is poetic. We find it in the classics: for instance, in Theocritus, when he praises Nais, whose beauty draws even Nature under her sway, and whose coming makes spring everywhere:

> Where has my light hidden herself from my straying eyes? When I see not thee, I am ne'er satisfied. Though the heavens be bright, though the clouds have fled, yet for me is the day sunless, if it hide thee from me.

The most touching evidence of this friendship is the poem *On the Downfall of Thuringia*.

'One must,' says Leo,[13] 'refer the chief excellence

of the poem to the lady who tells the tale, must grant that the irresistible power of the description, the spectacle of the freshly open wounds, the sympathy in the consuming sorrow of a friend, gave unwonted power of the wing to this low-flying pen.'

Radegunde is thinking of her only remaining relative, Amalafried:

> When the wind murmurs, I listen if it bring me some news, but of all my kindred not even a shadow presents itself to me. . . . And thou, Amalafried, gentle son of my father's brother, does no anxiety for me consume thy heart? Hast thou forgotten what Radegunde was to thee in thy earliest years, and how much thou lovedst me, and how thou heldst the place of the father, mother, brother, and sister whom I had lost? An hour absent from thee seemed to me eternal; now ages pass, and I never hear a word from thee. A whole world now lies betwixt those who loved each other and who of old were never separate. If others, for pity alone, cross the Alps to seek their lost slaves, wherefore am I forgotten?—I who am bound to thee by blood? Where art thou? I ask the wind as it sighs, the clouds as they pass—at least some bird might bring me news of thee. If the holy enclosure of this monastery did not restrain me, thou shouldst see me suddenly appear beside thee. I could cross the stormy seas in winter if it were necessary. The tempest that alarms the sailors should cause no fear to me who love thee. If my vessel were dashed to pieces by the tempest, I should cling to a plank to reach thee, and if I could find nothing to cling to, I should go to thee swimming, exhausted. If I could but see thee once more, I should deny all the perils of the journey. . . .

There is little about Nature in this beautiful avowal of love and longing, but the whole colouring of the mood forms a background of feeling for his longer descriptions. His very long and tedious poem about the bridal journey of Gelesiuntha, the Spanish princess, who married King Chilperic, shews deep and touching feeling in parts. She left her Toledo home with a heavy heart, crossing the Pyrenees, where 'the mountains shining with snow reach to the stars, and their sharp peaks project over the rain clouds.' In the same vein as Ausonius, when he urged Paulinus to write to him, she begs her sister for news :

> By thy name full oft I call thee, Gelesiuntha, sister mine : with this name fountains, woods, rivers, and fields resound. Art thou silent, Gelesiuntha ? Answer as to thy sister stones and mountains, groves and waters and sky, answer in language mute.

In troubled thought and care she asked the very breezes, but of her sister's safety all were silent.

Fortunatus, like Ausonius, not only looked at Nature with sympathy, but was a master in description of scenery. His lengthy descriptions of spring are mostly only decorative work, but here and there we find a really poetic idea. For example :

> At the first spring, when earth has doffed her frost, the field is clothed with variegated grass ; the mountains stretch their leafy heads towards the sky, the shady tree renews its verdant foliage, the lovely vine is swelling with budding branches, giving promise that a weight of grapes shall hang from its prolific stems. While all joys return, the earth is dead and dull.

And :

> The soft violets paint the field with their own purple, the meadows are green with grass, the grass is bright with its fresh shoots. Little by little, like stars, the bright flowers spring up, and the sward is joyous and gay with flecks of colour, and the birds that through the winter cold have been numb and silent, with imprisoned song, are now recalled to their song.

He describes the cold winter, and a hot summer's day, when

> Even in the forests no shade was to be found, and the traveller almost fainted on the burning roads, longing for shade and cool drinks. At last the rustle of a crystal stream is heard, he hurries to it with delight, he lies down and lays his limbs in the soft kisses of the grass.

His poems about beautiful and noteworthy places include some on the Garonne and Gers (Egircius):

> So dried up by heat that it is neither river nor land, and the grumbling croak of the frog, sole ruler of the realm from which the fish are banished, is heard in the lonely swamp ; but when the rain pours down, the flood swells, and what was a lake suddenly becomes a sea.

He has many verses of this sort, written with little wit but great satisfaction.

More attractive are descriptions of the Rhine and Moselle, recalling Ausonius, and due to love partly of Nature, partly of verbal scene-painting. The best and most famous of these is on his journey by the Moselle from Metz to Andernach on the Rhine. Here he shews a keen eye and fine taste for wide views and high mountains, as well as for the minutiæ of scenery, with artistic treatment. He also blends his own thoughts and feelings with his impressions of Nature, making it clear that he values her not merely for decoration, but for her own sake.

He has been called the last Roman poet ; in reality, he belonged not only to the period which directly succeeded his own, when the Roman world already lay in ruins, but to the fully-developed Middle Ages — the time when Christianity and Germanism had mated with Roman minds.

In his best pieces, such as his famous elegy, he caught the classic tone to perfection, feeling himself in vital union with the great of bygone centuries ; but in thought and feeling he was really modern and under the influence of the Christian Germanic spirit with all its depth and intensity. His touching friendship with Radegunde is, as it were, a symbol of the blending of the two elements out of which the modern sprang. It was the stimulating influence of the noble Germanic princess, herself

Christian in soul, which fanned the dying sparks
of classic poetry into a flame.

Fortunatus stood upon a borderland. Literature
was retreating further and further from the classic
models, and culture was declining to its fall. In
Gaul, as in Spain and Italy, the shadows of coming
night were broadening over literary activity, thought,
and feeling.

It is a characteristic fact in Roman literature,
that not only its great lights, but the lesser ones
who followed them, were enthusiastically imitated.
Latin poetry of the Middle Ages lived upon recollec-
tions of the past, or tried to raise itself again by its
help ; even so late a comer as Fortunatus became
in his turn an object of marvel, and was copied by
poets who never reached his level.

It is not surprising that feeling for Nature shewed
a corresponding shallowness and lassitude.

Not only bucolic but didactic writing was modelled
upon the classic. Isodorus and Beda, in their
works with identical titles ' concerning the existence
of things,' relied on Roman models no less than
Alcuin, who had formed himself on the pattern of
Augustine's time in his *Conflict between Winter
and Spring*, as well as in many single verses, directly
inspired by Virgil.[16]

His *Farewell to his Cell* caught the idyllic tone
very neatly :

Beloved cell, retirement's sweet abode !
Farewell, a last farewell, thy poet bids thee !
Beloved cell, by smiling woods embraced,
Whose branches, shaken by the genial breeze,
To meditation oft my mind disposed.
Around thee too, their health-reviving herbs
In verdure gay the fertile meadows spread ;
And murmuring near, by flowery banks confined,
Through fragrant meads the crystal streamlets glide,
Wherein his nets the joyful fisher casts,
And fragrant with the apple bending bough,
With rose and lily joined, the gardens smile ;
While jubilant, along thy verdant glades

> At dawn his melody each songster pours,
> And to his God attunes the notes of praise.

These heartfelt effusions express a feeling which certainly inspired many monks when they turned from their gloomy cells to the gardens and woods beyond—a feeling compounded of renunciation of the world with idyllic comfort in their surroundings. If their fundamental feeling was worship and praise of the Creator, their constant outdoor work, which, during the first centuries, was strenuous cultivation of the soil, must have roused a deep appreciation of Nature in the nobler minds among them. Their choice of sites for monasteries and hermitages fully bears out this view."

The Conflict between Spring and Winter, with its classic suggestions, is penetrated by a truly German love of spring." It described the time when the cuckoo sings high in the branches, grass clothes earth with many tints, and the nightingale sings untiringly in the red-gold butcher's broom, captivating us with her changing melodies.

Among the savants whom Charlemagne gathered round him was Angilbert. Virgil was his model, but the influence of the lighter fluency of Fortunatus was visible, as in so many of his contemporaries. With a vivid and artistic pen he described the wood and park of Aachen and the Kaiser's brilliant hunt "; the great forest grove, the grassy meadows with brooks and all sorts of birds flitting about, the thicket stocked with many kinds of game.

At the same time, his writing betrayed the conventional tone of courts in its praise of his great secular lord, and a 'thoughtful romantic inclination' for the eternal feminine, for the beautiful women with splendid ornaments, and necks shining like milk or snow or glowing like a rose, who, as Ebert puts it, 'lay far from the asceticism of the poetry of the saints.'

Naso Muadorinus in his pastorals took Calpurnius

and Nemesianus for his models, just as they had taken Virgil, and Virgil Theocritus. Muadorinus imitated the latter in his pastorals.

In an alternate song of his between an old man and a boy, the old man draws an artistic contrast between the shady coolness of the wood and the mid-day glow of the sun, while the boy praises Him whose songs the creatures follow as once they followed Orpheus with his lute; and at the end, Charlemagne, who was extolled at the beginning as a second Cæsar, is exalted to heaven as the founder of a new Golden Age.

In the Carolingian Renaissance of the Augustine epoch of literature, Theodulf, Bishop of Orleans, takes first place. At any rate, he described in a very superior way, and, like Fortunatus, with some humour, the draining of the Larte at Le Mans, Feb. 820; also, in a light and lively strain, the Battle of the Birds, and, with the same strong colouring, Paradise.

The idyll of the cloister garden, so often treated, became famous in the much-read *Hortulus* of Wahlafried.[40]

Despite classical flourishes from Virgil and Columella, and pharmaceutical handling of plants, there is a good deal of thoughtful observation of Nature in these 444 hexameters.

They contain descriptions of seasons, of recipes, flowers and vegetables, of the gardener's pleasure in digging his fields in spring, clearing them of nettles, and levelling the ground thrown up by the moles, in protecting his seedlings from rain and sun, and, later on, in his gay beds of deciduous plants.

There is a touch here and there which is not unpoetic—for instance:

A bright green patch of dark blue rue paints this shady grove; it has short leaves and throws out short umbels, and passes the breath of the wind and the rays of the sun right down to the end of the stalk, and at a gentle touch gives forth a heavy scent.

and :

> With what verse, with what song, can the dry thinness of my meagre muse rightly extol the shining lily, whose whiteness is as the whiteness of gleaming snow, whose sweet scent is as the scent of Sabian woods ?

He closes pleasantly too, adjuring Grimald to read the book under the shade of the peach tree, while his school-fellows play round and pick the great delicate fruit which they can barely grasp with one hand. In the poem to the layman Ruodbern (100 hexameters) he described the dangers of Alpine travelling, both from weather and other foes. In those days the difficulties of the road excluded all interest in mountain beauty. There is a tender and expressive poem in Sapphic metre, in which, homesick and cold in winter, he sang his longing for beautiful Reichenau. But even he, like most of his predecessors and all his followers, wielded his pen with labour, expression often failing to keep pace with thought.

It only remains to mention Wandalbert, a monk of the monastery at Prün, who, in a postscript to the *Conclusio des Martyrologium*, gives a charming account of a landowner's life in field, garden, and hunt.

In the cloister, then, idyllic comfort, delighting in Nature and a quiet country life, was quite as much at home as scholarship and classical study. But we shall look there in vain for any trace of the sentimental, the profoundly melancholy attitude of the Fathers of the Church, Basil and Gregory, or for Augustine's deep faith and devout admiration of the works of creation : even the tone of Ausonius and Fortunatus, in their charming descriptions of scenery, was now a thing of the past. Feeling for Nature—sentimental, sympathetic, cosmic, and dogmatic—had dwindled down to mere pleasure in cultivating flowers in the garden, to the level Aachen landscape and such like; and the power to describe the impression made by scenery was, like the impression itself, lame and weary.

It was the night of the decline breaking over Latin literature.

And how did it stand with German literature up to the eleventh century? A German Kingdom had existed from the treaties of Verdun and Mersen (842), but during this period traces of German poetry are few, outweighed by Latin.

The two great Messianic poems, *Heliand* and *Krist*, stand out alone. In the *Heliand* the storm on the lake of Gennesaret is vividly painted:

> Then began the power of the storm; in the whirl-wind the waves rose, night descended, the sea broke with uproar, wind and water battled together; yet, obedient to the command and to the controlling word, the water stilled itself and flowed serenely.

In *Krist* there is a certain distinction in the description of the Ascension, as the rising figures soar past the constellations of stars, which disappear beneath their feet; for the rest, the symbolic so supplants the direct meaning, that in place of an epic we have a moralizing sermon. But there are traces of delight in the beauty of the outer world, in the sunshine, and sympathy is attributed to Nature:

> She grew very angry at such deeds.

The poem *Muspilli* (the world fire) shews the old northern feeling for Nature; still more the few existing words of the *Wessobrunner Prayer*:

> This I heard as the greatest marvel among men,
> That once there was no earth nor heaven above,
> The bright stars gave no light, the sun shone not,
> Nor the moon, nor the glorious sea.

How plainly 'the bright stars' and the 'glorious sea' shew joy in the beauty of the world!

In the oldest Scandinavian poems the inflexible

character of the Northerner and the northern land-scape is reflected; the descriptions are short and scanty; it is not mountain, rock, and sea which count as beautiful, but pleasant, and, above all, fruitful scenery. The imagery is bold : (Kenninger) the wind is the wolf of wood or sail, the sea the pathway of the whale, the bath of the diving bird, etc.

The Anglo-Saxon was especially distinguished by his forcible images and epithets. In Rynerwulf we have 'night falls like a helmet, dark brown covers the mountains.' 'The sky is the fortress of the storm, the sun the torch of the world, the jewel of splendour.' 'Fire is eager, wild, blind, and raging; the sea is the gray sea, and the sparkling splendid sea; waves are graves of the dead,' etc.

Vivid feeling for Nature is not among the characteristic features of either Scandinavian or old German poetry.

It is naive and objective throughout, and seldom weighty or forcible.

The Waltharius shews the influence of Virgil's language, in highly-coloured and sympathetic descriptions like those of the Latin poetry of the Carolingian Renaissance.

Animal saga probably first arose just before the twelfth century, and their home was probably Franconia.

Like the genial notices of plant life in the Latin poems of the Carlovingian period, the animal poems shewed interest in the animal world—the interest of a child who ponders individual differences and peculiarities, the virtues and failings so closely allied to its own. It was a naive ' hand-and-glove' footing between man and the creatures, which attributed all his wishes and weaknesses to them, wiped out all differences between them with perfect impartiality, and gave the characteristics of each animal with exactness and poetry.

The soil for the cultivation of poetry about animals was prepared by the symbolic and allegorical way of looking at Nature which held sway all through the Middle Ages.

The material was used as a symbolic language for the immaterial, the world of sense conceived of as a great picture-book of the truths of salvation, in whose pages God, the devil, and, between them man, figured : thus plant life suggested the flower of the root of Jesse, foretold by Isaiah, red flowers the Saviour's wounds, and so forth. In the earliest Christian times, a remarkable letter existed in Alexandria, the so-called 'Physiologus,' which has affected the proverbial turns of speech in the world's literature up to the present day to an almost unequalled degree.

It gave the symbolic meanings of the different animals. The lamb and unicorn were symbols of Christ; sheep, fish, and deer, of his followers; dragons, serpents, and bears, of the devil; swine, hares, hyenas, of gluttony; the disorderly luxuriance of snow meant death, the phœnix the resurrection, and so forth, indeed, whole categories of animals were turned into allegories of the truths of salvation.[41] The cleverest fables of animals were in *Isengrimen*, published in Ghent about 1140 in Latin verse—the story of the sick lion and his cure by the fox, and the outwitting of the wolf. Such fables did not remain special to German national literature, but became popular subjects in the literature of the whole world; and it is a significant fact that they afterwards took root especially in Flanders, where the taste for still life and delight in Nature has always found a home, and which became the nursery, in later times, of landscape, animal, and genre painting.

CHAPTER III

THE NAÏVE FEELING AT THE TIME OF THE CRUSADES

In the development and maturing of the race, as of the individual, nothing is more helpful than contact with foreign elements, people of other manners, thoughts, and feelings. Intimate intercourse between different nationalities rouses what is best in the soul of a nation, inviting, as it does, to discussion and opposition, as well as to the acquisition of new ideas. The conquests of Alexander the Great opened up a new world to the Greek, and a new culture arose—Hellenism. It was a new world that rose before the astonished eyes of the Crusader—in his case too, the East; but the resulting culture did not last. The most diverse motives fused to bring about this great migration to a land at once unknown and yet, through religion, familiar; and a great variety of characters and nations met under the banner of the Cross.

Naturally this shaking up together, not only of Europeans among themselves, but of the eastern with the western world, brought about a complete revolution in manners, speech, art, science, trade, manufacture, thought, and feeling, and so became an important factor in general progress.

The narrow boundaries of nationality, race, and education were broken through; all felt equal before the leading idea; men, places, plants, and animals were alike new and wonderful. Little wonder if German knights returning home from the East wove fiction with their fact, and produced the most fantastic and adventurous heroic songs.

Many of the noblest of the nations joined the Crusades in pious ardour for the cause, and it is easy to imagine the effect of the complete novelty of scene upon them. With such tremendous new impressions to cope with, it is not surprising that even the best minds, untrained as they were, were unequal to the task, and that the descriptions of real experiences or events in poetic form failed to express what they meant. Besides this, there is no doubt that in many ways the facts fell below their ideals ; also that the Crusader's mantle covered at the same time a rabble, which joined from the lowest motives, the scum of Europe. It must also be remembered that it is far easier to experience or feel than to pass on that experience and feeling to others ; that those who wrote did not always belong to the most educated; and that they wrote, for the most part, with difficulty in Greek or Latin. When all this has been weighed and admitted, the fact remains that in existing accounts of the Crusades there is great poverty of description of scenery, and lack of much feeling for Nature. The historian, as such, was bound to give first place to matters of fact and practical importance, and so to judge a place by its value to an army passing through or occupying it ; by its fertility, water-supply, its swamps or stony ground, and so forth ; but still the modern reader is astonished to see how little impression the scenery of the Holy Land made, judged by the accounts we possess, upon the Crusaders. Even when it is conceded that other important concerns came first, and that danger, want, and hunger must often have made everything disagreeable, still, references to Nature are very scanty, and one may look in vain for any interest in beautiful scenery for its own sake.

There is only matter-of-fact geographical and

mythological information in William of Tours'
History of the Crusades; for instance, in his descrip-
tion of the Bosphorus he does not waste a word
over its beauty. But, as 'fruitful' and 'pleasant'
are ever-recurring adjectives with him, one cannot
say that he absolutely ignored it.

He said of Durazzo: 'They weather the bad
seasons of the year in fruitful districts rich in woods
and fields, and all acceptable conditions'; of Tyre,
'The town has a most excellent position on a plain,
almost entirely surrounded by mountains. The soil
is productive, the wood of value in many ways.'
Of Antioch, 'Its position is very convenient and
pleasant, it lies in valleys which have excellent and
fertile soil, and are most pleasantly watered by
springs and streams. The mountains which enclose
the town on both sides are really very high; but
send down very clear water, and their sides and
slopes are covered by buildings up to the very
summits.' There is nothing about beautiful views,
unless one takes this, which really only records a
meteorological curiosity: 'From the top of one
mountain one can see the ball of the sun at the
fourth watch of the night, and if one turns round at
the time when the first rays light up the darkness,
one has night on one side and day on the other.'

Tyre is described again as 'conspicuous for the
fertility of its soil and the charm of its position.'
Its great waterworks are especially admired, since
by their means 'not only the gardens and most
fruitful orchards flourish, but the cane from which
sugar is made, which is so useful to man for health
and other purposes, and is sent by merchants to the
most distant parts of the world.' Other reporters
were charmed by the fertility and wealth of the
East. 'On those who came from the poorer and
colder western countries, the rich resources of the
sunny land in comparison with the poverty of home
made an impression of overflowing plenty, and at

times almost of inexhaustibleness. The descriptions of certain districts, extolled for their special richness, sound almost enthusiastic.'[1]

Burkhard von Monte Sion was enthusiastic about Lebanon's wealth of meadows and gardens, and the plain round Tripolis, and considered the Plain of Esdraelon the most desirable place in the world; but, on exact and unprejudiced examination, there is nothing in his words beyond homely admiration and matter-of-fact discussion of its great practical utility.

He says of La Boneia, 'That plain has many homesteads, and beautiful groves of olive and fig and other trees of various kinds, and much timber. Moreover, it abounds in no common measure in rivers and pasture land'; closes a geographical account of Lebanon thus, 'There are in Libanus and Antilibanus themselves fertile and well-tilled valleys, rich in pasture land, vineyards, gardens, plantations—in a word, in all the good things of the world'; and says of the Plain of Galilee, 'I never saw a lovelier country, if our sins and wrong-doing did not prevent Christians from living there.'

He had some feeling too for a distant view. He wrote of Samaria: 'The site was very beautiful; the view stretched right to the Sea of Joppa and to Antipatris and Cæsarea of Palestine, and over the whole mountain of Ephraim down to Ramathaym and Sophim and to Carmel near Accon by the sea. And it is rich in fountains and gardens and olive groves, and all the good things this world desires.' But it would be going too far to conclude from the following words that he appreciated the contrast between simple and sublime scenery: 'It must be noticed too, that the river, from the source of Jordan at the foot of Lebanon as far as the Desert of Pharan, has broad and pleasant plains on both sides, and beyond these the fields are surrounded by very high mountains as far as the Red Sea.'

In dealing with Gethsemane and the Mount of Olives, religious enthusiasm suppresses any reference to scenery.

These descriptions shew that the wealth and fertility of the country were praised before its beauty, and that this was only referred to in short, meagre phrases, which tell less about it than any raptures without special knowledge.

It was much the same with Phokas, who visited the Holy Land in 1135.[2]

He was greatly impressed by the position of Antioch, 'with its meadows and fruitful gardens, and the murmur of waters as the river, fed by the torrents of the Castalian spring, flows quietly round the town and besprinkles its towers with its gentle waves . . . . but most to be admired of all is the mountain between town and sea, a noble and remarkable sight—indeed, a delight to the beholder's eye . . . . the Orontes flows with countless windings at the foot of it, and discharges itself into the sea.'

He thought Lebanon very beautiful and worthy its praise in Holy Scripture: 'The sun lies like white hair upon its head; its valleys are crowned with pines, cedars, and cypresses; streams, beautiful to look at and quite cold, flow from the ravines and valleys down to the sea, and the freshly melted snow gives the flowing water its crystal clearness.'

Tyre, too, was praised for its beauty: 'Strangers were particularly delighted with one spring, which ran through meadows; and if one stands on the tower, one can see the dense growth of plants, the movement of the leaves in the glow of noon.'

The plain of Nazareth, too, was ' a heaven on earth, the delight of the soul.'

But recollections of the sacred story were dearer to Phokas than the scenery, and elsewhere he limited himself to noting the rich fruit gardens, shady groups of trees, and streams and rivers with pleasant banks.

Epiphanius Monachus Hagiopolitæ, in his *Enarratio Syriæ*, was a very dry pioneer; so, too, the *Anonymus de locis Hierosolymitanis*; Perdiccas, in his *Hierosolyma*, describes Sion thus: 'It stands on an eminence so as to strike the eye, and is beautiful to behold, owing to a number of vines and flower gardens and pleasant spots.'

It must be admitted then, that, beside utilitarian admiration of a Paradise of fruitfulness, there is some record of simple, even enthusiastic delight in its beauty; but only as to its general features, and in the most meagre terms. The country was more interesting to the Crusaders as the scene of the Christian story than as a place in which to rest and dream and admire Nature for her own sake.

The accounts of German pilgrimages[5] of the fourteenth and fifteenth centuries only contain dry notices, such as those of Jacob von Bern (1346–47), Pfintzing (1436–40), and Ulrich Leman (1472–80). The last-mentioned praises Damascus in this clumsy fashion: 'The town is very gay, quite surrounded by orchards, with many brooks and springs flowing inside and out, and an inexpressible number of people in it,' etc. Dietrich von Schachten describes Venice in this way: 'Venice lies in the sea, and is built neither on land nor on mountain, but on wooden piles, which is unbelievable to one who has not seen it'; and Candia: 'Candia is a beautiful town in the sea, well built; also a very fruitful island, with all sorts of things that men need for living.' He describes a ride through Southern Italy: 'Saturday we rode from Trepalda, but the same day through chestnut and hazel woods; were told that these woods paid the king 16,000 gulden every year. After that we rode a German mile through a wood, where each tree had its vine—many trees carried 3 ohms of wine, which is pleasant to see—and came to Nola.'

He called Naples 'very pretty and big,' and went

on: 'Then the king took us to the sea and shewed us the ports, which are pretty and strong with bulwarks and gates; we saw many beautiful ships too,' etc. One does not know which is the more wonderful here, the poverty of the description or the utter lack of personal observation: what the wood produced, and how one was protected from the sea, was more important to the writer than wood and sea themselves, and this, even in speaking of the Bay of Naples, perhaps the most beautiful spot in Europe. But instances like these are typical of German descriptions at the time, and their Alpine travels fared no better.'

Geographical knowledge of the Alps advanced very slowly; there was as yet no æsthetic enjoyment of their beauty. The Frankish historians (Gregory of Tours, Fredegar) chronicled special events in the Alps, but very briefly. Fredegar, for instance, knew of the sudden appearance of a hot spring in the Lake of Thun, and Gregory of Tours notes that the land-slip in 563 at the foot of the Dent du Midi, above the point where the Rhine enters the Lake of Geneva, was a dreadful event. Not only was the Castle of Tauretunum overwhelmed, but the blocking of the Rhine caused a deluge felt as far as Geneva. The pious prince of the Church explained this as a portent of another catastrophe, the pest, which ravaged Gaul soon after.

There was much fabling at that time in the legends of saints, about great mines of iron, gold, and silver, and about chamois and buck, cattle-breeding and Alpine husbandry in the 'regio montana'; for example, in von Aribo's *Vita S. Emmerani*. When the Alps became more frequented, especially when, through Charlemagne, a political bridge came to unite Italy and Germany, new roads were made and the whole region was better known—in fact, early in mediæval times, not only political, but ecclesiastical and mercantile life spread its threads over a great

part of the known world, and began to bind the
lives of nations together, so that the Alps no
longer remained *terra incognita* to dwellers far and
near.

We have accounts of Alpine journeys by the Abbé
Majolus v. Clugny (970), Bernard v. Hildesheim
(1101), Aribert v. Mailand, Anno v. Coeln'), but
without a trace of orography. They scarcely refer
to the snow and glacier regions from the side of
physical geography, or even of æsthetic feeling; and
do not mention the mountain monarchs so familiar
to-day—Mt. Blanc, the Jungfrau, Ortner, Glockner,
etc.—which were of no value to their life, practical
or scientific. These writers record nothing but names
of places and their own troubles and dangers in
travelling, especially in winter. And even at the end
of the fifteenth century, German travels across the
Alps were written in the same strain—for example,
the account of the voyage of the Elector-Palatine
Alexander v. Zweibrücken and Count Joh. Ludwig
zu Nassau (1495–96) from Zurich Rapperschwyl and
Wesen to Wallensee: ' This is the real Switzerland;
has few villages, just a house here and a house there,
but beautiful meadows, much cattle, and very high
mountains, on which snow lies, which falls before
Christmas, and is as hard as any rock.' As an
exception to this we have a vivid and poetic de-
scription of the famous Verona Pass in Latin verse
by Guntherus Ligurinus.

Günther's description of this notorious ravine,
between sky-high Alps, with the torrent rushing
at the bottom and a passage so narrow that men
could only move forward one by one, sounds like
a personal experience. This twelfth-century poem
comes to us, in fact, like a belated echo of Fortunatus.

We must now enquire whether the chief representa-
tives of German literature at this time shewed any
of the national love of Nature, whether the influence
of the Crusades was visible in them, how far scenery

took a place in epic and song, and whether, as
moderns have so often stated, mediæval Germany
stood high above antiquity in this respect. Gervinus,
a classic example on the last point, in the section of
his history of German poetry which treats of the
difference between the German fables about animals
on the one hand, and Esop's and the Oriental on the
other, said :

> The way in which animals are handled in the fables
> demanded a far slighter familiarity between them and
> men ; so exact a knowledge as we see in the German
> fables, often involving knowledge of their natural
> history, such insight into the 'privacy of the animal
> world,' belonged to quite another kind of men. Antiquity
> did not delight in Nature, and delight in Nature is
> the very foundation of these poems. Remote antiquity
> neither knew nor sought to know any natural history ;
> but only wondered at Nature. The art of hunting
> and the passion for it, often carried to excess in the
> Middle Ages, was unknown to it. It is a bold remark
> of Grimm's that he could smell the old smell of the
> woods in the German animal poems, but it is one whose
> truth every one will feel, who turns to this simple
> poetry with an open mind, who cares for Nature and
> life in the open.

This is a very tangle of empty phrases and mis-
statements. No people stood in more heartfelt and
naive relation to Nature, especially to the animal
world, than the Hindoos and Persians. In earlier
enquiries[6] we have reviewed the naive feeling dis-
played in Homer and the sentimental in Hellenism,
and have seen that the taste for hunting increased
knowledge of Nature in the open in Hellenic days
far more than in the Middle Ages. We shall see now
that the level of feeling reached in those and imperial
Roman days was not regained in European literature
until long after the fall of Latin poetry, and that it
was the fertilizing influence of that classic spirit, and
that alone, which enabled the inborn German taste
for Nature, and for hunting, and plant and animal
life, to find artistic expression. It was a too super-

ficial knowledge of classic literature, and an inclination to synthesis, and clever *a priori* argument (a style impressed upon his day by Hegel's method, and fortunately fast disappearing), which led Gervinus to exalt the Middle Ages at the expense of antiquity. It sounds like a weak concession when he says elsewhere :

> Joy in Nature, which is peculiar to modern times, in contrast to antiquity, which is seen in the earliest mediæval poems, and in which, moreover, expiring antiquity came to meet the German—this joy in Nature, in dwelling on plant and animal life, is the very soul of this (animal) poetry. As in its plastic art, so in all its poetry, antiquity only concerned itself with gods and heroes ; its glance was always turned upwards.

But, as a fact, no one has ever stood with feet more firmly planted on this earth than the Greek, enjoying life and undeterred by much scruple or concern as to the powers above ; and centuries of development passed before German literature equalled Greek in love of Nature and expressive representation of her beauty.

To rank the two national epics of Germany, the *Nibelungenlied* and *Gudrun*, side by side with the *Iliad* and *Odyssey* is to exaggerate their value. And here, as ever, overstraining the comparison is mischievous.

The *Nibelungenlied* is undeniably charming with its laconic and yet plastic descriptions, its vigorous heroes, and the tragic course of their fate ; so is *Gudrun*, that melodious poem of the North Sea. But they never, either in composition, method of representation, or descriptive epithets, reach the perfect art of the Greek epics. What moral beauty and plastic force there is in Homer's comparisons and in his descriptions of times and seasons ! what a clear eye and warm heart he has for Nature in all her moods ! and what raw and scanty beginnings of such things we have in the *Nibelungenlied* !

It is true Homer had not attained to the degree of sympathy which finds in Nature a friend, a sharer of one's joys and sorrows; she is pictured objectively in the form of epic comparisons; but how faithfully, and with what range and variety!

There can scarcely be another epic in the world so poor in descriptions of time and place as the *Nibelungenlied*; it cannot be used to prove German feeling for Nature!

India, Persia, and Greece made natural phenomena the counterparts of human life, weaving into the tale, by way of comparison or environment, charming genre pictures of plant and animal life, each complete in itself; in the *Nibelungenlied* Nature plays no part at all, not even as framework.

Time is indicated as sparsely as possible:

'Upon the 7th day at Worms on the Rhine shore, the gallant horsemen arrived.'

'On a Whitsun morning we saw them all go by'; or 'When it grew towards even, and near the sun's last ray, seeing the air was cooler'; or 'He must hang, till light morning threw its glow through the window.' The last is the most poetic; elsewhere it is 'Day was over, night fell.'

Terseness can be both a beauty and a force; but, in comparison with Greece, how very little feeling for Nature these expressions contain!

It is no better with descriptions of place:

'From the Rhine they rode through Hesse, their warriors as well, towards the Saxon country, where they to fighting fell.'

'He found a fortress placed upon a mountain.'

'Into a wide-roomed palace of fashion excellent, for there, beneath it rushing, one saw the Danube's flood.'

Even the story of the hunt and the murder of Siegfried is quite matter-of-fact and sparse as to scenery: 'By a cold spring he soon lost his life . . . .

then they rode from there into a deep wood . . . .
there they encamped by the green wood, where they
would hunt on the broad mead . . . . one heard
mountain and tree echo.'

'The spring of water was pure and cool and
good.' . . .

'There fell Chriemhild's husband among the
flowers . . . . all round about the flowers were
wetted with his blood.'

One thinks instinctively of Indian and Greek
poetry, of Adonis and the death of Baldur in the
Northern Saga. But even here, where the subject
almost suggests it, there is no trace of Nature's
sympathy with man.

References to the animal world too—Chriemhild's
dreams of the falcons seized by two eagles, and
the two wild boars which attacked Siegfried, the
game hunted in the forests by the heroes who run
like panthers—all show it to be of no importance.

Even such phrases as rosy-red, snow-white, etc.,
are rare—'Her lovely face became all rosy-red with
pleasure'; but there is a certain tenderness in the
comparisons of Chriemhild:

'Then came the lovely maiden, even as morning
red from sombre clouds outbreaking,' and, 'just
as the moon in brightness excels the brightest
stars, and suddenly outshining, athwart the clouds
appears,' so she excelled all other women.

It has been said that one can hear the sighing of
the north wind and the roar of the North Sea in
Gudrun, but this is scarcely more than a pretty
phrase. The 'dark tempestuous' sea, 'wild un-
fathomable' waves, the shore 'wet from the
blood of the slain,' are indeed mentioned, but
that is all.

Wat of Sturmland says to the young warriors :
'The air is still and the moon shines clear ~ . . . .
when the red star yonder in the south dips his head
in the brine, I shall blow on my great horn that all

the hosts shall hear'; but it is hope of morning, not delight in the starry sky, that he is expressing.

Indications of place too are of the briefest, just ' It was a broad neck of land, called the Wülpen-sand,' or, ' In a few hours they saw the shores where they would land, a little harbour lay in sight enfolded by low hills clothed with dark fir trees.'

The first trace of sympathy with Nature occurs in the account of the effect of Horand's song.

Like Orpheus, he charms the little birds and other creatures : ' He sang with such a splendid voice, that the little birds ceased their song.'

' And as he began to sing again, all the birds in the copse round ceased their sweet songs.'

' The very cattle left their green pastures to hearken, the little gold beetles stopped running among the grass, the fishes ceased to shoot about in the brooks. He sang long hours, and it seemed but a brief moment. The very church bells sounded sweet no longer ; the folk left the choir songs of the priests and ran to hear him. All who heard his voice were heart-sick after the singer, so grand and sweet was the strain.'

Indications of time are rarely found more short and concise than here :

> When night ended and day began.
> On the 12th day they quitted the country.
> In Maytime. On a cool morning.

This is a little richer :

> It was the time when leaves spring up delightfully and birds of all sorts sing their best in the woods.

Much more definite and distinct is :

> It was about that time of the year when departing winter sheds his last terrors upon the earth ; a sharp breeze was blowing and the sea was covered with broken up ice ; but there were gleams of sunshine upon the hills, and the little birds began to tune their throats tremulously, that they might be ready to sing their lay when the March weather was past.

> Gudrun trembled with cold; her wet garment clung close to her white limbs; the wind dashed her golden hair about her face.

And later, when the morning of Gudrun's deliverance breaks, the indications of time, though short, are plastic enough:

> After the space of an hour the red star went down upon the edge of the sea, and Wat of Sturmland, standing upon the hill, blew a great blast on his horn, which was heard in the land for miles round. . . . The sound of Wat's horn . . . . wakened a young maid, who, stealing on tiptoe to the window, looked over the bay and beheld the glimmering of spears and helms upon the sands. . . . 'Awake, mistress,' she cried, 'the host of the Hegelings is at hand.'

Companions are few:

> He sprang like a wild lion.

The shower of stones flung down upon Wat 'is but an April shower.'

Images are few too:

> This flower of hope, to find repose here on the shore, Hartmouth and his friends did not bring to blossom.

Wilhelm Grimm rightly observes:

> At this epoch the poetry of the Fatherland gave no separate descriptions of Nature—descriptions, that is, whose only object was to paint the impression of the landscape in glowing colours upon the mind. The old German masters certainly did not lack feeling for Nature, but they have left us no other expression of it than such as its connection with historical events demanded.

And further:

> The question, whether contact with Southern Italy, or, through the Crusades, with Asia Minor, Syria, and Palestine, did not enrich German poetry with new pictures of Nature, can only, as a general rule, be answered in the negative.

In the courtly epics of chivalry, the place of real Nature was taken by a fabulous wonderworld, full of the most fantastic and romantic scenery, in which wood, field, plants, and animals were all distorted. For instance, in the Alexander saga (of Pfaffen Lamprecht) Alexander the Great describes to his teacher Aristotle the wonders he has seen, and how one day he came with his army to a dark forest, where the interlacing boughs of tall trees completely shut out the sunlight. Clear, cool streams ran through it down to the valley, and birds' songs echoed in the shade. The ground was covered by an enormous quantity of flower buds of wondrous size, which looked like great balls, snow-white and rose-coloured, closely folded up. Presently, the fragrant goblets opened, and out of all these wonder-flowers stepped lovely maidens, rosy as dawn and white as day, and about twelve years old. All these thousands of charming beings raised their voices together and competed with the birds in song, swaying up and down in charming lines, singing and laughing in the cool shade. They were dressed in red and white, like the flowers from which they were born ; but if sun rays fell on them, they would fade and die. They were only children of the woodland shade and the summer, and lived no longer than the flowers, which May brings to life and Autumn kills. In this wood Alexander and his host pitched their tents, and lived through the summer with the little maids. But their happiness only lasted three months and twelve days :

> When the time came to an end, our joy passed away too ; the flowers faded, and the pretty girls died ; trees lost their leaves, springs their flow, and the birds their song ; all pleasure passed away. Discomfort began to touch my heart with many sorrows, as day by day I saw the beautiful maidens die, the flowers fade : with a heavy heart, I departed with my men.

This fairy-like tale, with its blending of human and plant life, is very poetically conceived ; but it is only a play of fancy, one of the early steps towards the modern feeling.

The battle scenes, as well as other scenes in this poem, are bold and exaggerated. Armies meet like roaring seas; missiles fly from both sides as thick as snow; after the dreadful bath of blood, sun and moon veil their light and turn away from the murder committed there.

Hartmann von der Aue, too, did not draw real Nature, but only one of his own invention.

For example, the wild forest with the magic spring in *Iwein*:

> I turned to the wilds next morning, and found an extensive clearing, hidden in the forest, solitary and without husbandmen. There, to my distress, I descried a sad delight of the eyes—beasts of every kind that I know the names of, attacking each other . . . . this spring is cold and very pure; neither rain, sun, or wind reach it; it is screened by a most beautiful lime tree. The tree is excessively tall and thick, so that neither sun nor rain can penetrate its foliage, winter does not injure it, nor lessen its beauty by one hair; 'tis green and blossoming the whole year round. . . . Over the spring there is a wonderfully fine stone . . . . the tree was so covered with birds that I could scarcely see the branches, and even the foliage almost disappeared. The sweet songs were pleasant and resounded through the forest, which re-echoed them. . . .

> As I poured water upon the ruby, the sun, which had just come out, disappeared, the birds' song round about ceased, a black storm approached, dark heavy storm-clouds came from all four quarters of the vault of heaven. It seemed no longer bright day . . . . soon a thousand flashes of lightning played round me in the forest . . . . there came storm, rain, and hail . . . . the storm became so great that the forest broke down.

He never shews a real love for Nature even in his lyrics, for the wish for flowers in *Winter Complaint* can hardly be said to imply that:

> He who cares for flowers must lament much at this heavy, dismal time; a wife helps to shorten the long nights. In this way I will shorten long winter without the birds' song.

Wolfram von Eschenbach, too, is very sparing of references to Nature : time is given by such phrases as 'when twilight began,' or 'as the day broke,' 'at the bright glow of morning' . . . . 'as day already turned to evening.'

His interest in real things was driven into the background by love-making and adventures— *Arthur's Round Table* and the *Holy Grail* ; all the romance of knighthood. When he described a forest or a garden, he always decked it out lavishly.

For instance, the garden in Orgeluse :

> A garden surrounding a mountain, planted with noble trees where pomegranates, figs, olives, vines, and other fruits grew richly . . . . a spring poured from the rock, and (for all this would have been nothing to him without a fair lady) there he found what did not displease him—a lady so beautiful and fair that he was charmed at the sight, the flower of womanly beauty.

Comparisons are few and not very poetic. In *Songs of the Heart*—

> The lady of the land watered herself with her heart's tears.
>
> Her eyes rained upon the child.
>
> Her joy was drowned in lamentation.

Gawan and Orgeluse,

> Spite their outer sweetness, as disagreeable as a shower of rain in sunshine.
>
> There were many fair flowers, but their colours could not compare with that of Orgeluse.

His heroes are specially fond of birds. Young Parzival

> Felt little care while the little birds sang round him ; it made his heart swell, he ran weeping into the house.

and Gawan

> Found a door open into a garden ; he stept in to look round and enjoy the air and the singing of the birds.

So we see that in the *Nibelungenlied* scarcely a plant grew, and Hartmann and Wolfram's gardens belonged almost entirely to an unreal region; there are no traces of a very deep feeling for Nature in all this.

But Gottfried von Strassburg, with his vivid, sensuous imagination and keen eye for beauty, shewed a distinct advance both in taste and achievement. He, too, notes time briefly: 'And as it drew towards evening,' 'Now day had broke.' He repeats his comparisons: fair ladies are 'the wonder rose of May,' 'the longing white rose.' The two Isolts are sun and dawn. Brangäne is the full moon. The terrified girl is thus described:

> Her rosy mouth paled; the fair colour, which was her ornament, died out of her skin; her bright eyes grew dim like night after day.

Another comparison is:

> Like the siren's song, drawing a bark to the reef as by a magnet, so the sweet young queen attracted many hearts.

Love is a usurious plant, whose sun never goes down; a romance sweetens the mood as May dew sweetens the blood.

Constant friendship is one which takes the pleasure with the pain, the thorn with the rose. The last comparisons shew more thought, and still more is seen in the beginning of the poem, *Riwalin and Blancheflur*, which has a charming description of Spring.

> Now the festival was agreed upon and arranged
> For the four flowering weeks
> When sweet May attracts, till he flies off again.
> At Tinkapol upon a green plain
> High up on a wonderful meadow with spring colour
> Such as no eye has seen before or since. Soft sweet May
> Had dressed it with his own charming extravagance.

There were little wood birds, a joy to the ear,
Flowers and grass and green plants and summer
    meads
That were a delight to eye and heart.
One found there whatever one would, whatever May
    should bring—
Shade from the sun, limes by the brook,
A gentle breeze which brought the prattle
Of Mark's court people. May's friend, the green
    turf,
Had made herself a charming costume of flowers,
In which she shone back at the guests with a festival
    of her own ;
The blossoming trees smiled so sweetly at every
    one,
That heart and mind smiled back again.
The pure notes of the birds, blessed and beautiful,
Touched heart and senses, filling hill and dale with
    joy.
The dear nightingale,
Sweet bird, may it ever be blessed !
Sang so lustily upon the bough
That many a heart was filled with joy and good
    humour.
There the company pitched itself
With great delight on the green grass.
The limes gave enough shade,
And many covered their tent roofs with green
    boughs.

There is a heartfelt ring in this. We see that even
this early period of German mediæval poetry was
not entirely lacking in clear voices to sing of
Nature with real sympathy.

The description of the Minne grotto is famous,
with its magical accessories, its limes and other trees,
birds, songs, and flowers, so that 'eye and ear alike
found solace'; but the romantic love episode,
interwoven as it is by the poet with the life of Nature,
is more interesting for our purpose.

They had a court, they had a council which brought
them nought but joy. Their courtiers were the green
trees, the shade and the sunlight, the streamlet and
the spring ; flowers, grass, leaf, and blossom, which

refreshed their eyes. Their service was the song of the birds, the little brown nightingales, the throstlets and the merles and other wood birds. The siskin and the ringdove vied with each other to do them pleasure, all day long their music rejoiced ear and soul. Their love was their high feast. . . . The man was with the woman, and the woman with the man; they had the fellowship they most desired, and were where they fain would be. . . .

In the dewy morning they gat them forth to the meadow where grass and flowers alike had been refreshed. The glade was their pleasure-ground; they wandered hither and thither hearkening each other's speech, and waking the song of the birds by their footsteps. Then they turned them to where the cool clear spring rippled forth, and sat beside its stream and watched its flow till the sun grew high in the heaven, and they felt its shade. Then they betook them to the linden, its branches offered them a welcome shelter, the breezes were sweet and soft beneath its shade, and the couch at its feet was decked with the fairest grass and flowers.

With these lovers, love of Nature is only second to love of each other. So in the following :

That same morning had Tristan and his lady-love stolen forth hand in hand and come full early, through the morning dew, to the flowery meadow and the lovely vale. Dove and nightingale saluted them sweetly, greeting their friends Tristan and Iseult. The wild wood birds bade them welcome in their own tongue . . . . it was as if they had conspired among themselves to give the lovers a morning greeting. They sang from the leafy branches in changeful wise, answering each other in song and refrain. The spring that charmed their eye and ear whispered a welcome, even as did the linden with its rustling leaves. The blossoming trees, the fair meadow, the flowers, and the green grass— all that bloomed laughed at their coming; the dew which cooled their feet and refreshed their heart offered a silent greeting.

The amorous passion was the soil in which, in its early narrow stages, sympathy for Nature grew up. Was it the thirteenth-century lyrics, the love-songs of the Minnesingers, which unfolded the germ ? For the lyric is the form in which the deepest expression can be given to feeling for Nature, and in which she either appears as background, frame, or ornament, or, by borrowing a soul or symbolizing thought and feeling, blends with the inner life.

As the German court epics took their material from France, so the German love-songs were inspired by the Provençal troubadours. The national differeuces stand out clear to view: the vivid glowing Provençal is fresher, more vehement, and mettlesome; the dreamy German more monotonous, tame, and melancholy. The one is given to proud daring, wooing, battle, and the triumph of victory; the other to musing, loving, and brooding enthusiasm. The stamp of the occasional, of improvisation, is upon all Provençal work; while with the German Minnesingers, everything—Nature as well as love—tends to be stereotyped, monotonous.

The scanty remains of Troubadour songs' often shew mind and Nature very strikingly brought together, either in harmony or contrast. For example, Bernard von Ventadour (1195):

It may annoy others to see the foliage fall from the trees, but it pleases me greatly; one cannot fancy I should long for leaves and flowers when she, my dear one, is haughty to me.

Cold and snow become flowers and greenery under her charming glance.

As I slumber at night, I am waked by the sweet song of the nightingale; nothing but love in my mind quite thrilled by shudders of delight.

God! could I be a swallow and sweep through the air, I would go at midnight to her little chamber.

When I behold the lark up spring
To meet the bright sun joyfully,
How he forgets to poise his wing
In his gay spirit's revelry.
Alas! that mournful thoughts should spring
E'en from that happy songster's glee!
Strange that such gladdening sight should bring
Not joy but pining care to me.

A very modern thought which calls to mind
Theodore Storm's touching lines after the death
of his wife:

> But this I cannot endure, that the sun smiles as
> before, clocks strike and bells ring as in thy lifetime,
> and day and night still follow each other.

He connects spring with love:

> When grass grows green and fresh leaves spring
> And flowers are budding on the plain,
> When nightingales so sweetly sing
> And through the greenwood swells the strain,
> Then joy I in the song and in the flower,
> Joy in myself but in my lady more;
> All objects round my spirit turns to joy,
> But most from her my rapture rises high.

Arnold von Mareuil (about 1200) sings in the same
way:

> O! how sweet the breeze of April
> Breathing soft, as May draws near,
> While through nights serene and gentle
> Songs of gladness meet the ear.
> Every bird his well-known language
> Warbling in the morning's pride,
> Revelling on in joy and gladness
> By his happy partner's side . . . .
> With such sounds of bliss around me,
> Who could wear a saddened heart?

He calls his lady-love

> The fairest creature which Nature has produced here
> below, fairer than I can express and fairer than a beauti-
> ful May day, than sunshine in March, shade in summer,
> than May roses, April rain, the flower of beauty, mirror
> of love, the key of Fame.

Bertran de Born too sings:

> The beautiful spring delights me well
> When flowers and leaves are growing,
> And it pleases my heart to hear the swell
> Of the bird's sweet chorus flowing
> In the echoing wood, etc.

The Greek lyrists up to Alexandrian times contented themselves with implying indirectly that nothing delighted them so much as May and its delights; but these singers implicitly state it. The German Minnesingers too[8] are loud in praise of spring, as in that anonymous song:

> I think nothing so good nor worthy of praise
> As a fair rose and my good man's love;
> The song of the little birds in the woods is clear to
> many a heart.

and summer is greeted with:

> The good are glad that summer comes. See what
> a benefit it is to many hearts.

The Troubadour motive is here too:

> Winter and snow seem as beautiful flowers and clover
> to me, when I have embraced her.

and Kürenberg makes a lady sing:

> When I stand there alone in my shift and think of
> thee, noble knight, I blush like a rose on its thorn.

Delight in summer, complaint of winter—this is the fundamental chord struck again and again; there is scarcely any trace of blending the feelings of the lover with those of Nature. It is a monotonous repetition of a few themes, of flowers and little birds as messengers of love, and lady-loves who are brighter than the sun, whose presence brings spring in winter or cheers a grey and snowy day.

Deitmar von Eist greets spring with:

> Ah! now the time of the little birds' singing is
> coming for us, the great lime is greening, the long
> winter is past, one sees well-shaped flowers spread their
> glory over the heath. 'Tis a joy to many hearts, and
> a comfort too to mine.

In another song the birds and roses remind him of a happy past and of the lady of his heart.

A little bird sang on the lime o'erhead,
Its song resounded through the wood
And turned my heart back to another place ;
And once again I saw the roses blow,
And they brought back the many thoughts
I cherish of a lady.

A lady says to a falcon :

You happy falcon you ! You fly whither you will !
And choose the tree you like in the wood.
I have done the same. I chose a husband
For myself, whom my eyes chose.
So 'tis fitting for beautiful women.

In winter he complains :

Alas for summer delight ! The birds' song has
disappeared with the leaves of the lime. Time has
changed, the nightingales are dumb. They have given
up their sweet song and the wood has faded from
above.

Uhland's beautiful motive in *Spring Faith*, that
light and hope will come back to the oppressed heart
with the flowers and the green, is given, though stiffly
and dimly, by Heinrich von Veldegge :

I have some delightful news ; the flowers are sprout-
ing on the heath, the birds singing in the wood. Where
snow lay before, there is now green clover, bedewed in
the morning. Who will may enjoy it. No one forces
me to, I am not free from cares.

and elsewhere :

At the time when flowers and grass come to us, all
that made my heart sad will be made good again.

The loss of the beauty of summer makes him sad :

Since the bright sunlight has changed to cold, and
the little birds have left off singing their song, and cold
nights have faded the foliage of the lime, my heart is
sad.

Ulrich von Guotenberg makes a pretty com-
parison :

She is my summer joy, she sows flowers and clover
In my heart's meadow, whence I, whate'er befall,
Must teem with richer bliss : the light of her eyes
Makes me bloom, as the hot sun the dripping
    trees. . . .
Her fair salute, her mild command
Softly inclining, make May rain drop down into my
    heart.

Heinrich von Rugge laments winter :

The dear nightingale too has forgotten how beauti-
fully she sang . . . . the birds are mourning every-
where.

and longs for summer :

I always craved blissful days . . . . I liked to hear
the little birds' delightful songs. Winter cannot but
be hard and immeasurably long. I should be glad
if it would pass away.

Heinrich von Morungen :

How did you get into my heart ?
It must ever be the same with me.
As the noon receives her light from the sun,
So the glance of your bright eyes, when you leave
    me,
Sinks into my heart.

He calls his love his light of May, his Easter Day :

She is my sweetheart, a sweet May
Bringing delights, a sunshine without cloud.

and says, in promising fidelity : ' My steady mind
is not like the wind.'
Reinmar says :

When winter is over
I saw the heath with the red flowers, delightful
    there. . . .
The long winter is past away ; when I saw the green
    leaves
I gave up much of my sorrow.

In a time of trouble he cried :

To me it must always be winter.

So we see that Troubadour references to Nature were drawn from a very limited area. Individual grasp of scenery was entirely lacking, it did not occur to them to seek Nature for her own sake. Their comparisons were monotonous, and their scenes bare, stereotyped arabesques, not woven into the tissue of lyric feeling. Their ruling motives were joy in spring and complaint of winter. Wood, flowers, clover, the bright sun, the moon (once), roses, lilies, and woodland birds, especially the nightingale, served them as elementary or landscape figures.

Wilhelm Grimm says :

> The Minnesingers talk often enough of mild May, the nightingale's song, the dew shining on the flowers of the heath, but always in relation only to their own feelings reflected in them. To indicate sad moods they used faded leaves, silent birds, seed buried in snow.

and Humboldt :

> The question, whether contact with Southern Italy, or the Crusades in Asia Minor, Syria, and Palestine, have enriched the art of poetry in Germany with new natural pictures, can only generally be answered by the negative. It is not remarked that the acquaintance with the East gave any new direction to the songs of the minstrels. The Crusaders came little into actual contact with the Saracens ; they even lived in a state of great restraint with other nations who fought in the same cause. One of the oldest lyric poets was Friedrich of Hausen. He perished in the army of Barbarossa. His songs contain many views of the Crusades ; but they chiefly express religious sentiments on the pain of being separated from his dear friends. He found no occasion to say anything concerning the country or any of those who took part in the wars, as Reinmar the Elder, Rubin, Neidhart, and Ulrich of Lichtenstein. Reinmar came a pilgrim to Syria, as it appears, in the train of Leopold the 6th, Duke of Austria. He complains that the recollections of his country always haunted him, and drew away his thoughts from God. The date tree has here been mentioned sometimes, when they speak of the palm branches which pious

pilgrims bore upon their shoulders. I do not remember
that the splendid scenery in Italy has excited the fancy
of the minstrels who crossed the Alps.   Walther, who
had wandered about, had only seen the river Po ;
but Friedank was at Rome. He merely remarked
that grass grew in the palaces of those who formerly
bore sway there.

As a fact, even the greatest Minnesinger, Walther,
the master lyrist of the thirteenth century, was not
ahead of his contemporaries in this matter.   His
Spring Longing begins :

> Winter has wrought us harm everywhere,
> Forest and field are dreary and bare
> Where the sweet voices of summer once were,
> Yet by the road where I see maiden fair
> Tossing the ball, the birds' song is there.

and *Spring and Women* :

> When flowers through the grass begin to spring
> As though to greet with smiles the sun's bright rays,
> On some May morning, and in joyous measure,
> Small songbirds make the dewy forest ring
> With a sweet chorus of sweet roundelays,
> Hath life in all its store a purer pleasure ?
> 'Tis half a Paradise on earth.
> Yet ask me what I hold of equal worth,
> And I will tell what better still
> Ofttimes before hath pleased mine eyes,
> And, while I see it, ever will.
> When a noble maiden, fair and pure,
> With raiment rich and tresses deftly braided,
> Mingles, for pleasure's sake, in company,
> High bred, with eyes that, laughingly demure,
> Glance round at times and make all else seem faded,
> As, when the sun shines, all the stars must die.
> Let May bud forth in all its splendour ;
> What sight so sweet can he engender
> As with this picture to compare ?
> Unheeded leave we buds and blooms,
> And gaze upon the lovely fair !

The grace in this rendering of a familiar motive,
and the individuality in the following *Complaint
of Winter*, were both unusual at the time :

Erewhile the world shone red and blue
And green in wood and upland too,
And birdlets sang on the bough.
But now it's grown grey and lost its glow,
And there's only the croak of the winter crow,
Whence—many a ruffled brow!

Elsewhere he says that his lady's favour turns his winter to spring, and adds:

Cold winter 'twas no more for me,
Though others felt it bitterly;
To me it was mid May.

He has many pictures of Nature and pretty comparisons, but the stereotyped style predominates— heath, flowers, grass, and nightingales. The pearl of the collection is the naive song which touches sensuous feeling, like the *Song of Solomon*, with the magic light of innocence:

Under the lime on the heath where I sat with my
     love,
There you would find
The grass and the flowers all crushed—
Sweetly the nightingale sang in the vale by the wood.
Tandaradei!
When I came up to the meadow my lover was waiting
     me there.
Ah! what a greeting I had! Gracious Mary, 'tis bliss
     to me still!
Tandaradei! Did he kiss me, you ask? Look at the
     red of my lips!
Of sweet flowers of all sorts he made us a bed,
I wager who passes now smiles at the sight,
The roses would still show just where my head lay.
Tandaradei!
But how he caressed me, that any but one
Should know that, God forbid! I were shamed if
     they did;
Only he and I know it,
And one little birdie who never will tell.

So we see that interest in Nature in the literature of the Crusaders very seldom went beyond the utilitarian bounds of pleasure and admiration in fertility and pleasantness; and the German national epics rarely alluded to her traits even by way of comparison. The court epics shewed some advance, and sympathy was distinctly traceable in Gottfried, and even attained to artistic expression in his lyrics, where his own feelings chimed with Nature.

For the rest, the Minnesingers' descriptions were all alike. The charm of Nature apart from other considerations, delight in her for her own sake alone, was unknown to the time.

Hitherto we have only spoken of literature.

Feeling for Nature reveals itself in plastic art also, especially in painting; and since the mind of a people is one united organism, the relation between poetry and painting is not one of opposition and mutual exclusion — they rather enlarge and explain, or condition each other.

As concerns feeling for Nature, it may be taken as a universal rule that landscape - painting only develops when Nature is sought for her own sake, and that so long as scenery merely serves the purpose of ornament in literature, so long it merely serves as accessory and background in painting; whereas, when Nature takes a wider space in prose and poetry, and becomes an end of representation in herself, the moment for the birth of landscape-painting has come. We will follow the stages of the development of painting very briefly, from Woltmann and Woermann's excellent book,' which, if it throws no fresh light upon our subject, illustrates what has just been said in a striking manner.

In the first centuries *Anno Domini*, painting was wholly proscribed by Christendom. Its technique did not differ from that of antiquity; but Christendom took up an attitude of antagonism. The picture worship of the old religions was opposed to its very origin and essence, and was only gradually introduced into the Christian cult through heathen influences. It is a fact too, easy to explain, especially through its Jewish origin, that Christianity at first felt no need of art, and that this one-sidedness only ceased when the specifically Jewish element in it had died out, and Christendom passed to cultivated Greeks and Romans. In the cemeteries and catacombs of the first three centuries, we find purely decorative work, light vines with Cupids, but also remains of landscapes ; for instance, in the oldest part of the cemetery of Domitilla at Rome, where the ceiling decoration consists of shepherds, fishers, and biblical scenes. The ceiling picture in St Lucina (second century) has apparently the Good Shepherd in the middle, and round it alternate pictures of Him and of the praying Madonna ; whilst in the middle it has also charming divisions with fields, branches with leaves and flowers, birds, masks, and floating genii.

In Byzantine painting too, the influence of antiquity was still visible, especially in a Psaltery with a Commentary and fourteen large pictures. David appears here as a shepherd ; a beautiful woman's form, exhibiting the melody, is leaning with her left arm upon his shoulder ; a nymph's head peeps out of the foliage ; and in front we have Bethlehem, and the mountain god resting in a bold position under a rock ; sheep, goats, and water are close by, and a landscape with classic buildings, streams, and mountains forms the background ; it is very poetically conceived. Elsewhere, too, personifications recur, in which classic beauty is still visible, mixed with severe Christian forms.

At the end of the tenth century began the Romantic period, which closed in the thirteenth.

The brilliant progress made by architecture paved the way for the other arts ; minds trained in its laws began to look for law in organic Nature too, and were no longer content with the old uncertain and arbitrary shapes. But as no independent feeling for Nature, in the widest sense of the term, existed, mediæval art treated her, not according to her own laws, but to those of architecture. With the development of the Gothic style, from the thirteenth century on, art became a citizen's craft, a branch of industry. Heretofore it had possessed but one means of expression—religious festival or ceremony, severely ecclesiastical. This limit was now removed. The artist lived a wide life, open to impressions from Nature, his imagination fed by poetry with new ideas and feelings, and constantly stimulated by the love of pleasure, which was so vehement among all classes that it turned every civil and ecclesiastical event to histrionic purposes, and even made its influence felt upon the clergy. The strong religious feeling which pervaded the Middle Ages still ruled, and even rose to greater enthusiasm, in accordance with the spirit of the day; but it was no longer a matter of blind submission of the will, but of conscious acceptance.

It is true that knowledge of the external world was as yet very limited; the painter had not explored and mastered it, but only used it as a means to represent a certain realm of feeling, studying it just so far as this demanded. We have seen the same in the case of poetry. The beginnings of realistic painting were visible, although, as, for example, in representing animals, no individuality was reached.

From the middle of the fourteenth century a new French school sprang up. The external world was more keenly and accurately studied, especially on its graceful side. It was only at the end of that period that painting felt the need to develop the background, and indicate actual surroundings by blue sky, hills, Gothic buildings, and conventional trees. These were given in linear perspective; of aerial perspective there was none. The earlier taste still ruled in initialling and border decorations; but little flowers were added by degrees to the thorn-leaf pattern, and birds, sometimes angels, introduced.

The altar-piece at Cologne, at the end of the fourteenth century, is more subjective in conception, and full of lyric feeling. Poetic feeling came into favour, especially in Madonna pictures of purely idyllic character, which were painted with most charming surroundings. Instead of a throne and worshipping figures, Mary was placed sitting comfortably with the Child on flowery turf, and saints around her; and although the background might be golden instead of landscape, yet all the stems and blossoms in the grass were naturally and accurately treated. In a little picture in the town museum at Frankfort, the Madonna is seated in a rose garden under fruit trees gay with birds, and reading a book; a table with food and drinks stands close by, and a battlemented wall surrounds the garden. She is absorbed in contemplation; three female saints are attending to mundane business close by, one drawing water from a brook, another picking cherries, the third teaching the child Christ to play the zither. There is real feeling in the whole picture, and the landscape is worked in with distinct reference to the chief idea.

Hence, although there were many isolated attempts to shew that realistic and individual study of Nature had begun, landscape-painting had not advanced beyond the position of a background, treated in a way more or less suited to the main subject of the picture; and trees, rocks, meadows, flowers, were still only framework, ornament, as in the poetry of the Minnesingers.[10]

CHAPTER IV

INDIVIDUALISM AND SENTIMENTAL FEELING
AT THE RENAISSANCE

In a certain sense all times are transitional to those who live in them, since what is old is always in process of being destroyed and giving way to the new. But there are landmarks in the general development of culture, which mark off definite periods and divide what has been from what is beginning. Hellenism was such a landmark in antiquity, the Renaissance in the Middle Ages.

Without overlooking the differences between Greek and Italian, classic and modern, which are relative and not absolute, it is instructive to note the great likeness between these two epochs. The limits of their culture will stand out more clearly, if, by the aid of Helbig's researches and Burckhardt's masterly account of the Renaissance, we range the chief points of that likeness side by side.

They were epochs in which an icy crust, which had been lying over human thought and feeling, melted as if before a spring breeze. It is true that the theory of life which now began to prevail was not absolutely new; the stages of growth in a nation's culture are never isolated; it was the result of the enlargement of various factors already present, and their fusion with a flood of incoming ones.

The Ionic-Doric Greek kingdom widened out in Alexander's time to a Hellenic-Asiatic one, and the

barriers of the Romano-Germanic Middle Ages fell
with the Crusades and the great voyages of dis-
covery. Hellenism and the Renaissance brought
about the transition from antiquity and the mediæval
to the specifically modern; the Roman Empire
inherited Hellenism, the Reformation the Renais-
sance. Both had their roots in the past, both made
new growth which blossomed at a later time. In
Hellenism, Oriental elements were mixed with the
Greek; in the Renaissance, it was a mixture of
Germanic with the native Italian which caused the
revival of classic antiquity and new culture.

Burckhardt says[1]:

> Elsewhere in Europe men deliberately and with re-
> flection borrowed this or the other element of classical
> civilization; in Italy, the sympathies both of the learned
> and of the people were naturally engaged on the side
> of antiquity as a whole, which stood to them as a
> symbol of past greatness. The Latin language too
> was easy to an Italian, and the numerous monuments
> and documents in which the country abounded
> facilitated a return to the past. With this tendency,
> other elements—the popular character which time had
> now greatly modified, the political institutions im-
> ported by the Lombards from Germany, chivalry
> and northern forms of civilization, and the influence
> of religion and the Church—combined to produce the
> modern Italian spirit, which was destined to serve as
> the model and ideal for the whole western world.

The distance between the works of the Greek
artists and poets—between Homer, Sophocles, and
Phidias on the one hand, and the Alexandrian
Theocritus and Kallimachos and the Pergamos
sculptures on the other—is greater than lies between
the *Nibelungenlied* and the Minnesingers, and Dante
and Petrarch. In both cases one finds oneself in a
new world of thought and feeling, where each and
all bears the stamp of change, in matters political
and social as well as artistic. If, for example, by the
aid of Von Helbig's researches,[2] we conjure up a

picture of the chief points in the history of Greek culture, we are astonished to see how almost every point recurred at the Renaissance, as described by Burckhardt.

The chief mark of both epochs was individualism, the discovery of the individual. In Hellenism it was the barriers of race and position which fell; in the Renaissance, the veil, woven of mysticism and delusion, which had obscured mediæval faith, thought, and feeling. Every man recognized himself to be an independent unit of church, state, people, corporation—of all those bodies in which in the Middle Ages he had been entirely merged.

Monarchical institutions arose in Hellenism; but the individual was no longer content to serve them only as one among many; he must needs develop his own powers. Private affairs began to preponderate over public; the very physiognomy of the race shewed an individual stamp.

> After the time of Alexander the Great, portrait shewed most marked individuality. Those of the previous period had a certain uniform expression; one would have looked in vain among them for the diversities in contemporary types shewn by comparing Alexander's vivid face full of stormy energy, Menander's with its peculiar look of irony, and the elaborate savant-physiognomy of Aristotle. (HELBIG.)

And Burckhardt says:

> At the close of the thirteenth century Italy began to swarm with individuality; the charm laid upon human personality was dissolved, and a thousand figures meet us each in its own special shape and dress. . . . Despotism, as we have already seen, fostered in the highest degree the individuality, not only of the tyrant or Condottiere himself, but also of the men whom he protected or used as his tools—the secretary, minister, poet, or companion.

Political indifference brought about a high degree of cosmopolitanism, especially among those who were banished. 'My country is the whole world,' said Dante; and Ghiberti: 'Only he who has learned everything is nowhere a stranger; robbed of his fortune and without friends, he is yet a citizen of every country, and can fearlessly despise the changes of fortune.'

In both Hellenism and the Renaissance, an effort was made in art and science to see things as they really were. In art, detail was industriously cultivated; but its naturalism, especially as to undraped figures, was due to a sensuous refinement of gallantry and erotic feeling. The sensuous flourished no less in Greek times than in those of Boccaccio; but the most characteristic peculiarity of Hellenism was its intentional revelling in feeling—its sentimentality. There was a trace of melancholy upon many faces of the time, and unhappy love in endless variations was the poet's main theme. Petrarch's lyre was tuned to the same key; a melancholy delight in grief was the constant burden of his song.

In Greece the sight of foreign lands had furthered the natural sciences, especially geography, astronomy, zoology, and botany; and the striving for universality at the Renaissance, which was as much a part of its individualism as its passion for fame, was aided by the widening of the physical and mental horizons through the Crusades and voyages of discovery. Dante was not only the greatest poet of his time, but an astronomer; Petrarch was geographer and cartographer, and, at the end of the fifteenth century, with Paolo Toscanelli, Lucca Baccioli, and Leonardo da Vinci, Italy was beyond all comparison the first nation in Europe in mathematics and natural science.

A significant proof of the wide-spread interest in natural history is found in the zeal which shewed itself at an early period for the collection and comparative study of plants and animals. Italy claims

> to be the first creator of botanical gardens . . . .
> princes and wealthy men, in laying out their pleasure
> gardens, instinctively made a point of collecting the
> greatest possible number of different plants in all their
> species and varieties.   (BURCKHARDT.)

Leon Battista Alberti, a man of wide theoretical
knowledge as well as technical and artistic facility
of all sorts, entered into the whole life around him
with a sympathetic intensity that might almost be
called nervous.

> At the sight of noble trees and waving corn-fields
> he shed tears . . . . more than once, when he was ill,
> the sight of a beautiful landscape cured him.
>   (BURCKHARDT.)

He defined a beautiful landscape as one in which
one could see in its different parts, sea, mountain,
lake or spring, dry rocks or plains, wood and valley.
Therefore he cared for variety ; and, what is more
striking, in contrast to level country, he admired
mountains and rocks !

In Hellenism, hunting, to which only the Mace-
donians had been addicted before, became a
fashion, and was enjoyed with Oriental pomp in
the *paradeisoi*. Writers drew most of their compari-
sons from it. In the Renaissance, Petrarch did the
same, and animals often served as emblems of state
—their condition ominous of good or evil—and
were fostered with superstitious veneration, as, for
example, the lions at Florence.

Thus the growth of the natural sciences increased
interest in the external world, and sensitiveness
brought about a sentimental attitude towards Nature
in Hellenism and in the Renaissance.

Both discovered in Nature a source of purest
pleasure ; the Renaissance feeling was, in fact, the
extension and enhancement of the Hellenic. Burck-
hardt overlooked the fact that beautiful scenery
was appreciated and described for its own sake in
Hellenism, but he says very justly :

> The Italians are the first among modern peoples by
> whom the outward world was seen and felt as some-
> thing beautiful. . . .   By the year 1200, at the height
> of the Middle Ages, a genuine hearty enjoyment of
> the external world was again in existence, and found
> lively expression in the minstrelsy of different nations,
> which gives evidence of the sympathy felt with all the
> simple phenomena of Nature—spring with its flowers,
> the green fields and the woods.   But these pictures
> are all foreground without perspective.

Among the Minnesingers there were traces of
feeling for Nature ; but only for certain stereotyped
phases. Of the individuality of a landscape, its
characteristic colour, form, and light, not a word
was said.

Even the Carmina Burana were not much ahead
of the Minnesingers in this respect, although they
deserve a closer examination.

These Latin poems of wandering clerks probably
belong to the twelfth century, and though no doubt
a product in which the whole of Europe had a share,
their best pieces must be ascribed to a French hand.
Latin poetry lives again in them, with a freshness
the Carlovingian Renaissance never reached ; they
are mediæval in form, but full of a frank enjoy-
ment of life and its pleasures, which hardly any
northerner of that day possessed. Often enough
this degenerated into frivolity ; but the stir of
national awakening after the long sleep of the Middle
Ages is felt like a spring breeze through them all.

It is a far cry from the view of Nature we saw
in the Carlovingian monks, to these highly-coloured
verses. The dim light of churches and bare cell
walls may have doubled the monks' appreciation
of blue skies and open-air life ; but they were
fettered by the constant fight with the senses ;
Nature to them must needs be less a work of God
for man's delight, than a dangerous means of
seduction. 'They wandered through Nature with
timid misgiving, and their anxious fantasy depicted

forms of terror or marvellous rescues.'¹ The idyllic pleasure in the simple charms of Nature, especially in the monastery garden of the Carlovingian time, contrasts strikingly with the tone of these very mundane *vagantes clerici*, for whom Nature had not only long been absorbed and freed from all demoniac influence, but peopled by the charming forms of the old mythic poems, and made for the joy and profit of men, in the widest and naivest sense of the words.

Spring songs, as with the Minnesingers, take up most of the space ; but the theme is treated with greater variety. Enjoyment of life and Nature breathes through them all.

One runs thus :

> Spring cometh, and the earth is decked and studded with vernal flowers. The harmony of the birds' returning song rouses the heart to be glad. It is the time of joy.

Songs 98 to 118 rejoice that winter is gone; for instance :

> Now in the mild springtime Flora opens the lap which the cold frost had locked in cruel time of winter ; the zephyr with gentle murmur cometh with the spring ; the grove is clad in leaves. The nightingale is singing, the fields are gay with divers hues. It is sweet to walk in the wooded glens, it is sweeter to pluck the lily with the rose, it is sweetest of all to sport with a lovely maiden.

Another makes a similar confession, for Nature and amorous passion are the two strings of these lyres :

> Beneath the pleasant foliage of a tree 'tis sweet to rest, while the nightingale sings her plaintive song; sweeter still, to sport in the grass with a fair maiden. . . . O, to what changeful moods is the heart of the lover prone ! As the vessel that wanders o'er the waves without an anchor, so doth Love's uncertain warfare toss 'twixt fear and hope.

The beauties of Nature are drawn upon to describe the fair maiden ; her eyes are compared to stars, her colour to lilies and snow, her mouth to a rose, her kiss 'doth rend in sunder all the clouds of care.'

> In the flowery season I sat beneath a shady tree while the birds sang in the groves . . . . and listened to my Thisbe's talk, the talk I love and long for ; and we spoke of the sweet interchange of love, and in the doubtful balance of the mind wanton love and chastity were wavering.
> I have seen the bright green of flowers, I have seen the flower of flowers, I have seen the rose of May ; I have seen the star that is brighter than all other, that is glorious and fair above all other, through whom may I ever spend my life in love.

On such a theme the poet rings endless changes. The most charming is the poem *Phyllis and Flora*. Actual landscape is not given, but details are treated with freshness and care :

> In the flowery season of the year, under a sky serene, while the earth's lap was painted with many colours, when the messenger of Aurora had put to flight the stars, sleep left the eyes of Phyllis and of Flora, two maidens whose beauty answered to the morning light. The breeze of spring was gently whispering, the place was green and gay with grass, and in the grass itself there flowed a living brook that played and babbled as it went. And that the sun's heat might not harm the maidens, near the stream there was a spreading pine, decked with leaves and spreading far its inter-weaving branches, nor could the heat penetrate from without. The maidens sat, the grass supplied the seat. . . . They intend to go to Love's Paradise : at the entrance of the grove a rivulet murmurs ; the breeze is fragrant with myrrh and balsam ; they hear the music of a hundred timbrels and lutes. All the notes of the birds resound in all their fulness ; they hear the sweet and pleasant song of the blackbird, the garrulous lark, the turtle and the nightingale, etc. . . . He who stayed there would become im-mortal ; every tree there rejoices in its own fruit ; the ways are scented with myrrh and cinnamon and amomum ; the master could be forced out of his house.

The first to shew proof of a deepening effect of Nature on the human spirit was Dante.

Dante and Petrarch elaborated the Hellenistic feeling for Nature; hence the further course of the Renaissance displayed all its elements, but with increased subjectivity and individuality.

No one, since the days of Hellenism, had climbed mountains for the sake of the view—Dante was the first to do it. And although, in ranging heaven, earth, hell, and paradise in the *Divina Commedia*, he rarely described real Nature, and then mostly in comparisons; yet, as Humboldt pointed out, how incomparably in a few vigorous lines he wakens the sense of the morning airs and the light on the distant sea in the first canto of Purgatorio:

> The dawn was vanquishing the matin hour,
> Which fled before it, so that from afar
> I recognized the trembling of the sea.

And how vivid this is:

>   The air
> Impregnate changed to water. Fell the rain:
> And to the fosses came all that the land
> Contain'd not, and, as mightiest streams are wont,
> To the great river with such headlong sweep
> Rush'd, that naught stayed its course.
>
> Through that celestial forest, whose thick shade
> With lively greenness the new-springing day
> Attempered, eager now to roam and search
> Its limits round, forthwith I left the bank;
> Along the champaign leisurely my way
> Pursuing, o'er the ground that on all sides
> Delicious odour breathed. A pleasant air,
> That intermitted never, never veered,
> Smote on my temples gently, as a wind
> Of softest influence, at which the sprays,
> Obedient all, lean'd trembling to that part
> Where first the holy mountain casts his shade;
> Yet were not so disordered; but that still
> Upon their top the feather'd quiristers
> Applied their wonted art, and with full joy
> Welcomed those hours of prime, and warbled shrill

Amid the leaves, that to their jocund lays
Kept tenour ; even as from branch to branch
Along the piny forests on the shore
Of Chiassi rolls the gathering melody,
When Eolus hath from his cavern loosed
The dripping south. Already had my steps,
Tho' slow, so far into that ancient wood
Transported me, I could not ken the place
Where I had enter'd ; when behold ! my path
Was bounded by a rill, which to the left
With little rippling waters bent the grass
That issued from its brink.

and this of the heavenly Paradise :

                        I looked,
And, in the likeness of a river, saw
Light flowing, from whose amber-seeming waves
Flash'd up effulgence, as they glided on
'Twixt banks, on either side, painted with spring,
Incredible how fair ; and, from the tide,
There, ever and anon outstarting, flew
Sparkles instinct with life ; and in the flowers
Did set them, like to rubies chased in gold ;
Then, as if drunk with odours, plunged again
Into the wondrous flood, from which, as one
Re-entered, still another rose.

His numerous comparisons conjure up whole
scenes, perfect in truth to Nature, and shewing a
keen and widely ranging eye. For example :

            Bellowing, there groaned
A noise, as of a sea in tempest torn
By warring winds.   (Inferno.)

O'er better waves to steer her rapid course
The light bark of my genius lifts the sail,
Well pleased to leave so cruel sea behind.
                              (Purgatorio.)

All ye, who in small bark have following sail'd,
Eager to listen on the adventurous track
Of my proud keel, that singing cuts her way.
                                (Paradiso.)

As sails full spread and bellying with the wind
Drop suddenly collapsed, if the mast split,
So to the ground down dropp'd the cruel fiend.
                                (Inferno.)

As, near upon the hour of dawn,
Through the thick vapours Mars with fiery beam
Glares down in west, over the ocean floor.
                                        (Purgatorio.)

            As 'fore the sun
That weighs our vision down, and veils his form
In light transcendent, thus my virtue fail'd
Unequal.   (Purgatorio.)

            As sunshine cheers
Limbs numb'd by nightly cold, e'en thus my look
Unloosed her tongue.

And now there came o'er the perturbed waves,
Loud crashing, terrible, a sound that made
Either shore tremble, as if of a wind
Impetuous, from conflicting vapours sprung,
That, 'gainst some forest driving all his might,
Plucks off the branches, beats them down, and
        hurls
Afar ; then, onward pressing, proudly sweeps
His whirlwind rage, while beasts and shepherds fly.
                                          (Inferno.)

As florets, by the frosty air of night
Bent down and closed, when day has blanch'd their
        leaves
Rise all unfolded on their spiry stems,
So was my fainting vigour new restored.
                                          (Inferno.)

        As fall off the light autumnal leaves,
One still another following, till the bough
Strews all its honours on the earth beneath.
                                          (Inferno.)

Bees, dolphins, rays of sunlight, snow, starlings,
doves, frogs, a bull, falcons, fishes, larks, and rooks
are all used, generally with characteristic touches of
detail.

Specially tender is this :

E'en as the bird, who 'mid the leafy bower
Has, in her nest, sat darkling through the night
With her sweet brood ; impatient to descry
Their wished looks, and to bring home their food,
In the fond quest, unconscious of her toil ;

She, of the time prevenient, on the spray
That overhangs their couch, with wakeful gaze
Expects the sun, nor, ever, till the dawn
Removeth from the east her eager ken,
So stood the dame erect.

The most important forward step was made by
Petrarch, and it is strange that this escaped Hum-
boldt in his famous sketch in the second volume of
Cosmos, as well as his commentator Schaller, and
Friedlander.

For when we turn from Hellenism to Petrarch, it
does not seem as if many centuries lay between ; but
rather as if notes first struck in the one had just
blended into distinct harmony in the other.

The modern spirit arose from a union of the genius
of the Italian people of the thirteenth century with
antiquity, and the feeling for Nature had a share
in the wider culture, both as to sentimentality and
grasp of scenery. Classic and modern joined hands
in Petrarch. Many Hellenic motives handed on by
Roman poets reappear in his poetry, but always
with that something in addition of which antiquity
shewed but a trace — the modern subjectivity and
individuality. It was the change from early bud
to full blossom. He was one of the first to deserve
the name of modern—modern, that is, in his whole
feeling and mode of thought, in his sentimentality
and his melancholy, and in the fact that ' more than
most before. and after him, he tried to know himself
and to hand on to others what he knew.' (Geiger.)
It is an appropriate remark of Hettner's, that the
phrase, ' he has discovered his heart,' might serve
as a motto for Petrarch's songs and sonnets. He
knew that he had that sentimental disorder which
he called ' acedia,' and wished to be rid of it. This
word has a history of its own. To the Greeks, to
Apollonius, for instance,' it meant carelessness, in-
difference ; and, joined with the genitive νόοιο—that
is, of the mind—it meant, according to the scholiasts,

as much as λυπη (Betrübnis)—that is, distress or grief. In the Middle Ages it became ' dislike of intellect so far as that is a divine gift '—that disease of the cloister which a monkish chronicler defined as ' a sadness or loathing and an immoderate distress of mind, caused by mental confusion, through which happiness of mind was destroyed, and the mind thrown back upon itself as from an abyss of despair.'

To Dante it meant the state—

> Sad
> In the sweet air, made gladsome by the sun,

distaste for the good and beautiful.

The modern meaning which it took with Petrarch is well defined by Geiger as being neither ecclesiastic nor secular sin,' but

> Entirely human and peculiar to the cleverest—the battle between reality and seeming, the attempt to people the arid wastes of the commonplace with philosophic thought—the unhappiness and despair that arise from comparing the unconcern of the majority with one's own painful unrest, from the knowledge that the results of striving do not express the effort made—that human life is but a ceaseless and unworthy rotation, in which the bad are always to the fore, and the good fall behind .... as pessimism, melancholy, world pain (Weltschmerz)—that tormenting feeling which mocks all attempt at definition, and is too vitally connected with erring and striving human nature to be curable—that longing at once for human fellowship and solitude, for active work and a life of contemplation.

Petrarch knew too the pleasure of sadness, what Goethe called ' Wonne der Wehmuth,' the *dolendi voluptas*.

> Lo, what new pleasure human wits devise !
> For oftentimes one loves
> Whatever new thing moves
> The sighs, that will in closest order go ;
> And I'm of those whom sorrowing behoves ;
> And that with some success
> I labour, you may guess,
> When eyes with tears, and heart is brimmed with woe.

In Sonnet 190:

My chiefest pleasure now is making moan.

Oh world, oh fruitless thought,
Oh luck, my luck, who'st led me thus for spite !...
For loving well, with pain I'm rent . . . .
Nor can I yet repent,
My heart o'erflowed with deadly pleasantness.
Now wait I from no less
A foe than dealt me my first blow, my last.
And were I slain full fast,
'Twould seem a sort of mercy to my mind. . . .
My ode, I shall i' the field
Stand firm ; to perish flinching were a shame,
In fact, myself I blame
For such laments ; my portion is so sweet.
Tears, sighs, and death I greet.
O reader that of death the servant art,
Earth can no weal, to match my woes, impart.

His poems are full of scenes and comparisons from
Nature ; for the sympathy for her which goes with
this modern and sentimental tone is a deep one:

In that sweet season of my age's prime
Which saw the sprout and, as it were, green blade
Of the wild passion. . . .

                        Changed me
From living man into green laurel whose
Array by winter's cold no leaf can lose.
                                        (Ode 1.)

Love is that by which

My darknesses were made as bright
As clearest noonday light.   (Ode 4.)

Elsewhere it is the light of heaven breaking in his
heart, and springtime which brings the flowers.
    In Sonnet 44 he plays with impossibilities, like
the Greek and Roman poets :

Ah me ! the sea will have no waves, the snow
Will warm and darken, fish on Alps will dwell,
And suns droop yonder, where from common cell

> The springs of Tigris and Euphrates flow,
> Or ever I shall here have truce or peace
> Or love . . . .·

and uses the same comparisons, Sestina 7 :

> So many creatures throng not ocean's wave,
> So many, above the circle of the moon,
> Of stars were never yet beheld by night ;
> So many birds reside not in the groves ;
> So many herbs hath neither field nor shore,
> But my heart's thoughts outnumber them each eve.

Many of his poems witness to the truth that the love-passion is the best interpreter of Nature, especially in its woes. The woes of love are his constant theme, and far more eloquently expressed than its bliss :

> So fair I have not seen the sun arise,
> When heaven was clearest of all cloudy stain—
> The welkin-bow I have not after rain
> Seen varied with so many shifting dyes,
> But that her aspect in more splendid guise
> Upon the day when I took up Love's chain
> Diversely glowed, for nothing mortal vies
> Therewith . . . .   (Sonnet 112.)

> From each fair eyelid's tranquil firmament
> So brightly shine my stars untreacherous,
> That none, whose love thoughts are magnanimous,
> Would from aught else choose warmth or guidance lent.
> Oh, 'tis miraculous, when on the grass
> She sits, a very flower, or when she lays
> Upon its greenness down her bosom white.
>   (Sonnet 127.)

> Oh blithe and happy flowers, oh favoured sod,
> That by my lady in passive mood are pressed,
> Lawn, which her sweet words hear'st and treasurest,
> Faint traces, where her shapely foot hath trod,
> Smooth boughs, green leaves, which now raw juices
>   load,
> Pale darling violets, and woods which rest
> In shadow, till that sun's beam you attest,
> From which hath all your pride and grandeur flowed ;

Oh land delightsome, oh thou river pure
Which bathest her fair face and brilliant eyes
And winn'st a virtue from their living light,
I envy you each clear and comely guise
In which she moves.   (Sonnet 129.)

These recall Nais in Theocritus :

When she crept or trembling footsteps laid,
Green bright and soft she made
Wood, water, earth, and stone ; yea, with conceit
The grasses freshened 'neath her palms and feet.
And her fair eyes the fields around her dressed
With flowers, and the winds and storms she stilled
With utterance unskilled
As from a tongue that seeketh yet the breast.
                                       (Sonnet 25.)

As oft as yon white foot on fresh green sod
Comelily sets the gentle step, a dower
Of grace, that opens and revives each flower,
Seems by the delicate palm to be bestowed.
                                       (Sonnet 132.)

I seem to hear her, hearing airs and sprays,
And leaves, and plaintive bird notes, and the brook
That steals and murmurs through the sedges green.
Such pleasure in lone silence and the maze
Of eerie shadowy woods I never took,
Though too much tow'r'd my sun they intervene.
                                       (Sonnet 143.)

and like Goethe's :

I think of thee when the bright sunlight shimmers
Across the sea;
When the clear fountain in the moonbeam glimmers
I think of thee. . . .

I hear thee, when the tossing waves' low rumbling
Creeps up the hill;
I go to the lone wood and listen trembling
When all is still. . . .

So Petrarch sings in Ode 15 :

Now therefore, when in youthful guise I see
The world attire itself in soft green hue,
I think that in this age unripe I view
That lovely girl, who's now a lady's mien.

Then, when the sun ariseth all aglow,
I trace the wonted show
Of amorous fire, in some fine heart made queen. . . .
When leaves or boughs or violets on earth
I see, what time the winter's cold decays,
And when the kindly stars are gathering might,
Mine eye that violet and green portrays
(And nothing else) which, at my warfare's birth,
Armed Love so well that yet he worsts me quite.
I see the delicate fine tissue light
In which our little damsel's limbs are dressed. . . .
Oft on the hills a feeble snow-streak lies,
Which the sun smiteth in sequestered place.
Let sun rule snow ! Thou, Love, my ruler art,
When on that fair and more than human face
I muse, which from afar makes soft my eyes. . . .
I never yet saw after mighty rain
The roving stars in the calm welkin glide
And glitter back between the frost and dew,
But straight those lovely eyes are at my side. . . .
If ever yet, on roses white and red,
My eyes have fallen, where in bowl of gold
They were set down, fresh culled by virgin hands,
There have I seemed her aspect to behold. . . .
But when the year has flecked
Some deal with white and yellow flowers the braes,
I forthwith recollect
That day and place in which I first admired
Laura's gold hair outspread, and straight was fired. . . .
That I could number all the stars anon
And shut the waters in a tiny glass
Belike I thought, when in this narrow sheet
I got a fancy to record, alas,
How many ways this Beauty's paragon
Hath spread her light, while standing self-complete,
So that from her I never could retreat. . . .
She's closed for me all paths in earth and sky.

The reflective modern mind is clear in this, despite its loquacity. He was yet more eloquent and intense, more fertile in comparisons, when his happiest days were over.

In Ode 24, standing at a window he watches the strange forms his imagination conjures up—a wild creature torn in pieces by two dogs, a ship wrecked by a storm, a laurel shattered by lightning :

Within this wood, out of a rock did rise
A spring of water, mildly rumbling down,
Whereto approached not in any wise
The homely shepherd nor the ruder clown,
But many muses and the nymphs withal. . . .
But while herein I took my chief delight,
I saw (alas!) the gaping earth devour
The spring, the place, and all clean out of sight—
Which yet aggrieves my heart unto this hour. . . .
At last, so fair a lady did I spy,
That thinking yet on her I burn and quake,
On herbs and flowers she walked pensively. . . .
A stinging serpent by the heel her caught,
Wherewith she languished as the gathered flower.

Now Zephyrus the blither days brings on,
With flowers and leaves, his gallant retinue,
And Progne's chiding, Philomela's moan,
And maiden spring all white and pink of hue ;
Now laugh the meadows, heaven is radiant grown,
And blithely now doth Love his daughter view ;
Air, water, earth, now breathe of love alone,
And every creature plans again to woo.
Ah me ! but now return the heaviest sighs,
Which my heart from its last resources yields
To her that bore its keys to heaven away.
And songs of little birds and blooming fields
And gracious acts of ladies, fair and wise,
Are desert land and uncouth beasts of prey.

(Sonnet 269.)

The nightingale, who maketh moan so sweet
Over his brood belike or nest-mate dear,
So deft and tender are his notes to hear,
That fields and skies are with delight replete ;
And all night long he seems with me to treat,
And my hard lot recall unto my ear.

(Sonnet 270.)

In every dell
The sands of my deep sighs are circumfused.

(Ode 1.)

Oh banks, oh dales, oh woods, oh streams, oh fields
Ye vouchers of my life's o'erburdened cause,
How often Death you've heard me supplicate.

(Ode 8.)

Whereso my foot may pass,
A balmy rapture wakes

When I think, here that darling light hath played.
If flower I cull or grass,
I ponder that it takes
Root in that soil, where wontedly she strayed
Betwixt the stream and glade,
And found at times a seat
Green, fresh, and flower-embossed.   (Ode 13.)

Whenever plaintive warblings, or the note
Of leaves by summer breezes gently stirred,
Or baffled murmur of bright waves I've heard
Along the green and flowery shore to float,
Where meditating love I sat and wrote,
Then her whom earth conceals, whom heaven
        conferred,
I hear and see, and know with living word
She answereth my sighs, though so remote.
'Ah, why art thou,' she pityingly says,
'Pining away before thy hour?'
                                    (Sonnet 238.)

The waters and the branches and the shore,
Birds, fishes, flowers, grasses, talk of love,
And me to love for ever all invite.
                                    (Sonnet 239.)

Thou'st left the world, oh Death, without a sun. . . .
Her mourners should be earth and sea and air.
                                    (Sonnet 294.)

Here we have happiness and misery felt in the
modern way, and Nature in the modern way drawn
into the circle of thought and feeling, and personified.

Petrarch was the first, since the days of Hellenism,
to enjoy the pleasures of solitude quite consciously.

How often to my darling place of rest,
Fleeing from all, could I myself but flee,
I walk and wet with tears my path and breast.
                                    (Sonnet 240.)

He shared Schiller's thought:

Oh Nature is perfect wherever we stray,
'Tis man that deforms it with care.

As love from thought to thought, from hill to hill,
Directs me, when all ways that people tread
Seem to the quiet of my being, foes,

If some lone shore, or fountain-head, or rill
Or shady glen, between two slopes outspread,
I find—my daunted soul doth there repose. . . .
On mountain heights, in briary woods, I find
Some rest ; but every dwelling place on earth
Appeareth to my eyes a deadly bane. . . .
Where some tall pine or hillock spreads a shade,
I sometimes halt, and on the nearest brink
Her lovely face I picture from my mind. . . .
Oft hath her living likeness met my sight,
(Oh who'll believe the word ?) in waters clear,
On beechen stems, on some green lawny space,
Or in white cloud. . . .
Her loveliest portrait there my fancy draws,
And when Truth overawes
That sweet delusion, frozen to the core,
I then sit down, on living rock, dead stone,
And seem to muse, and weep and write thereon. . . .
Then touch my thoughts and sense
Those widths of air which hence her beauty part,
Which always is so near, yet far away. . . .
Beyond that Alp, my Ode,
Where heaven above is gladdest and most clear,
Again thou'lt meet me where the streamlet flows
And thrilling airs disclose
The fresh and scented laurel thicket near,
There is my heart and she that stealeth it.
(Ode 17.)

It is the same idea as Goethe's in *Knowest thou
the Land ?* Again :

Alone, engrossed, the least frequented strands
I traverse with my footsteps faint and slow,
And often wary glances round me throw,
To flee, should human trace imprint the sands.
(Sonnet 28.)

A life of solitude I've ever sought,
This many a field and forest knows, and will.
(Sonnet 221.)

Love of solitude and feeling for Nature limit or
increase each other ; and Petrarch; like Dante, took
scientific interest in her, and found her a stimulant
to mental work.

Burckhardt says : 'The enjoyment of Nature is
for him the favourite accompaniment of intellectual

pursuits; it was to combine the two that he lived in learned retirement at Vaucluse and elsewhere, that he from time to time fled from the world and from his age.'

He wrote a book *On a Life of Solitude* (*De Vita Solitaria*) by the little river Sorgue, and said in a letter from Vaucluse: 'O if you could imagine the delight with which I breathe here, free and far from the world, with forests and mountains, rivers and springs, and the books of clever men.'

Purely objective descriptions, such as his picture of the Gulf of Spezzia and Porto Venere at the end of the sixth book of the *Africa*, were rare with him ; but, as we have already seen, he admired mountain scenery.   He refers to the hills on the Riviera di Levante as 'hills distinguished by most pleasant wildness and wonderful fertility.'[6]

The scenery of Reggio moved him, as he said,[7] to compose a poem.   He described the storm at Naples in 1343, and the earthquake at Basle.   As we have seen from one of his odes, he delighted in the wide view from mountain heights, and the freedom from the oppression of the air lower down.   In this respect he was one of Rousseau's forerunners, though his 'romantic' feeling was restrained within characteristic limits.   In a letter of April 26, 1335, interesting both as to the period and the personality of the writer, he described to Dionisius da Borgo San Sepolchro the ascent of Mt. Ventoux near Avignon which he made when he was thirty-two, and greatly enjoyed, though those who were with him did not understand his enjoyment.   When they had laboured through the difficulties of the climb, and saw the clouds below them, he was immensely impressed.   It was in accordance with his love of solitude that lonely mountain tops should attract him, and the letter shows that he fully appreciated both climb and view.

'It was a long day, the air fine.   We enjoyed the

advantages of vigour of mind, and strength and agility of body, and everything else essential to those engaged in such an undertaking, and so had no other difficulties to face than those of the region itself.'

. . . ' At first, owing to the unaccustomed quality of the air and the effect of the great sweep of view spread out before me, I stood like one dazed. I beheld the clouds under our feet, and what I had read of Athos and Olympus seemed less incredible as I myself witnessed the same things from a mountain of less fame. I turned my eyes towards Italy, whither my heart most inclined. The Alps, rugged and snow-capped, seemed to rise close by, although they were really at a great distance. . . . The Bay of Marseilles, the Rhone itself, lay in sight.'

It was a very modern effect of the wide view that ' his whole past life with all its follies rose before his mind ; he remembered that ten years ago, that day, he had quitted Bologna a young man, and turned a longing gaze towards his native country : he opened a book which was then his constant companion, *The Confessions of St Augustine*, and his eye fell on the passage in the tenth chapter :

> And men go about and admire lofty mountains and broad seas, and roaring torrents and the ocean, and the course of the stars, and forget their own selves while doing so.

His brother, to whom he read these words, could not understand why he closed the book and said no more. His feeling had suddenly changed.

He knew, when he began the climb, that he was doing something very unusual, even unheard of among his contemporaries, and justified himself by the example of Philip V. of Macedon, arguing that a young man of private station might surely be excused for what was not thought blamable in a grey-haired king. Then on the mountain top, lost in the view, the passage in St Augustine suddenly occurred to him, and he started blaming himself

for admiring earthly things so much. ' I was amazed
. . . . angry with myself for marvelling but now at
earthly things, when I ought to have learnt long
ago that nothing save the soul was marvellous, and
that to the greatness of the soul nought else was
great'; and he closed with an explanation flavoured
with theology to the taste of his confessor, to whom
he was writing. The mixture of thoroughly modern
delight in Nature ⁸ with ascetic dogma in this letter,
gives us a glimpse into the divided feelings of
one who stood upon the threshold between two
eras, mediæval and modern, into the reaction of
the mediæval mind against the budding modern
feeling.

This is, at any rate, the first mountain ascent
for pleasure since Hellenic days, of which we have
detailed information. From Greece before Alexander
we have nothing ; but the Persian King Darius, in
his expedition against the Scythians in the region
of Chalcedon, ascended the mountain on which stood
the Urios temple to Zeus, and there ' sitting in the
temple, he took a view of the Euxine Sea, which is
worthy of admiration.' (Herodotus.)

Philip V. of Macedon ascended the Hæmus B.C. 181,
and Apollonios Rhodios describes the panorama
spread out before the Argonauts as they ascended
the Dindymon, and elsewhere recalls the view from
Mt. Olympus. These are the oldest descriptions of
distant views conceived as landscape in the classic
literature preserved to us. Petrarch's ascent comes
next in order.

This sentimental and subjective feeling for Nature,
half - idyllic, half - romantic, which seemed to arise
suddenly and spontaneously in Petrarch, is not to
be wholly explained by a marked individuality,
nourished by the tendencies of the period ; the influ-
ence of Roman literature, the re-birth of the classic,
must also be taken into account. For the Renais-
sance attitude towards Nature was closely allied to

the Roman, and therefore to the Hellenic; and the fact that the first modern man arose on Italian soil was due to the revival of antiquity plus its union with the genius of the Italian people. Many direct analogies can be traced between Petrarch and the Roman poets; it was in their school that his eyes opened to the wonders of Nature, and he learnt to blend the inner with the outer life.

Boccaccio does not lead us much further. There is idyllic quality in his description of a wood in the *Ameto*,¹ and especially in *Fiammetta*, in which he praises country life and describes the spring games of the Florentine youth.

This is the description of a valley in the *Decameron*:

' After a walk of nearly a mile, they came to the Ladies' Valley, which they entered by a straight path, whence there issued forth a fine crystal current, and they found it so extremely beautiful and pleasant, especially at that sultry season, that nothing could exceed it, and, as some of them told me afterwards, the plain in the valley was so exact a circle, as if it had been described by a pair of compasses, though it seemed rather the work of Nature than of art, and was about half a mile in circumference, surrounded by six hills of moderate height, on each of which was a palace built in the form of a little castle. . . . The part that looks toward the south was planted as thick as they could stand together with vines, olives, almonds, cherries, figs, and most other kinds of fruit trees, and on the northern side were fine plantations of oak, ash, etc., so tall and regular that nothing could be more beautiful. The vale, which had only that one entrance, was full of firs, cypress trees, laurels, and pines, all placed in such order as if it had been done by the direction of some exquisite artist, and through which little or no sun could penetrate to the ground, which was covered with a thousand different flowers. . . . But what gave no less delight than any of the rest was a rivulet that came through a valley which divided two of the mountains, and running through the vein of a rock, made a most agreeable murmur with its fall, appearing, as it was dashed and sprinkled into drops, like so much quicksilver.'

Description of scenery for its own sake is scarcely more than attempted here, nor do Petrarch's lyrics, with their free thought of passion and overpowering consciousness of the joys and sorrows of love, reach the level of Hellenism in this respect. Yet it advanced with the Renaissance. Pope Pius II. (Æneas Sylvius) was the first to describe actual landscape (Italian), not merely in a few subjective lines, but with genuine modern enjoyment. He was one of those figures in the world's history in whom all the intellectual life and feeling of a time come to a focus.

He had a heart for everything, and an all-round enthusiasm for Nature unique in his day. Antiquity and Nature were his two passions, and the most beautiful descriptions of Nature before Rousseau and Goethe are contained in his *Commentaries*.

Writing of the country round his home, he says :

'The sweet spring time had begun, and round about Siena the smiling hills were clothed with leaves and flowers, and the crops were rising in plenty in the fields. Even the pasture land quite close to the town affords an unspeakably lovely view ; gently sloping hills, either planted with homely trees or vines, or ploughed for corn, look down on pleasant valleys in which grow crops, or green fields are to be seen, and brooks are even flowing. There are, too, many plantations, either natural or artificial, in which the birds sing with wondrous sweetness. Nor is there a mound on which the citizens have not built a magnificent estate ; they are thus a little way out of the town. Through this district the Pope walked with joyous head.'

Again and again love of Nature drew him away

even in old age from town life and the circle of
courtiers and flatterers; he was for ever finding
new reasons to prolong his *villeggiatura*, despite
the grumbling of his court, which had to put up with
wretched inns or monasteries overrun by mice, where
the rain came through the roofs and the necessaries
of life were scanty.[10]

His taste for these beautifully-situated monastic
solitudes was a riddle to those around him.   He
wrote of his summer residence in Tibur :

' On all sides round the town in summer there are
most lovely plantations, to which the Pope with his
cardinals often retired for relaxation, sitting some-
times on some green sward beneath the olives, some-
times in a green meadow on the bank of the river
Aino, whence he could see the clear waters.   There
are some meadows in a retired glen, watered by
many streams ; Pius often rested in these meadows
near the luxuriant streams and the shady trees.   He
lived at Tibur with the Minorites on an elevation
whence he could see the town and the course of the
Aino as it flowed into the plain beneath him and
through the quiet gardens, nor did anything else
give him pleasure.

' When the summer was over, he had his bedroom
in the house overlooking the Aino ; from there the
most beautiful view was to be seen, and also from
a neighbouring mountain on the other side of the
river, still covered with a green and leafy grove . . .
he completed a great part of his journey with the
greatest enjoyment.'

In May 1462 he went to the baths at Viterbo, and,
old man as he was, gives this appreciative description
of spring beauties by the way :

' The road by which he made for Sorianum was
at that time of the year delightful ; there was a
tremendous quantity of genista, so that a great part
of the field seemed a mass of flowering yellow, while
the rest, covered as it was by shrubs and various

grasses, brought purple and white and a thousand different colours before the eyes. It was the month of May, and everything was green. On one side were the smiling fields, on the other the smiling woods, in which the birds made sweet harmony. At early dawn he used to walk into the fields to catch the exquisite breeze before the day should grow hot, and gaze at the green crops and the flowering flax, which then, emulating heaven's own blue, gave the greatest joy to all beholders. . . . Now the crows are holding vigil, and the ringdoves; and the owl at times utters lament with funeral note. The place is most lovely; the view in the direction of Siena stretches as far as Amiata, and in the west reaches Mt. Argentarius.'

In the plains the plague was raging; the sight of the people appealing to him as to a god, moved him to tears as he thought how few of the children would survive in the heat. He travelled to a castle charmingly placed on the lake of Bolsena, where ' there is a shady circular walk in the vineyard under the big grapes; stone steps shaded by the vine leaves lead down to the bank, where ilex oaks, alive with the songs of blackbirds, stand among the crags.' Halfway up the mountain, in the monastery of San Salvatore, he and his court took up their quarters.

'The most lovely scenery met the eye. As you look to the west from the higher houses, the view reaches beyond Ilcinum and Siena as far as the Pistorian Alps. To the north a variety of hills and the pleasant green of woods presents itself, stretching a distance of five miles; if your sight is good, your eye will travel as far as the Apennine range and can see Cortona.'

There he passed the time, shooting birds, fishing, and rowing.

'In the cool air of the hills, among the old oaks and chestnuts, on the green meadows where there were no thorns to wound the feet, and no snakes

or insects to hurt or annoy, the Pope passed days
of unclouded happiness.'

This is thoroughly modern : 'Silvarum amator,' as
he calls himself, he includes both the details of the
near and the general effect of the far-distant land-
scape.

And with age his appreciation of it only seemed
to increase ; for instance, he says of Todi :

' A most lovely view meets the eye wherever you
turn ; you can see Perusia and all the valley that lies
between, full of wide - spreading forts and fertile
fields, and honoured by the river Tiber, which, draw-
ing its coils along like a snake, divides Tuscia from
Umbria, and, close to the city itself, enters many a
mountain, passing through which it descends to the
plain, murmuring as it goes, as though constrained
against its will.'

This is his description of a lake storm, during an
excursion to the Albanian Mountains :

As far as Ostia ' he had a delightful voyage ; at
night the sea began to be most unwontedly troubled,
and a severe storm arose. The east wind rolled up
the waters from their lowest depths, huge waves
beat the shore ; you could have heard the sea, as it
were, groaning and wailing. So great was the force
of the winds, that nothing seemed able to resist it ;
they raged and alternately fled and put one another
to rout, they overturned woods and anything that
withstood them. The air glittered with frequent
lightning, the sky thundered, and terrific thunder-
bolts fell from the clouds. . . . The night was
pitch dark, though the flashes of lightning were
continuous.'

And of a lake at rest he says :

' The beauty of that lake is remarkable ; every-
where it is surrounded by high rocks, the water is
transparently clear. Nature, so far superior to art,
provided a most pleasant journey. The Nemorian
lake, with its crystal-clear waters, reflects the faces

of those that look into it, and fills a deep basin. The descent from the top to the bottom is wooded. The poetic genius would never be awakened if it slept here; you would say it was the dwelling-place of the Muses, the home of the Nymphs, and, if there is any truth in legends, the hiding-place of Diana.'

He visited the lakes among the mountains, climbing and resting under the trees; the view from Monte Cavo was his favourite, from which he could see Terracina, the lakes of Nemi and Albano, etc. He noted their extent and formation, and added:

'The genista, however, was especially delightful, covering, as it did with its flowers, the greater part of the plains. Then, moreover, Rome presented itself fully to the eyes, together with Soracte and the Sabine Land, and the Apennine range white with snow, and Tibur and Præneste.'

It is clear that it was a thoroughly modern enthusiasm which attracted Æneas Sylvius to the country and gave him this ready pen for everything in Nature—everything, that is, except bare mountain summits.

It is difficult to attribute this faculty for enjoying and describing scenery to the influence of antiquity alone, for, save the younger Pliny, I know of no Roman under the Empire who possessed it, and, besides, we do not know how far Pius II. was acquainted with Roman literature. We know that the re-awakening of classic literature exerted an influence upon the direction of the feeling for Nature in general, and, for the rest, very various elements coalesced. Like times produce like streams of tendency, and Hellenism, the Roman Empire, and the Renaissance were alike to some extent in the conditions of their existence and the results that flowed from them; the causal nexus between them is undeniable, and makes them the chief stepping-stones on the way to the modern.

Theocritus, Meleager, Petrarch, and Æneas Sylvius

may serve as representatives of the development of the feeling for Nature from classic to modern ; they are the ancestors of our enthusiasm, the links in the chain which leads up to Rousseau, Goethe, Byron, and Shelley.

From the autobiography of Æneas Sylvius and the lyrics of Petrarch we gain a far truer picture of the feeling of the period up to the sixteenth century than from any poetry in other countries. Even the epic had a more modern tone in Italy; Ariosto's descriptions were far ahead of any German epic.

Humboldt pointed out very clearly the difference between the epic of the people and the epic of art —between Homer and Ariosto. Both, he said, are true painters of the world and Nature ; but Ariosto pleases more by his brilliance and wealth of colour, Homer by purity of form and beauty of composition. Ariosto achieves through general effect, Homer through perfection of form. Nature is more naive in Homer, the subject is paramount, and the singer disappears ; in Ariosto, Nature is sentimental, and the poet always remains in view upon the stage. In Homer all is closely knit, while Ariosto's threads are loosely spun, and he breaks them himself in play. Homer almost never describes, Ariosto always does.

Ariosto's scenes and comparisons from Nature, being calculated for effect, are more subjective, and far more highly-coloured than Homer's. But they shew a sympathetic grasp.

The modern bloom, so difficult to define, lies over them — something at once sensuous, sentimental, and chivalrous. He is given to describing lonely woodland scenery, fit places for trysts and lovers' rendezvous.

In the 1st Canto of *Mad Orlando* :

> With flowery thorns, vermilion roses near
> Her, she upon a lovely bush doth meet,
> That mirrored doth in the bright waves appear,
> Shut out by lofty oaks from the sun's heat.

> Amidst the thickest shades there is a clear
> Space in the middle for a cool retreat ;
> So mixed the leaves and boughs are, through them
>   none
> Can see ; they are impervious to the sun.

In the 6th Canto the Hippogriff carries Roger
into a country :

> Nor could he, had he searched the whole world
>   through,
> Than this a more delightful country see . . . .
> Soft meads, clear streams, and banks affording
>   shade,
> Hillocks and plains, by culture fertile made.
> Fair thickets of the cedar, palm and no
> Less pleasant myrtle, of the laurel sweet,
> Of orange trees, where fruit and flow'rs did grow,
> And which in various forms, all lovely, meet
> With their thick shades against the fervid glow
> Of summer days, afforded a retreat ;
> And nightingales, devoid of fear, among
> Those branches fluttered, pouring forth their song.
> Amid the lilies white and roses red,
> Ever more freshened by the tepid air,
> The stag was seen, with his proud lofty head,
> And feeling safe, the rabbit and the hare . . . .
> Sapphires and rubies, topazes, pearls, gold,
> Hyacinths, chrysolites, and diamonds were
> Like the night flow'rs, which did their leaves unfold
> There on those glad plains, painted by the air
> So green the grass, that if we did behold
> It here, no emeralds could therewith compare ;
> As fair the foliage of the trees was, which
> With fruit and flow'r eternally were rich.
> Amid the boughs, sing yellow, white, and blue,
> And red and green small feathered creatures gay ;
> The crystals less limpidity of hue
> Than the still lakes or murmuring brooks display.
> A gentle breeze, that seemeth still to woo
> And never change from its accustomed way,
> Made all around so tremulous the air
> That no annoyance was the day's hot glare.
>   (Canto 34.)

Descriptions of time are short :

> From the hard face of earth the sun's bright hue
> Not yet its veil obscure and dark did rend ;

The Lycaonian offspring scarcely through
The furrows of the sky his plough did send.
(Canto 80.)

Comparisons, especially about the beauty of women, are very artistic, recalling Sappho and Catullus :

The tender maid is like unto the rose
In the fair garden on its native thorn;
Whilst it alone and safely doth repose,
Nor flock nor shepherd crops it; dewy morn,
Water and earth, the breeze that sweetly blows,
Are gracious to it; lovely dames adorn
With it their bosoms and their beautiful
Brows; it enamoured youths delight to cull.
(Canto 1.)

Only, Alcina fairest was by far
As is the sun more fair than every star. . . .
Milk is the bosom, of luxuriant size,
And the fair neck is round and snowy white;
Two unripe ivory apples fall and rise
Like waves upon the sea-beach when a slight
Breeze stirs the ocean.   (Canto 7.)

Now in a gulf of bliss up to the eyes
And of fair things, to swim he doth begin.
(Canto 7.)

So closely doth the ivy not enlace
The tree where firmly rooted it doth stand,
As clasp each other in their warm embrace
These lovers, by each other's sweet breath fanned.
Sweet flower, of which on India's shore no trace
Is, or on the Sabæan odorous sand.
(Canto 7.)

Her fair face the appearance did maintain
That sometimes shewn is by the sky in spring,
When at the very time that falls the rain,
The sun aside his cloudy veil doth fling.
And as the nightingale its pleasant strain
Then on the boughs of the green trees doth sing,
Thus Love doth bathe his pinions at those bright
But tearful eyes, enjoying the clear light.
(Canto 11.)

But as more fickle than the leaf was she,
When it in autumn doth more sapless grow,
And the old wind doth strip it from the tree,
And doth before it in its fury grow.

(Canto 21.)

He uses the sea :

As when a bark doth the deep ocean plough,
That two winds strike with an alternate blast,
'Tis now sent forward by the one, and now
Back by the other in its first place cast,
And whirled from prow to poop, from poop to prow,
But urged by the most potent wind at last
Philander thus irresolute between
The two thoughts, did to the least wicked lean.

(Canto 21.)

As comes the wave upon the salt sea shore
Which the smooth wind at first in thought hath
    fanned ;
Greater the second is than that before
It, and the third more fiercely follows, and
Each time the humour more abounds, and more
Doth it extend its scourge upon the land :
Against Orlando thus from vales below
And hills above, doth the vile rabble grow.

(Canto 24.)

These comparisons not only shew faithful and
personal observation, but are far more subjective
and subtle than, for instance, Dante's. The same
holds good of Tasso. How beautiful in detail,
and how sentimental too, is this from *Jerusalem
Delivered* :

Behold how lovely blooms the vernal rose
When scarce the leaves her early bud disclose,
When, half unwrapt, and half to view revealed,
She gives new pleasure from her charms concealed.
But when she shews her bosom wide displayed,
How soon her sweets exhale, her beauties fade !
No more she seems the flower so lately loved,
By virgins cherished and by youths approved.
So swiftly fleeting with the transient day
Passes the flower of mortal life away.

Not less subjective is :

> Like a ray of light on water
> A smile of soft desire played in her liquid eyes.
>
> (Sonnet 18.)

The most famous lines in this poem are those which describe a romantic garden so vividly that Humboldt says 'it reminds one of the charming scenery of Sorrento.' It certainly proves that even epic poetry tried to describe Nature for her own sake :

> The garden then unfolds a beauteous scene,
> With flowers adorned and ever living green;
> There silver lakes reflect the beaming day,
> Here crystal streams in gurgling fountains play.
> Cool vales descend and sunny hills arise,
> And groves and caves and grottos strike the eyes.
> Art showed her utmost power ; but art concealed
> With greater charm the pleased attention held.
> It seemed as Nature played a sportive part
> And strove to mock the mimic works of art :
> By powerful magic breathes the vernal air,
> And fragrant trees eternal blossoms bear :
> Eternal fruits on every branch endure,
> Those swelling from their buds, and these mature:
> The joyous birds, concealed in every grove,
> With gentle strife prolong the notes of love.
> Soft zephyrs breathe on woods and waters round,'
> The woods and waters yield a murmuring sound ;
> When cease the tuneful choir, the wind replies,
> But, when they sing, in gentle whisper dies ;
> By turns they sink, by turns their music raise
> And blend, with equal skill, harmonious lays.

But even here the scene is surrounded by an imaginary atmosphere ; flowers, fruit, creatures, and atmosphere all lie under a magic charm. Tasso's importance for our subject lies far more in his much-imitated pastorals.

The *Arcadia* of Jacopo Sannazaro, which appeared in 1504, a work of poetic beauty and still greater literary importance,[11] paved the way for pastoral poetry, which, like the sonnet, was interwoven with prose. The shepherd's occupations are described with care, though many of the songs and terms of expression rather fit the man of culture than the child of Nature, and he had that genuine enthusiasm for the rural which begets a convincing eloquence.

' 'Tis you,' he says at the end, addressing the Muse, ' who first woke the sleeping woods, and taught the shepherds how to strike up their lost songs.'

Bembo wrote this inscription for his grave :

> Strew flowers o'er the sacred ashes, here lies Sannazaro;
> With thee, gentle Virgil, he shares Muse and grave.

Virgil too was industriously imitated in the didactic poetry of his country.

Giovanni Rucellai (born 1475) wrote a didactic poem, *The Bees*, which begins :

' O chaste virgins, winged visitants of flowery banks, whilst I prepared to sing your praise in lofty verse, at peep of day I was o'ercome by sleep, and then appeared a chorus of your tiny folk, and from their rich mellifluous haunts, in a clear voice these words flowed forth. . . . And I will sing how liquid and serene the air distils sweet honey, heavenly gift, on flowerets and on grass, and how the bees, chaste and industrious, gather it, and thereof with care and skill make perfumed wax to grace the altars of our God.'

And a didactic poem by Luigi Alamanni (born 1495), called *Husbandry*, has : ' O blessed is he who dwells in peace, the actual tiller of his joyous fields, to whom, in his remoteness, the most righteous earth brings food, and secure in well-being, he rejoices in his heart. If thou art not surrounded by society rich with purple and gems, nor with houses adorned with costly woods, statues, and gold ; . . . at least, secure in the humble dwelling of wood from the copse hard by, and common stones collected close at hand, which thine own hand has founded and built, whenever thou awakenest at the approach of dawn, thou dost not find outside those who bring news of a thousand events contrary to thy desires. . . . Thou wanderest at will, now quickly, now slowly, across the green meadow, through the wood, over the grassy hill, or by the stream. Now here, now there . . . thou handlest the hatchet, axe, scythe, or hoe. . . . To enjoy in sober comfort at almost all seasons, with thy dear children, the fruits of thine own tree, the tree planted by thyself, this brings a sweetness sweet beyond all others.'

These didactic writings, inspired by Virgilian Georgics, show a distinct preference for the idyllic.

Sannazaro's *Arcadia* went through sixty editions in the sixteenth century alone. Tasso reckoned with the prevalent taste of his day in *Aminta*, which improved the then method of dramatizing a romantic idyll. The whole poem bears the stamp of an idealizing and romantic imagination, and embodies in lyric form his senti- mental idea of the Golden Age and an ideal world of Nature. Even down to its details *Aminta* recalls the pastorals of Longos; and Daphne's words (Act I. Scene 1) suggest the most feeling outpourings of Kallimachos and Nonnos:

And callest thou sweet spring-time
The time of rage and enmity,
Which breathing now and smiling,
Reminds the whole creation,
The animal, the human,
Of loving! Dost thou see not
How all things are enamoured
Of this enamourer, rich with joy and health?
Observe that turtle-dove,
How, toying with his dulcet murmuring,
He kisses his companion. Hear that nightingale
Who goes from bough to bough
Singing with his loud heart, 'I love!' 'I love!' . . .

       The very trees
Are loving. See with what affection there,
And in how many a clinging turn and twine,

The vine holds fast its husband. Fir loves fir,
The pine the pine, and ash and willow and beech
Each towards the other yearns, and sighs and trembles.
That oak tree which appears
So rustic and so rough,
Even that has something warm in its sound heart;
And hadst thou but a spirit and sense of love,
Thou hadst found out a meaning for its whispers.
Now tell me, would thou be
Less than the very plants and have no love ?

One seems to hear Sakuntala and her friends talking, or Akontios complaining. So, too, when the unhappy lover laments (Aminta) :

In my lamentings I have found
A very pity in the pebbly waters,
And I have found the trees
Return them a kind voice :
But never have I found,
Nor ever hope to find,
Compassion in this hard and beautiful
What shall I call her ?

Aminta describes to Tirsis how his love grew from boyhood up :

There grew by little and little in my heart,
I knew not from what root,
But just as the grass grows that sows itself,
An unknown something which continually
Made me feel anxious to be with her.

Sylvia kisses him :

Never did bee from flower
Suck sugar so divine
As was the honey that I gathered then
From those twin roses fresh.

In Act II. Scene 1, the rejected Satyr, like the rejected Polyphemus or Amaryllis in Theocritus, complains in antitheses which recall Longos :

The woods hide serpents, lions, and bears under their green shade, and in your bosom hatred, disdain, and cruelty dwell. . . . Alas, when I bring the earliest flowers, you refuse them obstinately, perhaps because

lovelier ones bloom on your own face; if I offer beauti-
ful apples, you reject them angrily, perhaps because
your beautiful bosom swells with lovelier ones . . . .
and yet I am not to be despised, for I saw myself lately
in the clear water, when winds were still and there
were no waves.

This is the sentimental pastoral poetry of
Hellenism reborn and intensified.

So with the elegiac motive so loved by Alexandrian
and Roman poets, praise of a happy past time; the
chorus sings in *Aminta*:

O lovely age of gold,
Not that the rivers rolled
With milk, or that the woods wept honeydew;
Not that the ready ground
Produced without a wound,
Or the mild serpent had no tooth that slew . . . .
But solely that . . . . the law of gold,
That glad and golden law, all free, all fitted,
Which Nature's own hand wrote—What pleases is
    permitted ! . . .
Go ! let us love, the daylight dies, is born ;
But unto us the light
Dies once for all, and sleep brings on eternal night.

Over thirty pastoral plays can be ascribed to Italy
in the last third of the sixteenth century. The
most successful imitator of Tasso was Giovanni
Battista Guarini (born 1537) in *The True Shepherd*
(*Il Pastor Fido*). One quotation will shew how he
outvied *Aminta*. In Act I. Scene 1, Linko says:

Look round thee, Sylvia ; behold
All in the world that's amiable and fair
Is love's sweet work : heaven loves, the earth, the sea,
Are full of love and own his mighty sway.
Love through the woods
The fiercest beasts ; love through the waves attends
Swift gliding dolphins and the sluggish whales.
That little bird which sings . . . .
Oh, had he human sense,
' I burn with love,' he'd cry, ' I burn with love,'
And in his heart he truly burns,
And in his warble speaks
A language, well by his dear mate conceived,
Who answering cries, ' And I too burn with love,'

He praises woodland solitude :

Dear happy groves !
And thou all silent, solitary gloom,
True residence of peace and of repose !
How willingly, how willingly my steps
To you return, and oh ! if but my stars
Benightly had decreed
My life for solitude, and as my wish
Would naturally prompt to pass my days—
No, not the Elysian fields,
Those happy gardens of the demi-gods,
Would I exchange for yon enchanting shades.

The love lyrics of the later Renaissance are
remarkably rich in vivid pictures of Nature com-
bined with much personal sentiment. Petrarch's
are the model ; he inspired Vittoria Colonna, and
she too revelled in sad feelings and memories,
especially about the death of her husband : [12]
‘When I see the earth adorned and beautiful
with a thousand lovely and sweet flowers, and how
in the heavens every star is resplendent with varied
colours ; when I see that every solitary and lively
creature is moved by natural instinct to come out
of the forests and ancient caverns to seek its fellow
by day and by night ; and when I see the plains
adorned again with glorious flowers and new leaves,
and hear every babbling brook with grateful mur-
murs bathing its flowery banks, so that Nature,
in love with herself, delights to gaze on the beauty
of her works, I say to myself, reflecting : “ How
brief is this our miserable mortal life ! ” Yesterday
this plain was covered with snow, to-day it is green
and flowery. And again in a moment the beauty
of the heavens is overclouded by a fierce wind, and
the happy loving creatures remain hidden amidst
the mountains and the woods ; nor can the sweet
songs of the tender plants and happy birds be heard,
for these cruel storms have dried up the flowers on
the ground ; the birds are mute, the most rapid

streams and smallest rivulets are checked by frost,
and what was one hour so beautiful and joyous, is;
for a season, miserable and dead.'

Here the two pictures in the inner and outer life
are equally vivid to the poetess; it is the real
' pleasure of sorrow,' and she lingers over them with
delight.

Bojardo, too, reminds us of Petrarch; for example,
in Sonnet 89:[13]

> Thou shady wood. inured my griefs to hear,
> So oft expressed in quick and broken sighs;
> Thou glorious sun, unused to set or rise
> But as the witness of my daily fear;
>
> Ye wandering birds, ye flocks and ranging deer,
> Exempt from my consuming agonies;
> Thou sunny stream to whom my sorrow flies
> 'Mid savage rocks and wilds, no human traces near.
>
> O witnesses eternal, how I live!
> My sufferings hear, and win to their relief
> That scornful beauty—tell her how I grieve!
>
> But little 'tis to her to hear my grief.
> To her, who sees the pangs which I receive,
> And seeing, deigns them not the least relief.

Lorenzo de Medici's idylls were particularly rich
in descriptions of Nature and full of feeling. ' Here
too that delight in pain, in telling of their unhappiness
and renunciation; here too those wonderful tones
which distinguish the sonnets of the fourteenth and
fifteenth centuries so favourably from those of a
later time.' (Geiger.)

There is a delicate compliment in this sonnet:

> O violets, sweet and fresh and pure indeed,
> Culled by that hand beyond all others fair!
> What rain or what pure air has striven to bear
> Flowers far excelling those 'tis wont to yield?
> What pearly dew, what sun, or sooth what earth
> Did you with all these subtle charms adorn;
> And whence is this sweet scent by Nature drawn,

Or heaven who deigns to grant it to such worth ?
O, my dear violets, the hand which chose
You from all others, that has made you fair,
'Twas that adorned you with such charm and worth ;
Sweet hand ! which took my heart altho' it knows
Its lowliness, with that you may compare.
To that give thanks, and to none else on earth.

Thus we see that the Italians of the thirteenth, fourteenth, and fifteenth centuries were penetrated through and through by the modern spirit—were, indeed, its pioneers. They recognized their own individuality, pondered their own inner life, delighted in the charms of Nature, and described them in prose and poetry, both as counterparts to feeling and for her own sake.

Over all the literature we have been considering—whether poetic comparison and personification, or sentimental descriptions of pastoral life and a golden age, of blended inner and outer life, or of the finest details of scenery—there lies that bloom of the modern, that breath of subjective personality, so hard to define. The rest of contemporary Europe had no such culture of heart and mind, no such marked individuality, to shew.

The further growth of the Renaissance feeling, itself a rebirth of Hellenic and Roman feeling, was long delayed.

Let us turn next to Spain and Portugal—the countries chiefly affected by the great voyages of discovery, not only socially and economically, but artistically—and see the effect of the new scenery upon their imagination.

CHAPTER V

ENTHUSIASM FOR NATURE AMONG THE DISCOVERERS
AND CATHOLIC MYSTICS

THE great achievement of the Italian Renaissance
was the discovery of the world within, of the whole
deep contents of the human spirit. Burckhart,
praising this achievement, says:

> If we were to collect the pearls from the courtly and
> knightly poetry of all the countries of the West during
> the two preceding centuries, we should have a mass of
> wonderful divinations and single pictures of the inward
> life, which at first sight would seem to rival the poetry
> of the Italians. Leaving lyrical poetry out of account,
> Godfrey of Strassburg gives us, in his *Tristram
> and Isolt*, a representation of human passion, some
> features of which are immortal. But these pearls lie
> scattered in the ocean of artificial convention, and
> they are altogether something very different from a
> complete objective picture of the inward man and his
> spiritual wealth.

The discovery of the beauty of scenery followed
as a necessary corollary of this awakening of in-
dividualism, this fathoming of the depths of human
personality. For only to fully-developed man
does Nature fully disclose herself.

This had already been stated by one of the most
philosophic minds of the time, Pico della Mirandola,
in his speech on the dignity of man. God, he tells
us, made man at the close of creation to know the
laws of the universe, to love its beauty, to admire its

greatness. He bound him to no fixed place, to no prescribed form of work, and by no iron necessity ; but gave him freedom to will and to move.

'I have set thee,' said the Creator to Adam, 'in the midst of the world, that thou mayest the more easily behold and see all that is therein. I created thee a being neither heavenly nor earthly, neither mortal nor immortal, only that thou mightest be free to shape and to overcome thyself. Thou mayest sink into a beast, and be born again to the Divine likeness. The brutes bring with them from their mothers' body what they will carry with them as long as they live ; the higher spirits are from the beginning, or soon after, what they will be for ever. To thee alone is given a growth and a development depending on thine own free will. Thou bearest in thee the germs of a universal life.'

The best men of the Renaissance realized this ideal of an all-round development, and it was the glory of Italy in the fourteenth and fifteenth centuries, that she found a new realm in the inner man at the very time that her discoveries across the seas were enlarging the boundaries of the external world, and her science was studying it. Mixed as the motives of the discoverers must have been, like those of the crusaders before them, and probably, for the most part, self-interested, it is easy to imagine the surprise they must have felt at seeing ignorant people, who, to quote Peter Martyr (de rebus oceanicis) : [1]

> Naked, without weights or measures or death-dealing money, live in a Golden Age without laws, without slanderous judges, without the scales of the balance. Contented with Nature, they spend their lives utterly untroubled for the future. . . . Theirs is a Golden Age ; they do not enclose their farms with trench or wall or hurdle ; their gardens are open. Without laws, without the scales of the balance, without judges, they guard the right by Nature's light.

And their wonder at the novelties in climate and vegetation, the strange forests, brilliant birds, and splendid stars of the tropics, must have been no less.

Yet it is one thing to feel, and another to find words to convey the feeling to others; and the explorers often expressed regret for their lack of skill in this respect.

Also, and this is more important in criticizing what they wrote, these seamen were mostly simple, unlettered folk, to whom a country's wealth in natural products and their practical value made the strongest appeal, and whose admiration of bays, harbours, trees, fields of grain, etc., was measured by the same standard of utility. Even such unskilled reporters did not entirely fail to refer to the beauty of Nature ; but had it not been for the original and powerful mind of Christopher Columbus, we should have had little more in the way of description than ' pleasant,' ' pretty,' and such words.

Marco Polo described his journey to the coast of Cormos² in very matter-of-fact fashion, but not without a touch of satisfaction at the peculiarities of the place:

> You then approach the very beautiful plain of Formosa, watered by fine rivers, with plantations of the date palms, and having the air filled with francolins, parrots, and other birds unknown to our climate. You ride two days to it, and then arrive at the ocean, on which there is a city and a fort named Cormos. The ships of India bring thither all kinds of spiceries, precious stones, and pearls, cloths of silk and gold, elephants' teeth, and many other articles. . . . They sow wheat, barley, and other kinds of grain in the month of November, and reap them in March, when they become ripe and perfect ; but none except the date will endure till May, being dried up by the extreme heat.

Elsewhere he wrote of scenery in the same strain : of the Persian deserts, and the green table-lands and wild gorges of Badachshan, Japan with its golden roofed palaces, paradisaical Sunda Islands with their 'abundance of treasure and costly spices,' Java the less with its eight kingdoms, etc.; but naturally his chief interest was given to the manners and customs of the various races, and the fertility and uses of their countries.

In Bishop Osorio's *History of Emmanuel, King of Portugal*, we see some pleasure in the beauties of Nature peeping through the matter-of-fact tone of the day.

Thus, speaking of the companions of Vasco da Gama, he says that they admired the far coast of Africa :

> They descried some little islands, which appeared extremely pleasant; the trees were lofty, the meadows of a beautiful verdure, and great numbers of cattle frisked about everywhere; they could see the inhabitants walking upon the shore in vast numbers. . . .

Of Mozambique he says :

> The palm trees are of a great height, covered with long prickly leaves; broad-spreading boughs afford an agreeable shade, and bear nuts of a great size, called cocoes.

Of Melinda :

> The city stands in a beautiful plain, surrounded with a variety of fine gardens; these are stocked with all sorts of trees, especially the orange, the flowers of which yield a most graceful diffusive smell. The country is rich and plentiful, abounding not only with tame and domestic cattle, but with game of all kinds, which the natives hunt down or take with nets.

Of Zanzibar :

> The soil of this place is rich and fertile, and it abounds with springs of the most excellent water; the whole island is covered with beautiful woods, which are extremely fragrant from the many wild citrons growing there, which diffuse the most grateful scent.

Of Brazil, which is ' extremely pleasant and the soil fruitful ' :

Clothed with a beautiful verdure, covered with tall trees, abounding with plenty of excellent water . . . . and so healthy that the inhabitants make no use of medicines, for almost all who die here are not cut off by any distemper, but worn out by age. Here are many large rivers, besides a vast number of delightful springs. The plains are large and spacious, and afford excellent pasture. . . . In short, the whole country affords a most beautiful prospect, being diversified with hills and valleys, and these covered with thick shady woods stocked with great variety of trees, many of which our people were quite strangers to: of these there was one of a particular nature, the leaves of which. when cut, sent forth a kind of balsam. The trees used in dyeing scarlet grow here in great plenty and to a great height. The soil likewise produces the most useful plants.

Of Ormuz, near Arabia :

The name of the island seems to be taken from the ancient city of Armuza in Caramania . . . the place is sandy and barren, and the soil so very poor that it produces nothing fit for human sustenance, neither by nature nor by the most laborious cultivation . . yet here you might see greater plenty of these, as well as all luxurious superfluities, than in most other countries of a richer and more fertile soil, for the place, poor in itself, having become the great mart for the commodities of India, Persia, and Arabia, was thus abundantly stocked with the produce of all these countries.

Peter Martyr's [3] point of view was much the same. He was full of surprise at the splendour round him, and the advantages such fertility offered to husbandry :

Thus after a few days with cheerful hearts they espied the land long looked for. . . .

As they coasted along by the shore of certain of these islands, they heard nightingales sing in the thick woods in the month of November.

They found also great rivers of fresh water and natural havens of capacity to harbour great navies of ships. . . . They found there wild geese, turtle-doves, and ducks, much greater than ours, and as white as swans, with heads of purple colour.   Also popinjays, of the which some are green, some ye ow, and having their feathers intermingled with lgreen, yellow, and purple, which varieties delighted the sense not a little. . . . They entered into a main large sea, having in it innumerable islands, marvellously differing one from another ; for some of them were very fruitful, full of herbs and trees, other some very dry, barren, and rough, with high rocky mountains of stone, whereof some were of bright blue, or azurine colour, and other glistening white.

He filled a whole page with descriptions of the wonderful wealth of flowers, fruit, and vegetables of all kinds, which the ground yields even in February.   The richness of the prairie grass, the charm of the rivers, the wealth of fruit, the enormous size of the trees (with a view to native houses), the various kinds of pines, palms, and chestnuts, and their uses, the immense downfall of water carried to the sea by the rivers—all this he noted with admiration ; but industrial interest outweighed the æsthetic, even when he called Spain happier than Italy. There is no trace of any real feeling for scenery, any grasp of landscape as a whole ; he did not advance beyond scattered details, which attracted his eye chiefly for their material uses.

But there is real delight in Nature in the account of a journey to the Cape Verde Islands, undertaken on the suggestion of Henry the Navigator by Aloise da Mosto,' an intelligent Venetian nobleman :

Cape de Verde is so called because the Portuguese, who had discovered it about a year before, found it covered with trees, which continue green all the year round.   This is ˙a high and beautiful Cape, which runs a good length into the sea, and has two hills or little mountains at the point thereof.   There are several villages of negroes from Senega, on and about the promontory, who dwell in thatched houses close to the shore, and in sight of those who sail by. . . . The coast is all low and full of fine large trees, which are constantly green ; that is, they never wither as those in Europe do, for the new leaves grow before the old ones fall off. These trees are so near the shore that they seem to drink out of the sea. It is a most beautiful coast to behold, and the author, who had sailed both in the East and West, never saw any comparable with it.

As Ruge says :

> The delight of this solid and prudent citizen of Strasburg in the beauty of the tropics is lost in translation, but very evident in the original account.[5]

After reading it, we cannot quite say with Humboldt that Columbus was the very first to give fluent expression to Nature's beauty on the shores of the New World ; none the less, and apart from his importance in other respects, he remains the chief representative of his time in the matter. Humboldt noted this in his critical examination of the history of geography in the fifteenth and sixteenth centuries, in which he pointed out his deep feeling for Nature, and also, what only those who know the difficulties of language at the time can appreciate, the beauty and simplicity of his expression of it.[6]

Columbus is a striking example of the fact that a man's openness to Nature increases with his general inner growth. No one doubts that uneducated sailors, like other unlettered people, are vividly impressed by fine scenery, especially when it is new to them, if they possess a spark of mental refinement. They have the feeling, but are unable to express it in words. But, as Humboldt says, feeling improves speech ; with increased culture, the power of expression increases.

We owe a debt of gratitude to Fernandez de Navarrete[7] for the Diary in which we can trace Columbus' love for Nature increasing to ' a deep and poetic feeling for the majesty of creation.'

He wrote, October 8th, 1492, in his diary :

> ' Thanks be to God,' says the Admiral, ' the air is very soft like the April at Seville, and it is a pleasure to be there, so balmy are the breezes.'

And Humboldt says :

> The physiognomy and forms of the vegetation, the
> impenetrable thickets of the forests, in which one can
> scarcely distinguish the stems to which the several
> blossoms and leaves belong, the wild luxuriance of the
> flowering soil along the humid shores, and the rose-
> coloured flamingoes which, fishing at early morning at
> the mouth of the rivers, impart animation to the
> scenery,—all in turn arrested the attention of the old
> mariner as he sailed along the shores of Cuba, between
> the small Lucayan Islands and the Jardinillos.

Each new country seemed to him more beautiful
than the last; he complained that he could not find
new words in which to give the Queen an impression
of the beauty of the Cuban coast.

It will repay us to examine the Diary more closely,
since Humboldt only treated it shortly and in
scattered extracts, and it has been partly falsified,
unintentionally, by attempts to modernize the
language instead of adhering to literal translation.
What Peschel says, for instance, is pretty but
distinctly exaggerated :

> Columbus was never weary of listening to the night-
> ingales, comparing the genial Indian climate with the
> Andalusian spring, and admiring the luxuriant wilder-
> ness on these humid shores, with their dense vegetation
> and forests so rich in all kinds of plants, and alive with
> swarms of parrots . . . with an open eye for all the
> beauties of Nature and all the wonders of creation, he
> looked at the splendour of the tropics very much as a
> tender father looks into the bright eyes of his child.[8]

The Diary of November 3rd says :

> He could see nothing, owing to the dense foliage of
> the trees, which were very fresh and odoriferous ; so that
> he felt no doubt that there were aromatic herbs among
> them.   He said that all he saw was so beautiful that his
> eyes could never tire of gazing upon such loveliness, nor
> his ears of listening to the songs of birds.

November 14th :

> He saw so many islands that he could not count them
> all, with very high land covered with trees of many
> kinds and an infinite number of palms.   He was much

astonished to see so many lofty islands, and assured the Sovereigns that the mountains and islands he had seen since yesterday seemed to him to be second to none in the world, so high and clear of clouds and snow, with the sea at their bases so deep.

November 25th :

He saw a large stream of beautiful water falling from the mountains above, with a loud noise. . . . Just then the sailor boys called out that they had found large pines. The Admiral looked up the hill and saw that they were so wonderfully large, that he could not exaggerate their height and straightness, like stout yet fine spindles. He perceived that here there was material for great store of planks and masts for the largest ships in Spain . . . the mountains are very high, whence descend many limpid streams, and all the hills are covered with pines, and an infinity of diverse and beautiful trees.

November 27th :

The freshness and beauty of the trees, the clearness of the water and the birds, made it all so delightful that he wished never to leave them. He said to the men who were with him that to give a true relation to the Sovereigns of the things they had seen, a thousand tongues would not suffice, nor his hand to write it, for that it was like a scene of enchantment.

December 13th :

The nine men well armed, whom he sent to explore a certain place, said, with regard to the beauty of the land they saw, that the best land in Castille could not be compared with it. The Admiral also said that there was no comparison between them, nor did the Plain of Cordova come near them, the difference being as great as between night and day. They said that all these lands were cultivated, and that a very wide and large river passed through the centre of the valley and could irrigate all the fields. All the trees were green and full of fruit, and the plants tall and covered with flowers. The roads were broad and good. The climate was like April in Castille ; the nightingale and other birds sang as they do in Spain during that month, and it was the most pleasant place in the world. Some birds sing sweetly at night, the crickets and frogs are heard a good deal.

All this shews a naive and spontaneous delight in Nature, as free from sentimentality as from any grasp of landscape as a distinct entity.

In a letter about Cuba, which Humboldt gives, he says :

> The lands are high, and there are many very lofty mountains . . . all most beautiful, of a thousand different shapes, accessible and covered with trees of a thousand kinds of such great height that they seemed to reach the skies. I am told that the trees never lose their foliage, and I can well believe it, for I observed that they were as green and luxuriant as in Spain in the month of May. Some were in bloom, others bearing fruit, and others otherwise according to their nature. There were palm trees of six or eight kinds, wonderful in their beautiful variety ; but this is the case with all the other trees ; fruits and grasses, trees, plants and fruits filled us with admiration. It contains extraordinary pine groves and very extensive plains.

Humboldt here comments that these often-repeated expressions of admiration prove a strong feeling for the beauty of Nature, since they are concerned with foliage and shade, not with precious metals. The next letter shews the growing power of description :

> Reaching the harbour of Bastimentos, I put in. . . . The storm and a rapid current kept me in for fourteen days, when I again set sail, but not with favourable weather. . . . I had already made four leagues when the storm recommenced and wearied me to such a degree that I absolutely knew not what to do ; my wound re-opened, and for nine days my life was despaired of. Never was the sea seen so high, so terrific, and so covered with foam ; not only did the wind oppose our proceeding onward, but it also rendered it highly dangerous to run in for any headland, and kept me in that sea, which seemed to me a sea of blood, seething like a cauldron on a mighty fire. Never did the sky look more fearful ; during one day and one night it burned like a furnace, and emitted flashes in such fashion that each time I looked to see if my masts and my sails were not destroyed ; these flashes came with such alarming fury that we all thought the ship must have been consumed. All this time the waters from heaven never ceased, not to say that it

rained, for it was like a repetition of the Deluge. The men were at this time so crushed in spirit, that they longed for death as a deliverance from so many martyr-doms. Twice already had the ships suffered loss in boats, anchors, and rigging, and were now lying bare without sails.

These extracts shew how feeling for Nature in unlettered minds could develop into an enthusiasm which begot to some extent its own power of expression. Columbus was entirely deficient in all previous knowledge of natural history ; but he was gifted with deep feeling (the account of the nocturnal visions in the *Lettera Rarissima* is proof of this)', mental energy, and a capacity for exact observation which many of the other explorers did not possess, and these faculties made up for what he lacked in education.

> In Cuba alone, he distinguishes seven or eight different species of palm more beautiful and taller than the date tree ; he informs his learned friend Anghiera that he has seen pines and palms wonderfully associ-ated together in one and the same plain, and he even so acutely observed the vegetation around him, that he was the first to notice that there were pines in the mountains of Cibao, whose fruits are not fir cones but berries like the olives of the Axarafe de Sevilla.
>
> (*Cosmos.*)

Most of Vespucci's narratives of travel, especially his letters to the Medici, only contain adventures and descriptions of manners and customs. He lacked the originality and enthusiasm which gave the power of the wing to Columbus.

That imposing Portuguese poem, the *Lusiad* of Camoens, is full of jubilation over the discovery of the New World. Camoens made his notes of foreign places at first hand ; he had served as a soldier, fought at the foot of Atlas in the Red Sea and Persian Gulf, had doubled the Cape twice, and, inspired by a deep love for Nature, had spent sixteen years in examining the phenomena of the ocean on the Indian and

Chinese shores.   He was a great sea painter. His poetic and inventive power remind one at times of Dante — for instance, in the description of the Dream Face; and he pictures foreign lands with the clearness and detail of the discoverers and later travellers.   Here and there his poetry is like the Diary of Columbus translated into verse—epic verse.

He had the same fiery spirit, nerve, and fresh insight, with the poet's gift added.

(None the less, the classic apparatus of deities in Thetys' *Apology* is no adornment.)

Comparisons from Nature and animals are few but detailed :

> E'en as the prudent ants which towards their nest
> Bearing the apportioned heavy burden go,
> Exercise all their forces at their best,
> Hostile to hostile winter's frost and snow ;
> There, all their toils and labours stand confessed,
> There, never looked-for energy they show ;
> So, from the Lusitanians to avert
> Their horrid Fate, the nymphs their power exert.

> Thus, as in some sequestered sylvan mere
> The frogs (the Lycian people formerly),
> If that by chance some person should appear
> While out of water they incautious be,
> Awake the pool by hopping here and there,
> To fly the danger which they deem they see,
> And gathering to some safe retreat they know,
> Only their heads above the water show — So fly the
>   Moors.

> E'en as when o'er the parching flame there glows
> A flame, which may from some chance cause ignite,
> (All while the whistling, puffing Boreas blows),
> Fanned by the wind sets all the growth alight,
> The shepherd's group, lying in their repose
> Of quiet sleep, aroused in wild afright
> At crackling flames that spread both wide and high,
> Gather their goods and to the village fly ;
> So doth the Moor.

> E'en as the daisy which once brightly smiled,
> Plucked by unruly hands before its hour,

And harshly treated by the careless child,
All in her chaplet tied with artless power,
Droops, of its colour and its scent despoiled,
So seems this pale and lifeless damsel flower ;
The roses of her lips are dry and dead,
With her sweet life the mingled white and red.

The following simile reminds us of the far-fetched
comparison of Apollonios Rhodios [11] :

As the reflected lustre from the bright
Steel mirror, or of beauteous crystal fine,
Which, being stricken by the solar light,
Strikes back and on some other part doth shine ;
And when, to please the child's vain curious sight,
Moved o'er the house, as may his hand incline,
Dances on walls and roof and everywhere,
Restless and tremulous, now here now there,
So did the wandering judgment fluctuate.

He says of Diana :

And, as confronted on her way she pressed,
So beautiful her form and bearing were,
That everything that saw her love confessed,
The stars, the heaven, and the surrounding air.

The Indus and Ganges are personified in stanza
xiv. 74, the Cape in v. 50.

His time references are mostly mixed up with
ancient mythology :

As soon, however, as the enamelled morn
O'er the calm heaven her lovely looks outspread,
Opening to bright Hyperion, new-born,
Her purple portals as he raised his head,
Then the whole fleet their ships with flags adorn.

and :

So soon, however, as great Sol has spread
His rays o'er earth, whom instantly to meet,
Her purple brow Aurora rising shews,
And rudely life around the horizon throws.

He is at his best in writing of the sea.
He says of the explorers on first setting sail :

Now were they sailing o'er wide ocean bright,
The restless waves dividing as they flew;
The winds were breathing prosperous and light,
The vessels' hollow sails were filled to view;
The seas were covered o'er with foaming white
Where the advancing prows were cutting through
The consecrated waters of the deep. . . .
Thus went we forth these unknown seas to explore,
Which by no people yet explored had been;
Seeing new isles and climes which long before
Great Henry, first discoverer, had seen.

Now did the moon in purest lustre rise
On Neptune's silvery waves her beams to pour,
With stars attendant glittered all the skies,
E'en like a meadow daisy-spangled o'er;
The fury of the winds all peaceful lies
In the dark caverns close along the shore,
But still the night-watch constant vigils keep,
As long had been their custom on the deep.

To tell thee of the dangers of the sea
At length, which human understanding scare,
Thunder-storms, sudden, dreadful in degree,
Lightnings, which seem to set on fire the air,
Dark floods of rain, nights of obscurity,
Rollings of thunder which the world would tear,
Were not less labour than a great mistake,
E'en if I had an iron voice to speak.

He describes the electric fires of St Elmo and the
gradual development of the waterspout:

I saw, and clearly saw, the living light
Which sailors everywhere as sacred hold
In time of storm and crossing winds that fight,
Of tempest dark and desperation cold;
Nor less it was to all a marvel quite,
And matter surely to alarm the bold,
To observe the sea-clouds, with a tube immense,
Suck water up from Ocean's deep expanse. . . .
A fume or vapour thin and subtle rose,
And by the wind begin revolving there;
Thence to the topmost clouds a tube it throws,
But of a substance so exceeding rare. . . .
But when it was quite gorged it then withdrew
The foot that on the sea beneath had grown,
And o'er the heavens in fine it raining flew,
The jacent waters watering with its own.

The storm at sea reminds us of Æschylus in
splendour :

> The winds were such, that scarcely could they shew
> With greater force or greater rage around,
> Than if it were this purpose then to blow
> The mighty tower of Babel to the ground. . . .
> Now rising to the clouds they seem to go
> O'er the wild waves of Neptune borne on end;
> Now to the bowels of the deep below ;
> It seems to all their senses, they descend ;
> Notus and Auster, Boreas,, Aquila,
> The very world's machinery would rend ;
> While flashings fire the black and ugly night
> And shed from pole to pole a dazzling light. . . .
> But now the star of love beamed forth its ray,
> Before the sun, upon the horizon clear,
> And visited, as messenger of day,
> The earth and spreading sea, with brow to cheer. . . .

And, as it subsides :

> The mountains that we saw at first appeared,
> In the far view, like clouds and nothing more.

Off the coast of India :

> Now o'er the hills broke forth the morning light
> Where Ganges' stream is murmuring heard to flow,
> Free from the storm and from the first sea's fight,
> Vain terror from their hearts is banished now.

His magic island, the Ilha of Venus, could only
have been imagined by a poet who had travelled
widely. All the delights of the New World are there,
with the vegetation of Southern Europe added. It
is a poet's triumphant rendering of impressions
which the discoverers so often felt their inability
to convey :

> From far they saw the island fresh and fair,
> Which Venus o'er the waters guiding drove
> (E'en as the wind the canvas white doth bear). . . .
> Where the coast forms a bay for resting-place,
> Curved and all quiet, and whose shining sand
> Is painted with red shells by Venus' hand. . . .
> Three beauteous mounts rise nobly to the view,
> Lifting with graceful pride their sweeling head,

O'er which enamelled grass adorning grew.
In this delightful lovely island glad,
Bright limpid streams their rushing waters threw
From heights with rich luxuriant verdure clad,
'Midst the white rocks above, their source derive,
The streams sonorous, sweet, and fugitive. . . .
A thousand trees toward heaven their summits raise,
With fruits odoriferous and fair;
The orange in its produce bright displays
The tint that Daphne carried in her hair;
The citron on the ground its branches lays,
Laden with yellow weights it cannot bear;
The beauteous melons, which the whole perfume
The virgin bosom in their form assume.
The forest trees, which on the hills combine
To ennoble them with leafy hair o'ergrown,
Are poplars of Alcides; laurels shine,
The which the shining God loved as his own;
Myrtles of Cytherea with the pine
Of Cybele, by other love o'erthrown;
The spreading cypress tree points out where lies
The seat of the ethereal paradise. . . .
Pomegranates rubicund break forth and shine,
A tint whereby thou, ruby, losest sheen.
'Twixt the elm branches hangs the jocund vine,
With branches some of red and some of green. . . .
Then the refined and splendid tapestry,
Covering the rustic ground beneath the feet,
Makes that of Achemeina dull to be,
But makes the shady valley far more sweet.
Cephisian flowers with head inclined we see
About the calm and lucid lake's retreat. . . .
'Twas difficult to fancy which was true,
Seeing on heaven and earth all tints the same,
If fair Aurora gave the flowers their time,
Or from the lovely flowers to her it came;
Flora and Zephyr there in painting drew
The violets tinted, as of lovers' flame,
The iris, and the rose all fair and fresh
E'en as it doth on cheek of maiden blush. . . .
Along the water sings the snow-white swan,
While from the branch respondeth Philomel. . . .
Here, in its bill, to the dear nest, with care,
The rapid little bird the food doth bear.

Subjective feeling for Nature is better displayed
in the lyric than the epic.

The Spaniard, Fray Luis de Leon, was a typical example of a sixteenth-century lyrist ; full of mild enthusiasm for Nature, the theosophico-mystical attitude of the Catholic.

A most fervid feeling for Nature from the religious side breathed in St Francis of Assisi—the feeling which inspired his hymn to Brother Sun (*Cantico del Sole*), and led his brother Egidio, intoxicated with love to his Creator, to kiss trees and rocks and weep over them ¹² :

> Praised by His creatures all,
> Praised be the Lord my God
> By Messer Sun, my brother above all,
> Who by his rays lights us and lights the day—
> Radiant is she, with his great splendour stored,
> Thy glory, Lord, confessing.
> By Sister Moon and Stars my Lord is praised,
> Where clear and fair they in the heavens are raised
> By Brother Wind, etc. . . .

His follower, Bonaventura, too, in his verses counted—

> The smallest creatures his brothers and sisters, and called upon crops, vineyards, trees, flowers, and stars to praise God.

Bernard von Clairvaux made it a principle ' to learn from the earth, trees, corn, flowers, and grass '; and he wrote in his letter to Heinrich Murdach (Letter 106) :

> Believe me, I have proved it ; you will find more in the woods than in books ; trees and stones will teach you what no other teacher can.

He looked upon all natural objects as ' rays of the Godhead,' copies of a great original.

His contemporary, Hugo von St Victor, wrote :

> The whole visible world is like a book written by the finger of God. It is created by divine power, and all human beings are figures placed in it, not to shew the free-will of man, but as a revelation and visible sign, by divine will, of God's invisible wisdom. But

> as one who only glances at an open book sees marks
> on it, but does not read the letters, so the wicked and
> sensual man, in whom the spirit of God is not, sees
> only the outer surface of visible beings and not their
> deeper parts.

German mystics wrote in the same strain; for
instance, the popular Franciscan preacher, Berthold
von Regensburg (1272),

> Whose sermons on fields and meadows drew many
> thousands of hearers, and moved them partly by
> the unusual freshness and vitality of his pious feeling
> for Nature,

in spite of many florid symbolical accessories, such
as we find again in Ekkehart and other fifteenth-
century mystics, and especially in Tauler, Suso, and
Ruysbroek.

The northern prophetess and foundress of an Order
Birgitta (1373) held that the breath of the Creator
was in all visible things: 'We feel it pervading us
in her visions,' says Hammerich,[13]

> Whether by gurgling brook or snow-covered firs.
> It is with us when the prophetess leads us along the
> ridges of the Swedish coast with their surging waves
> or down the shaft of a mine, or to wander in the quiet
> of evening through vineyards between roses and lilies,
> while the dew is falling and the bells ring out the
> Ave Maria.

Vincentius von Beauvais (1264) in his *Speculum
Naturæ* demonstrates the value of studying Nature
from a religious and moral point of view; and the
Carthusian general, Dionysius von Rickel (1471), in
his paper *On the beauty of the world and the glory of
God* (*De venustate mundi et de pulchritudine Dei*)
says in Chapter xxii.: 'All the beauty of the
animal world is nothing but the reflection and out-
flow of the original beauty of God,' and gives as
special examples:

> Roses, lilies, and other beautiful and fragrant
> flowers, shady woods, pine trees, pleasant meadows,

high, mountains, springs, streams and rivers, and the broad arm of the immeasurable sea . . . and above all shine the stars, completing their course in the clear sky in wonderful splendour and majestic order.

Raymundus von Sabieude, a Spaniard, who studied medicine and philosophy at Toulouse, and wrote his *Theologia Naturalis* in 1436, considered Nature, like Thomas Aquinas, from a mystical and scholastic point of view, as made up of living beings in a graduated scale from the lowest to the highest; and he lauded her in terms which even Pope Clement VII. thought exaggerated. Piety in him went hand in hand with a natural philosophy like Bacon's, and his interest in Nature was rather a matter of intellect than feeling.

God has given us two books—the book of all living beings, or Nature, and the Holy Scriptures. The first was given to man from the beginning when all things were created, for each living being is but a letter of the alphabet written by the finger of God, and the book is composed of them all together as a book is of letters . . . man is the capital letter of this book. This book is not like the other, falsified and spoilt, but familiar and intelligible; it makes man joyous and humble and obedient, a hater of evil and a lover of virtue.

Among the savants of the Renaissance who applied the inductive method to Nature before Bacon,[14] we must include the thoughtful and pious Spaniard Luis Vives (1540), who wrote concerning the useless speculations of alchemists and astrologers about occult things : ' It is not arguing that is needed here, but silent observation of Nature.' Knowledge of Nature, he said, would serve both body and soul.

The tender religious lyrics of the mystic, Luis de Leon, followed next.[16] His life (1521-1591) brings us up to the days of the Inquisition. He himself, an excellent teacher and man of science, was imprisoned for years for opinions too openly expressed in his writings ; but, with all his varied fortunes he never lost his innate manliness and tenderness. His biographer tells us, that as soon as the holidays began, he would hurry away from the gloomy lecture rooms and the noisy students at Salamanca, to the country, where he had taken an estate belonging to a monastery at the foot of a hill by a river, with a little island close by.

It had a large uncultivated garden, made beautiful by fine old trees, with paths among the vines and a stream running through it to the river, and a long avenue of poplars whose rustle blended with the noise of the mill-wheel. Beyond was a view of fields. Leon would sit for hours here undisturbed, dipping his feet in the brook under a poplar—the tree which was reputed to flourish on sand alone and give shelter to all the birds under heaven—while the rustle of the leaves sang his melancholy to sleep. His biographer goes on to say that he had the Spaniard's special delight in Nature, and understood her language and her secrets; and the veiled splendour of her tones, colours, and forms could move him to tears. As he sat there gazing at the clouds, he felt lifted up in heart by the insignificance of all things in comparison with the spirit of man.

In the pitching and tossing of his ' ships of thought ' he never lost the consciousness of Nature's beauty, and would pray the clouds to carry his sighs with them in their tranquil course through heaven. He loved the sunrise, birds, flowers, bees, fishes ; nothing was meaningless to him ; all things were letters in a divine alphabet, which might bring him a message from above. Nature was symbolic; the glow of dawn meant the glow of divine love; a wide view, true freedom ; rays of sunshine, rays of divine glory; the setting sun, eternal light; stars, flowers of light in an everlasting spring.

His love for the country, especially for its peacefulness, was free from the folly and excess of the pastoral poetry of his day. He did not paint Nature entirely for her own sake; man was always her master [16] in his poems, and he sometimes, very finely, introduced himself and his affairs at the close, and represented Nature as addressing himself.

His descriptions are short, and he often tries to represent sounds onomato-poetically.

This is from his ode, *Quiet Life* [17]:

O happy he who flies
Far from the noisy world away—
Who with the worthy and the wise
Hath chosen the narrow way.
The silence of the secret road
That leads the soul to virtue and to God! . . .
O streams, and shades, and hills on high,
Unto the stillness of your breast
My wounded spirit longs to fly—
To fly and be at rest.
Thus from the world's tempestuous sea,
O gentle Nature, do I turn to thee. . . .
A garden by the mountain side
Is mine, whose flowery blossoming
Shews, even in spring's luxuriant pride,
What Autumn's suns shall bring:
And from mountain's lofty crown
A clear and sparkling rill comes tumbling down;
Then, pausing in its downward force
The venerable trees among,
It gurgles on its winding course;
And, as it glides along,
Gives freshness to the day and pranks
With ever changing flowers its mossy banks.
The whisper of the balmy breeze
Scatters a thousand sweets around,
And sweeps in music through the trees
With an enchanting sound
That laps the soul in calm delight
Where crowns and kingdoms are forgotten quite.

The poem, *The Starry Sky*, [18] is full of lofty enthusiasm for Nature and piety:

When yonder glorious sky
Lighted with million lamps I contemplate,
And turn my dazzled eye
To this vain mortal state
All mean and visionary, mean and desolate,

A mingled joy and grief
Fills all my soul with dark solicitude. . . .
List to the concert pure
Of yon harmonious countless worlds of light.
See, in his orbit sure
Each takes his journey bright,
Led by an unseen hand through the vast maze of
    night.
See how the pale moon rolls
Her silver wheel. . . .
See Saturn, father of the golden hours,
While round him, bright and blest,
The whole empyrean showers
Its glorious streams of light on this low world of
    ours.
But who to these can turn
And weigh them 'gainst a weeping world like this,
Nor feel his spirit burn
To grasp so sweet a bliss
And mourn that exile hard which here his portion is ?
For there, and there alone,
Are peace and joy and never dying love :
Day that shall never cease,
No night there threatening,
No winter there to chill joy's ever-during spring.
Ye fields of changeless green
Covered with living streams and fadeless flowers;
Thou paradise serene,
Eternal joyful hours
Thy disembodied soul shall welcome in thy towers !

It was chiefly in Spanish literature at this time
that Nature was used allegorically.   Tieck [19] says:
' In Calderon's poetry, and that of his contemporaries,
we often find, in romances and song-like metres, most
charming descriptions of the sea, mountains, gardens,
and woody valleys, but almost always used alle-
gorically, and with an artistic polish which ends by
giving us, not so much a real impression of Nature,
as one of clever description in musical verse, re-
peated again and again with slight variations.'
This is true of Leon, but far more of Calderon, since
it belongs to the very essence of drama.   But,
despite his passion for description and his Catholic
and conventional tone, there is inexhaustible fancy,

splendid colour, and a modern element of individuality in his poems. His heroes are conscious of their own ego, feel themselves to be 'a miniature world,' and search out their own feelings 'in the wild waves of emotion' (as Aurelian, for example, in *Zenobia*).

Fernando says in *The Constant Prince*:

These flowers awoke in beauty and delight
At early dawn, when stars began to set;
At eve they leave us but a fond regret,
Locked in the cold embraces of the night.
These shades that shame the rainbow's arch of light,
Where gold and snow in purple pomp are met,
All give a warning man should not forget,
When one brief day can darken things so bright.
'Tis but to wither that the roses bloom—
'Tis to grow old they bear their beauteous flowers,
One crimson bud their cradle and their tomb.
Such are man's fortunes in this world of ours;
They live, they die; one day doth end their doom,
For ages past but seem to us like hours.

The warning which Zenobia gives her captor in his hour of triumph to beware of sudden reverses of fortune is finely conceived:

Morn comes forth with rays to crown her,
While the sun afar is spreading
Golden cloths most finely woven
All to dry her tear-drops purely.
Up to noon he climbs, then straightway
Sinks, and then dark night makes ready
For the burial of the sea
Canopies of black outstretching—
Tall ships fly on linen pinions,
On with speed the breezes send it,
Small the wide seas seem and straitened,
To its quick flight onward tending.
Yet one moment, yet one instant,
And the tempest roars, uprearing
Waves that might the stars extinguish,
Lifted for that ship's o'erwhelming.
Day, with fear, looks ever nightwards,
Calms must storm await with trembling
Close behind the back of pleasure
Evermore stalks sadness dreary.

In *Life's a Dream* Prince Sigismund, chained in a dark prison, says :

What sinned I more herein
Than others, who were also born ?
Born the bird was, yet with gay
Gala vesture, beauty's dower,
Scarcely 'tis a winged flower
Or a richly plumaged spray,
Ere the aerial halls of day
It divideth rapidly,
And no more will debtor be
To the nest it hates to quit ;
But, with more of soul than it,
I am grudged its liberty.
And the beast was born, whose skin
Scarce those beauteous spots and bars,
Like to constellated stars,
Doth from its greater painter win
Ere the instinct doth begin :
Of its fierceness and its pride,
And its lair on every side,
It has measured far and nigh ;
While, with better instinct, I
Am its liberty denied.
Born the mute fish was also,
Child of ooze and ocean weed ;
Scarce a finny bark of speed
To the surface brought, and lo !
In vast circuits to and fro
Measures it on every side
Its illimitable home ;
While, with greater will to roam,
I that freedom am denied.
Born the streamlet was, a snake
Which unwinds the flowers among,
Silver serpent, that not long
May to them sweet music make,
Ere it quits the flowery brake,
Onward hastening to the sea
With majestic course and free,
Which the open plains supply ;
While, with more life gifted, I
Am denied its liberty.

In Act II. Clotardo tells how he has talked to the young prince, brought up in solitude and confinement :

There I spoke with him awhile
Of the human arts and letters,
Which the still and silent aspect
Of the mountains and the heavens
Him have taught—that school divine
Where he has been long a learner,
And the voices of the birds
And the beasts has apprehended.

Descriptions of time and place are very rich in colour.

One morning on the ocean,
When the half-awakened sun,
Trampling down the lingering shadows
Of the western vapours dun,
Spread its ruby-tinted tresses
Over jessamine and rose,
Dried with cloths of gold Aurora's
Tears of mingled fire and snows
Which to pearl his glance converted.

Since these gardens cannot steal
Away your oft returning woes,
Though to beauteous spring they build
Snow-white jasmine temples filled
With radiant statues of the rose ;
Come into the sea and make
Thy bark the chariot of the sun,
And when the golden splendours run
Athwart the waves, along thy wake
The garden to the sea will say
(By melancholy fears deprest)—
'The sun already gilds the west,
How very short has been this day.'

There is a striking remark about a garden ; Menon says :

A beautiful garden surrounded by wild forest
Is the more beautiful the nearer it approaches its
    opposite.

Splendour of colour was everything with Calderon, but it was splendour of so stiff and formal a kind, that, like the whole of his intensely severe, even inquisitorial outlook, it leaves us cold.

We must turn to Shakespeare to learn how strongly

the pulse of sympathy for Nature could beat in contemporary drama. Goethe said : ' In Calderon you have the wine as the last artificial result of the grape, but expressed into the goblet, highly spiced and sweetened, and so given you to drink; but in Shakespeare you have the whole natural process of its ripening besides, and the grapes themselves one by one, for your enjoyment, if you will.'

In *Worship at the Cross* there is pious feeling for Nature and mystical feeling side by side with an obnoxious fanaticism, superstition, and other objectionable traits[20]; and mystical confessions of the same sort may be gathered in numbers from the works of contemporary monks and nuns. Even of such a fanatic and self-tormentor as the Spanish Franciscan Petrus von Alcantara (1562), his biographer says that despite his strict renunciation of the world, he retained a most warm and deep feeling for Nature.

' Whatever he saw of the outer world increased his devotion and gave it wings. The starry sky seen through his little monastery window, often kept him rapt in deep meditation for hours; often he was as if beside himself, so strong was his pious feeling when he saw the power and glory of God reflected in charming flowers and plants.'

When Gregorio Lopez (1596), a man who had studied many sides of Nature, was asked if so much knowledge confused him, he answered : ' I find God in all things, great and small.' Similar remarks are attributed to many others.

Next to Leon, as a poet in enthusiasm and mysticism, came St Teresa von Avila. She was especially notable for the ravishingly pretty pictures and comparisons she drew from Nature to explain the soul life of the Christian.[21]

In all these outpourings of mystic feeling for Nature, there was no interest in her entirely for her own sake; they were all more or less dictated by religious feeling. It was in the later German and Italian mystics—for example, Bruno, Campanella, and Jacob Boehme—that a more subjective and individual point of view was attained through Pantheism and Protestantism.

The Protestant free-speaking Shakespeare shewed a far more intense feeling for Nature than the Catholic Calderon.

CHAPTER VI

SHAKESPEARE'S SYMPATHY FOR NATURE

THE poetry of India may serve as a measure of the part which Nature can play in drama; it is full of comparisons and personifications, and eloquent expressions of intimate sympathy with plants and animals. In Greek tragedy, Nature stepped into the background; metaphors, comparisons, and personifications are rarer; it was only by degrees, especially in Sophocles and Euripides, in the choruses and monologues, that man's interest in her appeared, and he began to greet the light or the sky, land or sea, to attribute love, pity, or hate to her, or find comfort in her lonely places. During the Middle Ages, drama lay fallow, and the blossoming period of French tragedy, educated to the pathos of Seneca, only produced cold declamation, frosty rhetoric; of any real sympathy between man and Nature there was no question.

Over this mediæval void Calderon was the bridge to Shakespeare.

Shakespeare reached the Greek standpoint and advanced far beyond it. He was not only the greatest dramatist of modern times as to human action, suffering, and character, but also a genius in the interpretation of Nature.[1]

In place of the narrow limits of the old dramatists, he had the wider and maturer modern vision, and, despite his mastery of language, he was free both from the exaggeration and redundance of Oriental drama, and from the mere passion for describing, which so often carried Calderon away.

In him too, the subjectivity, which the Renaissance brought into modern art, was still more fully developed. His metaphors and comparisons shew this, and, most of all, the very perfect art with which he assigns Nature a part in the play, and makes her not only form the appropriate background, dark or bright as required, but exert a distinct influence upon human fate.

As Carrière points out :

> At a period which had painting for its leading art, and was turning its attention to music, his mental accord produced effects in his works to which antiquity . . . was a stranger.

Herder had already noted that Shakespeare gives colour and atmosphere where the Greek only gave outline. And although Shakespeare's outlines are drawn with more regard to fidelity than to actual beauty, yet, like a great painter, he brings all Nature into sympathy with man. We feel the ghostly shudder of the November night in *Hamlet*, breathe the bracing Highland air in *Macbeth*, the air of the woods in *As You Like It* ; the storm on the heath roars through Lear's mad outburst, the nightingale sings in the pomegranate outside Julia's window.

'How sweet the moonlight sleeps upon this bank,' when Love solves all differences in the *Merchant of Venice* ! On the other hand, when Macbeth is meditating the murder of Duncan, the wolf howls, the owl hoots, and the cricket cries. And since Shakespeare's characters often act out of part, so that intelligible motive fails, while it is important to the poet that each scene be raised to dramatic level and viewed in a special light, Goethe's words apply :

> Here everything which in a great world event passes secretly through the air, everything which at the very

moment of a terrible occurrence men hide away in their hearts, is expressed ; that which they carefully shut up and lock away in their minds is here freely and eloquently brought to light ; we recognize the truth to life, but know not how it is achieved.

Amorous passion in his hands is an interpreter of Nature; in one of his sonnets he compares it to an ocean which cannot quench thirst.

In Sonnet 130 he says :

My mistress' eyes are nothing like the sun ;
Coral is far more red than her lips' red ;
If snow be white, why then her breasts are dim ;
If hairs be wires, black wires grow on her head.
I have seen roses damask'd, red and white,
But no such roses see I in her cheeks ;
And in some perfumes is there more delight
Than in the breath that from my mistress reeks . . . .
And yet, by Heaven, I think my love as rare
As any she belied by false compare.

His lady-love is a mirror in which the whole world is reflected :

Since I left you, mine eye is in my mind . . . .
For if it see the rudest or gentlest sight,
The most sweet favour or deformed'st creature,
The mountain or the sea, the day or night,
The crow or dove, it shapes them to your feature.
(Sonnet 113.)

When she leaves him it seems winter even in spring:
'For summer and his pleasures wait on thee,
And thou away, the very birds are mute.'
(Sonnet 97.)

Here, as in the dramas,[2] contrasts in Nature are often used to point contrasts in life :

How sweet and lovely dost thou make the shame
Which like a canker in the fragrant rose
Doth spot the beauty of thy budding name !
O in what sweets dost thou thy sins enclose !
(Sonnet 95.)

and

No more be grieved at that which thou hast done;
Roses have thorns and silver fountains mud ;

> Clouds and eclipses stain both moon and sun,
> And loathsome canker lives in sweetest bud.
>
> (Sonnet 35.)

In an opposite sense is Sonnet 70 :

> The ornament of beauty is suspect
> A crow that flies in heaven's sweetest air,
> For canker vice the sweetest buds did love,
> And thou presentest a pure unstained prime.

Sonnet 7 has :

> Lo ! in the orient when the gracious light
> Lifts up his burning head, each under eye
> Doth homage to his new-appearing sight,
> Serving with looks his sacred majesty.

Sonnet 18 :

> Shall I compare thee to a summer's day ?
> Thou art more lovely and more temperate,
> Rough winds do shake the darling buds of May,
> And summer's lease hath all too short a date—
> But thy eternal summer shall not fade,
> Nor lose possession of that fair thou owest ;;
> Nor shall Death brag thou wanderest in his shade,
> When in eternal lines to time thou growest:
> So long as men can breathe or eyes can see,
> So long lives this, and this gives life to thee.

Sonnet 60 :

> Like as the waves make toward the pebbled shore,
> So do our minutes hasten to their end ;
> Each changing place with that which goes before,
> In sequent toil all forwards do contend.

Sonnet 73 :

> That time of life thou mayst in me behold,
> When yellow leaves, or none, or few do hang
> Upon those boughs which shake against the cold,
> Bare ruin'd choirs, where late the sweet birds sang
> In me thou see'st the twilight of such day
> As after sunset fadeth in the west,
> Which by-and-by black night doth take away,
> Death's second self, that seals up all in rest.
> In me thou see'st the glowing of such fire
> That on the ashes of his youth doth lie

As the death-bed whereon it must expire,
Consumed with that which it was nourished by.
This thou perceivest, which makes thy love more
  strong
To love that well which thou must leave ere long.

There are no better similes for the oncoming of age
and death, than the sere leaf trembling in the wind,
the twilight of the setting sun, the expiring flame.

Almost all the comparisons from Nature in his
plays are original, and rather keen and lightning-like
than elaborate, often with the terseness of proverbs:

The strawberry grows underneath the nettle.
(Henry V.)

Smooth runs the water where the brook is deep.
(Henry VI.)

The waters swell before a boisterous storm.
(Richard III.)

Sometimes they are heaped up, like Calderon's,
'making it' (true love)

Swift as a shadow, short as any dream,
Brief as the lightning in the collied night
That in a spleen unfolds both heaven and earth,
And ere a man hath power to say 'Behold!'
The jaws of darkness do devour it up.
(Midsummer Night's Dream.)

Compared with Homer's they are very bold, and
shew an astonishing play of imagination; in place
of the naive simplicity and naturalness of antiquity,
this modern genius gives us a dazzling display of wit
and thought. To quote only short examples [3]:

'Open as day,' 'deaf as the sea,' 'poor as winter,'
'chaste as unsunn'd snow.'

He ranges all Nature. These are characteristic
examples:

King Richard doth himself appear
As doth the blushing discontented sun
From out the fiery portal of the east,
When he perceives the envious clouds are bent
To dim his glory and to stain the track
Of his bright passage to the occident.
(Richard II.)

Since the more fair crystal is the sky,
The uglier seem the clouds that in it fly.

As when the golden sun salutes the morn,
And, having gilt the ocean with his beams,
Gallops the zodiac in his glistering coach
And overlooks the highest peering hills,
So Tamora.   (*Titus Andronicus.*)

As all the world is cheered by the sun,
So I by that; it is my day, my life.
                               (*Richard III.*)

So sweet a kiss the golden sun gives not
To those fresh morning drops upon the rose,
As thy eye-beams, when their fresh rays have smote
The night of dew that on my cheek down flows;
Nor shines the silver moon one half so bright
Through the transparent bosom of the deep,
As doth thy face through tears of mine give light;
Thou shinest on every tear that I do weep.
                               (*Love's Labour's Lost.*)

This is modern down to its finest detail, and much richer in individuality than the most famous comparisons of the same kind in antiquity.

Sea and stream are used :

Like an unseasonable stormy day
Which makes the silver rivers drown their shores
As if the world were all dissolved to tears,
So high above his limits swells the rage
Of Bolingbroke.   (*Richard II.*)

The current that with gentle murmur glides,
Thou know'st, being stopped, impatiently doth rage;
But when his fair course is not hindered,
He makes sweet music with the enamell'd stones,
Giving a gentle kiss to every sedge
He overtaketh on his pilgrimage;
And so by many winding nooks he strays
With willing sport to the wild ocean.
Then let me go, and hinder not my course.
                               (*Two Gentlemen of Verona.*)

Faster than spring-time showers comes thought on
    thought.

You are the fount that makes small brooks to flow.

And what is Edward but a ruthless sea ?
                               (*Henry VI.*)

If there were reason for these miseries,
Then into limits could I bind my woes;
When heaven doth weep, doth not the earth o'er-
flow?
If the winds rage, doth not the sea wax mad,
Threatening the welkin with his big-swoln face?
And wilt thou have a reason for this coil?
I am the sea: hark, how her sighs do blow!
She is the weeping welkin, I the earth;
Then must my sea be moved with her sighs;
Then must my earth with her continual tears
Become a deluge, overflow'd and drowned.
                        (*Titus Andronicus.*)

This battle fares like to the morning's war
When dying clouds contend with growing light,
What time the shepherd blowing of his nails
Can neither call it perfect day nor night.
Now sways it this way, like a mighty sea
Forced by the tide to combat with the wind;
Now sways it that way, like the self-same sea
Forced to retire by fury of the wind.
Sometime the flood prevails and then the wind:
Now one the better, then another best;
Both tugging to be victors, breast to breast,
Yet neither conqueror nor conquered.
So is the equal poise of this fell war.
                        (*Henry VI.*)

In the last five examples the epic treatment and the personifications are noteworthy.

Comparisons from animal life are forcible and striking:

How like a deer, stricken by many princes,
Dost thou lie here!   (*Julius Cæsar.*)

Richard III. is called;

The wretched bloody and usurping boar
That spoil'd your summer fields and fruitful vines,
Swills your warm blood like wash and makes his trough
In your embowell'd bosoms; this foul swine
Lies now even in the centre of this isle.
The tiger now hath seized the gentle hind.
                        (*Richard III.*)

The smallest objects are noted:

As flies to wanton boys are we to the gods;
They kill us for their sport.   (*King Lear.*)

Marcus : Alas! my lord, I have but kill'd a fly.

Titus : But how if that fly had a father and a mother ?
How would he hang his slender gilded wings,
And buzz lamenting doings in the air !
Poor harmless fly !
That, with his pretty buzzing melody,
Came here to make us merry ! and thou
Hast kill'd him !

(Titus Andronicus.)

Shakespeare has abundance of this idyllic miniature painting, for which all the literature of the day shewed a marked taste.

Tamora says :

My lovely Aaron, wherefore look'st thou sad,
When everything doth make a gleeful boast ?
The birds chant melody on every bush,
The snake lies rolled in the cheerful sun,
The green leaves quiver with the cooling wind
And make a chequer'd shadow on the ground.

(Titus Andronicus.)

And Valentine in *Two Gentlemen of Verona* :

This shadowy desert, unfrequented woods,
I better brook than flourishing peopled towns ;
Here can I sit alone, unseen of any,
And to the nightingale's complaining notes
Tune my distresses and record my woes.

Like this, in elegiac sentimentality, is Romeo :

Before the worshipp'd sun
Peer'd forth the golden window of the east . . . .
Many a morning hath he there been seen
With tears augmenting the fresh morning's dew.

Cymbeline, Winter's Tale, and *As You Like It* are particularly rich in idyllic traits ; the artificiality of court life is contrasted with life in the open ; there are songs, too, in praise of woodland joys :

Under the greenwood tree
Who loves to lie with me,
And tune his merry note
Unto the sweet bird's throat,

Come hither, come hither, come hither !
Here shall he see
No enemy
But winter and rough weather.

(*As You Like It.*)

Blow, blow, thou winter wind,
Thou art not so unkind
As man's ingratitude.
Thy tooth is not so keen,
Because thou art not seen,
Altho' thy breath be rude.
Heigh-ho, sing heigh-ho unto the green holly !
Most friendship is feigning, most loving mere folly !⁴

(*As You Like It.*)

Turning again to comparisons, we find birds used abundantly :

More pity that the eagle should be mewed
While kites and buzzards prey at liberty.

(*Richard III.*)

True hope is swift and flies with swallow's wings.

(*Richard III.*)

As wild geese that the creeping fowler eye,
Or russet-pated choughs, many in sort
Rising and cawing at the gun's report
Sever themselves and madly sweep the sky,
So at his sight away his fellows fly.

(*Midsummer Night's Dream.*)

And plant life is touched with special tenderness :

All the bystanders had wet their cheeks
Like trees bedashed with rain.

(*Richard III.*)

Why grow the branches when the root is gone ?
Why wither not the leaves that want their sap ?

(*Richard III.*)

Their lips were four red roses on a stalk,
Which in their summer beauty kiss'd each other.

(*Richard III.*)

Ah ! my tender babes !
My unblown flowers, new appearing sweets.

(*Richard III.*)

Romeo is

> To himself so secret and so close . . .
> As is the bud bit with an envious worm,
> Ere he can spread his sweet leaves to the air
> Or dedicate his beauty to the sun.

It is astonishing to see how Shakespeare noted the smallest and most fragile things, and found the most poetic expression for them without any sacrifice of truth to Nature.

Juliet is 'the sweetest flower of all the field.' Laertes says to Ophelia :

> For Hamlet and the trifling of his favour
> Hold it a fashion and a toy in blood,
> A violet in the youth of primy nature,
> Forward not permanent, sweet not lasting,
> The perfume and suppliance of a moment.
> The canker galls the infants of the spring
> Too oft before their buttons be disclosed ;
> And in the morn and liquid dew of youth
> Contagious blastments are most imminent.
>
> *(Hamlet.)*

Hamlet soliloquizes :

> How weary, stale, flat, and unprofitable
> Seems to me all the uses of this world.
> Fie on't, O fie ! 'tis an unweeded garden
> That grows to seed ; things rank and gross in nature
> Possess it merely.
>
> Indeed, it goes so heavily with my disposition that this goodly frame the earth seems to me a sterile promontory, this most excellent canopy the air, look you—this brave o'erhanging firmament, this majestical roof fretted with golden fire, why, it appears no other thing to me but a foul and pestilent congregation of vapours.

But the great advance which he made is seen far more in the sympathetic way in which he drew Nature into the action of the play.

He established perfect harmony between human fate and the natural phenomena around it.

There are moonlight nights for Romeo and Juliet's

brief dream, when all Nature, moon, stars, garden, seemed steeped in love together.

He places his melancholy, brooding Hamlet

> In a land of mist and long nights, under a gloomy sky, where day is only night without sleep, and the tragedy holds us imprisoned like the North itself, that damp dungeon of Nature. (BOERNE.)

What a dark shudder lies o'er Nature in *Macbeth*! And in *Lear*, as Jacobi says:

> What a sight! All Nature, living and lifeless, reasonable and unreasonable, surges together, like towering storm clouds, hither and thither; it is black oppressive Nature with only here and there a lightning flash from God—a flash of Providence, rending the clouds.

One must look at the art by which this is achieved in order to justify such enthusiastic expressions. Personification of Nature lies at the root of it, and to examine this in the different poets forms one of the most interesting chapters of comparative poetry, especially in Shakespeare.

With him artistic personification reached a pitch never attained before. We can trace the steps by which Greece passed from mythical to purely poetic personification, increasing in individuality in the Hellenic period; but Shakespeare opened up an entirely new region by dint of that flashlight genius of imagination which combined and illuminated all and everything.

Hense says:

> The personification is plastic when Æschylus calls the heights the neighbours of the stars; individual, when Shakespeare speaks of hills that kiss the sky. It is plastic that fire and sea are foes who conspire together and keep faith to destroy the Argive army; it is individual to call sea and wind old wranglers who enter into a momentary armistice. Other personifications of Shakespeare's, as when he speaks of the 'wanton wind,' calls laughter a fool, and describes time as having a wallet on his back wherein he puts alms for oblivion, are of a kind which did not, and could not, exist in antiquity.

The richer a man's mental endowment, the more individual his feelings, the more he can see in Nature.

Shakespeare's fancy revelled in a wealth of images ; new metaphors, new points of resemblance between the inner and outer worlds, were for ever pouring from his inexhaustible imagination.

The motive of amorous passion, for instance, was a very divining-rod in his hands, revealing the most delicate relations between Nature and the soul. Ibykos had pointed the contrast between the gay spring time and his own unhappy heart in which Eros raged like ' the Thracian blast.' Theocritus had painted the pretty shepherdess drawing all Nature under the spell of her charms ; Akontios (Kallimachos) had declared that if trees felt the pangs and longings of love, they would lose their leaves ; all such ideas, modern in their way, had been expressed in antiquity.

This is Shakespeare's treatment of them :

> How like a winter hath my absence been
> From thee, the pleasure of the fleeting year !
> What freezings have I felt, what dark days seen !
> What old December's bareness everywhere !
> And yet this time removed was summer time,
> The teeming autumn, big with rich increase . . .
> For summer and his pleasures wait on thee,
> And thou away the very birds are mute,
> Or, if they sing, 'tis with so dull a cheer
> That leaves look pale, dreading the winter's near.
> (Sonnet 97.)

> From you have I been absent in the spring,
> When proud-pied April dress'd in all his trim
> Hath put a spirit of youth in everything,
> That heavy Saturn laugh'd and leap'd with him.
> Yet nor the lays of birds nor the sweet smell
> Of different flowers in odour and in hue
> Could make me any summer's story tell. . . .
> Yet seem'd it winter still. . . .   (Sonnet 98.)

Or compare again the cypresses in Theocritus sole witnesses of secret love ; or Walther's

> One little birdie who never will tell,

with

> These blue-veined violets whereon we lean
> Never can blab, nor know not what we mean.
>
> *(Venus and Adonis.)*

Comparisons of ladies' lips to roses, and hands to lilies, are common with the old poets. How much more modern is :

> The forward violet thus did I chide ;
> Sweet thief, whence didst thou steal thy sweet that
>   smells
> If not from my love's breath ? . . .
> The lily I condemned for thy hand,
> And buds of marjoram had stolen thy hair ;
> The roses fearfully on thorns did stand,
> One blushing shame, another white despair. . . .
> More flowers I noted, yet I none could see
> But sweet or colour it had stolen from thee.
>
> (Sonnet 99.)

And how fine the personification in Sonnet 33 :

> Full many a glorious morning have I seen
> Flatter the mountain tops with sovereign eye,
> Kissing with golden face the meadows green,
> Gilding pale streams with heavenly alchemy ;
> Anon permit the basest clouds to ride ⁀
> With ugly rack on his celestial face,
> And from the forlorn world his visage hide,
> Stealing unseen to West with this disgrace :
> Even so my sun one early morn did shine
> With all triumphant splendour on my brow ;
> But out, alack ! he was but one hour mine ;
> The region cloud hath mask'd him from me now.
> Yet him for this my love no whit disdaineth ;
> Suns of the world may stain when heaven's sun
>   staineth.

This is night in *Venus and Adonis* :

> Look ! the world's comforter with weary gait
> His day's hot task hath ended in the West ;
> The owl, night's herald, shrieks 'tis very late ;
> The sheep are gone to fold, birds to their nest
> And coal-black clouds, that shadow heaven's light,
> Do summon us to part and bid good-night.

And this morning, in *Romeo and Juliet* :

> The grey-ey'd morn smiles on the frowning night,
> Checkering the Eastern clouds with streaks of light.
> And flecked darkness like a drunkard reels
> From forth day's path and Titan's fiery wheels ;
> Now, ere the sun advance his burning eye,
> The day to cheer, and night's dank dew to dry. . .

Such wealth and brilliance of personification was not found again until Goethe, Byron, and Shelley. He is unusually rich in descriptive phrases :

> The weary sun hath made a golden set,
> And by the bright track of his golden car
> Gives token of a goodly day to-morrow.

> The worshipp'd Sun
> Peered forth the golden window of the East.

> The all-cheering sun
> Should in the farthest East begin to draw
> The shady curtains from Aurora's bed.

The moon : .

> Like to a silver bow
> New bent in heaven.

Titania says :

> I will wind thee in my arms. . . .
> So doth the woodbine the sweet honeysuckle
> Gently entwist ; the female ivy so
> Enrings the barky fingers of the elm.
> O how I love thee !

> That same dew, which sometime on the buds
> Was wont to swell, like round and orient pearls,
> Stood now within the pretty flow'rets' eyes
> Like tears.
> > (*Midsummer Night's Dream.*)

> Daffodils
> That come before the swallow dares, and take
> The winds of March with beauty.
> > (*Winter's Tale.*)

> Pale primroses
> That die unmarried, ere they can behold
> Bright Phœbus in his strength.
> > (*Winter's Tale.*)

Goethe calls winds and waves lovers. In *Troilus and Cressida* we have :

> The sea being smooth,
> How many shallow bauble boats dare sail
> Upon her patient breast, making their way
> With those of nobler bulk !
> But let the ruffian Boreas once enrage
> The gentle Thetis, and anon behold
> The strong-ribb'd bark through liquid mountains cut,
> Bounding between two moist elements
> Like Perseus' horse.

And further on in the same scene :

> What raging of the sea ! shaking of earth !
> Commotion in the winds !
> . . . the bounded waters
> Should lift their bosoms higher than the shores.

The personification of the river in *Henry IV.* is half mythical :

> When on the gentle Severn's sedgy bank
> In single opposition, hand to hand,
> He did confound the best part of an hour
> In changing hardiment with great Glendower ;
> Three times they breath'd, and three times did they
> drink,
> Upon agreement, of swift Severn's flood ;
> Who, then affrighted with their bloody looks,
> Ran fearfully among the trembling reeds,
> And hid his crisp head in the hollow bank,
> Blood-stained with these valiant combatants.

Striking instances of personification from *Antony and Cleopatra* are :

> The barge she sat in, like a burnish'd throne
> Burn'd on the water ; the poop was beaten gold ;
> Purple the sails, and so perfumed, that
> The winds were lovesick with them ; the oars were
> silver,
> Which to the time of flutes kept stroke, and made
> The water which they beat to follow faster
> As amorous of their strokes.

And Antony, enthron'd in the market-place, sat alone

> Whistling to the air, which but for vacancy
> Had gone to gaze on Cleopatra too
> And made a gap in nature.

Instead of accumulating further instances of these very modern and individual (and sometimes far-fetched) personifications, it is of more interest to see how Shakespeare used Nature, not only as background and colouring, but to act a part of her own in the play, so producing the grandest of all personifications.

At the beginning of Act III. in *King Lear*, Kent asks:

> Who's there beside foul weather ?
> *Gentleman :* One minded like the weather, most unquietly.
> *Kent :* Where's the King ?
> *Gent :* Contending with the fretful elements.
> Bids the wind blow the earth into the sea,
> Or swell the curled waters 'bove the main,
> That things might change or cease ; tears his white hair,
> Which the impetuous blasts with eyeless rage
> Catch in their fury and make nothing of ;
> Strives in his little world of men to outscorn
> The to-and-fro conflicting wind and rain.

In the stormy night on the wild heath the poor old man hears the echo of his own feelings in the elements ; his daughters' ingratitude, hardness, and cruelty produce a moral disturbance like the disturbance in Nature ; he breaks out :

> Blow, wind, and crack your cheeks. Rage ! Blow !
> You cataracts and hurricanes, spout
> Till you have drench'd our steeples, drowned the cocks !
> You sulphurous and thought-executing fires,
> Vaunt couriers of oak-cleaving thunder-bolts,
> Singe my white head ! And thou, all-shaking thunder,
> Strike flat the thick rotundity o' the world !
> Crack nature's moulds, all germens spill at once
> That make ungrateful man . . . .
> Rumble thy bellyful ! Spit fire, spout rain !

> Nor rain, wind, thunder, fire are my daughters,
> I tax you not, you elements, with unkindness ;
> I never gave you kingdom, call'd you children,
> You owe me no subscription ; then, let fall
> Your horrible pleasure ; here I stand, your slave,
> A poor, infirm, weak, and despis'd old man :
> But yet I call you servile ministers,
> That will with two pernicious daughters join
> Your high engender'd battles 'gainst a head
> So old and white as this. O ! O ! 'tis foul !

How closely here animate and inanimate Nature are woven together, the reasoning with the unreasoning. The poet makes the storm, rain, thunder, and lightning live, and at the same time endues his human figures with a strength of feeling and passion which gives them kinship to the elements.

In *Othello*, too, there is uproar in Nature :

> Do but stand upon the foaming shore,
> The chidden billow seems to pelt the clouds . . . .
> I never did like molestation view
> On the enchafed flood.

but even the unruly elements spare Desdemona :

> Tempests themselves, high seas and howling winds,
> The gather'd rocks and congregated sands,
> Traitors ensteep'd to clog the guiltless keel—
> As having sense of beauty, do omit
> Their mortal natures, letting go safely by
> The divine Desdemona.

Cassio lays stress upon ' the great contention of the sea and skies '; but when Othello meets Desdemona, he cries :

> O my soul's joy !
> If after every tempest come such calms,
> May the winds blow till they have wakened death !
> And let the labouring bark climb hills of seas
> Olympus-high, and duck again as low
> As hell's from heaven. If it were now to die,
> 'Twere now to be most happy.

Iago calls the elements to witness his truthfulness :

> Witness, you ever-burning lights above,
> You elements that clip us round about,

> Witness, that here Iago doth give up
> The execution of his wit, hands, heart,
> To wrong'd Othello's service.

Nature is disgusted at Othello's jealousy :

> Heaven stops the nose at it, and the moon winks;
> The bawdy wind, that kisses all it meets,
> Is hush'd within the hollow mine of earth
> And will not hear it.

In terrible mental confusion he cries :

> O insupportable, O heavy hour !
> Methinks it should be now a huge eclipse
> Of sun and moon, and that the affrighted globe
> Should yawn at alteration.

Unhappy Desdemona sings :

> The poor soul sat sighing by a sycamore tree,
> Sing all a green willow;
> Her hand on her bosom, her head on her knee,
> Sing willow, willow, willow;
> The fresh streams ran by her and murmur'd her moans,
> Sing willow, willow, willow.

A song in *Cymbeline* contains a beautiful personification of flowers :

> Hark ! hark ! the lark at heaven's gate sings,
> And Phœbus 'gins arise,
> His steeds to water at those springs
> On chalic'd flowers that lies;
> And winking Mary-buds begin
> To ope their golden eyes;
> With everything that pretty is,
> My lady sweet, arise;
> Arise !   Arise !

The clearest expression of sympathy for Nature is in *Macbeth*.

Repeatedly we meet the idea that Nature shudders before the crime, and gives signs of coming disaster.

Macbeth himself says :

> Stars, hide your fires !
> Let not light see my black and deep desires;

> The eye wink at the hand ; yet let that be
> Which the eye fears, when it is done, to see.

and Lady Macbeth :

> . . . The raven himself is hoarse
> That croaks the fatal entrance of Duncan
> Under my battlements. . . . Come, thick night,
> And pall thee in the dunnest smoke of hell,
> That my keen knife see not the wound it makes,
> Nor heaven peep through the blanket of the dark
> To cry ' Hold ! hold ! ' . . .

The peaceful castle to which Duncan comes all unsuspectingly, is in most striking contrast to the fateful tone which pervades the tragedy. Duncan says :

> This castle hath a pleasant seat ; the air
> Nimbly and sweetly recommends itself
> Unto our gentle senses.

and Banquo :

> This guest of summer,
> The temple-haunting martlet, does approve
> By his loved masonry, that the heaven's breath
> Smells wooingly here ; no jetty, frieze,
> Buttress, nor coign of vantage but this bird
> Hath made his pendent bed and procreant cradle ;
> Where they most breed and haunt I have observ'd
> The air is delicate.

Perhaps the familiar swallow has never been treated with more discrimination ; and at this point of the tale of horror it has the effect of a ray of sunshine in a sky dark with storm clouds.

In Act II. Macbeth describes his own horror and Nature's :

> Now o'er the one half world
> Nature seems dead. . . . Thou sure and firm-set earth,
> Hear not my steps, which way they walk, for fear
> Thy very stones prate of my whereabouts.

Lady Macbeth says :

> It was the owl that shriek'd, the fatal bellman
> Which gives the stern'st good-night.

Lenox describes this night :

> The night has been unruly: where we lay
> Our chimneys were blown down; and, as they say,
> Lamentings heard i' the air ; strange screams of death
> And prophesying, with accents terrible,
> Of dire combustion and confus'd events,
> New hatch'd to the woeful time : the obscure bird
> Clamour'd the live-long night : some say, the earth
> Was feverish and did shake.

and later on, an old man says :

> Three score and ten I can remember well ;
> Within the volume of which time I have seen
> Hours dreadful and things strange ; but this sore night
> Hath trifled former knowings.

Rosse answers him :

> Ah, good father,
> Thou see'st the heavens, as troubled with man's act,
> Threaten his bloody stage ; by the clock 'tis day,
> And yet dark night strangles the travelling lamp.
> Is't night's predominance or the day's shame
> That darkness does the face of earth entomb
> When living light should kiss it ?

The whole play is a thrilling expression of the sympathy for Nature which attributes its own feelings to her—a human shudder in presence of the wicked—a human horror of crime, most thrilling of all in Macbeth's words :

> Come, seeling night,
> Scarf up the tender eye of pitiful day,
> And with thy bloody and invisible hand
> Cancel and tear to pieces that great bond
> Which keeps me pale.

In *Hamlet*, too, Nature is shocked at man's misdeeds :

> . . . Such an act (the queen's)
> That blurs the grace and blush of modesty
> . . . Heaven's face doth glow,
> Yea, this solidity and compound mass
> With tristful visage, as against the doom,
> Is thought-sick at the act.

But there are other personifications in this most wonderful of all tragedies, such as the magnificent one :

> But look, the dawn, in russet mantle clad,
> Walks o'er the dew of yon high eastern hill.

The first player declaims :

> But, as we often see, against some storm
> A silence in the heavens, the rack stand still,
> The bold winds speechless, and the orb below
> As hush as death. . . .

Ophelia dies :

> When down her weedy trophies and herself
> Fell in the weeping brook.

and Laertes commands :

> Lay her i' the earth,
> And from her fair and unpolluted flesh
> May violets spring.

Thus Shakespeare's great imagination gave life and soul to every detail of Nature, and he obtained the right background for his dramas, not only through choice of scenery, but by making Nature a sharer of human impulse, happy with the happy, shuddering in the presence of wickedness.

He drew every phase of Nature with the individualizing touch which stamps her own peculiar character, and also brings her into sympathy with the inner life, often with that poetic intuition which is so closely allied to mythology. And this holds good not only in dealing with the great elementary forces—storms, thunder, lightning, etc.— but with flowers, streams, the glow of sunlight. Always and everywhere the grasp of Nature was intenser, more individual, and subjective, than any we have met hitherto.

Idyllic feeling for Nature became sympathetic in his hands.

CHAPTER VII

THE DISCOVERY OF THE BEAUTY OF LANDSCAPE IN PAINTING

THE indispensable condition of landscape-painting—painting, that is, which raises the representation of Nature to the level of its main subject and paints her entirely for her own sake — is the power to compose separate studies into a whole and imbue that with an artistic idea. It was therefore impossible among people like the Hebrews,[1] whose eyes were always fixed on distance and only noted what lay between in a cursory way, and among those who considered detail without relation to a whole, as we have seen in mediæval poetry until the Renaissance. But just as study of the laws of aerial and linear perspective demands a trained and keen eye, and therefore implies interest in Nature, so the artistic idea, the soul of the picture, depends directly upon the degree of the artist's feeling for her. Literature and painting are equal witnesses to the feeling for Nature, and so long as scenery was only background in poetry, it had no greater importance in painting. Landscape painting could only arise in the period which produced complete pictures of scenery in poetry—the sentimental idyllic period.

We have seen how in the Italian Renaissance the fetters of dogma, tradition, and mediæval custom were removed, and servility and visionariness gave place to healthy individuality and realism ; how man and the world were discovered anew; and further, how among the other Romanic nations a lively feeling for Nature grew up, partly idyllic, partly mystic; and finally, how this feeling found dramatic expression in Shakespeare.

Natural philosophy also, in the course of its search for truth, as it threw off both one-sided Christian ideas and ancient traditions, came gradually to feel an interest in Nature; not only her laws, but her beauty, became an object of enthusiastic study.   By a very long process of development the Hellenic feeling for Nature was reached again in the Renaissance; but it always remained, despite its sentimental and pantheistic elements, sensual, superficial, and naive, in comparison with Christian feeling, which a warmer heart and a mind trained in scholastic wisdom had rendered more profound and abstract. Hence Nature was sometimes an object of attention in detail, sometimes in mass.[2]

As we come to the first landscape painters and their birthplace in the Netherlands, we see how steady and orderly is the development of the human mind, and how factors that seem isolated are really links in one chain.

In the Middle Ages, landscape was only background with more or less fitness to the subject. By the fifteenth century it was richer in detail, as we see in Pisanello and the Florentines Gozzoli and Mantegna. The poetry of earth had been discovered; the gold grounds gave way to field, wood, hill, and dale, and the blue behind the heads became a dome of sky.   In the sixteenth century, Giorgione shewed the value of effects of light, and Correggio's backgrounds were in harmony with his tender, cheerful scenes. Titian loved to paint, autumn; the sunny days of October with blue grapes, golden oranges, and melons; and evening with deep harmonies of colour over the sleeping earth.   He was a great pioneer in the realm of landscape. With Michael Angelo not a blade of grass grew ; his problem was man alone. Raphael's backgrounds, on the other hand, are life-like in detail : his little birds could fly out of the picture, the stems of his plants seem to curve and bend towards us, and we look deep into the flower they hold out.'

In the German Renaissance too, the great masters limited themselves to charming framework and ingenious arabesques for their Madonnas and Holy Families. But, as Lübke says,' one soon sees that Dürer depended on architecture for borders and backgrounds far less than Holbein ; he preferred landscape.

' The charm of this background is so great, the inwardness of German feeling for Nature so strongly expressed in it, that it has a special value of its own, and the master through it has become the father of landscape painting.''

This must be taken with a grain of salt ; but, at all events, it is true that Dürer combined ' keen and devoted study of Nature (in the widest sense of the word) with a penetration which aimed at tracing her facts up to their source.'' It is interesting to see how these qualities overcame his theoretical views on Nature and art.' Dürer's deep respect for Nature proved him a child of the new era. Melanchthon relates that he often regretted that he had been too much attracted in his younger days by variety and the fantastic, and had only understood Nature's simple truth and beauty later in life.

His riper judgment preferred her to all other models. Nature, in his remarks on the theory of art, includes the animate and the inanimate, living creatures as well as scenery, and it is interesting to observe that his admiration of her as a divine thing was due to deep religious feeling. In his work on Proportion' he says :

' Certainly art is hidden in Nature, and he who is able to separate it by force from Nature, he

possesses it.   Never imagine that you can or will
surpass Nature's achievements; human effort
cannot compare with the ability which her Creator
has given her.   Therefore no man can ever make
a picture which excels Nature's; and when, through
much copying, he has seized her spirit, it cannot
be called original work, it is rather something received
and learnt, whose seeds grow and bear fruit of their
own kind.   Thereby the gathered treasure of the
heart, and the new creature which takes shape and
form there, comes to light in the artist's work.'

Elsewhere Dürer says 'a good painter's mind
is full of figures,' and he repeatedly remarks upon
the superabundant beauty of all living things which
human intelligence rarely succeeds in reproducing.

The first modern landscapes in which man was
only accessory were produced in the Netherlands.
Quiet, absorbed musing on the external world was
characteristic of the nation; they studied the small-
est and most trifling objects with care, and set a high
value on minutiæ.

The still-life work of their prime was only possible
to such an easy-going, life-loving people; the delight-
ful animal pictures of Paul Potter and Adrian van de
Velde could only have been painted in the land of
Reineke Fuchs.   Carrière says about these masters
of genre painting: 'Through the emphasis laid upon
single objects, they not only revealed the national
characteristics, but penetrated far into the soul of
Nature and mirrored their own feelings there, so
producing works of art of a kind unknown to
antiquity.   That divine element, which the Greek
saw in the human form, the Germanic race divined
in all the visible forms of Nature, and so felt at one
with them and able to reveal itself through them.

' Nature was studied more for her own sake than in
her relation to man, and scenery became no longer
mere background, but the actual object of the
picture.   Animals, and even men, whether bathing

in the river, lying under trees, or hunting in the forest, were nothing but accessories; inorganic Nature was the essential element. The greatest Dutch masters did not turn their attention to the extraordinary and stupendous, the splendour of the high Alps or their horrible crevasses, or sunny Italian mountains reflected in their lakes or tropical luxuriance, but to common objects of everyday life. But these they grasped with a precision and depth of feeling which gave charm to the most trifling—it was the life of the universe divined in its minutiæ. In its treatment of landscape their genre painting displayed the very characteristics which had brought it into being.'[10]

The physical characters of the country favoured landscape painting too. No doubt the moist atmosphere and its silvery sheen, which add such freshness and brilliance to the colouring, influenced the development of the colour sense, as much as the absence of sharp contrasts in contour, the suggestive skies, and abundance of streams, woods, meadows, and dales.

But it was in devotional pictures that the Netherlanders first tried their wings; landscape and scenes from human life did not free themselves permauently from religion and take independent place for more than a century later. The fourteenth-century miniatures shew the first signs of the northern feeling for Nature in illustrations of the seasons in the calendar pictures of religious manuscripts. Beginnings of landscape can be clearly seen in that threshold picture of Netherland art, the altar-piece at Ghent by the brothers Van Eyck, which was finished in 1432. It shews the most accurate observation : all the plants, grasses, flowers, rose bushes, vines, and palms, are correctly drawn; and the luxuriant valley in which the Christian soldiers and the knights are riding, with its rocky walls covered by undergrowth jutting stiffly forward, is very like the valley of the Maas.

One sees that the charm of landscape has dawned upon the painters.

Their skies are no longer golden, but blue, and flecked with cloudlets and alive with birds ; wood and meadow shine in sappy green ; fantastic rocks lie about, and the plains are bounded by low hills. They are drinking deep draughts from a newly-opened spring, and they can scarcely have enough of it. They would like to paint all the leaves and fruit on the trees, all the flowers on the grass, even all the dewdrops. The effect of distance too has been discovered, for there are blue hill-tops beyond the nearer green ones, and a foreground scene opens back on a distant plain (in the Ghent altar-piece, the scene with the pilgrims); but they still possess very few tones, and their overcrowded detail is almost all, from foreground to furthest distance, painted in the same luminous strong dark-green, as if in insatiable delight at the beauty of their own colour. The progress made by Jan van Eyck in landscape was immense.

To the old masters Nature had been an unintelligible chaos of detail, but beauty, through ecclesiastical tradition, an abstract attribute of the Holy Family and the Saints, and they had used their best powers of imagination in accordance with this view. Hence they placed the Madonna upon a background of one colour, generally gilded. But now the great discovery was made that Nature was a distinct entity, a revelation and reflection of the divine in herself. And Jan van Eyck introduced a great variety of landscapes behind his Madonnas. One looks, for instance, through an open window to a wide stretch of country with fields and fortresses, and towns with streets full of people, all backed by mountains. And whether the scene itself, or only its background, lies in the open, the landscape is of the widest, enlivened by countless forms and adorned by splendid buildings.

Molanus, the savant of Löwen, proclaimed Dierick
Bouts, born like his predecessor Ouwater at Haarlem,
to be the inventor of landscape painting (claruit
inventor in describendo rure) ; but the van. Eycks
were certainly before him, though he increased
the significance of landscape painting and shewed
knowledge of aerial perspective and gradations of
tone. Landscape was a distinct entity to him, and
could excite the mood that suited his subject, as,
for instance, in the side picture of the Last Supper,
where the foreground is drawn with such exactness
that every plant and even the tiny creatures crawling
on the grass can be identified.

The scenery of Roger van der Weyden of Brabant
—river valleys surrounded by jagged rocks and
mountains, isolated trees, and meadows bright with
sappy green—is clearly the result of direct Nature
study; it has a uniform transparent atmosphere,
and a clear green shimmer lies over the foreground
and gradually passes into blue haze further back.

His pupil, Memling, shews the same fine gradations
of tone. The composition of his richest picture,
'The Marriage of St Catherine,' did not allow space
for an unbroken landscape, but the lines of wood
and field converge to a vista in such a way that the
general effect is one of unity.

Joachim de Patenir, who appeared in 1515, was
called a landscape painter by his contemporaries, be-
cause he reduced his sacred figures to a modest size,
enlarged his landscape, and handled it with extreme
care. He was very far from grasping it as a whole,
but his method was synthetical ; his river valleys,
with masses of tree and bush and romantic rocks,
fantastic and picturesque, with fortresses on the river
banks, all shew this.

Herry de Bles was like him, but less accurate ;
with all the rest of the sixteenth-century painters
of Brabant and Flanders, he did not rise to the idea
of landscape as a whole.

The most minute attention was given to the accurate painting of single objects, especially plants; the Flemings caring more for perfect truth to life, the Dutch for beauty. The Flemings generally sought to improve their landscape by embellishing its lines, while the Dutch gave its spirit, but adhered simply and strictly to Nature. The landscapes of Peter Brueghel the elder, with their dancing peasants surrounded by rocks, mills, groups of trees, are painful in their thoroughness; and Jan Brueghel carried imitation of Nature so far that his minutiæ required a magnifying-glass—it was veritable miniature work. He introduced fruit and flower painting as a new feature of art.

Rubens and Brueghel often painted on each other's canvas, Brueghel supplying landscape backgrounds for Rubens' pictures, and Rubens the figures for Brueghel's landscapes. Yet Rubens himself was the best landscapist of the Flemish school. He was more than that. For Brueghel and his followers, with all their patience and industry, their blue-green landscape with imaginary trees, boundless distance and endless detail, were very far from a true grasp of Nature. It was Rubens and his school who really made landscape a legitimate independent branch of art. They studied it in all its aspects, quiet and homely, wild and romantic, some taking one and some the other : Rubens himself, in his large way, grasping the whole without losing sight of its parts. They all lifted the veil from Nature and saw her as she was (Falke).

Brueghel put off the execution of a picture for which he had a commission from winter to spring, that he might study the flowers for it from Nature when they came out, and did not grudge a journey to Brussels now and then to paint flowers not to be had at Antwerp. There is a characteristic letter which he sent to the Archbishop of Milan with a picture :

'I send your Reverence the picture with the flowers, which are all painted from Nature. I have painted in as many as possible. I believe so many rare and different flowers have never been painted before nor so industriously. It will give a beautiful effect in winter; some of the colours almost equal Nature. I have painted an ornament under the flowers with artistic medallions and curiosities from the sea. I leave it to your reverence to judge whether the flowers do not far exceed gold and jewels in colour.'

He also painted landscapes in which people were only accessory, sunny valleys with leafage, golden cornfields, meadows with rows of dancing country folk or reapers in the wheat.

Rubens, though he felt the influence of southern light and sunshine as much as his fellows who had been in Italy, took his backgrounds from his native land, from parts round Antwerp, Mechlin, and Brussels. Foliage, water, and undulating ground were indispensable to him—were, to a certain extent, the actual bearers of the impression he wished to convey.

Brueghel always kept a childlike attitude, delighting in details, and proud of the clever brush which could carry imitation to the point of deception. Rubens was the first to treat landscape in a bold subjective way. He opened the book of Nature, so to speak, not to spell out the words syllable by syllable, but to master her secret, to descend into the depths of her soul, and then reflect what he found there—in short, he fully understood the task of the landscape painter. The fifty landscapes of his which we possess, contain the whole scale from a state of idyllic repose to one of dramatic excitement and tension. Take, for instance, the evening scene with the rainbow in the Louvre, marvellous in its delicate gradations of atmospheric tone, and the equally marvellous thunderstorm in the Belvedere at Vienna, where a rain-cloud bursts under sulphur lightning, and a mountain stream, swollen to a torrent and lashed by the hurricane, carries all before it—trees, rocks, animals, and men.

In France, scarcely a flower had been seen in literature since the Troubadour days, not even in the classical poetry of Corneille and Racine. There were idyllic features in Fénelon's *Telemachus*, and Ronsard borrowed motives from antiquity; but it was pastoral poetry which blossomed luxuriantly here as in Italy and Spain.

Honoré d'Urfé's famous *Astrée* was much translated; but both his shepherds and his landscape were artificial, and the perfume of courts and carpet knights was over the whole, with a certain trace of sadness.

The case was different with French painting. After the Netherlands, it was France, by her mediæval illustrated manuscripts, who chiefly aided in opening the world's eyes to landscape. Both the Poussins penetrated below the surface of Nature. Nicolas Poussin (1594–1665) painted serious stately subjects, such as a group of trees in the foreground, a hill with a classic building in the middle, and a chain of mountains in the distance, and laid more stress on drawing than colour. There was greater life in the pictures of his brother-in-law, Caspar Doughet, also called Poussin; his grass is more succulent, his winds sigh in the trees, his storm bends the boughs and scatters the clouds.

It was Claude Lorraine (1600–1682) who brought the ideal style to its perfection. He inspired the very elements with mind and feeling; his valleys, woods, and seas were just a veil through which divinity was visible. All that was ugly, painful, and confused was purified and transfigured in his hands. There is no sadness or dejection in his pictures, but a spirit of serene beauty, free from ostentation, far-fetched contrast, or artificial glitter. Light breezes blow in his splendid trees, golden light quivers through them, drawing the eye to a bright misty horizon ; we say with Uhland, 'The sky is solemn, as if it would say "this is the day of the Lord."'

Artistic feeling for Nature became a worship with Claude Lorraine.

The Netherlands recorded all Nature's phases in noble emulation with ever-increasing delight.

The poetry of air, cloudland, light, the cool freshness of morning, the hazy sultriness of noon, the warm light of evening, it all lives and moves in Cuyp's pictures and Wynant's, while Aart van der Meer painted moonlight and winter snow, and Jan van Goyen the melancholy of mist shot by sunlight. He, too—Jan van Goyen—was very clever in producing effect with very small means, with a few trees reflected in water, or a sand-heap—the art in which Ruysdael excelled all others. The whole poetry of Nature—that secret magic which lies like a spell over quiet wood, murmuring sea, still pool, and lonely pasture—took form and colour under his hands; so little sufficed to enchant, to rouse thought and feeling, and lead them whither he would. Northern seriousness and sadness brood over most of his work; the dark trees are overhung by heavy clouds and rain, mist and dusky shadows move among his ruins. He had painted, says Carrière, the peace of woodland solitude long before Tieck found the word for it.

Beechwoods reflected in a stream, misty cloud masses lighted by the rising sun ; he moves us with such things as with a morning hymn, and his picture of a swollen torrent forcing its way between graves which catch the last rays of the sun, while a cloud of rain shrouds the ruins of a church in the background, is an elegy which has taken shape and colour.

Ruysdael marks the culminating point of this period of development, which had led from mere backgrounds and single traits of Nature—even a flower stem or a blade of grass, up to elaborate compositions imbued by a single motive, a single idea.

To conjure up with slight material a complete little world of its own, and waken responsive feeling, is not this the secret of the charm in the pictures of his school—in the wooded hill or peasant's courtyard by Hobbema, the Norwegian mountain scene of Albert van Everdingen, the dusky fig-trees, rugged crags, and foaming cataract, or the half-sullen, half-smiling sea-pieces of Bakhuysen and Van der Velde ?

All these great Netherlanders far outstripped the poetry of their time; it was a hundred years later before mountain and sea found their painter in words, and a complete landscape picture was not born in German poetry until the end of the eighteenth century.

CHAPTER VIII

HUMANISM, ROCOCO, AND PIGTAIL

MANY decades passed before German feeling for Nature reached the heights attained by the Italian Renaissance and the Netherland landscapists. In the Middle Ages, Germany was engrossed with ecclesiastical dogma—man's relation, not only to God, but to the one saving Church—and had little interest for Science and Art ; and the great achievement of the fifteenth century, the Reformation, called for word and deed to reckon with a thousand years of old traditions and the slavery of intellectual despotism. The new time was born amid bitter throes. The questions at issue—religious and ecclesiastical questions concerned with the liberty of the Christian—were of the most absorbing kind, and though Germany produced minds of individual stamp such as she had never known before, characters of original and marked physiognomy, it was no time for the quiet contemplation of Nature. Mental life was stimulated by the new current of ideas and new delight in life awakened ; yet there is scarcely a trace of the intense feeling for Nature which we have seen in Petrarch and Æneas Sylvius.

Largely as it was influenced by the Italian Renaissance, it is certainly a mistake to reckon the Humanist movement in Germany, as Geiger does,[1] as a 'merely imported culture, entirely lacking independence.' The germ of this great movement

towards mental freedom was contained in the
general trend of the time, which was striving to free
itself from the fetters of the Middle Ages in customs
and education as well as dogma. It was chiefly
a polemical movement, a fight between contentious
savants. The writings of the Humanists at this
naively sensuous period were full of the joy of life
and love of pleasure; but scarcely any simple
feeling for Nature can be found in them, and there
was neither poet nor poem fit to be compared with
Petrarch and his sonnets.

Natural philosophy, too, was proscribed by
scholastic wisdom; the real Aristotle was only
gradually shelled out from under mediæval accre-
tions. The natural philosopher, Conrad Summen-
hart[?] (1450–1501) was quite unable to disbelieve
the foolish legend, that the appearance of a comet
foretold four certain events—heat, wind, war, and
the death of princes. At the same time, not being
superstitious, he held aloof from the crazy science
of astrology and all the fraud connected with it.
Indeed, as an observer of Nature, and still more as
a follower and furtherer of the scholastic Aristotelian
natural philosophy, he shewed a leaning towards
the theory of development, for, according to him,
the more highly organized structures proceed from
those of lower organization, and these again form
the inorganic under the influence of meteors and
stars. The poet laureate Conrad Celtes (b. 1459),
a singer of love and composer of four books about
it, was a true poet. His incessant wandering, for
he was always moving from place to place, was due
in part to love of Nature and of novelty, but still
more to a desire to spread his own fame. He lacked
the naivete and openness to impressions of the true
child of Nature; his songs in praise of spring, etc.,
scatter a colourless general praise, which is evidently
the result of arduous thought rather than of direct
impressions from without; and his many references

to ancient deities shew that he borrowed more than his phrases.

Though geography was then closely bound up with the writing of history, as represented by Beatus Rhenanus (1485-1547) and Johann Aventinus, and patriotism and the accounts of new lands led men to wish to describe the beauties and advantages of their own, the imposing discoveries across the seas did not make so forcible an impression upon the German humanist as upon savants elsewhere, especially in Italy and Spain. A mystico-theosophical feeling for Nature, or rather a magical knowledge of her, flourished in Germany at this time among the learned, both among Protestants and those who were partially true to Catholicism. One of the strangest exponents of such ideas was Cornelius Agrippa von Nettesheim of Cologne' (1535). His system of the world abounded in such fantastic caprices as these': everything depends on harmony and sympathy; when one of Nature's strings is struck, the others sound with it: the analogical correspondences are at the same time magical : symbolic relations between natural objects are sympathetic also: a true love-bond exists between the elm and vine; the sun bestows life on man; the moon, growth; Mercury, imagination; Venus, love, etc. God is reflected in the macrocosm, gives light in all directions through all creatures, is adumbrated in man microcosmically, and so forth.

Among others, Philippus Aureolus Theophrastus Bombastus Paracelsus von Hohenheim (1541), ranked Nature and the Bible, like Agrippa, as the best books about God and the only ones without falsehood.

'One must study the elements, follow Nature from land to land, since each single country is only one leaf in the book of creation. The eyes that find pleasure in this true experience are the true professors, and more reliable than all learned writings.'

He held man to be less God's very image than a microcosmic copy of Nature — the quintessence of the whole world. Other enthusiasts made similar statements. Sebastian Frank of Donauwörth (1543) looked upon the whole world as an open book and living Bible, in which to study the power and art of God and learn His will : everything was His image, all creatures are 'a reflection, imprint, and expression of God, through knowledge of which man may come to know the true Mover and Cause of all things.'

He shewed warm feeling for Nature in many similes and descriptions'—in fact, much of his pithy drastic writing sounds pantheistic. But he was very far from the standpoint of the great Italian philosophers, Giordano Bruno and Campanella. Bruno, a poet as well as thinker, distinguished Nature in her self-development—matter, soul, and mind—as being stages and phases of the One.

> The material of all things issues from the original
>   womb,
> For Nature works with a master hand in her own inner
>   depths ;
> She is art, alive and gifted with a splendid mind,
> Which fashions its own material, not that of others,
> And does not falter or doubt, but all by itself
> Lightly and surely, as fire burns and sparkles,
> Easily and widely, as light spreads everywhere,
> Never scattering its forces, but stable, quiet, and at one,
> Orders and disposes of everything together.

Campanella, even in a revolting prison, sang in praise of the wisdom and love of God, and His image in Nature. He personified everything in her ; nothing was without feeling ; the very movements of the stars depended on sympathy and antipathy ; harmony was the central soul of all things.

The most extraordinary of all German thinkers was the King of Mystics, Jacob Böhme. Theist and pantheist at once, his mind was a ferment of different

systems of thought.   It is very difficult to unriddle
his *Aurora*, but love of Nature, as well as love of
God, is clear in its mystical utterances :

> God is the heart or source of Nature.
> Nature is the body of God.

' As man's mind rules his whole body in every vein
and fills his whole being, so the Holy Ghost fills
all Nature, and is its heart and rules in the good
qualities of all things.'
' But now heaven is a delightful chamber of
pleasure, in which are all the powers, as in all Nature
the sky is the heart of the waters.'
In another place he calls God the vital power in the
tree of life, the creatures His branches, and Nature
the perfection and self-begotten of God.
Nature's powers are explained as passion, will, and
love, often in lofty and beautiful comparisons :
' As earth always bears beautiful flowers, plants,
and trees, as well as metals and animate beings, and
these finer, stronger, and more beautiful at one time
than another; and as one springs into being as
another dies, causing constant use and work, so it
is in still greater degree with the begetting of the
holy mysteries ' . . . creation is nothing else than a
revelation of the all-pervading superficial godhead
. . . and is like the music of many flutes combined
into one great harmony.'
But the most representative man, both of the
fifteenth century and, in a sense, of the German race,
was Luther. That maxim of Goethe's for teaching
and ethics, ' Cheerfulness is the mother of all virtues,'
might well serve as a motto for Luther.
The two men had much in common.
The one, standing half in the Middle Ages, had to
free himself from mental slavery by strength of will
and courage of belief.
The other, as the prophet of the nineteenth century,
the incarnation of the modern man, had to shake off

the artificiality and weak sentimentality of the eighteenth.

To both alike a healthy joy in existence was the root of being. Luther was always open to the influence of Nature, and, characteristically, the Psalter was his favourite book. ' Lord, how manifold are Thy works, in wisdom hast Thou made them all ! '

True to his German character, he could be profoundly sad ; but his disposition was delightfully cheerful and healthy, and we see from his letters and table-talk, that after wife and child, it was in ' God's dear world ' that he took the greatest pleasure. He could not have enough of the wonders of creation, great or small. ' By God's mercy we begin to see the splendour of His works and wonders in the little flowers, as we consider how kind and almighty He is; therefore we praise and thank Him. In His creatures we see the power of His word—how great it is. In a peach stone, too, for hard as the shell is, the very soft kernel within causes it to open at the right time.' ' Again, 'So God is present in all creatures, even the smallest leaves and poppy seeds.'

All that he saw of Nature inspired him with confidence in the fatherly goodness of God. He wrote, August 5th, 1530, to Chancellor Brneck :

> I have lately seen two wonderful things : the first, looking from the window at the stars and God's whole beautiful sky dome, I saw never a pillar to support it, and yet it did not fall, and is still firm in its place. Now, there are some who search for such pillars and are very anxious to seize them and feel them, and because they cannot, fidget and tremble as if the skies would certainly fall . . . the other, I also saw great thick clouds sweep over our heads, so heavy that they might be compared to a great sea, and yet I saw no ground on which they rested, and no vats in which they were contained, yet they did not fall on us, but greeted us with a frown and flew away. When they had gone, the rainbow lighted both the ground and the roof which had held them.

Luther often used very forcible images from

Nature. 'It is only for the sake of winter that we lie and rot in the earth; when our summer comes, our grain will spring up—rain, sun, and wind prepare us for it—that is, the Word, the Sacraments, and the Holy Ghost.'

His Bible was an orchard of all sorts of fruit trees; in the introduction to the Psalter, he says of the thanksgiving psalms: 'There one looks into the hearts of the saints as into bright and beautiful gardens—nay, as into heaven itself, where pure and happy thoughts of God and His goodness are the lovely flowers.'

His description of heaven for his little son John is full of simple reverent delight in Nature, quite free from platonic and mystical speculation as to God's relation to His universe; and Protestant divines kept this tone up to the following century, until the days of rationalism and pietism.

Of such spontaneous hearty joy in Nature as this, the national songs of a nation are always the medium. They were so now; for, while a like feeling was nowhere else to be found, the Volkslieder expressed the simple familiar relationship of the child of Nature to wood, tree, and flower in touching words and a half-mythical, half-allegorical tone which often revealed their old Germanic origin.

There is a fourteenth-century song, probably from the Lower Rhine,' which suggests the poems of the eighth and ninth centuries, about a great quarrel between Spring, crowned with flowers, and hoary-headed Winter, in which one praises and the other blames the cuckoo for announcing Spring.

In this song, Summer complains to mankind and other friends that a mighty master is going to drive him away; this mighty master, Winter, then takes up the word, and menaces Spring with the approach of frost, who will slight and imprison him, and then kill him; ice and hail agree with Winter, and storm, rain, snow, and bitter winds are called his vassals, etc.

There are naive verses in praise of Spring and
Summer :

> When that the breezes blow in May,
> And snow melts from the wood away,
> Blue violets lift their heads on high,
> And when the little wood-birds sing,
> And flow'rets from the ground up-spring,
> Then everybody's glad.

Others complaining of Winter, who must have leave
of absence, and the wrongs it has wrought are poured
out to Summer. The little birds are very human ;
the owlet complains :

> Poor little owlet me !
> I have to fly all alone through the wood to-night ;
> The branch I want to perch on is broken,
> The leaves are all faded,
> My heart is full of grief.

The cuckoo is either praised for bringing good
news, or made fun of as the ' Gutzgauch.'

> A cuckoo will fly to his heart's treasure, etc.

The fable songs [8] of animal weddings are full of
humour. The fox makes arrangements for his
wedding : ' Up with you now, little birds ! I am
going to take a bride. The starling shall saddle the
horses, for he has a grey mantle ; the beaver with the
cap of marten fur must be driver, the hare with his
light foot shall be outrider ; the nightingale with
his clear voice shall sing the songs, the magpie with
his steady hop must lead the dances,' etc.

The nightingale, with her rich tones, is beloved
and honoured before all the winged things ; she is
called ' the very dear nightingale,' and addressed
as a lady.

' Thou art a little woodbird, and flyest in and out
the green wood ; fair Nightingale, thou little wood-
bird, thou shalt be my messenger.'

It is she who warns the girl against false love, or is
the silent witness of caresses.

There were a great many wishing songs : ' Were I a little bird and had two wings, I would fly to thee,' or ' Were I a wild falcon, I would take flight and fly down before a rich citizen's house—a little maid is there,' etc. 'And were my love a brooklet cold, and sprang out of a stone, little should I grieve if I were but a green wood ; green is the wood, the brooklet is cold, my love is shapely.' The betrayed maiden cries: ' Would God I were a white swan ! I would fly away over mountain and deep valley o'er the wide sea, so that my father and mother should not know where I was.'

Flowers were used symbolically in many ways; roses are always the flowers of love. ' Pretty girls should be kissed, roses should be gathered,' was a common saying; and ' Gather roses by night, for then all the leaves are covered with cooling dew.' ' The roses are ready to be gathered, so gather them to-day. He who does not gather in summer, will not gather in winter.' There is tenderness in this: ' I only know a little blue flower, the colour of the sky; it grows in the green meadow, 'tis called forget-me-not.'

These are sadder :

> There is a lime tree in this valley,
> O God ! what does it there ?
> It will help me to grieve
> That I have no lover.

' Alas ! you mountains and deep valleys, is this the last time I shall see my beloved ? Sun, moon, and the whole sky must grieve with me till my death.'

Where lovers embrace, flowers spring out of the grass, roses and other flowers and grasses laugh, the trees creak and birds sing'; where lovers part, grass and leaves fade.[10]

Most touching of all is the idea, common to the national songs of all nations, that out of the grave of two lovers, lilies and roses spring up, or climbing plants, love thus outliving death.

We look in vain among the master singers of the fifteenth and sixteenth centuries for such fresh heart-felt tones as these, although honest Hans Sachs shews joy in Nature here and there; most charmingly in the famous comparison of 'the Wittenberg Night-ingale, which every one hears everywhere now,' in praise of Luther:

'Wake up, the dawn is nigh! I hear a joyous nightingale singing in the green hedge, it fills the hills and valleys with its voice. The night is stooping to the west, the day is rising from the east, the morn-ing red is leaping from the clouds, the sun looks through. The moon quenches her light; now she is pale and wan, but erewhile with false glamours she dazzled all the sheep and turned them from their pasture lands and pastor . . . . '

Fischart too, in his quaint description of a voyage on the Rhine in *Glückhaft Schiff*, shews little feeling for Nature; but in *Simplicissimus*, on the other hand, that monument of literature which reflected contemporary culture to a unique degree, it is very marked; the more so since it appeared when Germany lay crushed by the Thirty Years' War.

When the hero as a boy was driven from his village home and fled into the forest, he came upon a hermit who took care of him, and waking at midnight, he heard the old man sing:

Come, nightingale, comfort of the night,
Let your voice rise in a song of joy, come praise
    the Creator,
While other birds are sound asleep and cannot sing! . .
The stars are shining in the sky in honour of God. . . .
My dearest little bird, we will not be the laziest of all
And lie asleep; we will beguile the time with praise
Till dawn refreshes the desolate woods.

Simplicissimus goes on: 'During this song, methinks, it was as if nightingale, owl, and echo had combined

in song, and if ever I had been able to hear the morn-
ing star, or to try to imitate the melody on my
bagpipe, I should have slipt away out of the hut to
join in the melody, so beautiful it seemed ; but I
was asleep.'

What was the general feeling for Nature in other
countries during the latter half of the seventeenth
century ?   In Italy and Spain it had assumed a form
partly bucolic and idyllie, partly theosophically
mystical ; Shakespeare's plays had brought sym-
pathy to maturity in England ; the Netherlands had
given birth to landscape painting, and France had
the splendid poetic landscapes of Claude Lorraine.
But the idealism thus reached soon degenerated
into mannerism and artificiality, the hatching of
empty effect.

The aberrations of taste which found expression in
the periwig style of Louis XIV., and in the pigtails
of the eighteenth century, affected the feeling for
Nature too.   The histories of taste in general, and of
feeling for Nature, have this in common, that their
line of progress is not uniformly straightforward,
but liable to zigzags.   This is best seen in reviewing
the different civilized races together.   Moreover,
new ideas, however forcible and original, even epoch-
making, do not win acceptance at once, but rather
trickle slowly through resisting layers ; it is long
before any new gain in culture becomes the common
property of the educated, and hence opposite ex-
tremes are often found side by side—taste for what
is natural with taste for what is artificial.   Garden
style is always a delicate test of feeling for Nature,
shewing, as it does, whether we respect her ways
or wish to impose our own.   The impulse towards
the modern French gardening came from Italy.
Ancient and modern times both had to do with it.
At the Renaissance there was a return to Pliny's
style,[11] which the Cinque cento gardens copied.   In
this style laurel and box-hedges were clipt, and

marble statues placed against them, ' to break the uniformity of the dark green with pleasant silhouettes. One looks almost in vain for flowers and turf ; even trees were exiled to a special wilderness at the edge of the garden ; but the great ornament of the whole was never missing, the wide view over sunny plains and dome-capt towns, or over the distant shimmering sea, which had gladdened the eyes of Roman rulers in classic days.' [13]

The old French garden as Maître Lenotre laid it out in Louis XIV.'s time at Versailles, St Germain, and St Cloud, was architectural in design, and directly connected, like Pliny's, with various parts of the house, by open halls, pavilions, and colonnades. Every part of it—from neat turf parterres bordered by box in front of the terrace, designs worked out in flowers or coloured stones, and double rows of orange spaliers, to groups of statues and fountains—belonged to one symmetrical plan, the focus of which was the house, standing free from trees, and visible from every point. Farther off, radiating avenues led the eye in the same direction, and every little intersecting alley, true to the same principle, ran to a definite object — obelisk, temple, or what not. There was no lack of bowers, giant shrubberies, and water-courses running canal-wise through the park, but they all fell into straight lines ; every path was ruled by a ruler, the eye could follow it to its very end. Artifice was the governing spirit. As Falke says : ' Nature dared not speak but only supply material ; she had to sacrifice her own inventive power to this taste and this art. Hills and woods were only hindrances ; the straight lines of trees and hedges, with their medley of statues and " cabinets de verdure," demanded level ground, and the landscape eye of the period only tolerated woods as a finish to its cut and clipt artificialities.' [14]

Trees and branches were not allowed to grow at their own sweet will ; they were cut into cubes, balls, pyramids, even into shapes of animals, as the gardener's fancy or his principles decreed ; cypresses were made into pillars or hearts with the apex above or below ; and the art of topiary even achieved complete hunting scenes, with hunters, stags, dogs, and hares in full chase on a hedge. Of such a garden one could say with honest Claudius, ' 'Tis but a tailor's joke, and shews the traces of the scissors ; it has nothing of the great heart of Nature.'

It was Nature in bondage : ' green architecture,' with all its parts, walls, windows, roofs, galleries cut out of leafage, and theatres with stage and wings in which silk and velvet marquises with full-bottomed wigs and lace jabots, and ladies in hooped petticoats and hair in towers, played at private theatricals.

Where water was available, water devices were added. And in the midst of all this unnaturalness Greek mythology was introduced : the story of Daphne and Apollo appeared in one alley, Meleager and Atalanta in another, all Olympus was set in motion to fill up the walls and niches. And the people were like their gardens both in dress and manners ; imposing style was everything.

Then came the Rococo period of Louis XV. The great periwig shrivelled to a pigtail, and petty flourish took the place of Lenotre's grandezza.

' The unnatural remained, the imposing disappeared and caprice took its place,' says Falke. Coquetry too. All the artistic output of the time bears this stamp, painting included. Watteau's scenery and people were unnatural and affected— mere inventions to suit the gallant *fêtes*. But he knew and loved Nature, though he saw her with the intoxicated eye of a lover who forgets the individual but keeps a glorified impression of her beauty, whereas Boucher's rosy-blue landscapes look as if he had never seen their originals. His world had nothing in common with Nature, and with reality only this, that its sensuousness, gaiety, falsity, and coquetry were true to the period. But in both Watteau and Boucher there was a faint glimmer of the idyllic—witness the dash of melancholy in Watteau's brightest pictures. Feeling for Nature was seeking its lost path—the path it was to follow with such increased fervour.

German literature too, in the seventeenth century, stood under the sign manual of the Pigtail and Periwig ; it was baroque, stilted, bombastic, affected, feeling and form alike were forced, not spontaneous. Verses were turned out by machinery and glued together. Martin Opitz,[14] the recognized leader and king of poets, had travelled far, but there is no distinct feeling for Nature in his poetry. His words to a mountain :

' Nature has so arranged pleasure here, that he who takes the trouble to climb thee is repaid by delight,' scarcely admit the inference that he understood the charm of distance in the modern sense. He took warmer interest in the bucolic side of country life ; rhyming about the delightful places, dwellings of peace, with their myrtles, mountains, valleys, stones, and flowers, where he longed to be ; and his *Spring Song*, an obvious imitation of the classics (Horace's *Beatus ille* was his model for *Zlatna*), has this conventional contrast between his heart and Nature.

' The frosty ice must melt ; snow cannot last any longer, Favonius ; the gentle breeze is on the fields again. Seed is growing vigorously, grass greening in all its splendour, trees are budding, flowers growing . . . thou, too my heart, put off thy grief.'

There is more nostalgia than feeling for Nature in this :

' Ye birches and tall limes, waste places, woods and fields, farewell to you !

' My comfort and my better dwelling-place is elsewhere ! '

But (and this Winter, strange to say, ignores) his pastorals have all the sentimental elegiac style of the Pigtail period.

There had been German adaptations of foreign pastorals, such as Montreux, *Schäferei von der schönen Juliana*, since 1595 ; Urfé's *Astrée* and Montemayor's *Diana* appeared in 1619, and Sidney's *Arcadia* ten years later.

Opitz tried to widen the propaganda for this kind of poetry, and hence wrote, not to mention little pastorals such as *Daphne, Galatea, Corydon,* and *Asteria,* his *Schäferei von der 'Nymphen Hercinie.'*

His references to Nature in this are as exaggerated as everything else in the poem. He tells how he did not wake ' until night, the mother of the stars, had gone mad, and the beautiful light of dawn began to shew herself and everything with her. . . .

' I sprang up and greeted the sweet rays of the sun, which looked down from the tops of the mountains and seemed at the same time to comfort me.'

He came to a spring ' which fell from a crag with charming murmur and rustle,' cut a long poem in the fir bark, and conversed with three shepherds on virtue, love, and travelling, till the nymph Hercynia appeared and shewed him the source of the Silesian stream. One of the shepherds, Buchner, was particularly enthusiastic about water: ' Kind Nature, handmaid of the Highest, has shewn her best handiwork in sea, river, and spring.'

Fleming too, who already stood much higher as a lyrist and had travelled widely, lacked the power of describing scenery, and must needs call Oreads, Dryads, Castor and Pollux to his aid. He rarely reached the simple purity of his fine sonnet *An Sich,* or the feeling in this : ' Dense wild wood, where even the Titan's brightest rays give no light, pity my sufferings. In my sick soul 'tis as dark as in thy black hollow.'

In this time of decline the hymns of the Evangelical Church (to which Fleming contributed) were full of feeling, and brought the national songs to mind as nothing else did.

A few lines of Paul Gerhardt's seem to me to outweigh whole volumes of contemporary rhymes—lines of such beauty as the *Evening Song*:

> Now all the woods are sleeping,
> And night and stillness creeping
> O'er field and city, man and beast;
> The last faint beam is going,
> The golden stars are glowing
> In yonder dark-blue deep.

And after him, and more like him than any one else, came Andreas Gryphius.

There was much rhyming about Nature in the poet schools of Hamburg, Königsberg, and Nuremberg; but, for the most part, it was an idle tinkle of words without feeling, empty artificial stuff with high-flown titles, as in Philipp von Zesen's *Pleasure of Spring*, and *Poetic Valley of Roses and Lilies*.

' Up, my thoughts, be glad of heart, in this joyous pleasant March; ah! see spring is reviving, earth opens her treasury,' etc.

His romances were more noteworthy if not more interesting. He certainly aimed high, striving for simplicity and clearness of expressions in opposition to the Silesian poets, and hating foreign words.

His feeling for Nature was clear; he loved to take his reader into the garden, and was enthusiastic about cool shady walks, beds of tulips, birds' songs, and echoes. Idyllic pastoral life was the fashion—people of distinction gave themselves up to country life and wore shepherd costume—and he introduced a pastoral episode into his romance, *Die adriatische Rosemund*.[15]

Rosemund, whose father places arbitrary conditions in the way of her marriage with Markhold, becomes a shepherdess.

> Not far off was a delightful spot where limes and alders made shade on hot summer days for the shepherds and shepherdesses who dwelt around. The shady trees, the meadows, and the streams which ran round it, and through it, made it look beautiful . . . the celestial Rosemund had taken up her abode in a little shepherd hut on the slope of a little hill by a watercourse, and shaded by some lime trees, in which the birds paid her homage morning and evening. . . . Such a place and such solitude refreshed the more than human Rosemund, and in such peace she was able to unravel her confused thoughts.

She thought continually of Markhold, and spent her time cutting his name in the trees. The following description of a walk with her sister Stillmuth and her lover Markhold, gives some idea of the formal affected style of the time.

> The day was fine, the sky blue, the weather everywhere warm. The sun shone down on the globe with her pleasant lukewarm beams so pleasantly, that one scarcely cared to stay indoors. They went into the garden, where the roses had opened in the warmth of the sun, and first sat down by the stream, then went to the grottos, where Markhold particularly admired the shell decorations. When this charming party had had enough of both, they finally betook themselves to a leafy walk, where Rosemund introduced pleasant conversation on many topics. She talked first about the many colours of tulips, and remarked that even a painter could not produce a greater variety of tints nor finer pictures than these, etc.

In describing physical beauty, he used comparisons from Nature; for instance, in *Simson* [16]:

> The sun at its brightest never shone so brightly as her two eyes . . . no flower at its best can shew such red as blooms in the meadow of her cheeks, no civet rose is so milk-white, no lily so delicate and spotless, no snow fresh-fallen and untrodden is so white, as the heaven of her brows, the stronghold of her mind.

H. Anselm von Ziegler und Klipphausen also waxes eloquent in his famous *Asiatischen Banise*: ' The suns of her eyes played with lightnings; her

curly hair, like waves round her head, was some-
what darker than white; her cheeks were a pleasant
Paradise where rose and lily bloomed together in
beauty—yea, love itself seemed to pasture there.'
Elsewhere too this writer, so highly esteemed by the
second Silesian school of poets, indulged in showy
description and inflated rhetoric. Anton Ulrich von
Braunschweig-Wolfenbüttel tried more elaborate
descriptions of scenery ; so that Chovelius says :

> The Duke's German character shews pleasantly in
> his delight in Nature. The story often takes one into
> woods and fields ; already griefs and cares were carried
> to the running brook and mossy stone, and happy
> lovers listened to the nightingale.

His language is barely intelligible, but there is a
pleasant breadth about his drawing—for example, of
the king's meadow and the grotto in *Aramena* :

> Very cold crystal streams flowed through the fields
> and ran softly over the stony ground, making a
> pleasant murmur. Whilst the ear was thus contented,
> a distant landscape delighted the eye. No more
> delightful p ace, possessing all this at once, could have
> been found,1etc.

> Looking through the numerous air-holes, the eye
> lost itself in a deep valley, surrounded by nothing but
> mountains, where the shepherds tended their flocks, and
> one heard their flutes multiplied by the echo in the most
> delightful way.

Mawkish shepherd play is mixed here with such
verses as (Rahel) :

> Thou, Chabras, thou art the dear stream, where
> Jacob's mouth gave me the first kiss. Thou, clear
> brook, often bearest away the passionate words of my
> son of Isaac . . . on many a bit of wounded bark,
> the writing of my wounds is to be found.

The most insipid pastoral nonsense of the time
was produced by the Nuremberg poets, the Pegnitz
shepherds Klaj and Harsdörfer. Their strength lay
in imitating the sounds of Nature, and they were

much admired. What is still more astonishing, Lohenstein's writings were the model for thirty years, and it was the fashion for any one who wrote more simply to apologize for being unable to reach the level of so great a master ! To us the bombast, artificiality, and hidden sensuality of his poetry and Hoffmannswaldan's, are equally repulsive.

What dreary, manufactured stuff this is from Lohenstein's *Praise of Roses sung by the Sun* [17]:

> This is the queen of flowers and plants,
> The bride of heaven, world's treasure, child of stars !
> For whom love sighs, and I myself, the sun, do pant,
> Because her crown is golden, and her leaves are
>   velvet,
> Her foot and stylus emerald, her brilliance shames the
>   ruby.
>
> Other beings possess only single beauties,
> Nature has made the rose beautiful with all at once.
> She is ashamed, and blushes
> Because she sees all the other flowers stand ashamed
>   before her.

In *Rose Love* he finds the reflection of love in everything :

> In whom does not Love's spirit plant his flame ?
> One sees the oil of love burn in the starry lamps,
> That pleasant light can nothing be but love,
> For which the dew from Phœbus' veil doth fall.
> Heaven loves the beauteous globe of earth,
> And gazes down on her by night with thousand eyes ;
> While earth to please the heaven
> Doth clover, lilies, tulips in her green hair twine,
> The elm and vine stock intertwine,
> The ivy circles round the almond trees,
> And weeps salt tears when they are forced apart.
> And where the flowers burn with glow of Love,
> It is the rose that shews the brightest flame,
> For is the rose not of all flowers the queen,
> The wondrous beauty child of sun and earth ?

Artificiality and bombast reached its highest pitch in these poets, and feeling for Nature was entirely absent.

CHAPTER IX

SYMPTOMS OF A RETURN TO NATURE

It is refreshing to find, side by side with these mummified productions, the traces of a pure national poetry flowing clear as ever, ' breaking forth from the very heart of the people, ever renewing its youth, and not misled by the fashion of the day.'[1]

The traces prove that simple primitive love for Nature was not quite dead. For instance, this of the Virgin Mary : ' Mary, she went across the heath, grass and flowers wept for grief, she did not find her son.' And the lines in which the youth forced into the cloister asks Nature to lament with him : ' I greet you all, hill and dale, do not drive me away— grass and foliage and all the green things in the wild forest. O tree! lose your green ornaments, complain, die with me—'tis your duty.'

Then the Spring greetings :

Now we go into the wide, wide world,
With joy and delight we go ;
The woods are dressing, the meadows greening,
The flowers beginning to blow.
Listen here! and look there! We can scarce trust
     our eyes,
For the singing and soaring, the joy and life everywhere.

And :

What is sweeter than to wander in the early days of
     Spring
From one place to another in sheer delight and glee ;
While the sun is shining brightly, and the birds exult
     around
Fair Nightingale, the foremost of them all ?

This has the pulse of true and naive feeling (the hunter is starting for the hunt in the early morning) :

> When I come into the forest, still and silent everywhere,
> There's a look of slumber in it, but the air is fresh and cool.
> Now Aurora paints the fir tops at their very tips with gold,
> And the little finch sits up there launching forth his song of praise,
> Thanking for the night that's over, for the day that's just awake
> Gently blows the breeze of morning, rocking in the topmost twigs,
> And it bends them down like children, like good children when they pray ;
> And the dew is an oblation as it drops from their green hair.
> O what beauties in the forest lie that we may see and know !
> One could melt away one's heart before its wonders manifold !

The sixth line in the original has a melody that reminds one of Goethe's early work.

But even amidst the artificial poetry then in vogue, there were a few side streams which turned away from the main current of the great poet schools, from the unnaturalness and bombast affected especially by the Silesians. As Winter says, even the satirists Moscherosch and Logau were indirectly of use in paving the way for a healthier condition, through their severe criticisms of the corruption of the language ; and Logau's one epigram on May, ' This month is a kiss which heaven gives to earth, that she may be a bride now, a mother by-and-by,' outweighs all Harsdörfer's and Zesen's poetry about Nature.

But even by the side of Opitz and Fleming there was at least one poet of real feeling, Friedrich von Spee.[2] With all his mystic and pietist Christianity, he kept an open eye for Nature. His poems are full of disdain of the world and joy in Nature,[3] longings

for death and lamentations over sin; he delighted
in personifications of abstract ideas, childish playing
with words and feelings, and sentimental enthusi-
asm. But mawkish and canting as he was apt to
be, he often shewed a fine appreciation of detail.
He was even—a rare thing then—fascinated by the
sea.

> Now rages and roars the wild, wild sea,
> Now in soft curves lies quietly;
> Sweetly the light of the sun's bright glow
> Mirrors itself in the water below.
>
> Sad winter's past—the stork is here,
> Birds are singing and nests appear;
> Bowery homes steal into the day,
> Flow'rets present their full array;
> Like little snakes and woods about,
> The streams go wandering in and out.

His motives, like his diminutives, are constantly
recurring. He uses many bold and poetic personi-
fications; the sun 'combs her golden hair,' the
moon is a good shepherd who leads his sheep the
stars across the blue heath, blowing upon a soft
pipe; the sun adorns herself in spring with a crown
and a girdle of roses, fills her quiver with arrows,
and sends her horses to gallop for miles across the
smooth sky; the wind flies about, stopping for
breath from time to time; shakes its wings and
withdraws into its house when it is tired; the brook
of Cedron sits, leaning on a bucket in a hollow,
combing his bulrush hair, his shoulders covered
by grass and water; he sings a cradle song to his
little brooks, or drives them before him, etc.

But the most gifted poet of the set, and the most
doughty opponent of Lohenstein's bombast, was the
unhappy Christian Guenther.'

He vents his feelings in verse because he must.
There is a foretaste of Goethe in his lyrics, poured
out to free the soul from a burden, and melodious as
if by accident. As we turn over the leaves of his

book of songs, we find deep feeling for Nature mingled with his love and sorrows.[1]

> Bethink you, flowers and trees and shades,
> Of the sweet evenings here with Flavia !
> 'Twas here her head upon my shoulder pressed ;
> Conceal, ye limes, what else I dare not say.
> 'Twas here she clover threw and thyme at me,
> And here I filled her lap with freshest flowers.
> Ah ! that was a good time !
> I care more for moon and starlight than the pleasantest
>   of days,
> And with eyes and heart uplifted from my chamber
>   often gaze
> With an awe that grows apace till it scarcely findeth
>   space.

To his lady-love he writes :

> Here where I am writing now
> 'Tis lonely, shady, cool, and green ;
> And by the slender fig I hear
> The gentle wind blow towards Schweidnitz.
> And all the time most ardently
> I give it thousand kisses for thee.

And at Schweidnitz :

> A thousand greetings, bushes, fields, and trees,
> You know him well whose many rhymes
> And songs you've heard, whose kisses seen ;
> Remember the joy of those fine summer nights.

To Eleanora :

> Spring is not far away. Walk in green solitude
> Between your alder rows, and think . . .
> As in the oft-repeated lesson
> The young birds' cry shall bear my longing ;
> And when the west wind plays with cheek and dress
>   be sure
> He tells me of thy longing, and kisses thee a thousand
>   times for me.

In a time of despair, he wrote :

> Storm, rage and tear ! winds of misfortune, shew all
>   your tyranny !
> Twist and split bark and twig,
> And break the tree of hope in two

> Stem and leaves are struck by this hail and thunder,
> The root remains till storm and rain have laid their
>   wrath.

Again :

> The woods I'll wander through,
> From men I'll flee away,
> With lonely doves I'll coo,
> And with the wild things stay.
> When life's the prey of misery,
> And all my powers depart,
> A leafy grave will be
> Far kinder than thy heart.

True lyrist, he gave Nature her full right in his feelings, and found comfort in return ; but, as Goethe said of him, gifted but unsteady as he was, ' He did not know how to restrain himself, and so his life and poetry melted away.'

Among those who made use of better material than the Silesian poets, H. Barthold Brockes stood first. Nature was his one and only subject ; but in this he was not original, he was influenced by England. While France was dictating a taste like the baroque, and Germany enthusiastically adopting it (every petty prince in the land copied the gardens at Versailles, Schwetzingen more closely than the rest), a revolution which affected all Europe was brought about by England. The order of the following dates is significant: William Kent, the famous garden artist, died in 1748, James Thomson in the same year, Brockes a year earlier ; and about the same time the imitations of Robinson Crusoe sprang up like mushrooms.

We have considered Shakespeare's plays ; English lyrists too of the fifteenth and sixteenth centuries shewed deep feeling for Nature, and invested scenery with their own feelings in a very delicate way.

G. Chaucer (1400) praises the nightingale's song in *From the Floure and Leafe* :

> So was I with the song
> Thorow ravished, that till late and long

Ne wist I in what place I was ne where ; . . .
And at the last, I gan full well aspie
Where she sat in a fresh grene laurer tree
On the further side, even right by me,
That gave so passing a delicious smell
According to the eglentere full well. . . .

On the sote grass
I sat me downe, for, as for mine entent,
The birddes song was more convenient,
And more pleasant to me by many fold
Than meat or drink or any other thing.

Thomas Wyatt (1542) says of his lady-love :

The rocks do not so cruelly
Repulse the waves continually,
As she my suit and affection
So that I am past remedy.

Robert Southwell (1595), in *Love's Servile Lott*,
compares love to April :

May never was the month for love,
For May is full of floures,
But rather Aprill, wett by kinde,
For love is full of showers. . . .
Like winter rose and summer yce,
Her joyes are still untymelye ;
Before her hope, behind remorse,
Fayre first, in fyne unseemely.

Edmund Spenser (1598) describes a garden in *The
Faerie Queene* :

There the most daintie Paradise on ground
It selfe did offer to his sober eye,
In which all pleasures plenteously abownd,
And none does others' happinesse envye ;
The painted flowres, the trees upshooting hye,
The dales for shade, the hilles for breathing space,
The trembling groves, the christall running by,
And, that which all fair workes doth most aggrace,
The art which all that wrought appeared in no place.

Mountain scenery was seldom visited or described.
Michael Drayton (1731) wrote an ode on the Peak,
in Derbyshire :

Though on the utmost Peak
A while we do remain,

Amongst the mountains bleak
Exposed to sleet and rain,
No sport our hours shall break
To exercise our vein.

It is clear that he preferred his comfort to every-
thing, for he goes on :

Yet many rivers clear
Here glide in silver swathes,
And what of all most dear
Buxton's delicious baths,
Strong ale and noble chear
T' assuage breem winter's scathes.

Thomas Carew (1639) sings :

Ask me no more where Jove bestows,
When June is past, the fading rose,
For in your beauties' orient deep
These flowers, as in their causes, sleep.
Ask me no more whither do stray
The golden atoms of the day,
For in pure love Heaven did prepare
Those powders to enrich your hair.
Ask me no more whither doth haste
The nightingale, when May is past,
For in your sweet dividing throat
She winters and keeps warm her note.
Ask me no more where those stars shine
That downwards fall in dead of night,
For in your eyes they sit, and there
Fixed become, as in their sphere.
Ask me no more if east or west
The phœnix builds her spicy nest,
For unto you at last she flies
And in your fragrant bosom dies.

William Drummond (1746) avowed a taste which
he knew to be very unfashionable :

Thrice happy he, who by some shady grove,
Far from the clamorous world, doth live his own
Though solitary, who is not alone,
But doth converse with that eternal love.
O how more sweet is birds' harmonious moan
Or the soft sobbings of the widow'd dove,
Than those smooth whisp'rings near a prince's
    throne . . . .
O how more sweet is zephyr's wholesome breath
And sighs perfum'd, which new-born flowers unfold.

Another sonnet, to a nightingale, says :

> Sweet bird, that sing'st away the early hours
> Of winters past or coming void of care,
> Well pleased with delights which present are,
> Fair seasons, budding sprays, sweet-smelling flowers ;
> To rocks, to springs, to rills, from leafy bowers
> Thou thy Creator's goodness dost declare,
> And what dear gifts on thee He did not spare,
> A stain to human sense in sin that lowers,
> What soul can be so sick which by thy songs
> Attir'd in sweetness, sweetly is not driven
> Quite to forget earth's turmoils, spites, and wrongs ?

He greets Spring :

> Sweet Spring, thou turn'st with all thy goodly train
> Thy head with flames, thy mantle bright with flowers ;
> The zephyrs curl the green locks of the plain,
> The clouds for joy in pearls weep down their showers.

Robert Blair (1746) sings in *The Grave* :

> Oh, when my friend and I
> In some thick wood have wander'd heedless on,
> Hid from the vulgar eye, and sat us down
> Upon the sloping cowslip-cover'd bank,
> Where the pure limpid stream has slid along
> In grateful errors through the underwood,
> Sweet murmuring ; methought the shrill - tongu'd
>   thrush
> Mended his song of love, the sooty blackbird
> Mellowed his pipe and soften'd every note,
> The eglantine smell'd sweeter and the rose
> Assum'd a dye more deep, whilst ev'ry flower
> Vied with its fellow plant in luxury
> Of dress. Oh ! then the longest summer's day
> Seem'd too, too much in haste, still the full heart
> Had not imparted half ; half was happiness
> Too exquisite to last—Of joys departed
> Not to return, how painful the remembrance !

The great painter of Nature among the poets was James Thomson. He was not original, but followed Pope, who had lighted up the seasons in a dry, dogmatic way in *Windsor Forest*, and pastoral poems, and after the publication of his *Winter* the taste of the day carried him on. His deep and sentimental affection for Nature was mixed up with piety and moralizing. He said in a letter to his friend Paterson :

> Retirement and Nature are more and more my passion every day ; and now, even now, the charming time comes on ; Heaven is just on the point, or rather in the very act, of giving earth a green gown. The voice of the nightingale is heard in our lane. You must know that I have enlarged my rural domain . . . walled, no, no ! paled in about as much as my garden consisted of before, so that the walk runs round the hedge, where you may figure me walking any time of day, and sometimes of the night. . . . May your health continue till you have scraped together enough to return home and live in some snug corner, as happy as the Corycius senex in Virgil's fourth Georgic, whom I recommend both to you and myself as a perfect model of the truest happy life.

It is a fact that Solitude and Nature became a passion with him. He would wander about the country for weeks at a time, noting every sight and sound, down to the smallest, and finding beauty and divine goodness in all. His *Seasons* were the result.

There is faithful portraiture in these landscapes in verse ; some have charm and delicacy, but, for the most part, they are only catalogues of the external world, wholly lacking in links with the inner life.

Scene after scene is described without pause, or only interrupted by sermonizing ; it is as monotonous as a gallery of landscape paintings.

The human beings introduced are mere accessories, they do not live, and the undercurrent of all is praise of the Highest. His predilection is for still life in wood and field, but he does not neglect grander scenery ; his muse

> Sees Caledonia, in romantic view :
> Her airy mountains, from the waving main
> Invested with a keen diffusive sky,
> Breathing the soul acute ; her forests huge,
> Incult, robust, and tall, by Nature's hand
> Planted of old ; her azure lakes between,

Poured out extensive and of watery wealth
Full ; winding, deep and green, her fertile vales,
With many a cool translucent brimming flood
Washed lovely. . . ."

And in *A Hymn* we read :

Ye headlong torrents rapid and profound,
Ye softer floods that lead the humid maze
Along the vale ; and thou, majestic main,
A secret world of wonders in thyself.

It is the lack of human life, the didactic tone, and
the wearisome detail which destroys interest in the
Seasons—the lack of happy moments of invention.
Yet it had great influence on his contemporaries
in rousing love for Nature, and it contains many
beautiful passages.   For example :

Come, gentle Spring, ethereal mildness, come,
And from the bosom of yon dropping cloud,
While music wakes around, veiled in a shower
Of shadowing roses, on our plains descend.

His most artistic poem is Winter :

When from the pallid sky the sun descends
With many a spot, that o'er his glaring orb
Uncertain wanders, stained ; red fiery streaks
Begin to flush around.   The reeling clouds
Stagger with dizzy poise, as doubting yet
Which master to obey ; while rising slow,
Blank in the leaden-coloured east, the moon
Wears a wan circle round her blunted horns.
Seen through the turbid fluctuating air,
The stars obtuse emit a shivering ray ;
Or frequent seem to shoot, athwart the gloom,
And long behind them trail the whitening blaze.
Snatched in short eddies plays the withered leaf,
And on the flood the dancing feather floats.
With broadened nostrils to the sky upturned,
The conscious heifer snuffs the stormy gale. . . .
Retiring from the downs, where all day long
They picked their scanty fare, a blackening train
Of clamorous rooks thick urge their weary flight
And seek the closing shelter of the grove.
Assiduous, in his bower, the wailing owl
Plies his sad song.   The cormorant on high
Wheels from the deep, and screams along the land.

Loud shrieks the soaring heron, and with wild wing
The circling sea-fowl cleave the flaky skies.
Ocean, unequal pressed, with broken tide
And blind commotion heaves, while from the shore,
Eat into caverns by the restless wave
And forest-rustling mountains, comes a voice
That solemn-sounding bids the world prepare.

The elaboration of detail in such painting is certain evidence, not only of a keen, but an enthusiastic eye for Nature. As he says in Winter :

Nature, great parent ! whose unceasing hand
Rolls round the seasons of the changeful year !
How mighty, how majestic, are thy works !
With what a pleasing dread they swell the soul
That sees astonish'd, and astonish'd sings !

Brockes was directly influenced by Pope and Thomson, and translated the *Seasons,* when he had finished his *Irdisches Vergnügen in Gott.* This unwieldy work, insipid and prosaic as it is, was still a literary achievement, thanks to the dignity of the subject and the high seriousness of its aim, at a time when frivolity was the fashion in poetry. Its long pious descriptions of natural phenomena have none of the imposing flow of Thomson's strophes. It treats of fire in 138 verses of eight lines each, of air in 79, water in 78, earth in 74, while flowers and fruit are dissected and analyzed at great length ; and all this rhymed botany and physics is loosely strung together, but it shews a warm feeling for Nature of a moralizing and devotional sort. He says himself[7] that he took up the study of poetry first as an amusement, but later more seriously, and chose Nature as his theme, not only because her beauty moved him, but as a means ' whereby man might enjoy a permissible pleasure and be edified at the same time.'

So I resolved to sing the praises of the Creator to the best of my powers, and felt the more bound to do it, because I held that such great and almost inexcusable neglect and ingratitude was a wrong to the Creator, and unbecoming in Christendom. I therefore composed different pieces, chiefly in Spring, and tried my best to describe the beauties of Nature, in order, through my own pleasure, to rekindle the praise of the wise Creator in myself and others, and this led at last to the first part of my *Irdisches Vergnugen*. (1721.)

His evidence from animal and plant life for the teleological argument is very laughable; take, for example, the often-quoted chamois :

The fat is good for phthisis, the gall for the face, chamois flesh is good to eat, and its blood cures vertigo—the skin is no less useful. Doth not the love as well as the wisdom and almightiness of the Creator shine forth from this animal ?

For the rest, the following lines from *Irdisches Vergnügen in Gott* will serve to give an idea of his style ; they certainly do honour to his laborious attempt to miss none of the charms of the wood :

Lately as I sat on the green grass
Shaded by a lime tree, and read,
I raised my eyes by chance and saw
Different trees here and there, some far, some near,
Some half, some all in light, and some in shade,
Their boughs bowed down by leaves.
I saw how beautifully both air and flowery mead
Were crowned and adorned.
To describe the green grace
And the landscape it makes so sweet,
And at the same time prolong my pleasure,
I took pencil and paper
And tried to describe the beautiful trees in rhyme,
To the glory of God their Creator.
Of all the beauty the world lays before our eyes,
There certainly is none which does not pale
Beside green boughs,
Nothing to compare for pure beauty with a wood.
The green roofing overhead
Makes me feel young again ;
It hangs there, a living tapestry,
To the glory of God and our delight. . . .
Beyond many trees that lay in shade
I often saw one in full light ;

A human eye would scarce believe
How sweetly twilight, light and darkness
Meet side by side in leafy trees.
Peering through the leaves with joy
We notice, as we see the leaves
Lighted from one side only,
That we can almost see the sun
Mixing gold with the tender green, etc.

and so on for another twenty lines.

Yet this rich Burgomaster of Hamburg, for all that he dealt chiefly in rhymed prose, had his moments of rare elevation of thought and mystical rapture about Nature; for instance, in the introduction to *Ueber das Firmament*:

As lately in the sapphire depths,
Not bound by earth nor water, aim nor end,
In the unplumbed aerial sea I gazed,
And my absorbed glance, now here, now there,
But ever deeper sank—horror came over me,
My eye grew dizzy and my soul aghast.
That infinite vast vault,
True picture of Eternity,
Since without birth or end
From God alone it comes . . . .
It overwhelmed my soul.
The mighty dome of deep dark light,
Bright darkness without birth or bound,
Swallowed the very world—burying thought.
My being dwindled to an atom, to a nought;
I lost myself,
So suddenly it beat me down,
And threatened with despair.
But in that salutary nothingness, that blessed loss,
All present God! in Thee—I found myself again.

While English poetry and its German imitations were shewing these signs of reaction from the artificiality of the time, and science and philosophy often lauded Nature to the skies, as, for instance, Shaftesbury[8] (1671-1713), a return to Nature became the principle of English garden-craft in the first half of the eighteenth century.[9] The line of progress here, as in taste generally, did not run straightforward, but fluctuated. From the geometric gardens of Lenotre, England passed to the opposite extreme ; in the full tide of periwig and hoop petticoat, minuets, beauty - patches and rouge, Addison and Pope were banishing everything that was not strictly natural from the garden. Addison would even have everything grow wild in its own way, and Pope wrote :

> To build, to plant, whatever you intend,
> To rear the column, or the arch to bend,
> To swell the terrace or to sink the grot,
> In all let Nature never be forgot.

William Kent made allowance for this idea ; but, as a painter, and looking at his native scenery with a painter's eye, he noted its characteristic features —the gentle undulations, the freshness of the green, the wealth of trees—and based his garden-craft on these.

The straight line was banished ; in its place came wide spaces of lawn and scattered groups of trees of different sorts — dark fir and alder here, silver birch and grey poplar there ; and flowery fields with streams running through them stood out in relief against dark woodland.

Stiff walls, balustrades, terraces, statues, and so forth, disappeared ; the garden was not to contrast with the surrounding landscape, but to merge into it—to be not Art, but a bit of Nature. It was, in fact, to be a number of such bits, each distinct from the rest — waterfall, sheltered sunny nook, dark wood, light glade. Kent himself soon began to vary this mosaic of separate scenes by adding ruins and pavilions ; but it was Chambers the architect who developed the idea of variety by his writings on the dwellings and manners of the Chinese.[10]

The fundamental idea that the garden ought to be a sample of the landscape was common both to Kent and the Chinese ; but, as China is far richer than England in varieties of scenery, her gardens included mountains, rocks, swamps, and deserts, as well as sunny fields and plains, while English gardens were comparatively monotonous. When the fashion for the Chinese style came in, as unluckily it did just when we were trying to oust the Rococo, so that one pigtail superseded the other, variety was achieved by groups of buildings in all sorts of styles. Stables, ice-houses, gardeners' cottages took the form of pavilions, pagodas, kiosks, and temples.

Meanwhile, as a reaction against the Rococo, enthusiasm for Nature increased, and feeling was set free from restraint by the growing sentimentality. Richardson's novels fed the taste for the pleasures of weeping sensibility, and garden-craft fell under its sway. In all periods the insignificant and non-essential is unable to resist the general stamp, if that only shews a little originality.

These gardens, with temples to friendship and love, melancholy, virtue, re-union, and death, and so forth, were suitable backgrounds for the sentimental scenes described in the English novels, and for the idyllic poets and moonshine singers of Germany. Here it was the fashion to wander, tenderly inter-twined, shedding floods of tears and exchanging kisses, and pausing at various places to read the inscriptions which directed them what to feel. At one spot they were to laugh, at another to weep, at a third to be fired with devotion.

Hermitages sprang up everywhere, with hermits, real or dummy. Any good house near a wood, or in a shady position, was called a hermitage, and dedicated to arcadian life, free from care and cere-mony. Classic and romantic styles competed for favour in architecture ; at one moment everything must needs be purely classic, each temple Corinthian, Ionic, or Doric ; at another Gothic, with the ruins and fortresses of mediæval romance. And not only English gardens, but those of Europe generally, though to a less degree, passed through these stages of development, for no disease is so infectious as fashion.

It was not till the end of the eighteenth century that a healthy reaction set in in England, when Repton turned back to Kent's fundamental principle and freed it from its unnatural excrescences, with the formula : the garden should be an artistic representation of the landscape, a work of art whose materials are provided by Nature herself, whether grass, flowers, bushes, trees, water, or whatever it may be that she has to offer. Thus began our modern landscape gardening.

In another region too, a change was brought about from the Rococo to a more natural style. It is true that Nature plays no direct *rôle* in *Robinson Crusoe*, and wins as little notice there as in its numberless imitations ; yet the book roused a longing for healthier, more natural conditions in thousands of minds. It led the idyllic tendency of the day back to its source, and by shewing all the stages, from the raw state of Nature up to the culture of the community, in the life of one man, it brought out the contrast between the far-off age of innocence and the perverted present.

The German *Simplicissimus* closed with a Robinsonade, in which the hero, after long wandering, found rest and peace on an island in the ocean of the world, alone with himself and Nature. The readers of *Robinson Crusoe* were in much the same position. Defoe was not only a true artist, but a man of noble, patient character, and his romance proved a healing medicine to many sick minds, pointing the way back to Nature and a natural life, and creating a longing for the lost innocence of man.

Rousseau, who was also a zealous advocate of

the English gardens, and disgusted by the French Pigtail style, was more impressed by *Robinson Crusoe* than by any other book. It was the first book his Emilia gave him, as a gospel of Nature and unspoilt taste.

CHAPTER X

THE SENSITIVENESS AND EXAGGERATION OF THE ELEGIAC IDYLLIC FEELING

THIS longing to return to the lost paradise of Nature gradually produced a state of melancholy hypersensitiveness, an epidemic of wòrld pain, quite as unnatural as the Rococo.

The heart came into its rights again and laid claim to absolute dominion in its kingdom, and regret that it had lain so long deprived of its own, gave rise to a tearful pensiveness, which added zest to restitution. It was convalescence, but followed at once by another complaint. Feeling swung from one extreme to the other.

German feeling in the first half of the eighteenth century was chiefly influenced, on the one hand, by Richardson's novels, which left no room for Nature, and by the poetry of Young and Thomson; on the other, by the pastoral idylls interspersed with anacreontic love-passages, affected by the French. At first description and moralizing preponderated.

In 1729 Haller's *Alps* appeared. It had the merit of drawing the eyes of Europe to Alpine beauty and the moral worth of the Swiss, but shewed little eye for romantic scenery. It is full of descriptive painting, but not of a kind that appeals: scene follows scene with considerable pathos, especially in dealing with the people; but landscape is looked at almost entirely from the moralizing or utilitarian standpoint.

' Here, where the majestic Mount Gothard elevates its summit above the clouds, and where the earth itself seems to approach the sun, Nature has assembled in one spot all the choicest treasure of the globe. The deserts of Libya, indeed, afford us greater novelties, and its sandy plains are more fertile in monsters : but thou, favoured region, art adorned with useful productions only, productions which can satisfy all the wants of man. Even those heaps of ice, those frowning rocks in appearance so sterile, contribute largely to the general good, for they supply inexhaustible fountains to fertilize the land. What a magnificent picture does Nature spread before the eye, when the sun, gilding the top of the Alps, scatters the sea of vapours which undulates below ! Through the receding vale the theatre of a whole world rises to the view ! Rocks, valleys, lakes, mountains, and forests fill the immeasurable space, and are lost in the wide horizon. We take in at a single glance the confines of divers states, nations of various characters, languages, and manners, till the eyes, overcome by such extent of vision, drop their weary lids, and we ask of the enchanted fancy a continuance of the scene.

' When the first emotion of astonishment has subsided, how delightful is it to observe each several part which makes up this sublime whole ! That mass of hills, which presents its graceful declivity covered with flocks of sheep whose bleatings resound through the meadows ; that large clear lake, which reflects from its level surface sunbeams gently curved ; those valleys, rich in verdure, which compose by their various outlines points of perspective which contract in the distance of the landscape ! Here rises a bare steep mountain laden with the accumulated snow of ages ; its icy head rests among the clouds, repelling the genial rays of the moon and the fervid heat of the dog-star : there a chain of cultivated hills spreads before the delighted eye ; their green pastures are enlivened by flocks, and their golden corn waves in the wind : yet climates so different as those are only separated by a cool, narrow valley.   Behold that foaming torrent rushing from a perpendicular height !   Its rapid waves dash among the rocks, and shoot even beyond their limits.   Divided by the rapidity of its course and the depth of the abyss where it falls, it changes into a grey moving veil ; and, at length scattered into humid atoms, it shines with the tints of the rainbow, and, suspended over the valley, refreshes it with plenteous dew.   The traveller beholds with astonishment rivers flowing towards the sky, and issuing from one cloud, hide themselves in the grey veil of another.

' Those desert places uncheered by the rays of the sun, those frozen abysses deprived of all verdure, hide beneath their sterile sands invaluable treasures, which defy the rigour of the seasons and all the injuries of time !   'Tis in dark and marshy recesses, upon the damp grottos, that crystal rocks are formed.   Thus splendour is diffused through their melancholy vaults, and their shadowy depths glitter with the colours of the rainbow.   O Nature, how various are thy operations, how infinite thy fertility ! '

We cannot agree with Frey[1] that ' these few strophes may serve as sufficient proof that Haller's poetry is still, even among the mass of Alpine poetry, unsurpassed for intense power of direct vision, and easily makes one forget its partial lack of flexibility of diction.'

The truth is, flexibility is entirely lacking ; but the lines do express the taste for open-air life among the great sublimities and with simple people.   The poem is not romantic but idyllic, with a touch of the elegiac. It is the same with the poem *On the Origin of Evil* (Book I.) :

On those still heights whence constant springs flow
    down,
I paused within a copse, lured by the evening breeze ;
Wide country lay spread out beneath my feet,
Bounded by its own size alone. . . .
Green woods covered the hills, through which the pale
    tints of the fields
Shone pleasantly.   ‐
Abundance and repose held sway far as the eye
    could reach . . . .
And yonder wood, what left it to desire
With the red tints upon the half-bare beeches
And the rich pine's green shade o'er whitened moss ?
While many a sun-ray through the interstices
A quivering light upon the darkness shed,
Blending in varying hues green night with golden day
How pleasant is the quiet of the copse ! . . .
Yea, all I see is given by Providence,
The world itself is for its burgher's joy ;
Nature's inspired with the general weal,
The highest goodness shews its trace in all.

Friedrich von Hagedorn, too, praises country pleasures[1] in *The Feeling of Spring* :

Enamelled meadows ! freshly decked in green,
I sing your praises constantly ;
Nature and Spring have decked you out. . . .
Delightful quiet, stimulant of joy,
How enviable thou art !

This idyllic taste for country life was common at the time, especially among the so-called ' anacreontists.' Gleim, for instance, in his *Praise of Country Life* : ' Thank God that I have fled from the bustle of the world and am myself again under the open sky.'

And in *The Countryman* :

How happy is he who, free from cares, ploughs his father's fields ; every morning the sun shines on the grass in which he lies.

And Joh. Friedrich von Cronegk :

> Fly from sordid cares and the proud tumult of cities
> . . . here in the peaceful valley shy wisdom sports
> at ease, where the smiling Muse crowns herself with
> dewy roses.

With this idyllic tone it is not surprising to find the religious feeling of many hymn writers ; for instance, Gleim in *The Goodness of God* :

> For whom did Thy goodness create the world so beautiful, O God ? For whom are the flowers on hill and dale ? . . . Thou gavest us power to perceive the beauty.

And above all, honest Gellert :

> The skies, the globe, the seas, praise the eternal glory. O my Creator, when I consider Thy might and the wisdom of Thy ways. . . . Sunshine and storm preach Thee, and the sands of the sea.

Ewald von Kleist excelled Haller as much as Haller had excelled Brockes.

Julian Schmidt says[3] : 'Later on, descriptive poetry, like didactic, fell into disgrace ; but at that time this dwelling upon the minutiæ of Nature served to enrich the imagination ; Kleist's descriptions are thoughtful and interesting.' It is easy to see that his longer poems cost him much labour ; they were not the pure songs of feeling that gush out spontaneously like a spring from the rock. But in eloquence and keenness of observation he excelled his contemporaries, although he, too, followed the fashion of eighteenth - century literature, and coquetted with Greek nymphs and deities, and the names of winds and maidens.

The tendency to depression, increased by his failure to adapt himself to military life, made him incline more and more to solitude.

To Doris begins :

> Now spring doth warm the flakeless air,
> And in the brook the sky reflects her blue,
> Shepherds in fragrant flowers find delight . . .

The corn lifts high its golden head,
And Zephyr moves in waves across the grain,
Her robe the field embroiders ; the young rush
Adorns the border of each silver stream,
Love seeks the green night of the forest shade,
And air and sea and earth and heaven smile.

Sighs for Rest :

O silver brook, my leisure's early soother,
When wilt thou murmur lullabies again ?
When shall I trace thy sliding smooth and smoother,
While kingfishers along thy reeds complain :
Afar from thee with care and toil opprest,
Thy image still can calm my troubled breast.

O ye fair groves and odorous violet valleys,
Girt with a garland blue of hills around,
Thou quiet lake, where, when Aurora sallies,
Her golden tresses seem to sweep the ground :
Soft mossy turf, on which I wont to stray,
For me no longer bloom thy flow'rets gay.
As when the chilly nights of March arise
And whirl the howling dust in eddies swift,
The sunbeams wither in the dimmer skies,
O'er the young ears the sand and pebbles drift :
So the war rages, and the furious forces
The air with smoke bespread, the field with corses.

The vineyard bleeds, and trampled is the corn,
Orchards but heat the kettles of the camp. . . .

As when a lake which gushing rains invade
Breaks down its dams, and fields are overflowed,
So floods of fire across the region spread,
And standing corn by crackling flames is mowed :
Bellowing the cattle fly ; the forests burn,
And their own ashes the old stems in-urn.

He too, who fain would live in purity,
Feels nature treacherous, hears examples urge,
As one who, falling overboard at sea,
Beats with his arms and feet the buoyant surge,
And climbs at length against some rocky brink,
Only beneath exhausted strength to sink.

My cheek bedewed with holy tears in vain,
To love and heaven I vowed a spotless truth :

> Too soon the noble tear exhaled again,
> Example conquered, and the glow of youth
> To live as live one's comrades seems allowed;
> He who would be a man, must quit the crowd.

He, too, wrote with hymn-like swing in praise of the Creator: 'Great is the Lord! the unnumbered heavens are the chambers of his fortress, storm and thunder-clouds his chariot.'

The most famous of his poems, and the one most admired in his own day, was *Spring*. This is full of love for Nature. It describes a country walk after the muggy air of town, and conveys a vivid impression of fresh germinating spring, though it is overlaid by monotonous detail:

> Receive me, hallowed shades! Ye dwellings of sweet bliss!
> Umbrageous arches full of sleeping dark delights . . .
> Receive me! Fill my soul with longing and with rest . . .
> And you, ye laughing fields,
> Valleys of roses, labyrinths of streams,
> I will inhale an ecstasy with your balsamic breath,
> And, lying in the shade, on strings of gold
> Sing your indwelling joys. . . .
> On rosy clouds, with rose and tulip crowned,
> Spring has come down from heaven. . . .
> The air grew softer, fields took varied hues,
> The shades were leafy, and soft notes awoke
> And flew and warbled round the wood in twilight greenery.
> Brooks took a silver tint, sweet odours filled the air,
> The early shepherd's pipe was heard by Echo in the dale. . . .
> Most dear abode! Ah, were I but allowed
> Down in the shade by yon loquacious brook
> Henceforth to live! O sky! thou sea of love,
> Eternal spring of health, will not thy waters succour me?
> Must my life's blossom wither, stifled by the weeds?

Johann Peter Uz, who was undervalued because of his sickly style, wrote many little songs full of feeling for Nature, though within narrow limits. Their titles shew the pastoral taste':—*Spring,*

Morning, Shepherd's Morning Song, The Muse with the Shepherds, The Meadow in the Country, Vintage, Evening, May, The Rose, Summer and Wine, Winter Night, Longing for Spring, etc.

Many are fresh and full of warm feeling, especially the Spring Songs':

> See the blossoming of Spring !
> Will 't not taste the joys it showers ?
> Dost not feel its impulse thrill ?
> Friends ! away our cares we'll fling !
> In the joyous time of flowers,
> Love and Bacchus have their will.

and

> O forest, O green shady paths,
> Dear place of spring's display !
> My good luck from the thronging town
> Has brought me here away.
>
> O what a fresh breeze flows
> Down from the wooded hill,
> How pleasantly the west wind flies
> With rustling dewy wing
> Across the vale,
> Where all is green and blossoming.

The personification is more marked in this :

> Thou hast sent us the Spring in his gleaming robe
> With roses round his head. Smiling he comes, O
>   God !
> The hours conduct him to his flowery throne.
> Into the groves he enters and they bloom ; fresh green
>   is on the plain,
> The forest shade returns, the west wind lovingly un-
>   furls
> Its dewy plumes, and happy birds begin to sing.
> The face of Nature Thou hast deckt with beauty that
>   enchants,
> O Thou rich source of all the beautiful . . .
> My heart is lifted up to Thee in purest love.

His feeling for Nature was warm enough, although most of his writing was so artificial and tedious from much repetition of a few ideas, that Kleist could write to Gleim[5]: 'The odes please me more the more I read them. With a few exceptions, they have only one fault, too many laurel woods; cut them down a little. Take away the marjoram too, it is better in a good sausage than in a beautiful poem.'

Joh. Georg Jacobi also belonged to the circle of poets gathered round Gleim; but in many respects he was above it. He imitated the French style[6] far less than the others—than Hagedorn, for example; and though the Anacreontic element was strong in him, he overcame it, and aimed at pure lyrical feeling. From his Life, written by a devoted friend, we see that he had all the sentimentality of the day,[7] but with much that was healthy and amiable in addition, and he touched Nature with peculiar freshness and genuineness.

In a poem to his brother, about the Saale valley near Halle, he wrote:

Lie down in early spring on yon green moss,
By yon still brook where heart with heart we spoke,
My brother . . . .
Will't see the little garden and the pleasant heights
   above,
So quiet and unspoilt? O friend, 'tis Nature speaks
In distant wood, near plain and careless glade,
Here on my little hill and in the clover . . . .
Dost hear the rustle of the streamlet through the wood?

Jacobi was one whose heart, as he said of Gleim, took a warm interest in all that breathed, even a violet, and sought sympathy and companionship in the whole range of creation.

This is from his *Morning Song*:

See how the wood awakes, how from the lighted heights
With the soft waving breeze
The morning glory smiles in the fresh green. . . .
Here by the rippling brook and quivering flower,
We catch Love's rustle as she gently sweeps
Like Spring's own breath athwart the plains.

Another song is:

Tell me, where's the violet fled,
Late so gayly blowing,

Springing 'neath fair Flora's tread,
Choicest sweets bestowing ?
Swain, the vernal scene is o'er,
And the violet blooms no more.

Say, where hides the blushing rose,
Pride of fragrant morning,
Garland meet for beauty's brows,
Hill and dale adorning ?
Gentle maid, the summer's fled,
And the hapless rose is dead.

Bear me then to yonder rill,
Late so freely flowing,
Watering many a daffodil
On its margin glowing.
Sun and wind exhaust its store,
Yonder rivulet glides no more.

Lead me to the bowery shade,
Late with roses flaunting,
Loved resort of youth and maid,
Amorous ditties chanting.
Hail and wind with fury shower,
Leafless mourns the rifled bower !

Say, where bides the village maid,
Late yon cot adorning ?
Oft I've met her in the glade
Fair and fresh as morning.
Swain, how short is beauty's bloom,
Seek her in her grassy tomb.

Whither roves the tuneful swain
Who, of rural pleasures,
Rose and violet, rill and plain,
Sang in deftest measures ?
Maiden, swift life's vision flies,
Death has closed the poet's eyes.

To Nature runs thus :

Leaves are falling, mists are twining, and to winter
    sleep inclining
Are the trees upon the plain,
In the hush of stillness ere the snowflakes hide them,
Friendly Nature, speak to me again !
Thou art echo and reflection of our striving,

> Thou art painter of our hopes and of our fears,
> Thou art singer of our joys and of our sorrows,
> Of our consolations and our groans. . . .

While feeling for Nature was all of this character, idyllic, sensitive, sympathetic, but within very narrow bounds, and the poets generally were wandering among Greek and Latin bucolics and playing with Damon, Myrtil, Chloe, and Daphnis, Salomon Gessner made a speciality of elegiac pastoral poetry. He was a better landscapist than poet, and his drawings to illustrate his idylls were better than the poems themselves. The forest, for instance, and the felling of the tree, are well drawn; whereas the sickly sweet Rococo verse in imitation of the French, and reminding one more of Longos than Theocritus, is lifeless. His rhapsody about Nature is uncongenial to modern readers, but his love was real.

The introduction 'to the Reader'[8] is characteristic:

> These Idylls are the fruits of some of my happiest hours; of those hours when imagination and tranquillity shed their sweetest influence over me, and, excluding all which belongs to the period in which we live, recalled all the charms and delights of the Golden Age. A noble and well-regulated mind dwells with pleasure on these images of calm tranquillity and uninterrupted happiness, and the scenes in which the poet delineates the simple beauties of uncorrupted nature are endeared to us by the resemblance we fancy we perceive in them to the most blissful moments that we have ourselves enjoyed. Often do I fly from the city and seek the deepest solitudes; there, the beauties of the landscape soothe and console my heart, and gradually disperse those impressions of solicitude and disgust which accompanied me from the town; enraptured, I give up my whole soul to the contemplation of Nature, and feel, at such moments, richer than an Utopian monarch, and happier than a shepherd of the Golden Age.

This is a true picture of the time! Man knew that he was sick, and fled from town and his fellows into solitude, there to dream himself back to a happier past, and revel in the purity and innocence, the healing breath, of forest and field.

The magic of moonlight began to be felt. Mirtilla

> perceived his old father slumbering in the moon-beams. . . . Mirtilla stood long contemplating him, and his eyes rested fondly on the old man except when he raised them toward heaven through the glistening leaves of the vine, and tears of filial love and joy bedewed his cheeks. . . . How beautiful! how beautiful is the landscape! How bright, how clear appears the deep blue of heaven through the broken clouds! They fly, they pass away, these towering clouds; but strew a shadow as they pass over the sunny landscape. . . . Oh, what joy overwhelms my soul! how beautiful, how excellent is all around, what an inexhaustible source of rapture! From the enlivening sun down to the little plant that his mild influence nourishes, all is wonderful! What rapture overpowers me when I stand on the high hill and look down on the wide-spread landscape beneath me, when I lay stretched along the grass and examine the various flowers and herbs and their little inhabitants; when at the midnight hour I contemplate the starry heavens! . . . Wrapt in each other's arms, let us contemplate the approach of morning, the bright glow of sunset, or the soft beams of moonlight; and as I press thee to my trembling heart, let us breathe out in broken accents our praises and thanksgivings. Ah! what inexpressible joy, when with such raptures are blended the transports of the tenderest love.

Many prosaic writings of a different kind shew how universally feeling, in the middle of the eighteenth century, turned towards Nature.

The æsthetic writer Sulzer (1750) wrote *On the Beauty of Nature.* Crugot's widely-read work of edification, *Christ in Solitude* (1761), shewed the same point of view among the mystical and pietist clergy; and Spalding's *Human Vocation*[9] (written with a warmth that reminds one of Gessner) among the rationalists, whom he headed. He says:

> Nature contains numberless pleasures, which, through my great sensitiveness, nourish my mind. . . . I open

eye and ear, and through these openings pleasures flow into my soul from a thousand sides : flowers painted by the hand of Nature, the rich music of the forest, the bright daylight which pours life and light all round me. . . . How indifferent, tasteless, and dead is all the fantastic glamour of artificial splendour and luxuriance in comparison with the living radiance of the real beautiful world of Nature, with the joyousness, repose, and admiration I feel before a meadow in blossom, a rustling stream, the pleasant awesomeness of night, or of the majesty of innumerable worlds. Even the commonest and most familiar things in Nature give me endless delight, when I feel them with a heart attuned to joy and admiration. . . . I lose myself, absorbed in delight, in the consideration of all this general beauty, of which I hold myself to be a not disfigured part.

Klopstock, the torch-bearer of Germany's greatest poets, owed much of his power of the wing to religion. He introduced that new epoch in the literature of his country which culminated in Goethe. As so often happens in mental development, the reaction against prevailing conditions and the advance to higher ones, in the middle of the eighteenth century, led first of all to the opposite extreme—balance was only reached by degrees. What chiefly made Klopstock a literary reformer was the glowing enthusiasm and powerful imagination which compelled the stiff poetic forms, clumsy as they were, to new rhythm and melodious cadence. And although his style degenerated into mannerism in the *Messias*, for the youthful impetus which had carried his Pegasus over the clouds to the stars could not keep it there without artificial aid, the immense value of his influence remained. He is one of the most interesting representatives, not only of his own, but of all similar periods of exaggerated feelings and ideals. Despite his loftiness of thought and speech, and his seraphic raptures, he was not without a full share of sensuous development, and women's eyes, or a girl's rosy lips, would draw him away from the finest view in the world.

A mind so intent upon the noble and beautiful was sure to be enthusiastic about Nature; his correspondence is the best witness to this, and at the same time throws side-lights upon the period.

It is difficult to-day to understand the influence which the *Messias* had upon its readers; even Friedenkende spent happy hours reading it with pious tears of delight, and young and old were of the same opinion.

There is a pretty letter from Gustchen Stolberg [10] to Klopstock, which runs thus :

UETERSEN,
25 April 1776.

> In the garden. Yes, in the garden, dearest Klopstock! I have just been walking about, it was so beautiful: the little birds were singing, violets and other flowers wafted their fragrance to me, and I began thinking very warmly of all whom I dearly, dearly love, and so very soon came to my dear Klopstock, who certainly has no truer friend than I am, though perhaps others express it better. . . . Thanks, thanks, for your very delightful little letter—how dear to me I don't tell you—can't tell you.

C. F. Cramer was his enthusiastic panegyrist. It is not only what he says of the private life and special taste of his adored friend which is note-worthy, but the way in which he does it—the tone in which, as a cultivated man of the day, he judged him. 'He will paint and paint Nature. For this he must be acquainted with her. This is why he loves her so well. This is why he strays by the brook and weeps. This is why in spring he goes out into the fields of blossoms, and his eyes run over with tears. All creation fills him with yearning and delight. He goes from mountain to valley like a man in a dream. When he sees a stream, he follows its course; when a hill, he must climb it; when a river—oh! if only he could rush with it to the sea! A rock—oh! to look down from its crags to the land below! A hawk hovers over him—oh ! to have its wings and fly so much nearer to the stars ! He stands for hours looking at a flower or moss, throws himself down on the grass and decks his hat with ivy and cornflowers. He goes by moonlight to visit the graves and think of death, immortality, and eternal life. Nothing hinders his meditations. He sees everything in relation to something else. Every visible object has an invisible companion, so ardently, so entirely, so closely does he feel it all.'

This, coming straight from life, tells us more than a volume of odes ; it contains the real feeling of the time, sensitive, dreamy, elegiac.

His friend goes on : ' He walks often and likes it, but generally looks for sunny places ; he goes very slowly, which is fatal for me, for I run when I walk. . . . Often he stands still and silent, as if there were knots which he could not untie (in his thoughts). And truly there are unknown depths of feeling as well as thought.'

In another place : ' He went out and gloated over the great scene of immeasurable Nature. Orion and the Pleiades moved over his head, the dear moon was opposite. Looking intently into her friendly face, he greeted her repeatedly : " Moon, Moon, friend of my thoughts ; hurry not away, dear Moon, but stay. What is thy name ? Laura, Cynthia, Cyllene ? Or shall I call thee beautiful Betty of the Sky ? " . . . He loved country walks ; we made for lonely places, dark fearsome thickets, lonel unfrequented paths, scrambled up all the hills, spied out every bit of Nature, came to rest at last under a shady rock. . . . Klopstock's life is one constant enjoyment. He gives himself up to feeling, and revels in Nature's feast. . . . Winter is his favourite time of year. . . ." He preaches skating with the unction of a missionary to the heathen, and not without working miracles, . . . the ice by moonlight is a feast of the Gods to him . . . only

one rule, we do not leave the river till the moon
has gone.' Klopstock described this in his *Skating*:

> O youth, whose skill the ice-cothurn
> Drives glowing now, and now restrains,
> On city hearths let faggots burn,
> But come with me to crystal plains.
> The scene is filled with vapouring light,
> As when the winter morning's prime
> Looks on the lake. Above it night
> Scatters, like stars, the glittering rime.
> How still and white is all around!
> How rings the track with new sparr'd frost!
> Far off the metal's cymbal sound
> Betrays thee, for a moment lost. . . .

Cramer tells how Klopstock paid a long-remem-
bered visit to Count Bernstoff at Schloss Stintenburg:

> It has a most romantic situation in a bewitching
> part of Mecklenburg; 'tis surrounded by forest full of
> delightful gloom, and a large lake, with a charming
> little island in the centre, which wakes echoes. Klop-
> stock is very fond of echoes, and is always trying to
> find them in his walks.

This illustrates the lines in *Stintenburg*:

> Isle of pious solitude,
> Loved playmate of the echo and the lake, etc.

but in this ode, as in so many of his, simple personal
feeling gives way to the stilted mannerism of the
bard poetry.

He wrote of Soroe,[12] one of the loveliest places in
the Island of Zealand, as ' an uncommonly pleasant
place '; where ' By a sacred tree, on a raised grass
plot two hundred paces from the great alley, and
from a view over the Friedensburg Lake towards
a little wooded island . . . Fanny appeared to him
in the silver evening clouds over the tree-tops.'

The day on which he composed *The Lake
of Zurich* was one of the pleasantest in his life.
Cramer says: ' He has often told me and still tells,
with youthful fervour, about those delightful days

and this excursion : the boat full of people, mostly young, all in good spirits ; charming girls, his wife Herzel, a lovely May morning.' '

But, unlike St Preux, he 'seemed less impressed by our scenery than by the beauty of our girls,' and his letters bear out the remark.' Yet delight in Nature was always with him : Klopstock's lofty morality pours forth all through it. Nature, love, fame, wine, everything is looked at from an ennobling point of view.'

> Fair is the majesty of all thy works
> On the green earth, O Mother Nature fair !
> But fairer the glad face
> Enraptured with their view.
> Come from the vine banks of the glittering lake,
> Or—hast thou climbed the smiling skies anew—
> Come on the roseate tip
> Of evening's breezy wing,
> And teach my song with glee of youth to glow,
> Sweet joy, like thee—with glee of shouting youths,
> Or feeling Fanny's laugh.

> Behind us far already Uto lay.
> At whose feet Zurich in the quiet vale
> Feeds her free sons : behind—
> Receding vine-clad hills.
> Uncloud'd beamed the top of silver Alps,
> And warmer beat the heart of gazing youths,
> And warmer to their fair
> Companions spoke its glow.
> And Haller's Doris sang, the pride of song ;
> And Hirzel's Daphne, dear to Kleist and Gleim ;
> And we youths sang and felt
> As each were—Hagedorn.

> Soon the green meadow took us to the cool
> And shadowy forest, which becrowns the isle.
> Then cam'st thou, Joy ; thou cam'st
> Down in full tide to us ;
> Yes, goddess Joy, thyself ; we felt, we clasp'd,
> Best sister of humanity, thyself,
> With thy dear innocence
> Accompanied, thyself.

Sweet thy inspiring breath, O cheerful Spring;
When the meads cradle thee, and their soft airs
Into the hearts of youths
And hearts of virgins glide,
Thou makest feeling conqueror. Ah! through thee
Fuller, more tremulous, heaves each blooming breast;
With lips spell-freed by thee
Young love unfaltering pleads.
Fair gleams the wine, when to the social change
Of thought, or heart-felt pleasure, it invites,
And the 'Socratic' cup
With dewy roses bound,
Sheds through the bosom bliss, and wakes resolves,
Such as the drunkard knows not—proud resolves
Emboldening to despair
Whate'er the sage disowns.

Delightful thrills against the panting heart
Fame's silver voice—and immortality
Is a great thought. . . .
But sweeter, fairer, more delightful, 'tis
On a friend's arm to know oneself a friend. . . .
O were ye here, who love me though afar . . .
How would we build us huts of friendship, here
Together dwell for ever.

This is of Fredensborg on an August day:

Here, too, did Nature tarry, when her hand
Pour'd living beauty over dale and hill,
And to adorn this pleasant land
Long time she lingered and stood still. . . .
The lake how tranquil! From its level brim
The shore swells gently, wooded o'er with green,
And buries in its verdure dim
The lustre of the summer e'en. . . .

The inner and outer life are closely blended in
The Early Grave:

Welcome, O silver moon,
Fair still companion of the night!
Friend of the pensive, flee not soon;
Thou stayest, and the clouds pass light.

Young waking May alone
Is fair as summer's night so still,
When from his locks the dews drop down,
And, rosy, he ascends the hill.

Ye noble souls and true,
Whose graves with sacred moss are strawn,
Blest were I, might I see with you
The glimmering night, the rosy dawn.

This is true lyric feeling, spontaneous, not forced. Many of his odes, and parts of the *Messias*, shew great love for Nature.   There is a fine flight of imagination in *The Festival of Spring* :

Not into the ocean of all the worlds would I plunge —not hover where the first created, the glad choirs of the sons of light, adore, deeply adore and sunk in ecstasy.   Only around the drop on the bucket, only around the earth, would I hover and adore.   Hallelujah ! hallelujah ! the drop on the bucket flowed also out of the hand of the Almighty.

When out of the hand of the Almighty the greater earth flowed, when the streams of light rushed, and the seven stars began to be—then flowedst thou, drop, out of the hand of the Almighty.

When a stream of light rushed, and our sun began to be, a cataract of waves of light poured, as adown the rock a storm-cloud, and girded Orion, then flowedst thou, drop, out of the hand of the Almighty.   Who are the thousandfold thousands, who all the myriads that inhabit the drop ? . . .

But thou, worm of Spring, which, greenly golden, art fluttering beside me, thou livest and art, perhaps, ah ! not immortal. . . .

The storm winds that carry the thunder, how they roar, how with loud waves they stream athwart the forest !   Now they hush, slow wanders the black cloud. . . .

Ah ! already rushes heaven and earth with the gracious rain ; now is the earth refreshed. . . .

Behold Jehovah comes no longer in storm ; in gentle pleasant murmurs comes Jehovah, and under him bends the bow of peace.

In another ode, *The Worlds*, he calls the stars 'drops of the ocean.'

Again, in *Death* he shews the sense of his own nothingness, in presence of the overpowering greatness of the Creator :

> Ye starry hosts that glitter in the sky,
> How ye exalt me! Trancing is the sight
> Of all Thy glorious works, Most High.
> How lofty art Thou in Thy wondrous might;
> What joy to gaze upon these hosts, to one
> Who feels himself so little, God so great,
> Himself but dust, and the great God his own!
> Oh, when I die, such rapture on me wait!

As regards our subject, Klopstock performed this function—he tuned the strings of feeling for Nature to a higher pitch, thereby excelling all his contemporaries. His poetry always tended to extravagance; but in thought, feeling, and language alike, he was ahead of his time.

The idyllic was now cultivated with increased fervour, especially by the Göttingen Brotherhood of Poets. The artificial and conventional began to wane, and Nature's own voice was heard again. The songs of Claudius were like a breath of spring.[16] His peasant songs have the genuine ring; they are hail-fellow-well-met with Nature. Hebel is the only modern poet like him.

EVENING SONG

> The lovely day-star's run its course . . . .
> Come, mop my face, dear wife,
> And then dish up. . . .
> The silvery moon will look down from his place
> And preside at our meal over dishes and grace.

He hated artificiality :

> Simple joy in Nature, free from artifice, gives as great a pleasure as an honest lover's kiss.

His *Cradle Song to be sung by Moonlight* is delightful in its naive humour (the moon was his special favourite) :

Sleep then, little one. Why dost thou weep ?
Moonlight so tender and quiet so deep,
Quickly and easily cometh thy sleep.
Fond of all little ones is the good moon ;
Girls most of all, but he even loves boys.
Down from up there he sends beautiful toys. . . .
He's old as a raven, he goes everywhere ;
Even when father was young, he was there.

The pearl of his poems is the exquisite *Evening
Song* :

> The moon hath risen on high,
> And in the clear dark sky
> The golden stars all brightly glow ;
> And black and hushed the woods,
> While o'er the fields and floods
> The white mists hover to and fro.
>
> How still the earth, how calm !
> What dear and home-like charm
> From gentle twilight doth she borrow !
> Like to some quiet room,
> Where, wrapt in still soft gloom,
> We sleep away the daylight's sorrow.·

Boie's *Evening Song* is in the same key. None
of the moonshine poets of his day expressed night-
fall like this :

> How still it is ! How soft
> The breezes blow !
> The ime leaves lisp in whisper and echo answers
>   lbw ;
> Scarce audibly the rivulet running amid the flower
> With murmuring ripple laps the edge of yonder
>   mystic bower.
> And e' er darker grows the veil thou weavest o'er the
>   land,
> And ever quieter the hush—a hush as of the grave. . . .
> Listen ! 'tis Night ! she comes, unlighted by a star,
> And with the slow sweep of her heavy wing
> Awes and revives the timid earth.

Bürger sings in praise of idyllic comfort in *The
Village*, and Hoelt'ys mild enthusiasm, touched
with melancholy, turned in the same direction.

> My predilection is for rural poetry and melancholy enthusiasm; all I ask is a hut, a forest, a meadow with a spring in it, and a wife in my hut.

The beginning of his *Country Life* shews that moralizing was still in the air:

Happy the man who has the town escaped!
To him the whistling trees, the murmuring brooks,
The shining pebbles preach
Virtue's and wisdom's lore. . . .
The nightingale on him sings slumber down;
The nightingale rewakes him, fluting sweet,
When shines the lovely red
Of morning through the trees.
Then he admires Thee in the plain, O God!
In the ascending pomp of dawning day,
Thee in Thy glorious sun.
The worm—the budding branch—
Where coolness gushes in the waving branch
Or o'er the flowers streams the fountain, rests,
Inhales the breadth of prime
The gentle airs of eve.
His straw-decked thatch, where doves bask in the
       sun,
And play, and hop, invites to sweeter rest
Than golden halls of state
Or beds of down afford.
To him the plumy people sporting chirp,
Chatter and whistle on his basket perch,
And from his quiet hand
Peck crumbs or peas or grains

His *Winter Song* runs:

Summer joys are o'er,
Flow'rets bloom no more;
Wintry joys are sweeping,
Through the snow-drifts peeping;
Cheerful evergreen
Rarely now is seen.

No more plumèd throng
Charms the woods with song;
Ice-bound trees are glittering,
Merry snow-birds twittering,
Fondly strive to cheer
Scenes so cold and drear.

> Winter, still I see
> Many charms in thee,
> Love thy chilly greeting,
> Snow-storms fiercely beating,
> And the dear delights
> Of the long, long nights.

Hoeltz was the most sentimental of this group; Joh. Heinrich Voss was more robust and cheerful. He put his strength into his longer poems; the lyrics contain a great deal of nonsense. An extract from *Luise* will shew his idyllic taste:

> Wandering thus through blue fields of flax and acres of barley, both paused on the hill-top, which commands such a view of the whole lake, crisped with the soft breath of the zephyr and sparkling in sunshine; fair were the forests of white barked birch beyond, and the fir-trees, lovely the village at the foot half hid by the wood. Lovely Luise had welcomed her parents and shewn them a green mound under an old beech tree, where the prospect was very inviting. 'There we propose,' said she, ' to unpack and to spread the breakfast. Then we'll adjourn to the boat and be rowed for a time on the water,' etc.

We find the same taste, often expressed in a very original way, in both the brothers Stolberg. In Christian Stolberg's *Elegy to Hangwitz*, for instance, another poem has these lines:

> Thither, where 'mong the trees of life,
> Where in celestial bowers
> Under your fig-tree, bowed with fruit
> And warranting repose,
> Under your pine, inviting shady joy,
> Unchanging blooms
> Eternal Spring!

Friedrich Stolberg was a very prophet of Nature; in his ode *Nature* he says:

> He who does not love Nature cannot be my friend.

His prayer may serve as the motto of his day:

> Holy Nature, heavenly fair,
> Lead me with thy parent care;

In thy footsteps let me tread
As a willing child is led.
When with care and grief opprest,
Soft I sink me on thy breast;
On thy peaceful bosom laid,
Grief shall cease, nor care invade.
O congenial power divine,
All my votive soul is thine.
Lead me with thy parent care,
Holy Nature, heavenly fair!

He, too, sang the moon; but Klopstock's influence seems to have carried him to higher flights than his contemporaries. He wrote in fine language of wild scenery, even sea and mountains, which had played no part in German poetry before.

To the Sea

Thou boundless, shining, glorious sea,
With ecstasy I gaze on thee;
Joy, joy to him whose early beam
Kisses thy lip, bright ocean stream.
Thanks for the thousand hours, old sea,
Of sweet communion held with thee;
Oft as I gazed, thy billowy roll
Woke the deep feelings of my soul.

There are beautiful notes, reminding one of Goethe, in his *Unsterbliche Jüngling, Ode to a Mountain Torrent.*

Immortal youth!
Thou streamest forth from rocky caves;
No mortal saw
The cradle of thy might,
No ear has heard
Thy infant stammering in the gushing Spring.
How lovely art thou in thy silver locks!
How dreadful thundering from the echoing crags!
At thy approach
The firwood quakes;
Thou castest down, with root and branch, the fir
Thou seizest on the rock,
And roll'st it scornful like a pebble on.
Thee the sun clothes in dazzling beams of glory,
And paints with colours of the heavenly bow
The clouds that o'er thy dusky cataracts climb.

Why hasten so to the cerulean sea ?
Is not the neighbourhood of heaven good ?
Not grand thy temple of encircling rocks ?
Not fair the forest hanging o'er thy bed ?
Hasten not so to the cerulean sea ;
Youth, thou art here,
Strong as a god,
Free as a god,
Though yonder beckon treacherous calms below,
The wavering lustre of the silent sea,
Now softly silvered by the swimming moon,
Now rosy golden in the western beam ;
Youth, what is silken rest,
And what the smiling of the friendly moon,
Or gold or purple of the evening sun,
To him who feels himself in thraldom's bonds ?
Here thou canst wildly stream
As bids thy heart ;
Below are masters, ever-changeful minds,
Or the dead stillness of the servile main.
Hasten not so to the cerulean sea ;
Youth, thou art here,
Strong as a god,
Free as a god.

Here we have, with all Klopstock's pathos, a love
for the wild and grandiose in Nature, almost unique
in Germany, in this time of idyllic sentimentality.
But the discovery of the beauty of romantic moun-
tain scenery had been made by Rousseau some
time before, for Rousseau, too, was a typical fore-
runner, and his romances fell like a bomb-shell
among all the idyllic pastoral fiction of the day.

CHAPTER XI

THE AWAKENING OF FEELING FOR THE ROMANTIC

ROUSSEAU was one of those rare men who bring about a complete change in the culture of their time by their revolutionary originality. In such beings the world's history, so to speak, begins again. Out of touch with their own day, and opposed to its ruling taste and mode of thought, they are a law unto themselves, and naturally tend to measure all things by themselves, while their too great subjectivity is apt to be increased by a morbid sophistry of passion and the conviction of the prophet.

Of this type, unchecked by a broad sense of humanity, full of subversive wilfulness, and not only untrained in moderation, but degenerating into crass exaggeration, Rousseau was the first example. Hellenism, the Roman Empire, the Renaissance, had only produced forerunners. What in Petrarch was a tendency, became an established condition in Rousseau: the acedia reached its climax. All that went on in his mind was so much grit for his own mill, subject-matter for his observation, and therefore of the greatest value to him. He lived in introspection, a spectator of his own struggles, his own waverings between an ideal of simple duty and the imperious demands of a selfish and sensuous ego. His passion for Nature partially atoned for his unamiable and doubtful character ; he was false in many ways ; but that feeling rang true—it was the best part of him, and of that 'idealism of the heart' whose right of rule he asserted in an age of artificiality and petty formalism. Those were no empty words in his third letter to Malesherbes:

'Which time of my life do you suppose I recall most often and most willingly in my dreams? Not the pleasures of youth; they were too few, too much mixed with bitterness, and they are too far away now. It is the time of my retreat, of my solitary walks—those fast-flying delicious days that I passed all alone by myself, with my good and simple Thérèse, my beloved dog, my old cat, with the wild birds and the roes of the forest, with all Nature and her inconceivable Maker.

'When I got up early to go and watch the sunrise from my garden, when I saw a fine day begin, my first wish was that neither letters nor visitors might come to break its charm. . . .

'Then I would seek out some wild place in the forest, some desert spot where there was nothing to shew the hand of man, and so tell of servitude and rule—some refuge which I could fancy I was the first to discover, and where no importunate third party came between Nature and me. . . .

'The gold broom and the purple heather touched my heart; the majestic trees that shaded me, the delicate shrubs around, the astonishing variety of plants and flowers that I trod under foot, kept me alternately admiring and observing.'

His writings shew that with him return to Nature was no mere theory, but real earnest; they condemned the popular garden-craft and carpet fashions, and set up in their place the rights of the heart, and free enjoyment of Nature in her wild state, undisturbed by the hand of man.

It was Rousseau who first discovered that the Alps were beautiful. But to see this fact in its true light, we must glance back at the opinions of preceding periods.[1]

Though the Alpine countries were the arena of all sorts of enterprise, warlike and peaceful, in the fifteenth century, most of the interest excited by foreign parts was absorbed by the great voyages of discovery; the Alps themselves were almost entirely omitted from the maps.

To be just to the time, it must be conceded that security and comfort in travelling are necessary preliminaries to our modern mountain rapture, and in the Middle Ages these were non-existent. Roads and inns were few; there was danger from robbers as well as weather, so that the prevailing feelings on such journeys were misery and anxiety, not pleasure. Knowledge of science, too, was only just beginning; botany, geology, and geognosy were very slightly diffused; glacier theories were undreamt of. The sight of a familiar scene near the great snow-peaks roused men's admiration, because they were surprised to find it there; this told especially in favour of the idyllic mountain valleys.

Felix Fabri, the preacher monk of Ulm, visited the East in 1480 and 1483, and gave a lifelike description of his journeys through the Alps in his second account. He said² :

'Although the Alps themselves seem dreadful and rigid from the cold of the snow or the heat of the sun, and reach up to the clouds, the valleys below them are pleasant, and as rich and fruitful in all earthly delights as Paradise itself. Many people and animals inhabit them, and almost every metal is dug out of the Alps, especially silver. 'Mid such charms as these men live among the mountains, and Nature blooms as if Venus, Bacchus, and Ceres reigned there. No one who saw the Alps from afar would believe what a delicious Paradise is to be found amid the eternal snow and mountains of perpetual winter and never-melting ice.'

Very limited praise only extended to the valleys !

In the sixteenth century we have the records of

those who crossed the Alps with an army, such as Adam Reissner, the biographer of the Frundsberg, and mention their 'awe' at sight of the valleys, and of those who had travelled to Italy and the East, and congratulated themselves that their troublesome wanderings through the Alps were over. Savants were either very sparing of words about their travels, or else made rugged verses which shewed no trace of mountain inspiration. There were no outbursts of admiration at sight of the great snow-peaks; 'horrible' and 'dreadful' were the current epithets. The æsthetic sense was not sufficiently developed, and discount as we will for the dangers and discomforts of the road, and, as with the earlier travellers to the East, for some lack of power of expression, the fact remains that mountains were not appreciated. The prevalent notion of beautiful scenery was very narrow, and even among cultured people only meant broad, level country.

B. Kiechel[3] (1585) was enthusiastic about 'the beautiful level scenery' of Lichfeld, and found it difficult to breathe among the Alps. Schickhart wrote: 'We were delighted to get away from the horrible tedious mountains,' and has nothing to say of the Brenner Pass except this poor joke: 'It did not burn us much, for what with the ice and very deep snow and horribly cold wind, we found no heat.' The most enthusiastic description is of the Lake of Como, by Paulus Jovius (1552), praising Bellagio.[4] In the seventeenth century there was some admiration for the colossal proportions of the Alps, but only as a foil to the much admired valleys.

J. J. Grasser wrote of Rhœtia[5]: 'There are marble masses projecting, looking like walls and towers in imitation of all sorts of wonderful architecture. The villages lie scattered in the valleys, here and there the ground is most fruitful. There is luxuriance close to barrenness, gracefulness close to dreadfulness, life close to loneliness. The delight of the painter's eye is here, yet Nature excels all the skill of art. The very ravines, tortuous foot-paths, torrents, alternately raging and meagre, the arched bridges, waves on the lakes, varied dress of the fields, the mighty trees, in short, whatever heaven and earth grant to the sight, is an astonishment and a pastime to the enraptured eye of the wanderer.'

But this pastime depended upon the contrast between the charming valleys and the dreadful mountains.

Joseph Furttenbach (1591) writing about the same district of Thusis, described ' the little bridges, under which one hears the Rhine flowing with a great roar,' and sees what a horrible cruel wilderness the place is.'

In Conrad Gessner's *De admiratione Montium* (1541)[6] a passage occurs which shews that even in Switzerland itself in the sixteenth century one voice was found to praise Alpine scenery in a very different way, anticipating Rousseau. ' I have re-solved that so long as God grants me life I will climb some mountains every year, or at least one mountain, partly to learn the mountain flora, partly to strengthen my body and refresh my soul. What a pleasure it is to see the monstrous mountain masses, and lift one's head among the clouds. How it stimulates worship, to be surrounded by the snowy domes, which the Great Architect of the world built up in one long day of creation ! How empty is the life, how mean the striving of those who only crawl about on the earth for gain and home-baked pleasures ! The earthly paradise is closed to them.'

Yet, just as after Rousseau, and even in the nine-teenth century, travellers were to be found who thought the Alps ' dreadful' (I refer to Chateau-briand's ' hideux '), so such praise as this found no echo in its own day.

But with the eighteenth century came a change.

Travelling no longer subserved the one practical end of making acquaintance with the occupations, the morals, the affairs generally, of other peoples ; a new scientific interest arose, geologists and physicists ventured to explore the glaciers and regions of perpetual snow, and first admiration, and then love, supplanted the old feeling of horror.

Modern methods began with Scheuchzer's (1672-1733) *Itinera Alpina.* Every corner of the Alps was explored — the Splugen, Julier, Furka, Gotthard, etc.—and glaciers, avalanches, ores, fossils, plants examined. Haller, as his verses shew, was botanist as well as theologian, historian, and poet ; but he did not appreciate mountain beauty.

Brockes to some extent did. He described the Harz Mountains in the Fourth Book of his *Earthly Pleasure in God* (*Irdisches Vergüngen in Gott*) ; and in his *Observations on the Blankenburg Marble* he said : ' In many parts the rough mountain heights were monstrously beautiful, their size delights and appals us ' ; and wound up a discussion of wild scenery in contrast to cultivated with : ' Ponder this with joy and reverence, my soul. The mountain heights wild and beautiful shew us a picture of earthly disorder.'' It was very long before expressions of horror and fear entirely disappeared from descriptions of the Alps. In Richardson's *Sir Charles Grandison* we read : ' We bid adieu to France and found ourselves in Savoy, equally noted for its poverty and rocky mountains. We had left behind us a blooming Spring, which enlivened with its verdure the trees and hedges on the road we passed, and the meadows already smiled with flowers. . . . Every object which here presents itself is excessively miserable.' Savoy is ' one of the worst countries under Heaven.'

Addison,' on the other hand, wrote of the Alps from Ripaille : ' It was the pleasantest voyage in the world to follow the windings of this river Inn through such a variety of pleasing scenes as the course of it naturally led us. We had sometimes on each side of us a vast extent of naked rocks and mountains, broken into a thousand irregular steps and precipices . . . but, as the materials of a fine landscape are not always the most profitable to the owner of them, we met with but little corn or pasturage,' etc. Lady Mary Wortley Montagu wrote from Lyons, Sept. 25, 1718: ' The prodigious aspect of mountains covered with eternal snow, clouds hanging far below our feet, and the vast cascades tumbling down the rocks with a confused roaring, would have been solemnly entertaining to me, if I had suffered less from the extreme cold that reigns here.'

On the whole, Switzerland was little known at the beginning of the eighteenth century. Many travellers still measured the value of scenery entirely by fertility, like Keyssler,[10] who praised garden-like level country such as that round Mantua, in contrast to the useless wild Tyrolese mountains and the woods of Westphalia; and Lüneburg or Moser,[11] who observed ironically to Abbt (1763), after reading *Emilia* and *La Nouvelle Héloise*: ' The far-famed Alps, about which so much fuss has been made.'

Rousseau was the real exponent of rapture for the high Alps and romantic scenery in general. Isolated voices had expressed some feeling before him, but it was he who deliberately proclaimed it, and gave romantic scenery the first place among the beauties of Nature. He did not, as so many would have it—Du Bois Reymond, for example—discover our modern feeling for Nature; the great men of the Renaissance, even the Hellenic poets, fore-ran him; but he directed it, with feeling itself in general, into new channels.[12]

In French literature he stood alone; the descriptions of landscape before him were either borrowed blossoms of antiquity or sentimental and erotic pastorals. He opened up again for his country the taste for wood and field, sunshine and moonlight, for the idyllic, and, above all, for the sublime, which had been lost under artificiality and false taste.

The primitive freshness, the genuine ring of his enthusiasm for country life, was worth all the laboured pastorals and fables of previous periods of literature.

His *Confessions* opened not only the eyes of France, but the heart.

A Swiss by birth, and living in one of the most beautiful parts of Europe, Rousseau was devotedly fond of his home on the Lake of Geneva. As a boy he loved to leave the city and rove in the country.

He describes how once on a Sunday in 1728 he wandered about, forgetting the time. 'Before me were fields, trees, flowers; the beautiful lake, the hill country, and high mountains unfolded themselves majestically before my eyes. I gloated over the beautiful spectacle while the sun was setting. At last, too late, I saw that the city gates were shut.'

From that time on he felt more drawn to Nature than to men. In the Fourth Book of the *Confessions* he says, speaking of 1732:

'A view of the Lake of Geneva and its beautiful banks has had even in my idea a particular attraction that I cannot describe, not arising merely from the beauty of the prospect, but something, I know not what, more interesting which affects and softens me. Every time I have approached the Vaudois country, I have experienced an impression composed of the remembrance of Mademoiselle de Warens, who was born there; of my father, who lived there; of Mademoiselle de Wulson, who had been my first love; and of several pleasant journeys I had made there in my childhood, mingled with some nameless charm, more powerfully attractive than all the rest. When that ardent desire for a life of happiness and tranquillity (which ever follows me, and for which I was born) inflames my mind, 'tis ever to the country of Vaud, near the lake, on those charming plains, that imagination leads me.   An orchard on the banks of that lake, and no other, is absolutely necessary ; a firm friend, an amiable woman, a cow, and a little boat ; nor could I enjoy perfect happiness on earth without these concomitants. . . .   On my way to Vevey I gave myself up to the soft melancholy . . . I sighed and wept like a child.'

He clung to Nature, and most of all when surrounded by human beings ; a morbid impulse to flee from them was always present as a negative element in the background of his love for her.   His Fifth Reverie, the most beautiful one, shews this.

He had gone to the Peter Island on the Lake of Bienne.   So far as he knew, no other traveller had paid any attention to the place ; but that did not disturb his confidence in his own taste.

'The shores of the Lake of Bienne are wilder and more romantic than those of the Lake of Geneva, because the rocks and woods come nearer to the water ; but they are not less radiant.   With less cultivation and fewer vineyards, towns, and houses, there are more green fields and shady sheltered spots, more contrasts and irregularities.   As there are no good carriage roads on these happy shores, the district is little frequented by travellers ; but it is interesting for the solitary contemplation of those who like to intoxicate themselves at their leisure with Nature's charms, and to retire into a silence unbroken by any sound but the eagle's cry, the intermittent warbling of birds, and the roar of torrents falling from the mountains.'

Here he had a delightful Robinson Crusoe existence.   The only other human beings were the Bernese manager with his family and labourers. He counted his two months among the happiest of his life, and would have liked to stay for ever.

True to his character, he proceeded to analyze the charm of the episode, and decided that it was made up of the *dolce far niente*, solitude, absence of books and writing materials, dealing with simple folk, healthy movement in the open air, field labour, and, above all, intercourse with Nature, both in admiring and studying her. He was seized with a passion for botanizing, and planned a comprehensive Flora Petrinsularis, dividing the whole island into quarters, so that no part might escape notice.

'There is nothing more strange than the ravishment, the ecstasy, I felt at each observation I made upon vegetable structure and organization.

'I would go by myself, throw myself into a boat when the water was calm, and row to the middle of the lake, and then, lying full-length in the boat with my eyes to the sky, I would let myself drift, sometimes for hours, lost in a thousand confused but delicious reveries. . . . Often when the sunset reminded me that it was time to return, I found myself so far from the island that I was forced to pull with all my strength to get back before nightfall. At other times, instead of wandering about the lake, I amused myself by skirting the green shores of the island where the limpid water and cool shade often invited to a bathe. . . . When the lake was too rough for rowing, I would spend the afternoon scouring the island, botanizing right and left. I often sat down to dream at leisure in sunny, lonely nooks, or on the terraces and hillocks, to gaze at the superb ravishing panorama of the lake and its shores—one side crowned by near mountains, the other spread out in rich and fertile plains, across which the eye looked to the more distant boundary of blue mountains. . . . When evening fell, I came down from the higher parts of the mountains and sat by the shore in some hidden spot, and there the sound of the waves and the movements of the water, making me oblivious of all other distraction, would

plunge me into delicious reverie.   The ebb and flow
of the water, and the sound of it, restrained and
yet swelling at intervals, by striking eye and ear
without ceasing, came to the aid of those inner
movements of the mind which reverie destroys,
and sufficed to make me pleasantly conscious of
existence without the trouble of thinking. . . .
There is nothing actual in all this to which the heart
can attach itself ; even in our most intense enjoy-
ment there is scarcely a moment of which the heart
can truly say " I should like it to stay for ever." '

One thinks of Faust : ' O moment ! tarry awhile,
thou art so fair ! '

However, at the close of the Reverie he admits
that he has often had such moments—moments free
from all earthly passion—on the lake and on the
island. His feeling was increased by botanical
knowledge, and later on in life the world of trees
and plants became his one safe refuge when pursued
by delusions of persecution.

The Seventh Reverie has a touching account of
his pleasure in botany, of the effect of ' earth in her
wedding-dress, the only scene in the world of which
eyes and heart never weary,' the intoxicating sense
that he was part of a great system in which individual
detail disappears, and he only sees and hears the
whole.

' Shunning men, seeking solitude, no longer
dreaming, still less thinking, I began to concern
myself with all my surroundings, giving the prefer-
ence to my favourites . . . brilliant flowers, emerald
meadows, fresh shade, streams, thickets, green turf,
these purified my imagination. . . . Attracted by
the pleasant objects around, I note them, study
them, and finally learn to classify them, and so
become at one stroke as much of a botanist as one
need be when one only studies Nature to find ever
new reasons for loving her.

' The plants seem sown in profusion over the

earth like the stars in the sky, to invite man, through pleasure and curiosity, to study them ; but the stars are far off ; they require preliminary knowledge . . . while plants grow under our very feet— lie, so to speak, in our very hands.'

He had a peaceful sense of being free from his enemies when he was pursuing his botany in the woods. He described one never-to-be-forgotten' ramble when he lost himself in a dense thicket close to a dizzy precipice, where, save for some rare birds, he was quite alone. He was just feeling the pride of a Columbus in the discovery of new ground, when his eye fell upon a manufactory not far off. His first feeling was a flash of delight at finding himself again among men ; but this gave way to the more lasting and painful one, that even among the Alps there was no escape from his tormentors.

Years later, when he knew that he would never revisit the spot, the leaves in his herbarium would carry him back to it in memory.

So strong a personal attachment to Nature, solitude, and retirement had not been known before ; but it was thrown into this high relief by the morbid dread of man and hatred of culture, which formed a constant dark background to his mind. It was a state of mind which naturally led to intense dislike of formal French gardens and open admiration of the English park. He rejected all the garnish of gardencraft, even grafted roses and fruit trees, and only admitted indigenous plants which grew outdoors.[15] It is greatly due to his feeling for English Park style that a healthier garden-craft gained ground in Germany as well as France. The foremost maxim of his philosophy and teaching, that everything is good as it comes from the bosom of mother Nature, or rather from the hand of God, and that man and his culture are responsible for all the evil, worked out in his attitude towards Nature.

He placed her upon a pedestal, worshipping her,

and the Creator through her, and this made him the first to recognize the fact that study of Nature, especially of botany, should be an important factor in the education of children.

His *Confessions*, the truest photographs of a human character in existence, shew at once the keenest introspection and intense love for Nature. No one before Rousseau had been so aware of his own individuality—that is, of himself, as a being—who in this particular state only exists once, and has therefore not only relative but absolute value. He gave this peculiarity its full value, studying it as a thing outside himself, of which every detail was important, watching with great interest his own change of moods, the fluctuations of that double self which now lifted him to the ideal, now cast him down to the lowest and commonest. His relation to Nature was the best thing about him, and when he was happy, as he was for the first time in the society of Mademoiselle de Warens, Nature seemed lovelier than ever.

The scattered passages about Nature in the *Confessions* have a youthful freshness:

'The appearance of Aurora seemed so delightful one morning, that, putting on my clothes, I hastened into the country to see the rising of the sun. I enjoyed that pleasure to its utmost extent. It was one week after midsummer : the earth was covered with verdure and flowers ; the nightingales, whose soft warblings were almost over, seemed to vie with each other, and, in concert with birds of various kinds, to bid adieu to spring and hail the approach of a beautiful summer's day.'

He loved rambling over hill and dale, even by night ; thus, when he was at Lyons :

'It had been a very hot day, the evening was delightful, the dew moistened the parched grass, no wind was stirring ; the air was fresh without chilliness, the setting sun had tinged the clouds with a beautiful crimson, which was again reflected by the water, and the trees bordering the terrace were filled with nightingales that were constantly answering each other's songs. I walked along in a kind of ecstasy, surrendering my heart and senses to the enjoyment of so many delights, and sighing only from regret at enjoying them alone. Absorbed in this pleasing reverie, I lengthened my walk till it grew very late, without perceiving I was tired. At length I threw myself on the steps of a kind of niche in a terrace wall. How charming was that couch ! The trees formed a stately canopy, a nightingale sat directly over me, and with his soft notes lulled me to rest. How delicious my repose ! my awakening more so. It was broad day ; on opening my eyes, I saw the water, the verdure, and an adorable landscape before me.'

At the end of the Fourth Book he states his idea of beautiful scenery :

' I love to walk at my ease and stop at leisure . . . travelling on foot in a fine country with fine weather ı . . and having an agreeable object to terminate my journey. It is already understood what I mean by a fine country ; never can a flat one, though ever so beautiful, appear such to my eyes. I must have torrents, fir trees, black woods, mountains to climb or descend, and rugged roads with precipices on either side to alarm me. I experienced this pleasure to its utmost extent as I approached Chambéry, not far from a mountain road called the Pas d'Échelle. Above the main road, hewn through the solid rock, a small river runs and rushes into fearful chasms, which it appears to have been millions of ages in forming. The road has been hedged by a parapet to prevent accidents, and I was thus enabled to contemplate the whole descent and gain vertigoes at pleasure, for a great part of my amusement in these steep rocks lies in their causing a giddiness and swimming in my head, which I am particularly fond of, provided I am in safety. Leaning therefore on the parapet, I remained whole hours, catching from time to time a glance of the froth and blue water whose rushing caught my ear, mingled with the cries of ravens and other birds of prey that flew from rock to rock and bush to bush at 600 feet below me.'

His preference was for the wild and sublime, and he was glad that this was not a popular taste; but he could write glowing descriptions of more idyllic scenery and of village life.

He said of a day at the Charmettes, a property near Chambéry, with his beloved friend Madame de Warens, at the end of 1736 :

' I arose with the sun and was happy; I walked and was happy; I saw Madame de Warens and was happy ; I quitted her and still was happy. Whether I rambled through the woods, over the hills, or strolled along the valley; read, was idle, worked in the garden, or gathered fruits, happiness continually accompanied me.'

He offered his morning prayer from a hill-top, and in the evening, before he left, stooped to kiss the ground and the trees, gazing till they were out of sight at the places where he had been so happy.

At the Hermitage with Thérèse there was a similar idyll.

The most epoch - making event in European feeling for Nature was the appearance of *La Nouvelle Héloise* (1761). The book overflows with Rousseau's raptures about the Lake of Geneva. St Preux says :

' The nearer I drew to Switzerland, the greater were my emotions. That instant in which I discovered the Lake of Geneva from the heights of Jura, was a moment of ecstasy and rapture. The sight of my country, my beloved country, where a deluge of pleasure had overflowed my heart; the pure and wholesome air of the Alps, the gentle breeze of the country, more sweet than the perfumes of the East; that rich and fertile spot, that unrivalled landscape, the most beautiful that ever struck the eye of man, that delightful abode, to which I found nothing comparable in the vast tour of the globe; the mildness of the season, the serenity of the climate, a thousand pleasing recollections which recalled to my mind the pleasures I had enjoyed;—all these circumstances together threw me into a kind of transport which I cannot describe, and seemed to collect the enjoyment of my whole life into one happy moment.'

La Nouvelle Héloise shewed the world three things in quite a new light: the inner consciousness which was determined to give feeling its rights again, though well aware that 'a feeling heart is an unhappy gift from heaven'; the taste for solitude, 'all noble passions are formed in solitude'; and closely bound up with these, the love of romantic scenery, which it described for the first time in glowing language.

Such expressions as these of St Preux were unheard of at that time: 'I shall do my best to be free quickly, and able to wander at my ease in the wild places that to my mind make the charm of this country.' 'I am of opinion that this unfrequented country deserves the attention of speculative curiosity, and that it wants nothing to excite admiration but a skilful spectator'; and 'Nature seems desirous of hiding her real charms from the sight of men, because they are too little sensible of them, and disfigure them when within their reach; she flies from public places; it is on the tops of mountains, in the midst of forests, on desert islands, that she displays her most affecting charms.'

Rousseau certainly announced his views with all the fervour of a prophet proclaiming a newly-discovered truth. The sketch St Preux gives of the country that 'deserved a year's study,' in the twenty-third letter to Julia, is very poetic. He is ascending a rocky path when a new view breaks upon him :

> One moment I beheld stupendous rocks hanging ruinous over my head ; the next, I was enveloped in a drizzling cloud, which arose from a vast cascade that, dashing, thundered against the rocks below my feet. On one side a perpetual torrent opened to my view a yawning abyss, which my eyes could hardly fathom with safety ; sometimes I was lost in the obscurity of a hanging wood, and then was greatly astonished with the sudden opening of a flowery plain.

He was always charmed by ' a surprising mixture of wild and cultivated Nature ' :

> Here Nature seems to have a singular pleasure in acting contradictory to herself, so different does she appear in the same place in different aspects. Towards the east, the flowers of spring ; to the south, the flowers of autumn ; and northwards, the ice of winter. Add to that the illusions of vision, the tops of the mountains variously illumined, the harmonious mixture of light and shade. . . .

After climbing, he reflects :

> Upon the top of mountains, the air being subtle and pure, we respire with greater freedom, our bodies are more active, our minds more serene, our pleasures less ardent, and our passions much more moderate. Our meditations acquire a degree of sublimity from the grandeur of the objects around us. It seems as if, being lifted above all human society, we had left every low terrestrial sentiment behind.

He can find no words to express ' the amazing variety, magnitude, and beauty of a thousand stupendous objects, the pleasure of gazing at an entire new scene . . . and beholding, as it were, another Nature and a new world.'

Earlier in the year he wrote his letters to Julia upon a block of stone in his favourite wild spot, and the wintry landscape harmonized with his feelings :

> I run to and fro, climb the rocks and explore my whole district, and find everything as horrible without

as I experienced it within. There is no longer any verdure to be seen, the grass is yellow and withered, the trees are stripped of their foliage, and the north-east blast heaps snow and ice around me. In short, the whole face of Nature appears as decayed to my outward senses as I myself from within am dead to hope and joy.

Julia, too, is enthusiastic about places, where ' no vestiges are seen of human toil, no appearance of studied and laborious art; every object presents only a view of the tender care of Nature, our common mother.'

When St Preux knows that she returns his love, his sympathy for Nature overflows:

I find the country more delightful, the verdure fresher and livelier, the air more temperate, and the sky more serene than ever I did before; even the feathered songsters seem to tune their tender throats with more harmony and pleasure; the murmuring rills invite to love-inspiring dalliance, while the blossoms of the vine regale me from afar with the choicest perfumes ... let us animate all Nature, which is absolutely dead without the genial warmth of love.

St Preux escorts his old love to the Meillerie, and it was with his description of this that Rousseau unrolled the full charm of mountain scenery, and opened the eyes of his readers to see it.

They were climbing a mountain top on the Savoy side of the lake:

This solitary spot formed a wild and desert nook, but full of those sorts of beauties which are only agreeable to susceptible minds, and appear horrible to others. A torrent, occasioned by the melting of the snow, rolled in a muddy stream within twenty paces of us, and carried dust, sand, and stones along with it, not without considerable noise. Behind us, a chain of inaccessible rocks divided the place where we stood from that part of the Alps which they call the Ice house. . . . Forests of gloomy fir trees afforded us a melancholy shade on the right, while on the left was a large wood of oak, beyond which the torrent issued; and beneath, that vast body of water which the lake forms in the bay of the Alps, parted us from the rich coast of the Pays de Vaud, crowning the whole landscape with the top of the majestic Jura.

Rousseau's influence upon feeling in general, and feeling for Nature in particular, was an extraordinary one, widening and deepening at once.

By his strong personal impulse he impelled it into more natural paths, and at the same time he discovered the power of the mountains.

He brought to flower the germ which had lain dormant in Hellenism and the Renaissance; and although his readers imbibed a sickly strain of morbid sentimentality with this passion for the new region of feeling, the total effect of his individuality and his idealism was to intensify their love for Nature. His feelings woke the liveliest echo, and it was not France alone who profited by the lessons he taught.

He was no mountaineer himself, but he pointed out the way, and others soon followed it. Saussure began his climbing in 1760, exploring the Alps with the indomitable spirit of the discoverer and the scientist's craving for truth. He ascended Mont Blanc in 1787, and only too soon the valleys of Chamounix filled with tourists and speculators. One of the first results of Rousseau's imposing descriptions of scenery was to rouse the most ardent of French romance writers, Bernardin de St Pierre; and his writings, especially his beautiful pictures of the Ile de France, followed hard in the wake of *La Nouvelle Héloïse*.

In *Paul and Virginia* vivid descriptions of Nature were interwoven with an idyllic Robinson Crusoe romance:

> Within this enclosure reigns the most profound silence. The waters, the air, all the elements are at peace. Scarcely does the echo repeat the whispers of the palm trees spreading their broad leaves, the long points of which are gently agitated by the winds. A soft light illumines the bottom of this deep valley,

on which the sun shines only at noon. But even at
break of day the rays of light are thrown on the
surrounding rocks, and their sharp peaks, rising above
the shadows of the mountain, appear like tints of gold
and purple gleaming upon the azure sky.

Like Rousseau, St Pierre held that ‘to take
refuge in the wildest and most desert places is an
instinct common to all feeling and suffering beings,
as if rocks were ramparts against misfortune, and
Nature’s calm could appease the sorrows of the
soul’[14]; but he differed in caring for Nature far more
for her own sake, and not in opposition to culture and
a detested world. He wrote too, not as a philo-
sopher proclaiming a new gospel, but as a poet[15];
the poetry of Nature had been revealed to French
literature.

St Pierre drew the beauty of the tropics in a poem,
and George Forster’s *Voyage round the World*[16]
shewed how quickly Rousseau’s influence told upon
travels. It was a far cry from the Crusaders and
discoverers to the highly-cultured Forster, alive to
everything that was good and beautiful, and able
to express it. He was the first to describe countries
and peoples from both the scientific and artistic
standpoint—a style of writing which Humboldt per-
fected, and some later writers, Haeckel, for example,
in *Indischen Briefen*, have carried on with success.

To quote Forster :

> The town of Santa Cruz in Madeira was abreast of
> us at six in the afternoon. The mountains are here
> intersected by numerous deep glens and valleys.
> On the sloping ground we observed several country
> houses pleasantly situated amidst surrounding vine-
> yards and lofty cypresses, which gave the country
> altogether a romantic appearance. Early on the 29th
> we were agreeably surprised with the picturesque
> appearance of the city of Funchal. . . .

In October 1772, off South Africa :

> The night was scarcely begun when the water all
> round us afforded the most grand and astonishing sight

that can be imagined.   As far as we could see, the whole ocean seemed to be in a blaze.   Every breaking wave had its summit illuminated by a light similar to that of phosphorus, and the sides of the vessel, coming in contact with the sea, were strongly marked by a luminous line. . . . There was a singularity and a grandeur in the display of this phenomenon which could not fail of giving occupation to the mind, and striking it with a reverential awe, due to omnipotence.

The ocean was covered to a great extent with myriads of animalcules ; these little beings, organized, alive, endowed with locomotive power, a quality of shining whenever they please, of illuminating every body with which they come in contact . . . all these ideas crowded upon us, and bade us admire the Creator, even in His minutest works. . . . I hope I shall not have formed too favourable an opinion of my readers, if I expect that the generality will sympathize with me in these feelings.

In Dusky Bay :

We glided along by insensible degrees, wafted by light airs past numerous rocky islands, each of which was covered with wood and shrubberies, where numerous evergreens were sweetly contrasted and mingled with the various shades of autumnal yellow.   Flocks of aquatic birds enlivened the rocky shores, and the whole country resounded with the wild notes of the feathered tribe. . . . The view of rude sceneries in the style of Rosa, of antediluvian forests which clothed the rock, and of numerous rills of water which everywhere rolled down the steep declivity, altogether conspired to complete our joy.

Cascade Cove in New Zealand :

This waterfall at a distance of a mile and a half seems to be but inconsiderable on account of its great elevation ; but, after climbing about 200 yards upwards, we . . . found a view of great beauty and grandeur before us.   The first object which strikes the beholder is a clear column of water eight or ten yards in circumference, which is projected with great impetuosity from the perpendicular rock at the height of 100 yards.   Nearly at the fourth part of the whole height this column meeting a part of the same rock, which now acquires a little inclination, spreads on its broad back into a limpid sheet of about twenty-five yards in width. Here its surface is curled, and dashes upon every little eminence in its rapid descent, till it is all collected in a fine basin about sixty yards in circuit, included on three sides by the natural walls of the rocky chasm, and in front by huge masses of stone irregularly piled above each other. Between them the stream finds its way, and runs foaming with the greatest rapidity along the slope of the hill to the sea. The whole neighbourhood of the cascade . . . is filled with a steam or watery vapour. . . . We . . . were struck with the sight of a most beautiful rainbow of a perfectly circular form, produced by the meridian rays of the sun refracted in the vapour of the cascade.

The scenery on the left consists of steep brown rocks fringed on the summits with overhanging shrubs and trees; the enchanting melody of various birds resounded on all sides, and completed the beauty of this wild and romantic spot.

He described: ' A waterspout, a phenomenon which carried so much terrific majesty in it, and connected, as it were, the sea with the clouds, made our oldest mariners uneasy and at a loss how to behave.'

He begins his diary of August 1773 with O'Taheite:

It was one of those beautiful mornings which the poets of all nations have attempted to describe, when we saw the isle of O'Taheite within two miles before us. The east wind, which had carried us so far, was entirely vanished, and a faint breeze only wafted a delicious perfume from the land, and curled the surface of the sea. The mountains, clothed with forests, rose majestic in various spiry forms, on which we already perceived the light of the rising sun . . . everything seemed as yet asleep; the morning scarce dawned, and a peaceful shade still rested on the landscape. . . .

This spot was one of the most beautiful I had ever seen, and could not fail of bringing to remembrance the most fanciful descriptions of poets, which it eclipsed in beauty; we had a prospect of the plain below us, and of the sea beyond it. In the shade of trees, whose branches hung over the water, we enjoyed

> a pleasant gale, which softened the heat of the day;
> and, amidst the solemn uniform noise of the waterfall,
> which was but seldom interrupted by the whistling of
> birds, we sat down. . . .
>
> We could have been well pleased to have passed
> the whole day in this retirement . . . however, feast-
> ing our eyes once more with the romantic scenery, we
> returned to the plain.

It was such descriptions as these which stimu-
lated Humboldt. There is a breath of poetry in
his writings; his *Views of Nature* and *Cosmos* give
ample proof that love of Nature and knowledge of
Nature can condition and deepen each other.

It is not surprising that in the flood of scientific
'Travels' which followed, especially in imitation of
Forster, there were some that laid claim to a wonder-
ful grade of feeling. For example, the description of
a day at the Equator by von Spix and v. Martius
in their Travels in Brazil in 1817 to 1820:

> In these seas the sun rises from the ocean with great
> splendour, and gilds the clouds accumulated in the
> horizon, which in grand and various groups seem to
> present to the eye of the spectator continents with
> high mountains and valleys, with volcanoes and seas,
> mythological and other strange creations of fancy.
> The lamp of day gradually rises in the transparent
> blue sky; the damp grey fogs subside; the sea is calm
> or gently rises and falls, with a surface smooth as a
> mirror, in a regular motion. At noon a pale, faintly
> shining cloud rises, the herald of a sudden tempest,
> which at once disturbs the tranquillity of the sea.
> Thunder and lightning seem as if they would split our
> planet; but a heavy rain of a salt taste, pouring down
> in the midst of roaring whirlwinds, puts an end to
> the raging of the elements, and several semi-circular
> rainbows, extended over the ocean like gay triumphal
> arches, announce the peaceful termination of the great
> natural phenomenon. As soon as the air and sea have
> recovered their equilibrium, the sky again shews its
> transparent azure. . . . As the sun gradually sinks
> in the clouded horizon, the sea and sky assume a
> new dress, which is beyond description sublime and
> magnificent. The most brilliant red, yellow, violet, in

infinite shades and contrasts, are poured out in pro-
fusion over the azure of the firmament, and are reflected
in still gayer variety from the surface of the water.
The day departs amid continued lightning on the dusky
horizon, while the moon in silent majesty rises from
the unbounded ocean into the cloudless upper regions.
Variable winds cool the atmosphere ; numerous falling
stars, coming particularly from the south, shed a magic
light ; the dark - blue firmament, reflected with the
constellations on the untroubled bosom of the water,
represents the image of the wholly starry hemisphere ;
and the ocean, agitated even by the faintest breeze
of the night, is changed into a sea of waving fire. . . .
The variety of the light and foliage of the trees, which
is seen in the forests, on the slopes of the mountains :
the blending of the most diverse colours, and the dark
azure and transparency of the sky, impart to the land-
scapes of the tropical countries a charm to which even
the pencil of a Salvator Rosa and a Claude cannot do
justice. . . .

Except at noon, when all living creatures in the torrid
zone seek shade and repose, and when a solemn silence
is diffused over the scene, illumined by the dazzling
beams of the sun, every hour of the day calls into
action another race of animals. . . . When the sun
goes down, most of the animals retire to rest . . .
myriads of luminous beetles now begin to fly about
like *ignes fatui*, and the blood-sucking bats hover like
phantoms in the profound darkness of the night. . . .
The traveller does not here meet with the impressions
of those sublime and rugged high Alps of Europe, nor,
on the other hand, those of a meaner nature ; but the
character of these landscapes combines grandeur with
simplicity and softness. . . .

He who has not personally experienced the enchant-
ment of tranquil moonlight nights in these happy
latitudes can never be inspired, even by the most
faithful description, with those feelings which scenes
of such wondrous beauty excite in the mind of the
beholder.

A delicate transparent mist hangs over the country,
the moon shines brightly amid heavy and singularly
grouped clouds, the outlines of the objects illuminated
by it are clear and well defined, while a magic twilight
seems to remove from the eye those which are in
shade. Scarce a breath of air is stirring, and the
neighbouring mimosas, that have folded up their leaves
to sleep, stand motionless beside the dark crowns of

the manga, the jaca, and the ethereal jambos; or
sometimes a sudden wind arises and the juiceless leaves
of the acaju rustle, the richly flowered grumijama
and pitanga let drop a fragrant shower of snow-white
blossoms; the crowns of the majestic palms wave
slowly over the silent roof which they overshade, like
a symbol of peace and tranquillity.

Shrill cries of the cicada, the grasshopper, and tree
frog make an incessant hum, and produce by their
monotony a pleasing melancholy. . . . Every half-hour
different balsamic odours fill the air, and other flowers
alternately unfold their leaves to the night. . . .
While the silent vegetable world, illuminated by scores
of fireflies as by a thousand moving stars, charms the
night by its delicate effluvia, brilliant lightnings play
incessantly on the horizon, and elevate the mind in
joyful admiration to the stars, which, glowing in solemn
silence in the firmament above the continent and ocean,
fill the soul with a presentiment of still sublimer
wonders.

Travels by sea were described at much greater
length and with much more effusion than travels
by land; one might infer from the silence of the
people who moved about in Europe in the eight-
eenth century, that no love of Nature existed. The
extreme discomfort of the road up to a hundred
years ago may account for this silence within
Germany.

Lady Mary Wortley Montagu wrote in 1716 of
Saxon Switzerland :

We passed by moonshine the frightful precipices
that divide Bohemia from Saxony, at the bottom of
which runs the river Elbe . . . in many places the
road is so narrow that I could not discern an inch of
space between the wheels and the precipice. . . .

and her husband declared that

he had passed the Alps five times in different places,
without having gone a road so dangerous.

Scherr relates that in the late autumn of 1721
a citizen of Schwabisch-Gmünd travelled to Ell-
wangen, a distance of eight hours' posting.

Before starting, he had a mass performed in St John's Church ' for the safe conclusion of the coming journey.' He set off one Monday with his wife and a maid in a two - horse vehicle called a small tilt waggon (*Planwägelchen*), but in less than an hour the wheels stuck in mud, and the whole party had to get out and push the carriage, up to their knees in filth. In the middle of the village of Boebingen the driver inadvertently drove the front left wheel into a manure hole, the carriage was overturned, and the lady of the party had her nose and cheek badly grazed by the iron hoops.

From Moeggelingen to Aalen they were obliged to use three horses, and yet it took fully six hours, so that they were obliged to spend the night there. Next morning they set off early, and reached the village of Hofen by mid - day without accidents. Here for a time the travelling ceased, for a hundred paces beyond the village the carriage fell into a puddle, and they were all terribly soiled; the maid's right shoulder was dislocated, and the manservant's hand injured. The axle of one of the wheels was broken, and a horse completely lamed in the left forefoot. They had to put up a second time for the night, leave horses, carriage, man, and maid in Hofen, and hire a rack waggon, in which at last, pitifully shaken, they reached the gates of Ellwangen on Wednesday at vesper bells.

When Eva König, Lessing's *fiancée*, was on her way from Brunswick to Nuremberg in 1772, she wrote to him from Rattelsdorf (two miles north of Bamberg), on February 28th, as follows :

> You will certainly never in your life have heard of a village called Rattelsdorf ? We have been in it already twenty-four hours, and who knows if we shall not have to stay four times as long ! It depends on the Maine, whether it falls or not; as it is now, one could not cross it, even if one dared to. I have never in my life met with so many hindrances, so many dangers and hardships, as on this journey. I can

hardly think of any misfortunes which we have not already had.

She goes on to describe that in thirty-eight hours two axles and two poles had been broken, the horses had bolted with them, one horse had fallen and died, and so on; on March 2nd they were still prisoners in the wretched village.

In 1750 a day's journey was still reckoned at five miles, two hours to the mile; and when in July 1750 Klopstock travelled with Gleim from Halberstadt to Magdeburg in a light carriage drawn by four horses, at the rate of six miles in six hours, he thought this speed remarkable enough to merit comparison with the racing in the Olympian games. People of any pretensions shunned the discomforts of travelling on foot—the bad roads, the insecurity, the dirty inns, and the rough treatment in them; to walk abroad in good clothes and admire the scenery was an unknown thing. (G. Freytag.)

It was only after the widening of thoroughfares, the invention of steamboats (the first was on the Weser 1827) and railways (1835), that travelling became commoner and more popular, and feeling for Nature was thereby increased.

After the Swiss Alps had been discovered for them, people began to feel interest in their native mountains; Zimmermann led the way with his observations on a journey in the Harz 1775, and Gatterer in 1785 published *A Guide to Travelling in the Harz* in five volumes.

In 1806 appeared Nicolas's *Guide to Switzerland*, in 1777 J. T. Volkmar's *Journey to the Riesengebirge*, and before long each little country and province, be it Weimar, Mecklenburg, or the Mark, had discovered a Switzerland within its own boundaries, with mountains as much like the Swiss Alps as a charming little girl is like a giant.

It was the opening of men's eyes to the charms of romantic scenery at home.

The Isle of Rügen too, Swedish at that time, with its striking contrasts of deep blue bays and inlets, chalk rocks and beech woods, came into fashion with lovers of Nature, especially after the road from Sagard to Stubbenkamer had been improved "—so much so, in fact, that in 1805 Grümbke was complaining that many people only went there to feast, not to enjoy the scene:

> You know I am no foe to pleasure, and appreciate my food and drink after physical exertion as much as any one ; but it is desecration to make that the main object here. In this dreadfully beautiful wilderness, under these green corridors of beeches, on the battlements of this great dazzling temple, before this huge azure mirror of the sea, only high and serious thoughts should find a place—the whole scene, stamped as it is with majesty and mystery, seems designed to attract the mind to the hidden life of the unending world around it. For this, solitude and rest are necessary conditions, hence one must visit Stubbenkamer either alone or with intimate and congenial friends.

CHAPTER XII

THE UNIVERSAL PANTHEISTIC FEELING OF MODERN TIMES

THE eighteenth century, so proudly distinguished as the century of Frederic the Great and Maria Theresa, Kant and Lessing, Rousseau and Voltaire, the age of enlightenment, and, above all, of the Revolution, was the most sentimental period in history. Its feeling for Nature bore the same stamp. Many of the Anacreontists and Göttingen poets, as well as Klopstock, shewed genuine enthusiasm ; but their horizon was narrow, and though F. Stolberg sang of the sea and his native mountains, most of them only rang the changes on moonlight and star-light, pastoral idylls, the joys of spring, and winter excursions on the ice. Even Rousseau, the prophet of high mountains, was the child of the same senti-mental, self-adoring time ; a morbid strain, call it misanthropy, melancholy, what you will, underlay all his passion for Nature. It was Goethe who dissolved the spell which lay over the world, and, although born into the days of beautiful souls, moonshine poets, seraphic heaven stormers, pastoral poems, and *La Nouvelle Héloise*, ennobled and puri-fied the tone of the day and freed it from convention !

It was by dint of his genius for expression, the gift of finding the one right word, that he became the world's greatest lyrist : what he felt became a poem, what he saw a picture.

To see and to fashion into poetry were one with

him, whereas his predecessors had called out the
whole artillery of Olympus—nymphs, Oreads, Chloe,
Phyllis, Damon, Aurora, Echo, and Zephyr—even
the still heavier ordnance of the old Teutonic
gods and half-gods, only to repeat stereotyped ideas,
and produce descriptions of scenery, without lyric
thought and feeling.

But Goethe's genius passed through very evident
stages of development, and found forerunners in
Lessing and Herder.

Lessing's mind was didactic and critical, not lyric,
so that his importance here is a negative one. In
laying down the limits of poetry and painting in
Laocoon, he attacked the error of his day which
used poetry for pictures, debasing it to mere
descriptions of seasons, places, plants, etc.

He was dealing with fundamental principles when
he said :

> Simonides called painting dumb poetry, and poetry
> speaking painting ; but . . . many modern critics have
> drawn the crudest conclusions possible from this agree-
> ment between painting and poetry. At one time they
> confine poetry within the narrow limits of painting,
> and at another allow painting to fill the whole wide
> sphere of poetry. . . . This fault-finding criticism has
> partially misled the virtuosos themselves. In poetry
> a fondness for description, and in painting a fancy
> for allegory, has arisen from the desire to make the one
> a speaking picture without really knowing what it can
> and ought to paint, and the other a dumb poem without
> having considered in how far painting can express
> universal ideas without abandoning its proper sphere
> and degenerating into an arbitrary method of writing.
> . . . Since the artist can use but a single moment
> of ever-changing Nature, and the painter must further
> confine his study of this one moment to a single point
> of view, while their works are made not simply to be
> looked at, but to be contemplated long and often,
> evidently the most fruitful moment and the most fruit-
> ful aspect must be chosen. Now that only is fruitful
> which allows free play to the imagination. The more
> we see, the more we must be able to imagine ; and the
> more we imagine, the more we must think we see.

And against descriptive poetry he said :

> When a poetaster, says Horace, can do nothing else,
> he falls to describing a grove, an altar, a brook winding
> through pleasant meadows, a rushing river, or a rain-
> bow. Pope expressly enjoined upon every one who
> would not prove himself unworthy the name of poet, to
> abandon as early as possible this fondness for descrip-
> tion. A merely descriptive poem he declared to be a
> feast made up of sauces.

Acute as his distinction was between poetry as
the representative art of actions in time, and paint-
ing as the representative art of bodies in space, he
did not give due value to lyric feeling or landscape
painting.[1] They belong to a region in which his
sharp, critical acumen was not at home.

But his discussions established the position that
external objects of any sort, including Nature in all
her various shapes, are not proper subjects for
poetry when taken as Thomson, Brockes, and Haller
took them, by themselves alone, but must first be
imbued with human feeling. And the same holds
good of landscape painting. Goethe's lyrics are
the most perfect examples of this blending of the
outer and inner world.

Lessing's criticisms had a salutary, emancipating
effect upon prevalent taste ; but a more positive
influence came into play through Herder's warm
predilection for the popular songs, which had been
so long neglected, and for all that rises, as in the
Psalms, Homer, Shakespeare, Ossian, from primitive
sources of feeling, and finds spontaneous expression
in poetry. The effect of his pioneering was marked,
especially upon Goethe. Herder understood the
revulsion of feeling from the unnatural restraint
of the Pigtail period, and while holding up the
mirror to his own day, he at the same time led its
taste and the expression of it towards what was
simple and natural, by disclosing the treasures
which lay hidden in the poetry of the people. The
lyric was freed from the artificiality and convention

which had so long ruled it, and although he did
not carry out his plan of a history of poetry, his
collections and his profound remarks upon them
were of great service, sowing a seed that bore fruit
in succeeding days.

The popular songs to him were children of the
same mother as the plants and flowers. ' All the songs
of such unlettered folk,' [2] he said, ' weave a living
world around existing objects, actions, and events.
How rich and manifold they all become ! And
the eye can actually see them, the mind realize
them ; they are set in motion. The different parts
of the song are no more connected together than the
trees and bushes in a wood, the rocks in a desert,
or the scenes depicted.' In another place [3] he put
the history of feeling for Nature very tersely :
' There is no doubt that the spirit of man is made
gentler by studying Nature. What did the classics
aim at in their Georgics, but under various shapes
to make man more humane and raise him gradually
to order, industry, and prosperity, and to the power
to observe Nature ? . . .' Hence, when poetry re-
vived in the Middle Ages, she soon recollected
the true land of her birth among the plants and
flowers. The Provençal and the romantic poets
loved the same descriptions. Spenser, for instance,
has charming stanzas about beautiful wilds with
their streams and flowers ; Cowley's six books on
plants, vegetables, and trees are written with extra-
ordinary affection and a superfluity of imagination ;
and of our old Brockes, Gessner says : ' He observed
Nature's many beauties down to their finest
minutiæ, the smallest things move his tender feel-
ings ; a dewdrop on a blade of grass in the
sunshine inspires him. His scenes are often too
laboured, too wide in scope, but still his poems are
a storehouse of pictures direct from Nature. Haller's
Alps, Kleist's poems and Gessner's, Thomson's
Seasons, speak for themselves.'

He delighted in Shaftesbury's praises of Nature as the good and beautiful in the *Moralists*, and translated it[4]; in fact, in Herder we have already an æsthetic cult of the beauties of Nature.

After the moral disquisitions of Pope, Addison, Shaftesbury, etc., Nature's influence on man, moral and æsthetic, became, as we have already seen, a favourite theme in Germany too, both in pious and rationalistic circles[5]; but there are few traces of any æsthetic analysis.

The most important one was Kant's, in his *Observations on the Beautiful and Sublime* in 1764. He distinguished, in the finer feeling for Nature, a feeling for the sublime and a feeling for the beautiful.

> Both touch us pleasantly, but in different ways. The sight of a mountain with a snowy peak reaching above the clouds, the account of a storm . . . these excite pleasure, but mixed with awe; while flowery meadows, valleys with winding streams and covered by browsing herds, a description of Elysium, . . . also cause pleasant feelings, but of a gay and radiant kind. To appreciate the first sensations adequately, we must have a feeling for the sublime; to appreciate the second, a feeling for the beautiful.

He mentioned tall oaks, lonely shades in consecrated groves, and night-time, as sublime; day, beds of flowers, low hedges, and trees cut into shapes, as beautiful.

> Minds which possess the feeling for the sublime are inclined to lofty thoughts of friendship, scorn of the world, eternity, by the quiet stillness of a summer evening, when the twinkling starlight breaks the darkness. The light of day impels to activity and cheerfulness. The sublime soothes, the beautiful stimulates.

He goes on to subdivide the sublime :

> This feeling is sometimes accompanied by horror or by dejection, sometimes merely by quiet admiration, at other times by a sense of wide-spread beauty. I will call the first the terrible, the second the noble, the third the splendid sublime.

> Profound solitude is sublime, but in a terrible way. This is why great deserts, like the Desert of Gamo in Tartary, have always been the supposed abode of fearful shades, hobgoblins, and ghostly spectres. The sublime is always great and simple; the beautiful may be small, elaborate, and ornamental.

He tried, too, to define the romantic in Nature, though very vaguely:

> The dreadful variety of the sublime, when quite unnatural, is adventurous. When sublimity or beauty is excessive, it is called romantic.

In his *Kalligone*, which appeared in 1800, Herder quoted Kant in making one of the characters say, 'One calls day beautiful, night sublime,' and tried to carry the idea a step further; ' The sublime and beautiful are not opposed to each other, but stem and boughs of a tree whose top is the most sublimely beautiful of all,' that is the romantic. In the same book he attempted to analyze his impressions of Nature, calling a rugged place odious, an insignificant one without character tedious. ' In the presence of great mountains,' he says, ' the spirit is filled with bold aspirations, whereas in gentle valleys it lies quiet.' Harmony in variety was his ideal, like the sea in storm and cahn. ' An ocean of beautiful forms in rest and movement.',

And in reference to the contrast between a place made ' dreadful and horrible ' by a torrent dashing over rocks and a quiet and charming valley, he said: ' These changes follow unalterable laws, which are recognized by our minds, and in harmony with our feelings.' He saw the same order in variety among plants, from the highest to the lowest, from palm tree to moss. In the second part of the book he gave an enthusiastic description of the sublime in sky and sea.

His beautiful words on the inspiration of Nature shew his insight into her relation to the poet soul of the people:

Everything in Nature must be inspired by life, or it does not move me, I do not feel it. The cooling zephyr and the morning sunbeam, the wind blowing through the trees, and the fragrant carpet of flowers, must cool, warm, pervade us—then we feel Nature. The poet does not say he feels her, unless he feels her intensely, living, palpitating and pervading him, like the wild Nature of Ossian, or the soft luxuriant Nature of Theocritus and the Orientals. In Nature, the more varieties the better; for instance, in a beautiful country I rustle with the wind and become alive (and give life—inspire), I inhale fragrance and exhale it with the flowers; I dissolve in water; I float in the blue sky; I feel all these feelings.

Herder touched the lyre himself with a skilful hand. Thought predominated with him, but he could make Nature live in his song.' 'I greet thee. thou wing of heaven,' he sang to the lark; and to the rainbow, 'Beautiful child of the sun, picture and hope over dark clouds . . . hopes are colours, are broken sun-rays and the children of tears, truth is the sun.'

In *By the Sea at Naples* he wrote:

A-weary of the summer's fiery brand,
I sat me down beside the cooling sea,
Where the waves heaving, rolled and kissed the
    strand
Of the grey shore, . . .
And over me, high over in the air,
Of the blue skyey vault, rustled the tree . . .
Queen of all trees, slender and beautiful,
The pine tree, lifting me to golden dreams.

In *Recollections of Naples*:

Yes ! they are gone, those happy, happy hours,
Joyous but short, by Posilippo's bay !
Sweet dream of sea and lake, of rock and hill,
Grotto and island, and the mirrored sun
In the blue water—thou hast passed away !

and

When the glow of evening softly fades
From the still sea, and with her gleaming host
The moon ascends the sky.

Night is very poetic :

> And comest thou again,
> Thou Mother of the stars and heavenly thoughts ?
> Divine and quiet Mother, comest thou ?
> The earth awaits thee, from thy chalice cup
> But one drop of thy heavenly dew to quaff,
> Her flowers bend low their heads ;
> And with them, satiate with vision, droops
> My overcharged soul. . . .
> O starry goddess with the crown of gold,
> Upon whose wide-spread sable mantle gleam
> A thousand worlds . . .
> Silence divine, that filleth all the world,
> Flowing so softly to the eternal shores
> Of an eternal universe. . . .

And in *St John's Night*, he exclaims :

> Infinite, ah ! inexhaustible art thou, Mother Nature !

Like the rest, Herder suffered from the over-sensitiveness of his day. His correspondence with his *fiancée* shews this [8] ; one sees Rousseau's influence :

> My pleasantest hours are when, quite alone, I walk in a charming wood close to Bückeburg, or lie upon a wall in the shade of my garden, or lastly, for we have had capital moonlight for three nights, and the last was the best of all, when I enjoy these hours of sweetly sleeping night with all the songs of the nightingale.

> I reckon no hours more delightful than those of green solitude. I live so romantically alone, and among woods and churches, as only poets, lovers, and philosophers can live.

And his *fiancée* wrote :

> 'Tis all joy within and around me since I have known thee, my best beloved : every plant and flower, everything in Nature, seems beautiful to me.

and

> I went early to my little room ; the moon was quite covered by clouds, and the night so melancholy from the croaking of the frogs, that I could not leave the window for a long time : my whole soul was dark and cloudy; I thought of thee, my dear one, and that thought, that sigh, reduced me to tears.

and

> Do you like the ears of wheat so much ? I never
> pass a cornfield without stroking them.

Goethe focussed all the rays of feeling for Nature
which had found lyrical expression before him, and
purged taste, beginning with his own, of its un-
natural and sickly elements. So he became the
liberating genius of modern culture. Not only did
German lyric poetry reach its climax in him ; but
he was the most accurate, individual, and universal
interpreter of German feeling for Nature.

His wide original mind kept open house for the
most diverse elements of feeling, and exercised an
ennobling control upon each and all at will ; Homer's
naivete, Shakespeare's sympathy, Rousseau's en-
thusiasm, even Ossian's melancholy, found room
there.

While most love lyrics of his day were false in
feeling, mere raving extravagances, and therefore
poor in those metaphors and comparisons which
prove sympathy between Nature and the inner life,
it could be said of him that ' Nature wished to know
what she looked like, and so she created Goethe.'
He was the microcosm in which the macrocosm of
modern times was reflected.

He was more modern and universal than any of
his predecessors, and his insight into Nature and
love for her have been rarely equalled in later days.
He did not live, like so many of the elegiac and
idyllic poets of the eighteenth century, a mere dream-
life of the imagination : Goethe stood firmly rooted
among the actualities ; from boyhood up, as he said
in *Wahrheit und Dichtung,* he had ' a warm
feeling for all objective things.'

No poet, Klopstock not excepted, was richer in
verbal invention, and many of the phrases and
epithets which he coined form in themselves very
striking evidence (which is lost in translation) of
his close and original observation of Nature,

He has many beautiful comparisons to Nature:

His lady-love is 'brightly beautiful as morning clouds on yonder height.'

' I was wont to look at thee as one looks at the stars and moon, delighting in thee without the most distant wish in my quiet breast to possess thee.'

' I give kisses as the spring gives flowers.'

' My feeling for thee was like seed, which germinates slowly in winter, but ripens quickly in summer.'

The stars move ' with flower feet.'

The graces are ' pure as the heart of the waters, as the marrow of earth.'

A delicate poem is a rainbow only existing against a dark ground.

In *Stella*:

> Thou dost not feel what heavenly dew to the thirsty it is, to return to thy breast from the sandy desert world.
> I felt free in soul, free as a spring morning.

In *Faust*:

> The cataract bursting through the rocks is the image o: human effort ; its coloured reflection the image of life.

When Werther feels himself trembling between existence and non-existence, everything around him sinking away, and the world perishing with him :

> The past flashes like lightning over the dark abyss of the future.

These are among his still more numerous metaphors:

A sea of folly, an ocean of fragrance, the waves of battle, the stream of genius, the tiger claw of despair, the sun-ray of the past. Iphigenia says to Orestes :

> O let the pure breath of love blow lightly on thy heart's flame and cool it.

and Eleonora complains about Tasso :

> Let him go !   But what twilight falls round me now !
> Formerly the stream carried us along upon the light
> waves without a rudder.

In Goethe we see very clearly how the inner life,
under the pressure of its own intensity, will, so
to speak, overflow into the outer world, making
that live in its turn ; and how this is especially the
case when the amorous passion is present to add
its impetus to feeling, and attribute its own fervour
to all around.

May Song, On the Lake, Ganymede, are instances
of this.

Ganymede :

> Oh, what a glow
> Around me in morning's
> Blaze thou diffusest,
> Beautiful spring !
> With the rapture of love but intenser,
> Intenser and deeper and sweeter,
> Nestles and creeps to my heart
> The sensation divine
> Of thy fervour eternal,
> Oh, thou unspeakably fair !

Beautiful personifications abound :
The sun is proudly throned in heaven.
The glowing sun gazes at the rugged peak or
charms it with fiery love,
Or bathes like the moon in the ocean.
The parting glance of Mother Sun broods on the
grapes.
' Morning came frightening away light sleep with
its footsteps.'
' The young day arose with delight.'
The moon : ' Thou spreadest thy glance soothingly
over my abode.'
On a cloudy night : ' Evening already rocked
earth, and night hung on the mountains ; from a
hill of clouds the moon looked mournfully out of
the mist.'

' The lofty stars turn their clear eyes down to me.'

Even the rock lives: ' The hard rock opens its bosom, not envying earth its deep springs.'

ⱶ The stream: ' Thou hurriest on with joyful light mood; see the rock spring bright with the glance of the stars, yet no shady valley, no flowers make him tarry . . . his course winds downwards to the plain, then he scatters in delightful spray, in cloud waves . . . foams gloomily to the abyss.'

> With gradual step from out the far-off grey,
> Self-heralded draws on the storm.
> Birds on the wing fly low across the water, weighted
>   down,
> And seamen hasten to reef in the sail
> Before its stubborn wrath.

His flowers are alive:

> The beauteous snowdrops
> Droop o'er the plain,
> The crocus opens
> Its glowing bud . . .
> With saucy gesture
> Primroses flare,
> And roguish violets
> Hidden with care.

But these are only examples.   To obtain a clear idea of Goethe's attitude, we must take a more general survey of his work, for his poetic relationship to Nature, like his mental development in general, passed through various stages of growth. That it was a warm one even in youth is shewn by the letter in 1766 from Leipzig[9]:

> You live contented in M.   I even so here.   Lonely, lonely, altogether lonely.   Dearest Riese, this loneliness has impressed my soul with a certain sadness.

> This solitary joy is mine,
> When far apart from all mankind,
> By shady brook-side to recline.
> And keep my loved ones in my mind. . .

He goes on with these lines :

> Then is my heart with sorrow filled,
> Sad is mine eye.
> The flooded brook now rages by,
> That heretofore so gently rilled.
> No bird sings in the bushes now,
> The tree so green is dry,
> The zephyr which on me did blow
> So cheering, now storms northerly,
> And scattered blossoms bears on high.

He was already in full sympathy with Nature. A few of his earlier poems [10] shew prevalent taste, the allusions to Zephyr and Lima, for instance, in *Night*; but they are followed by lines which are all his own.

He had an incomparable way of striking the chords of love and Nature together.

Where his lady-love dwells, ' there is love, and goodness is Nature.' He thinks of her

> When the bright sunlight shimmers
> Across the sea,
> When the clear fountain in the moonbeam glimmers.
> Thou art seductive and charming ; flowers,
> Sun, moon, and stars only worship thee.

There is passionate feeling for Nature in the *May Song* of his Sesenheimer period :

> How gloriously gleameth
> All Nature to me !
> How bright the sun beameth,
> How fresh is the lea !
> White blossoms are bursting
> The thickets among,
> And all the gay greenwood
> Is ringing with song !
> There's radiance and rapture
> That nought can destroy,
> Oh earth, in thy sunshine,
> Oh heart, in thy joy.
> Oh love ! thou enchanter
> So golden and bright,
> Like the red clouds of morning
> That rest on yon height,

> It is thou that art clothing
> The fields and the bowers,
> And everywhere breathing
> The incense of flowers.

Looking back in old age to those happy days of youth, he saw in memory not only Frederica but the scenery around her. He said (*Wahrheit und Dichtung*): ' Her figure never looked more charming than when she was moving along a raised footpath ; the charm of her bearing seemed to vie with the flowering ground, and the indestructible cheerfulness of her face with the blue sky.' In Alsace he wrote :

> One has only to abandon oneself to the present in order to enjoy the charms of the sky, the glow of the rich earth, the mild evenings, the warm nights, at the side of one's love, or near her.

and one of the poems to Frederica says :

> The world lies round me buried deep in mist, but
> In one glance of thine lies sunshine and happiness.

There is a strong pulse of life—life that overflows into Nature—in *The Departure* :

> To horse ! Away, o'er hill and steep,
> Into the saddle blithe I spring ;
> The eve was cradling earth to sleep,
> And night upon the mountains hung.
> With robes of mist around him set,
> The oak like some huge giant stood,
> While, with its hundred eyes of jet,
> Peer'd darkness from the tangled wood.
> Amid a bank of clouds the moon
> A sad and troubled glimmer shed ;
> The wind its chilly wings unclosed,
> And whistled wildly round my head.
> Night framed a thousand phantoms dire,
> Yet did I never droop nor start ;
> Within my veins what living fire !
> What quenchless glow within my heart !

And very like it, though in a minor key, is the Elegy which begins, ' A tender, youthful trouble.'

He tells in *Wahrheit und Dichtung* how he found comfort for his love troubles in Frankfort :

> They were accustomed to call me, on account of wandering about the district, the 'wanderer.' In producing that calm for the mind, which I felt under the open sky, in the valleys, on the heights, in the fields, and in the woods, the situation of Frankfort was serviceable. . . . On the setting in of winter a new world was revealed to us, since I at once determined to skate. . . . For this new joyous activity we were also indebted to Klopstock, to his enthusiasm for this happy species of motion. . . . To pass a splendid Sunday thus on the ice did not satisfy us, we continued in movement late into the night. . . . The full moon rising from the clouds, over the wide nocturnal meadows which were frozen into fields of ice, the night breeze which rustled towards us on our course, the solemn thunder of the ice which sunk as the water decreased, the strange echo of our own movements, rendered the scenes of Ossian just present to our minds.

His attachment, to Lotte, stirred far deeper feelings than the earlier ones to Frederica and Lilli :

> (If I, my own dear Lilli, loved thee not,
> How should I joy to view this scene so fair !
> And yet if I, sweet Lilli, loved thee not,
> Should I be happy here or anywhere ?)

and drew him correspondingly nearer to Nature.
There is no book in any language which so lives and moves and has its being in Nature as *Werther*.[11] In *Wahrheit und Dichtung* Goethe said of the 'strange element' in which *Werther* was designed and written :

> I sought to free myself internally from all that was foreign to me, to regard the external with love, and to allow all beings, from man downwards, as low as they were comprehensible, to act upon me, each after its own kind. Thus arose a wonderful affinity with the single objects of Nature, and a hearty concord, a harmony with the whole, so that every change, whether of place or region, or of the times of the day and year, or whatever else could happen, affected me in the deepest manner. The glance of the painter associated itself with that of

the poet; the beautiful rural landscape, animated by the pleasant river, increased my love of solitude and favoured my silent observations as they extended on all sides.

The strong influence of *La Nouvelle Héloise* upon *Werther* was very evident, but there was a marked difference between Goethe's feeling for Nature and Rousseau's. Rousseau had the painter's eye, but not the keen poetic vision.

Goethe's romances are pervaded by the penetrating quality peculiar to his nation, and by virtue of which in *Werther*, the outer world, the scenery, was not used as framework, but was always interwoven with the hero's mood. The contrast between culture and Nature is always marked in Rousseau, and his religion was deism; Goethe resolves Nature into feeling, and his religion was a growing pantheism. As a work of art, *Werther* is excellent, *La Nouvelle Héloise* is not. Goethe used his hero's bearing towards Nature with marvellous effect to indicate the turns and changes of his moods, just as he indicated the threatening calamity and the growing apprehension of it by skilful stress laid upon some of her little traits—a faculty which only Theodore Storm among later poets has caught from him.

The growth of amorous passion is portrayed as an elementary force, and the revolutionary element in the book really consists in the strength of this passion and the assertion of its natural rights. Everything artificial, forced, conventional, in thought, act, and feeling—and what at that time was not?—was repugnant to Werther; what he liked most of all was the simplicity of children and uneducated people.

> Nothing distresses me more than to see men torment each other; particularly when in the flower of their age, in the very season of pleasure, they waste their few short days of sunshine in quarrels and disputes, and only perceive their error when it is too late to repair it.

To such intense sympathy as this, all that had been sung ere now by German poets had to give place. Nature, which hitherto had played no *rôle* at all in fiction, not even among the English, was Werther's truest and most intimate friend.

Werther is sensitive and sentimental, though in a single-hearted way, with a sentimentality that reminds us more and more, as the story proceeds, of the gloomy tone of Ossian and Young. He is a thoroughly original character, who feels that he is right so to be ; and although he falls a prey to his melancholy, yet there is much more force and thought in his outpourings than in all the moonshine tirades that preceded him. It is the work of a true poet, in the best days of a brilliant youth.

Werther, like Rousseau, was happiest in solitude. Solitude, in the ' place like paradise,' was precious balm to his feeling heart, which he considers ' like a sick child ' ; and the ' warm heavenly imagination of the heart ' illuminates Nature round him—his ' favourite valley,' the ' sweet spring morning,' Nature's ' unspeakable beauty.' He was absorbed in artistic feeling, though he could not draw ; ' I could not draw them, not a stroke, and have never been a greater artist than at that moment.' His power lay in imbuing his whole subject with feeling ; he felt the heart of Nature beating, and its echo in his own breast.

> When the lovely valley teems with vapour around me, and the meridian sun strikes the upper surface of the impenetrable foliage of my trees, and but a few stray gleams steal into the inner sanctuary, then I throw myself down in the tall grass by the trickling stream ; and as I lie close to the earth, a thousand unknown plants discover themselves to me. When I hear the buzz of the little world among the stalks, and grow familiar with the countless indescribable forms of the insects and flies, then I feel the presence of the Almighty who formed us in His own image, and the breath of that universal love which bears and sustains us, as it floats around us in an eternity of bliss ; and then, my

friend, when darkness overspreads my eyes, and heaven and earth seem to dwell in my soul and absorb its power, like the idea of a beloved mistress, then I often long and think : O that you could describe these conceptions, that you could impress upon paper all that lives so full and warm within you, that it might be the mirror of your soul, as your soul is the mirror of the infinite God !

O ! my friend ! but it is too much for my strength. I sink under the weight of the grandeur of these visions.

Werther could not express all his love for Nature, but the secret of it lay in the power to bring his own world of thought and feeling into communion with her, and so give her speech. He divined something immortal in her akin to himself. ' The true feeling of Nature,' he said, ' is love.' He poured ' the stream of his genius ' over her, and she became ' dear and familiar ' to him. . . . The simple homely scenery delighted him—the valley, the brook, the fine walnut trees.

When I go out at sunrise in the morning to Walheim, and with my own hands gather the peas in the garden, which are to serve for my dinner ; when I sit down to shell them and read my Homer during the intervals, and then, selecting a saucepan from the kitchen, fetch my own butter, put my mess on the fire, cover it up. . . . Nothing fills me with a more pure and genuine sense of happiness than those traits of patriarchal life, which, thank heaven, I can imitate without affectation.

With the growth of his love-passion his feeling for Nature increased ; on July 24th he wrote :

I never felt happier, I never understood Nature better, even down to the veriest stem or smallest blade of grass.

Then Albert came on the scene, and love became 'a torment, and Nature a tormentor :

August 18.—Must it ever be thus, that the source of our happiness must also be the fountain of our misery ? The full and ardent sentiment which animated my heart with the love of Nature, overwhelming me with a torrent of delight, and which brought all paradise before me, has now become an insupportable torment, a demon which perpetually pursues and harasses me. When in bye-gone days I gazed from these rocks upon yonder mountains across the river and upon the green flowery valley before me, and saw all nature budding and bursting around—the hills clothed from foot to peak with tall thick forest trees, the valleys in all their varied windings shaded with the loveliest woods, and the soft river gliding along amongst the lisping reeds, mirroring the beautiful clouds which the soft evening breeze wafted across the sky—when I heard the groves about me melodious with the music of birds, and saw the million swarms of insects dancing in the last golden beams of the sun, whose setting rays awoke the humming beetles from their grassy beds, whilst the subdued tumult around directed my attention to the ground, and I there observed the arid rock compelled to yield nutriment to the dry moss, whilst the heath flourished upon the barren sands below me—all this displayed to me the inner warmth which animates all Nature, and filled and glowed within my heart. I felt myself exalted by this overflowing fulness to the perception of the Godhead, and the glorious forms of an infinite universe became visible to my soul. . . . From the inaccessible mountains across the desert, which no mortal foot has trod, far as the confines of the unknown ocean, breathes the spirit of the eternal Creator, and every atom to which He has given existence finds favour in His sight. Ah! how often at that time has the flight of a bird soaring above my head inspired me with the desire of being transported to the shores of the immeasurable waters, there to quaff the pleasure of life from the foaming goblet of the infinite, and to partake, if but for a moment, even with the confined powers of my soul, the beatitude of the Creator, who accomplishes all things in himself and through himself. . . . It is as if a curtain had been drawn from before my eyes. . . . My heart is wasted by the thought of that destructive power which lies concealed in every part of universal nature—Nature has formed nothing that does not consume itself and every object near it ; so that, surrounded by earth, and air, and all the active powers, I wander on my way with aching heart, and the universe is to me a fearful monster, for ever devouring its own offspring. . . . If in such moments I find no sympathy . . . I either wander through the country, climb some precipitous cliff, or force a path through the trackless thicket, where I am lacerated and torn by thorns and briars, and thence I find relief.

Then, as he was going away, he felt how sympathetic the place had been to him :

I was walking up and down the very avenue which was so dear to me—a secret sympathy had frequently drawn me thither. . . .

the moon rose from behind a hill, increasing his melancholy, and Charlotte put his feeling into words, saying (like Klopstock) :

September 10.—Whenever I walk by moonlight, it brings to my remembrance all my beloved and departed friends, and I am filled with thoughts of death and futurity.

Even in his misery he realises the χάρις γόων of Euripides, Petrarch's *dolendi voluptas*—the *Wonne der Wehmuth.*

On September 4th he wrote :

It is even so ! As Nature puts on her autumn tints, it becomes autumn with me and around me. My leaves are sere and yellow, and the neighbouring trees are divested of their foliage.

It was due to this autumn feeling that he could say :

Ossian has superseded Homer in my heart. To what a world does the illustrious bard carry me ! To wander over pathless wilds, surrounded by impetuous whirlwinds, where, by the feeble light of the moon, we see the spirits of our ancestors ; to hear from the mountain tops, 'mid the roar of torrents, their plaintive sounds issuing from deep caverns. . . . And this heart is now dead ; no sentiment can revive it. My eyes are dry, and my senses, no more refreshed by the influence of soft tears, wither and consume my brain. I suffer much, for I have lost the only charm of life, that active sacred power which created worlds around me, and it is no more. When I look from my window at the distant hills and behold the morning sun breaking through the mists and illuminating the country round it which is still wrapt in silence, whilst the soft stream winds gently through the willows which have shed their leaves ; when glorious Nature displays all her beauties before me, and her wondrous prospects are ineffectual to attract one tear of joy from my withered heart. . . .

On November 30th he wrote : ' About dinner-time I went to walk by the river side, for I had no appetite,' and goes on in the tone of Ossian :

Everything around me seemed gloomy : a cold and damp easterly wind blew from the mountains, and black heavy clouds spread over the plain.

and in the dreadful night of the flood :

Upon the stroke of twelve I hastened forth. I beheld a fearful sight. The foaming torrents rolled from the mountains in the moonlight ; fields and meadows, trees and hedges, were confounded together, and the entire valley was converted into a deep lake which was agitated by the roaring wind. And when the moon shone forth and tinged the black clouds with silver, and the impetuous torrent at my feet foamed and resounded with awful and grand impetuosity, I was overcome by a mingled sensation of awe and delight. With extended arms I looked down into the yawning abyss, and cried ' Plunge ! ' For a moment my senses forsook me, in the intense delight of ending my sorrows and my sufferings by a plunge into that gulf.

To his farewell letter he adds :

Yes, Nature ! put on mourning. Your child, your friend, your lover, draws near his end.

The genuine poetic pantheism, which, for all his melancholy and sentimentality, was the spring of Werther's feeling, is seen in loftier and more comprehensive form in the first part of *Faust*, when Faust opens the book and sees the sign of macrocosmos :

How all things live and work, and ever blending,
Weave one vast whole from Being's ample range !
How powers celestial, rising and descending,
Their golden buckets ceaseless interchange.
Their flight on rapture-breathing pinions winging,
From heaven to earth their genial influence bringing,
Through the wide whole their chimes melodious ringing.

And the Earth spirit says :

> In the currents of life, in action's storm,
> I float and I wave
> With billowy motion,—
> Birth and the grave
> A limitless ocean.

Not only of knowledge of, but of feeling for, Nature, it is said :

> Inscrutable in broadest light,
> To be unveiled by force she doth refuse.

But Faust is in deep sympathy with her ; witness :

> Thou full-orbed moon ! Would thou wert gazing now
> For the last time upon my troubled brow !

and

> Loos'd from their icy fetters, streams and rills
> In spring's effusive, quick'ning mildness flow,
> Hope's budding promise every valley fills,
> And winter, spent with age, and powerless now,
> Draws off his forces to the savage hills.

and the idyllic evening mood, which gives way to a burst of longing :

> In the rich sunset see how brightly glow
> Yon cottage homes girt round with verdant green.
> Slow sinks the orb, the day is now no more ;
> Yonder he hastens to diffuse new light.
> Oh ! for a pinion from the earth to soar,
> And after, ever after him to strive !
> Then should I see the world outspread below,
> Illumined by the deathless evening beams,
> The vales reposing, every height aglow,
> The silver brooklets meeting golden streams. . . .
> Alas ! that when on Spirit wing we rise,
> No wing material lifts our mortal clay.
> But 'tis our inborn impulse, deep and strong,
> To rush aloft, to struggle still towards heaven,
> When far above us pours its thrilling song
> The skylark lost amid the purple even,
> When on extended pinion sweeps amain
> The lordly eagle o'er the pine-crowned height,
> And when, still striving towards its home, the crane
> O'er moor and ocean wings its onward flight.

But the most complete expression of Goethe's attitude, not only in the period of *Werther* and the first part of *Faust*, but generally, is contained in the *Monologue*, which was probably written not earlier than the spring of 1788:

> Spirit sublime! Thou gav'st me, gav'st me all
> For which I prayed. Not vainly hast thou turn'd
> To me thy countenance in flaming fire;
> Thou gav'st me glorious Nature for my realm,
> And also power to feel her and enjoy;
> Not merely with a cold and wond'ring glance,
> Thou didst permit me in her depths profound,
> As in the bosom of a friend, to gaze;
> Before me thou dost lead her living tribes,
> And dost in silent grove, in air and stream,
> Teach me to know my kindred. . . .

His feeling was not admiration alone, nor reverence alone, but the sympathy of *Childe Harold*:

> Are not the mountains, waves, and skies a part
> Of me and of my soul, as I of them?
> Is not the love of these deep in my heart
> With a pure passion? Should I not contemn
> All objects, if compared with these?

and the very confession of faith of such poetic pantheism is in Faust's words:

> Him who dare name,
> And yet proclaim,
> Yes, I believe? . . .
> The All-embracer,
> All-sustainer,
> Doth he not embrace, sustain
> Thee, me, himself?
> Lifts not the heaven its dome above?
> Doth not the firm-set earth beneath us rise?
> And beaming tenderly with looks of love,
> Climb not the everlasting stars on high?

The poems which date directly after the Wetzlar period are full of this sympathetic pantheistic love for Nature—*Mahomet's Song*, for example, with its splendid comparison of pioneering genius to a mountain torrent:

Ho! the spring that bursts
From the mountain height
Joyous and bright,
As the gleam of a star. . . .
Down in the vale below
Flowers bud beneath his tread . . .
And woo him with fond eyes.
And the streamlets of the mountains
Shout to him, and cry out 'Brother'!
Brother! take thy brothers with thee,
With thee to thine ancient father,
To the eternal Ocean,
Who with outstretch'd arms awaits us. . . .
And so beareth he his brothers
To their primal sire expectant,
All his bosom throbbing, heaving,
With a wild, tumultuous joy.

We see the same pathos—the pathos of Pindar and the Psalms—in the comparison:

Like water is the soul of man,
From heaven it comes, to heaven it goes,
And back again to earth in ceaseless change.

in the incomparable *Wanderer*, in *Wanderer's Storm Song*, and, above all, in *Ganymede*, already given, of which Loeper remarks:

The poem is, as it were, a rendering of that letter (Werther's of May 10th) in rhythm. The underlying pantheism had already shewn itself in the *Wanderer's Storm Song*. It was not the delight in God of a Brockes, not the adoration of a Klopstock, not æsthetic enjoyment of Nature, not, as in later years, scientific interest; it was rather a being absorbed in, identified with, Nature, a sympathy carried so far that the very ego was surrendered to the elements.

On the Lake of Zurich he wrote, June 15th, 1775:

And here I drink new blood, fresh food,
From world so free, so blest;
How sweet is Nature and how good,
Who holds me to her breast.

and Elmire sings in *Ermin and Elmire*:

From thee, O Nature, with deep breath
I drink in painful pleasure.

One of the gems among his Nature poems is *Autumn Feelings* (it was the autumn of his love for Lilli) :

> Flourish greener as ye clamber,
> O ye leaves, to seek my chamber ;
> Up the trellised vine on high
> May ye swell, twin-berries tender,
> Juicier far, and with more splendour
> Ripen, and more speedily.
> O'er ye broods the sun at even,
> As he sinks to rest, and heaven
> Softly breathes into your ear
> All its fertilizing fulness,
> While the moon's refreshing coolness,
> Magic-laden, hovers near.
> And alas ! ye're watered ever
> By a stream of tears that rill
> From mine eyes—tears ceasing never,
> Tears of love that nought can still.

The lyrical effect here depends upon the blending of a single impression of Nature with the passing mood—an occasional poem rare even for Goethe. In a letter to Frau von Stein he admitted that he was greatly influenced by Nature :

> I have slept well and am quite awake, only a quiet sadness lies upon my soul. . . . The weather agrees exactly with my state of mind, and I begin to believe that it is the weather around me which has the most immediate effect upon me, and the great world thrills my little one with her own mood.

Again, *To the Moon*, in the spring 1778, expresses perfect communion between Nature and feeling :

> Flooded are the brakes and dells
> With thy phantom light,
> And my soul receives the spell
> Of thy mystic night.
> To the meadow dost thou send
> Something of thy grace,
> Like the kind eye of a friend
> Beaming on my face.
> Echoes of departed times
> Vibrate in mine ear,
> Joyous, sad, like spirit chimes,
> As I wander here.

Flow, flow on, thou little brook,
Ever onward go !
Trusted heart and tender look
Left me even so !
Richer treasure earth has none
Than I once possessed—
Ah ! so rich, that when 'twas gone
Worthless was the rest.
Little brook ! adown the vale
Rush and take my song :
Give it passion, give it wail,
As thou leap'st along !
Sound it in the winter night
When thy streams are full,
Murmur it when skies are bright
Mirror'd in the pool.
Happiest he of all created
Who the world can shun,
Not in hate, and yet unhated,
Sharing thought with none,
Save one faithful friend, revealing
To his kindly ear
Thoughts like these, which o'er me stealing,
Make the night so drear.

In January 1778, he wrote to Frau von Stein about the fate of the unhappy Chr. von Lassberg, who had drowned himself in the Ilm :

> This inviting grief has something dangerously attractive about it, like the water itself ; and the reflections of the stars, which gleam from above and below at once, are alluring.

To the same year belongs *The Fisher*, which gave such melodious voice to the magic effect of a shimmering expanse of water, ' the moist yet radiant blue,' upon the mood ; just as, later on, *The Erlking*, with the grey of an autumn evening woven ghostlike round tree and shrub, made the mind thrill with foreboding.

Goethe was always an industrious traveller. In his seventieth year he went to Frankfort, Strassburg, the Rhine, Thuringia, and the Harz Mountains (Harzreise, 1777): ' We went up to the peaks, and down to the depths of the earth, and hammered at all the rocks.' His love for Nature increased with his science ; but, at the same time, poetic expression of it took a more objective form ; the passionate vehemence, the really revolutionary attitude of the *Werther* period, gave way to one equally spiritual and intellectual, but more temperate.

This transition is clearly seen in the Swiss letters. In his first Swiss travels, 1775, he was only just free from *Werther*, and his mind was too agitated for quiet observation :

> Hasten thee, Kronos ! . . .
> Over stock and stone let thy trot
> Into life straightway lead. . . .
> Wide, high, glorious the view
> Gazing round upon life,
> While from mount unto mount
> Hovers the spirit eterne,
> Life eternal foreboding. . . .

Far more significant and ripe—in fact, mature— are the letters in 1779, shewing, as they do, the attitude of a man of profound mind, in the prime of his life and time. He was the first German poet to fall under the spell of the mountains—the strongest spell, as he held, which Nature wields in our latitudes. ' These sublime, incomparable scenes will remain for ever in my mind ' ; and of one view in particular, over the mountains of Savoy and Valais, the Lake of Geneva, and Mont Blanc, he said: ' The view was so great, man's eye could not grasp it.'

He wrote of his feelings with perfect openness to Frau von Stein, and these letters extended farther back than those from Switzerland, and were partly mixed with them.

From Selz :

> An uncommonly fine day, a happy country—still all green, only here and there a yellow beech or oak leaf. Meadows still in their silver beauty—a soft welcome breeze everywhere. Grapes improving with every step and every day. Every peasant's house has a vine up to the roof, and every courtyard a great

overhanging arbour. The air of heaven soft, warm, and moist. The Rhine and the clear mountains near at hand, the changing woods, meadows, fields like gardens, do men good, and give me a kind of comfort which I have long lacked.

The pen remains as ever the pen of a poet, but he looks at Switzerland now with a mature, settled taste, analyzing his impressions, and studying mountains, glaciers, boulders, scientifically.

Of the Staubbach Fall, near Lauterbrunnen (Oct. 9th, 1779):

The clouds broke in the upper air, and the blue sky came through. Clouds clung to the steep sides of the rocks; even the top where the Staubbach falls over, was lightly covered. It was a very noble sight . . . then the clouds came down into the valley and covered all the foreground. The great wall over which the water falls, still stood out on the right. Night came on. . . . In the Munsterthal, through which we came, everything was lofty, but more within the mind's power of comprehension than these. In comparison with the immensities, one is, and must remain, too small.

And after visiting the Berne glacier from Thun (Oct. 14):

It is difficult to write after all this . . . the first glance from the mountain is striking, the district is surprisingly extensive and pleasant . . . the road indescribably beautiful . . . the view from the Lake of Brienz towards the snow mountains at sunset is great.

More eloquent is the letter of October 3rd, from the Munsterthal:

The passage through this defile roused in me a grand but calm emotion. The sublime produces a beautiful calmness in the soul, which, entirely possessed by it, feels as great as it ever can feel. How glorious is such a pure feeling, when it rises to the very highest without overflowing. My eye and my soul were both able to take in the objects before me, and as I was preoccupied by nothing, and had no false tastes to counteract their impression, they had on me their full and natural effect. When we compare such a feeling with that we are sensible of, when we laboriously harass ourselves with some trifle, and strain every nerve to gain as much as possible for it, and, as it were, to patch it out, striving to furnish joy and aliment to the mind from its own creation ; we then feel sensibly what a poor expedient, after all, the latter is. . . .

When we see such objects as these for the first time, the unaccustomed soul has to expand itself, and this gives rise to a sort of painful joy, an overflowing of emotion which agitates the mind and draws from us the most delicious tears. . . . If only destiny had bidden me to dwell in the midst of some grand scenery, then would I every morning have imbibed greatness from its grandeur, as from a lonely valley I would extract patience and repose.

One guesses in the dark about the origin and existence of these singular forms. . . . These masses must have been formed grandly and simply by aggregation. Whatever revolutions may subsequently have upheaved, rent, and divided them . . . the idea of such nightly commotions gives one a deep feeling of the eternal stability of the masses. . . . One feels deeply convinced that here there is nothing accidental, that here there is working an eternal law which, however slowly, yet surely governs the universe.

By the Lake of Geneva, where he thought of Rousseau, he went up the Dole :

The whole of the Pays de Vaux and de Gex lay like a plan before us . . . we kept watching the mist, which gradually retired . . . one by one we distinctly saw Lausanne . . . Vevey. . . . There are no words to express the beauty and grandeur of this view . . . the line of glittering glaciers was continually drawing the eye back again to the mountains.

From Cluse he wrote :

The air was as warm as it usually is at the beginning of September, and the country we travelled through beautiful. Many of the trees still green ; most of them had assumed a brownish-yellow tint, but only a few were quite bare. The crops were rich and verdant, the mountains caught from the red sunset a rosy hue blended with violet, and all these rich tints were combined with grand, beautiful, and agreeable forms of the landscape.

At Chamouni, about effects of light :

> Here too again it seemed to us as if the sun had first
> of all attracted the light mists which evaporated from
> the tops of the glaciers, and then a gentle breeze had,
> as it were, combed the fine vapours like a fleece of foam
> over the atmosphere. I never remember at home,
> even in the height of summer, to have seen any so
> transparent, for here it was a perfect web of light.

At the Col de Baume :

> Whilst I am writing, a remarkable phenomenon is
> passing along the sky. The mists, which are shifting
> about and breaking in some places, allow you through
> their openings, as through skylights, to catch a glimpse
> of the blue sky, while at the same time the mountain
> peaks, rising above our roofs of vapour, are illuminated
> by the sun's rays. . . .

At Leukertad, at the foot of the Gemmi, he wrote
(Nov. 9th) :

> The clouds which gather here in this valley, at one
> time completely hiding the immense rocks and absorb-
> ing them in a waste impenetrable gloom, or at another
> letting a part of them be seen like huge spectres, give
> to the people a cast of melancholy. In the midst of
> such natural phenomena the people are full of pre-
> sentiments and forebodings . . . and the eternal
> and intrinsic energy of his (man's) nature feels itself
> at every nerve moved to forebode and to indulge in
> presentiments.

On the way across the Rhine glacier to the Furka,
he felt the half-suggestive, half-distressing sense of
mountain loneliness :

> It was a strange sight . . . in the most desolate
> region of the world, in a boundless monotonous wilder-
> ness of mountains enveloped in snow, where for three
> leagues before and behind you would not expect to
> meet a living soul, while on both sides you had the deep
> hollows of a web of mountains, you might see a line
> of men wending their way, treading each in the deep
> footsteps of the one before him, and where, in the whole
> of the wide expanse thus smoothed over, the eye could
> discern nothing but the track they left behind them.
> The hollows, as we left them, lay behind us grey and

> boundless in the mist. The changing clouds continually passed over the pale disc of the sun, and spread over the whole scene a perpetually moving veil.

He sums up the impressions made on him with :

> The perception of such a long chain of Nature's wonders, excites within me a secret and inexpressible feeling of enjoyment.

The most profound change in his mental life was brought about by his visit to Italy, 1786–87. The poetic expression of this refining process, this striving towards the classic ideal, towards Sophrosyne, was *Iphigenia.*

Its effect upon his feeling for Nature appeared in a more matter-of-fact tone ; the man of feeling gave way to the scientific observer.

He had, as he said (Oct. 30th, 1887), lately 'acquired the habit of looking only at things, and not, as formerly, seeing with and in the things what actually was not there.'

He no longer imputed his feelings to Nature, and studied her influence on himself, but looked at her with impersonal interest. Weather, cloud, mountain formation, the species of stone, landscape, and social themes, were all treated almost systematically as so much diary memoranda for future use. There was no artistic treatment in such jottings ; meteorology, botany, and geology weighed too heavily.

The question, ' Is a place beautiful ? ' paled beside ' Is its soil clay ? ' 'Are its rocks quartz, chalk, or mica schist ? ' The problem of the archetypal plant was more absorbing than the finest groups of trees. The years of practical life at Weimar, and, above all, the ever-growing interest in science, were the chief factors in this change, which led him, as he said in his *Treatise on Granite,*

> from observation and description of the human heart, that part of creation which is the most youthful, varied, unstable, and destructible, to observation of that Son of Nature, which is the oldest, deepest, most stable, most indestructible.

The enthusiastic subjective realism of stormy youth was replaced by the measured objective realism of ripe manhood. Hence the difference between his letters from Switzerland and those from Italy, where this inner metamorphosis was completed ; as he said, ' Between Weimar and Palermo I have had many changes.'

For all that, he revelled in the beauty of Italy. As he once said ::

> It is natural to me to revere the great and beautiful willingly and with pleasure ; and to develop this predisposition day by day and hour by hour by means of such glorious objects, is the most delightful feeling.

The sea made a great impression upon him :

> I set out for the Lido . . . landed, and walked straight across the isthmus. I heard a loud hollow murmur—it was the sea ! I soon saw it ; it crested high against the shore as it retired, it was about noon and time of ebb. I have then at last seen the sea with my own eyes, and followed it on its beautiful bed, just as it quitted it.

But further on he only remarks : ' The sea is a great sight.' Elsewhere, too, it is only noticed very shortly.

Rome stimulated his mind to increased productiveness, and, partly for this reason, he could not assimilate all the new impressions which poured in upon him from without, from ruins, paintings, churches, palaces, the life of the people. He drew a great deal too ; from Frascati he wrote (Nov. 15th, 1786) :

> The country around is very pleasant ; the village lies on the side of a hill, or rather of a mountain, and at every step the draughtsman comes upon the most glorious objects. The prospect is unbounded. Rome lies before you, and beyond it on the right is the sea, the mountains of Tivoli, and so on.

In Rome itself (Feb. 2nd, 1787) :

> Of the beauty of a walk through Rome by moonlight it is impossible to form a conception without having witnessed it.

During Carnival (Feb. 21st) :

> The sky, so infinitely fine and clear, looked down
> nobly and innocently upon the mummeries.

In the voyage to Sicily :

> At noon we went on board ; the weather being ex-
> tremely fine, we enjoyed the most glorious of views.
> The corvette lay at anchor near to the Mole.   With an
> unclouded sun the atmosphere was hazy, giving to
> the rocky walls of Sorrento, which were in the shade,
> a tint of most beautiful blue.   Naples with its living
> multitudes lay in full sunshine, and glittered brilliantly
> with countless tints.

and on April 1st :

> With a cloudy sky, a bright but broken moonlight.
> the reflection on the sea was infinitely beautiful.

At first, Italy, and especially Rome, felt strange
to him, in scenery, sky, contour, and colour.   It
was only by degrees that he felt at home there.

He refers to this during his second visit to Rome
in a notable remark, which aptly expresses the
faculty of apperception—the link between us and
the unfamiliar, which enables mental growth.

June 16th, 1787 :

> One remark more ! Now for the first time do the
> trees, the rocks, nay, Rome itself, grow dear to me ;
> hitherto I have always felt them as foreign, though,
> on the other hand, I took pleasure in minor subjects
> having some resemblance to those I saw in youth.

On August 18th, 1787, he wrote :

> Yesterday before sunrise I drove to Acqua Acetosa.
> Verily, one might well lose his senses in contemplating
> the clearness, the manifoldness, the dewy transparency,
> the heavenly hue of the landscape, especially in the
> distance.

In October, when he heard of the engagement of
a beautiful Milanese lady with whom he had fallen
in love :

I again turned me instantly to Nature, as a subject for landscapes, a field I had been meanwhile neglecting, and endeavoured to copy her in this respect with the utmost fidelity. I was, however, more successful in mastering her with my eyes. . . . All the sensual fulness which that region offers us in rocks and trees, in acclivities and declivities, in peaceful lakes and lively streams, all this was grasped by my eye more appreciatively, if possible, than ever before, and I could hardly resent the wound which had to such degree sharpened my inward and outward sense.

On leaving Rome, he wrote :

Three nights before, the full moon shone in the clearest heaven, and the enchantment shed over the vast town, though often felt before, was never felt so keenly as now. The great masses of light, clear as in mild daylight, the contrast of deep shades, occasionally relieved by reflexions dimly portraying details, all this transported us as if into another, a simpler and a greater, world.

The later diaries on his travels are sketchy throughout, and more laconic and objective : for example, at Schaffhausen (Sept. 18th) :

Went out early, 7.30, to see the Falls of the Rhine ; colour of water, green — causes of this, the heights covered by mist — the depths clear, and we saw the castle of Laufen half in mist ; thought of Ossian. Love mist when moved by deep feeling.

At Brunnen :

Green of the lake, steep banks, small size of boatman in comparison to the enormous masses of rock. One saw precipices grown over by trees, summits covered by clouds. Sunshine over the scene, one felt the formless greatness of Nature.

He was conscious of the great change in himself since his last visit there, and wrote to Schiller (Oct. 14th, 1797) :

I remember the effect these things had upon me twenty years ago. The total impression remained with me, but the details faded, and I had a wonderful longing to repeat the whole experience and correct my impressions. I had become another man, and therefore it must needs appear different to me.

In later years he travelled a great deal in the Harz Mountains, to Carlsbad, Toplitz, the Maine, Marienbad, etc. After the death of his great friends, Schiller and Carl August, he was more and more lonely, and his whole outlook, with increasing years, grew more impersonal, his attitude to Nature more abstract and scientific ; the archetypal plant was superseded by the theory of colours. But he kept fresh eyes for natural beauty into ripe age ; witness this letter from Heidelberg, May 4th, 1808, to Frau von Stein :

> Yesterday evening, after finishing my work, I went alone to the castle, and first scrambled about among the ruins, and then betook myself to the great balcony from which one can overlook the whole country. It was one of the loveliest of May evenings and of sunsets. No ! I have really never seen such a fine view ! Just imagine ! One looked into the beautiful though narrow Neckar valley, covered on both sides with woods and vineyards and fruit trees just coming into flower. Further off the valley widened, and one saw the setting sun reflected in the Rhine as it flowed majestically through most beautiful country. On its further side the horizon was bounded by the Vosges mountains, lit up by the sun as if by a fire. The whole country was covered with fresh green, and close to me were the enormous ruins of the old castle, half in light and half in shade. You can easily fancy how it fascinated me. I stood lost in the view quite half an hour, till the rising moon woke me from my dreams.

Goethe's true lyrical period was in the seventies, before his Italian journeys ; during and after that time he wrote more dramatic and epic poetry, with ballads and the more narrative kind of epic. In sending *Der Jüngling und der Mühlbach* to Schiller from Switzerland in 1797, he wrote : ' I have discovered splendid material for idylls and elegies, and whatever that sort of poetry is called.'

Nature lyrics were few during his Italian travels, as in the journey to Sicily, 1787 ; among them were *Calm at Sea* :

Silence deep rules o'er the waters,
Calmly slumbering lies the main.

and *Prosperous Voyage* :

The mist is fast clearing,
And radiant is heaven,
Whilst Æolus loosens
Our anguish-fraught bond.

The most perfect of all such short poems was the *Evening Song*, written one September night of 1783 on the Gickelhahn, near Ilmenau. He was writing at the same time to Frau von Stein : ' The sky is perfectly clear, and I am going out to enjoy the sunset. The view is great and simple — the sun down.'

Every tree top is at peace,
E'en the rustling woods do cease
Every sound ;
The small birds sleep on every bough.
Wait but a moment—soon wilt thou
Sleep in peace.

The hush of evening, the stilling of desire in the silence of the wood, the beautiful resolution of all discords in Nature's perfect concord, the naive and splendid pantheism of a soul which feels itself at one with the world—all this is not expressed in so many words in the *Night Song* ; but it is all there, like the united voices in a great symphony. (SCHURÉ.)

The lines are full of that pantheism which not only brings subject and object, Mind and Nature, into symbolic relationship, but works them into one tissue. Taken alone with *The Fisher* and *To the Moon*, it would suffice to give him the first place as a poet of Nature.

He was not only the greatest poet, but the greatest and most universal thinker of modern times. With him feeling and knowledge worked together, the one reaching its climax in the lyrics of his younger days, the other gradually moderating the fervour of passion, and, with the more objective outlook of age, laying greater stress upon science. His feeling for Nature, which followed an unbroken course, like his mental development generally, stands alone as a type of perfectly modern feeling, and yet no one, despite the many intervening centuries, stood so near both to Homer and to Shakespeare, and in philosophy to Spinoza.

But because with Goethe poetry and philosophy were one, his pantheism is full of life and poetic vision, whilst that of the wise man of Amsterdam is severely mathematical and abstract. And the postulate of this pantheism was sympathy, harmony between Nature and the inner life. He felt himself a part of the power which upholds and encompasses the world. Nature became his God, love of her his religion. In his youth, in the period of *Werther*, *Ganymede*, and the first part of *Faust*, this pantheism was a nameless, unquenchable aspiration towards the divine—for wings to reach, like the rays of light, to unmeasured heights; as he said in the Swiss mountains, ' Into the limitless spaces of the air, to soar over abysses, and let him down upon inaccessible rocks.'

After the Italian journeys science took the lead, the student of Nature supplanted the lover, even his symbolism took a more abstract and realistic form. But he never, even in old age, lost his love for the beauties of Nature, and, holding to Spinoza's fundamental ideas of the unchangeableness and eternity of Nature's laws, and the oneness of the Cosmos, he sought to think it out and base it upon scientific grounds, through the unbroken succession of animal and vegetable forms of life, the uniform ' formation and transformation of all organic Nature.' He wrote to Frau von Stein : ' I cannot express to you how legible the book of Nature is growing to me; my long spelling out has helped me. It takes effect now all of a sudden ; my quiet delight is inexpressible ; I find much that is new, but nothing that is unexpected—everything fits in and

conforms, because I have no system, and care for
nothing but truth for its own sake. Soon every-
thing about living things will be clear to me.' [15]

Poetic and scientific intuition were simultaneous
with him, and their common bond was pantheism.
This pantheism marked an epoch in the history of
feeling. For Goethe not only transformed the un-
real feeling of his day into real, described scenery,
and inspired it with human feeling, and deciphered
the beauty of the Alps, as no one else had done,
Rousseau not excepted; but he also brought know-
ledge of Nature into harmony with feeling for her,
and with his wonderfully receptive and constructive
mind so studied the earlier centuries, that he gathered
out all that was valuable in their feeling.

As Goethe in Germany, so Byron in England led
the feeling for Nature into new paths by his
demoniac genius and glowing pantheism. Milton's
great imagination was too puritan, too biblical, to
allow her independent importance; he only assigned
her a *rôle* in relation to the Deity. In fiction, too,
she had no place; but, on the other hand, we find
her in such melancholy, sentimental outpourings as
Young's *Night Thoughts*:

> Night, sable Goddess! from her ebon throne
> In rayless majesty now stretches forth
> Her leaden sceptre o'er a slumb'ring world . . .
> Creation sleeps. 'Tis as the gen'ral pulse
> Of life stood still, and Nature made a pause;
> An awful pause, prophetic of her end . . . etc.

There is a wealth of imagery and comparison amid
Ossian's melancholy and mourning; clouds and mist
are the very shadows of his struggling heroes.
For instance:

> His spear is a blasted pine, his shield the rising moon.
> He sat on the shore like a cloud of mist on the rising
> hill.
>   Thou art snow on the heath; thy hair is the mist
> of Cromla, when it curls on the hill, when it shines to

the beam of the west. Thy breasts are two smooth
rocks seen from Branno of streams.

As the troubled noise of the ocean when roll the waves
on high ; as the last peal of the thunder of heaven, such
is the noise of battle.

As autumn's dark storms pour from two echoing
hills, towards each other approached the heroes.

The clouds of night came rolling down, Darkness
rests on the steeps of Cromla. The stars of the north
arise over the rolling of Erin's waves ; they shew their
heads of fire through the flying mist of heaven. A
distant wind roars in the wood. Silent and dark is the
plain of death.

Wordsworth's influence turned in another direc-
tion. His real taste was pastoral, and he preached
freer intercourse with Nature, glossing his ideas
rather artificially with a theism, through which one
reads true love of her, and an undeniable, though
hidden, pantheism.

In *The Influence of Natural Objects* he described
how a life spent with Nature had early purified him
from passion :

Nor was this fellowship vouchsafed to me
With stinted kindness. In November days,
When vapours, rolling down the valleys, made
A lonely scene more lonesome, among woods
At noon, and 'mid the calm of summer nights,
When by the margin of the trembling lake
Beneath the gloomy hills, I homeward went
In solitude, such intercourse was mine.
'Twas mine among the fields both day and night,
And by the waters all the summer long,
And in the frosty season, when the sun
Was set, and visible for many a mile,
The cottage windows through the twilight blazed,
I heeded not the summons. . . .

Like Klopstock, he delighted in sledging

while the stars
Eastward were sparkling bright, and in the west
The orange sky of evening died away.

Far more characteristic of the man is the con-
fession in *Tintern Abbey* :

Nature then
(The coarser pleasures of my boyish days
And their glad animal movements all gone by)
To me was all in all. I cannot paint
What then I was. The sounding cataract
Haunted me like a passion; the tall rock,
The mountain, and the deep and gloomy wood,
The colours and their forms, were then to me
An appetite, a feeling and a love
That had no need of a remoter charm
By thought supplied, or any interest
Unborrow'd from the eye.

Beautiful notes, to be struck again more forcibly by the frank pantheism of Byron.

What Scott had been doing for Scotland,[14] and Moore for Ireland, Wordsworth, with still greater fidelity to truth, tried to do for England and her people; in contrast to Byron and Shelley, who forsook home to range more widely, or Southey, whose *Thalaba* begins with an imposing description of night in the desert:

How beautiful is night!
A dewy freshness fills the silent air,
No mist obscures, nor cloud, nor speck, nor stain
Breaks the serene of heaven;
In full-orb'd glory yonder Moon divine
Rolls through the dark blue depths.
Beneath her steady ray
The desert-circle spreads
Like the round ocean, girdled with the sky.
How beautiful is night!

But all that previous English poets had done seemed harmless and innocent in comparison with Byron's revolutionary poetry. Prophecy in Rousseau became poetry in Byron.

There was much common ground between these two passionate aspiring spirits, who never attained to Goethe's serenity. Both were melancholy, and fled from their fellows; both strove for perfect liberty and unlimited self-assertion; both felt with the wild and uproarious side of Nature, and found idyllic scenes marred by thoughts of mankind.

Byron's turbulence never subsided ; and his love
for Nature, passionate and comprehensive as it was,
was always 'sickled o'er' with misanthropy and
pessimism, with the 'world-pain.'

He turned to her first through disdain of his kind
and love of introspection, and later on, when he was
spurned by the London world which had been at
his feet, and disdain grew into hatred and disgust,
from a wish to be alone.   But, as Boettger says :

> Though this heart, in which the whole universe is
> reflected, is a sick one, it has immeasurable depths,
> and an intensified spirit life which draws everything
> under its sway and inspires it, feeling and observing
> everything only as part of itself.

The basis of Byron's feeling for Nature was a
revolutionary one—elementary passion.   The genius
which threw off stanza after stanza steeped in
melody, was coupled with an unprecedented sub-
jectivity and individualism.   When the first part of
Childe Harold came out, dull London society was
bewitched by the music and novelty of this en-
thusiastic lyric of Nature, with its incomparable
interweaving of scenery and feeling :

> The sails were fill'd, and fair the light winds blew,
> As glad to waft him from his native home . . .
> But when the sun was sinking in the sea,
> He seized his harp . . .
> Adieu, adieu ! my native shore
> Fades o'er the waters blue ;
> The night winds sigh, the breakers roar,
> And shrieks the wild sea-mew ;
> Yon sun that sets upon the sea
> We follow in his flight ;
> Farewell awhile to him and thee,
> My native land, good-night !

He says of the beauty of Lusitania :

> Oh Christ ! it is a goodly sight to see
> What Heaven hath done for this delicious land.
> What fruits of fragrance blush on every tree !
> What goodly prospects o'er the hills expand ! . . .

The horrid crags, by toppling convent crown'd,
The cork trees hoar that clothe the shaggy steep,
The mountain moss, by scorching skies imbrown'd,
The sunken glen, whose sunless shrubs must weep,
The tender azure of the unruffled deep,
The orange tints that gild the greenest bough,
The torrents that from cliff to valley leap,
The vine on high, the willow branch below,
Mix'd in one mighty scene, with varied beauty glow.

Yet his spirit drives him away, 'more restless than the swallow in the skies.'

The charm of the idyllic is in the lines :

But these between, a silver streamlet glides . . .
Here leans the idle shepherd on his crook,
And vacant on the rippling waves doth look,
That peaceful still 'twixt bitterest foemen flow.

The beauty of the sea and night in this :

The moon is up ; by Heaven a lovely eve !
Long streams of light o'er dancing waves expand. . .
How softly on the Spanish shore she plays,
Disclosing rock, and slope, and forest brown
Distinct . . .
Bending o'er the vessel's laving side
To gaze on Dian's wave-reflected sphere.

He reflects that :

To sit on rocks, to muse o'er flood and fell,
To slowly trace the forest's shady scene . . .
To climb the trackless mountain all unseen
With the wild flock that never needs a fold,
Alone o'er steeps and foaming falls to lean,—
This is not solitude ; 'tis but to hold
Converse with Nature's charms, and view her stores
    unroll'd.
But 'midst the crowd, the hum, the shock of men,
To hear, to see, to feel, and to possess,
And roam along, the world's tired denizen,
Witbbl none who bless us, none whom we can
    ess . . .
This is to be alone—this, this is solitude.

His preference for wild scenery shews here :

Dear Nature is the kindest mother still,
Though always changing, in her aspect mild ;

From her bare bosom let me take my fill,
Her never-wean'd, though not her favour'd child.
O she is fairest in her features wild,
Where nothing polish'd dares pollute her path ;
To me by day or night she ever smiled,
Though I have mark'd her when none other hath,
And sought her more and more, and loved her best in
 wrath.

He observes everything — now 'the billows'
melancholy flow' under the bows of the ship, now
the whole scene at Zitza :

Where'er we gaze, around, above, below,
What rainbow tints, what magic charms are found !
Rock, river, forest, mountain, all abound,
And bluest skies that harmonize the whole ;
Beneath, the distant torrent's rushing sound
Tells where the volumed cataract doth roll
Between those hanging rocks, that shock yet please the
 soul.

This is full of poetic vision :

Where lone Utraikey forms its circling cove,
And weary waves retire to gleam at rest,
How brown the foliage of the green hill's grove,
Nodding at midnight o'er the calm bay's breast,
As winds come lightly whispering from the west,
Kissing, not ruffling, the blue deep's serene ;—
Here Harold was received a welcome guest ;
Nor did he pass unmoved the gentle scene,
For many a job could he from Night's soft presence
 glean.

Feeling himself 'the most unfit of men to herd
with man,' he is happy only with Nature :

Once more upon the waters ! yet once more !
And the waves bound beneath me as a steed
That knows his rider. Welcome to the roar !
Swift be their guidance, wheresoe'er it lead.

Where rose the mountains, there to him were friends ;
Where rolled the ocean, thereon was his home ;
Where a blue sky and glowing clime extends,
He had the passion and the power to roam ;
The desert, forest, cavern, breaker's foam,

Were unto him companionship ; they spake
A mutual language, clearer than the tome
Of his land's tongue, which he would oft forsake
For Nature's pages glass'd by sunbeams on the lake.

Again :

I live not in myself, but I become
Portion of that around me, and to me
High mountains are a feeling, but the hum
Of human cities torture ; I can see
Nothing to loathe in Nature save to be
A link reluctant in a fleshly chain,
Class'd among creatures, when the soul can flee,
And with the sky, the peak, the heaving plain
Of ocean, or the stars, mingle, and not in vain.

Are not the mountains, waves, and skies a part
Of me and of my soul, as I of them ?
Is not the love of these deep in my heart
With a pure passion ? Should I not contemn
All objects, if compared with these ?

Love of Nature was a passion with him, and
when he looked

Upon the peopled desert past
As on a place of agony and strife,

mountains gave him a sense of freedom.
He praised the Rhine :

Where Nature, nor too sombre nor too gay,
Wild but not rude, awful yet not austere,
Is to the mellow earth as autumn to the year.

and far more the Alps :

Above me are the Alps,
The palaces of Nature, whose vast walls
Have pinnacled in clouds their snowy scalps,
And throned eternity in icy halls
Of cold sublimity, where forms and falls
The avalanche, the thunderbolt of snow !
All that expands the spirit, yet appals,
Gather around these summits, as to shew
How Earth may pierce to Heaven, yet leave vain man
below.

On the Lake of Geneva :

> Ye stars which are the poetry of heaven . . .
> All heaven and earth are still—though not in sleep,
> But breathless, as we grow when feeling most ;
> And silent, as we stand in thoughts too deep.
> All heaven and earth are still : from the high host
> Of stars, to the lull'd lake and mountain coast,
> All is concenter'd in a life intense,
> Where not a beam, nor air, nor leaf is lost,
> But hath a part of being, and a sense
> Of that which is of all Creator and defence.
>
> And this is in the night. Most glorious night,
> Thou wert not sent for slumber ; let me be
> A sharer in thy fierce and far delight,
> A portion of the tempest and of thee !
> How the lit lake shines, a phosphoric sea,
> And the big rain comes dancing to the earth !
> And now again 'tis black—and now, the glee
> Of the loud hills shakes with its mountain mirth,
> As if they did rejoice o'er a young earthquake's birth.
> But where of ye, oh tempests, is the goal ?
> Are ye like those within the human breast ?
> Or do ye find, at length, like eagles, some high nest ?
>
> The morn is up again, the dewy morn
> With breath all incense, and with cheek all bloom,
> Laughing the clouds away with playful scorn,
> And living as if earth contained no tomb.

In Clarens :

> Clarens ! sweet Clarens, birthplace of deep Love,
> Thine air is the young breath of passionate thought,
> Thy trees take root in Love ; the snows above
> The very glaciers have his colours caught,
> And sunset into rose-hues sees them wrought
> By rays which sleep there lovingly ; the rocks,
> The permanent crags, tell here of Love.

Yet

> Ever and anon of griefs subdued
> There comes a token like a scorpion's sting,
> Scarce seen, but with fresh bitterness imbued ;
> And slight withal may be the things which bring
> Back on the heart the weight which it would fling
> Aside for ever ; it may be a sound,
> A tone of music, summer's eve or spring,

A flower, the wind, the ocean, which shall wound,
Striking the electric chain with which we are darkly
  bound.

The unrest and torment of his own heart he finds
reflected in Nature :

The roar of waters ! from the headlong height
Velino cleaves the wave-worn precipice ;
The fall of waters ! rapid as the light
The flashing mass foams, shaking the abyss ;
The hell of waters ! where they howl and hiss,
And boil in endless torture ; while the sweat
Of their great agony, wrung out from this
Their Phlegethon, curls round the rocks of jet
That gird the gulf around, in pitiless horror set,
And mounts in spray the skies, and thence again
Returns in an unceasing shower, which round
With its unemptied cloud of gentle rain
Is an eternal April to the ground,
Making it all one emerald ; how profound
The gulf, and how the giant element
From rock to rock leaps with delirious bound,
Crushing the cliffs, which downward, worn and rent
With his fierce footsteps, yields in chasms a fearful
  rent. . . .
Horribly beautiful ! but, on the verge
From side to side, beneath the glittering morn,
An Iris sits amidst the infernal surge,
Like Hope upon a deathbed.

The ' enormous skeleton ' of Rome impresses him
most by moonlight :

When the rising moon begins to climb
Its topmost arch, and gently pauses there ;
When the stars twinkle through the loops of time,
And the low night breeze waves along the air !

Underlying all his varying moods is this note :

There is a pleasure in the pathless woods,
There is a rapture on the lonely shore,
There is society, where none intrudes,
By the deep sea, and music in its roar :
I love not man the less, but Nature more,
From these our interviews, in which I steal
From all I may be, or have been before,
To mingle with the Universe and feel
What I can ne'er express, yet cannot all conceal.

The sea, the sky with its stars and clouds, and the mountains, are his passion:

Roll on, thou deep and dark blue Ocean—roll!
Ten thousand fleets sweep over thee in vain;
Man marks the earth with ruin—his control
Stops with the shore; upon the watery plain
The wrecks are all thy deed, nor doth remain
A shadow of man's ravage, save his own,
When, for a moment, like a drop of rain
He sinks into thy depths with bubbling groan,
Without a grave, unknell'd, uncoffin'd, and unknown.
                                        (*Childe Harold.*)

The day at last has broken. What a night
Hath usher'd it! How beautiful in heaven!
Though varied with a transitory storm,
More beautiful in that variety! . . .
                    And can the sun so rise,
So bright, so rolling back the clouds into
Vapours more lovely than the unclouded sky,
With golden pinnacles and snowy mountains,
And billows purpler than the ocean's, making
In heaven a glorious mockery of the earth.
                                    (*Sardanapalus.*)

He had loved the Scotch Highlands in youth:

Amidst Nature's native scenes,
Loved to the last, whatever intervenes
Between us and our childhood's sympathy
Which still reverts to what first caught the eye.
He who first met the Highlands' swelling blue
Will love each peak that shews a kindred hue,
Hail in each crag a friend's familiar face,
And clasp the mountain in his mind's embrace.
                                        (*The Island.*)

and in *The Island* he says:

How often we forget all time, when lone,
Admiring Nature's universal throne,
Her woods, her wilds, her waters, the intense
Reply of hers to our intelligence!
Live not the stars and mountains? Are the waves
Without a spirit? Are the dropping caves
Without a feeling in their silent tears?
No, no; they woo and clasp us to their spheres,
Dissolve this clog and clod of clay before
Its hour, and merge our soul in the great shore.
                                        (*The Island.*)

Byron's feeling was thus, like Goethe's in *Werther* and *Faust*, a pantheistic sympathy. But there was this great difference between them—Goethe's mind passed through its period of storm and stress, and attained a serene and ripe vision ; Byron's never did. Melancholy and misanthropy always mingled with his feelings ; he was, in fact, the father of our modern ' world-pain.'

Still more like a brilliant meteor that flashes and is gone was Shelley, the most highly strung of all modern lyrists. With him, too, love of Nature amounted to a passion ; but it was with her remote aerial forms that he was most at home. His imagination, a cosmic one, revelling among the spheres, was like Byron's in its preference for the great, wide, and distant ; but unlike his in giving first place to the serene and passionless. As Brandes says : ' In this familiarity with the great forms and movements of Nature, Shelley is like Byron ; but like him as a fair genius is like a dark one, as Ariel is like the flame-bringing angel of the morning star.'

We see his love for the sea, especially at rest, in the ' Stanzas written in dejection near Naples,' which contain the beautiful line which proved so prophetic of his death :

> The sun is warm, the sky is clear,
> The waves are dancing fast and bright ;
> Blue isles and snowy mountains wear
> The purple noon's transparent might. . . .
> I see the deep's untrampled floor
> With green and purple sea-weeds strewn ;
> I see the waves upon the shore
> Like light dissolved, in star showers thrown. . . .
> Yet now despair itself is mild,
> Even as the winds and waters are ;
> I could lie down like a tired child
> And weep away the life of care
> Which I have borne, and yet must bear,—
> Till death like sleep might steal on me,
> And I might feel in the warm air
> My cheek grow cold, and hear the sea
> Breathe o'er my dying brain its last monotony.

In his *Essay on Love*, speaking of the irresistible longing for sympathy, he says :

> In solitude, or in that deserted state when we are surrounded by human beings, and yet they sympathize not with us, we love the flowers, the grass, and the water and the sky.   In the motion of the very leaves of spring, in the blue air, there is then found a secret correspondence with our heart.   There is eloquence in the tongueless wind, and a melody in the flowing brooks and the rustling of the reeds beside them, which, by their inconceivable relation to something within the soul, awaken the spirits to a dance of breathless rapture, and bring tears of mysterious tenderness to the eyes, like the voice of one beloved singing to you alone.

As Brandes says : 'His pulses beat in secret sympathy with Nature's.   He called plants and animals his dear sisters and brothers, and the words which his wife inscribed upon his tombstone in Rome, "cor cordium," are true of his relation to Nature also.'

The Cloud, with its marvellously vivid personification, is a perfect example of his genius.

It gives the measure of his unlikeness to the more homekeeping imaginations of his contemporaries Wordsworth, Coleridge, Burns, and Moore ; and at the same time to Byron, for here there are no morbid reflections ; the poem is pervaded by a naive, child-like tone, such as one hears in the old mythologies.

The Cloud :

> I bring fresh showers for the thirsting flowers
> From the seas and the streams ;
> I bear light shade for the leaves when laid
> In their noonday dreams.
> From my wings are shaken the dews that waken
> The sweet buds every one,
> When rocked to rest on their Mother's breast
> As she dances about the sun.
> I wield the flail of the lashing hail,
> And whiten the green plains under ;
> And then again I dissolve it in rain,
> And laugh as I pass in thunder.

I sift the snow on the mountains below,
And their great pines groan aghast,
And all the night 'tis my pillow white
While I sleep in the arms of the Blast. . . .
From cape to cape, with a bridge-like shape,
Over a torrent sea,
Sunbeam-proof, I hang like a roof,
The mountains its columns be.
The triumphal arch through which I march,
With hurricane, fire, and snow,
When the Powers of the air are chained to my chair,
Is the million-coloured bow ;
The Sphere-fire above its soft colours wove
While the moist earth was laughing below.
I am the daughter of Earth and Water,
And the nursling of the Sky.

As Brandes puts it; When the cloud sings thus of
the moon :

When

That orbed maiden with white fire laden,
Whom Mortals call the Moon,
Glides glimmering o'er my fleece-like floor
By the midnight breezes strewn ;
And wherever the beat of her unseen feet,
Which only the angels hear,
May have broken the woof of my tent's thin roof,
The Stars peep behind her and peer.

or of—

The sanguine Sunrise, with his meteor eyes,

the reader is carried back, by dint of the virgin
freshness of the poet's imagination, to the time
when the phenomena of Nature were first moulded
into mythology.

This kinship to the myth is very clear in the
finest of all his poems, the *Ode to the West Wind*,
when the poet says to the wind :

O wild West Wind, thou breath of Autumn's being, . . .
Thou on whose stream, 'mid the steep sky's commotion,
Loose clouds like earth's decaying leaves are shed,
Shook from the tangled boughs of heaven and ocean.
Angels of rain and lightning, there are spread
On the blue surface of thine airy surge,
Like the bright hair uplifted from the head

> Of some fierce Mænad, even from the dim verge
> Of the horizon to the zenith's height,
> The locks of the approaching storm.

He calls the wind the ' breath of Autumn's being,' the one

> Who chariotest to their dark wintry bed
> The winged seeds.

And cries to it :

> If I were a dead leaf thou mightest bear ;
> If I were a swift cloud to fly with thee ;
> A wave to pant beneath thy power and share
> The impulse of thy strength, only less free
> Than thou, O uncontrollable ! . . .
> O lift me as a wave, a leaf, a cloud !
> I fall upon the thorns of life, I bleed !
> A heavy weight of hours has chained and bowed
> One too like thee, tameless, and swift, and proud.
> Make me thy lyre, even as the forest is ;
> What if my leaves are falling like its own ?
> The tumult of thy mighty harmonies
> Will take from both a deep autumnal tone,
> Sweet though in sadness. Be thou, Spirit fierce,
> My spirit. Be thou me, impetuous one !
> Drive my dead thoughts over the universe,
> Like withered leaves, to quicken a new birth ;
> And by the incantation of this verse,
> Scatter, as from an unextinguished hearth
> Ashes and sparks, my words among mankind !
> Be through my lips to unawakened earth
> The trumpet of a prophecy ! O Wind,
> If Winter comes, can Spring be far behind ?

His poems are full of this power of inspiring all the elements with life, breathing his own feeling into them, and divining love and sympathy in them ; for instance :

> The fountains mingle with the river,
> And the river with the ocean ;
> The winds of heaven mix for ever
> With a sweet emotion. . . .
> See the mountains kiss high heaven,
> And the waves clasp one another . . .
> And the sunlight clasps the earth,
> And the moonbeams kiss the sea.

and :

> I love all thou lovest,
> Spirit of Delight;
> The fresh earth in new leaves dressed,
> And the starry night,
> Autumn evening and the morn
> When the golden mists are born.
> I love snow and all the forms
> Of the radiant frost ;
> I love waves and winds and storms—
> Everything almost
> Which is Nature's, and may be
> Untainted by man's misery.

To Goethe, Byron, and Shelley, this pantheism, universal love, sympathy with Nature in all her forms, was the base of feeling ; but both of England's greatest lyrists, dying young, failed to attain perfect harmony of thought and feeling. There always remained a bitter ingredient in their poetry.

Let us now turn to France.

LAMARTINE AND VICTOR HUGO

Rousseau discovered the beauty of scenery for France ; St Pierre portrayed it poetically, not only in *Paul and Virginia*, but in *Chaumiére Indienne* and *Études de la Nature*. The science which these two writers lacked, Buffon possessed in a high degree ; but he had not the power to delineate Nature and feeling in combination : he lacked insight into the hidden analogies between the movements of the mind and the phenomena of the outer world. Chateaubriand, on the contrary, had this faculty to its full modern extent. It is true that his ego was constantly to the fore, even in dealing with Nature, but his landscapes were full of sympathetic feeling. He had Rousseau's melancholy and unrest, and cared nothing for those ' oppressive masses,' mountains, except as backgrounds ; but he was enthusiastic about the scenery which he saw in America, the virgin forests, and the Mississippi—above all, about the sea. His Réné, that life-like

figure, half-passionate, half-*blasé*, measuring every-
thing by himself, and flung hither and thither by
the waves of passion, shewed a lover's devotion to
the sea and to Nature generally."/ ' It was not
God whom I contemplated on the waves in the
magnificence of His works : I saw an unknown
woman, and the miracle of his smile, the beauties
of the sky, seemed to me disclosed by her breath.
I would have bartered eternity for one of her caresses.
I pictured her to myself as throbbing behind this
veil of the universe which hid her from my eyes.
Oh ! why was it not in my power to rend the veil
and press the idealized woman to my heart, to spend
myself on her bosom with the love which is the
source of my inspiration, my despair, and my life ? '

In subjectivity and dreaminess both Chateau-
briand and Lamartine were like the German roman-
ticists, but their fundamental note was theism, not
pantheism. The storm of the French Revolution,
which made radical changes in religion, as in all
other things, was followed by a reaction. Chris-
tianity acquired new power and inwardness, and
Nature was unceasingly praised as the mirror of the
divine idea of creation.

In his *Génie du Christianisme*, Chateaubriand said :

> The true God, in entering into His Works, has given
> his immensity to Nature . . . there is an instinct in
> man, which puts him in communication with the scenes
> of Nature.

Lamartine was a sentimental dreamer of dreams,
a thinker of lofty thoughts which lost themselves
in the inexpressible. His *Méditations* shew his
ardent though sad worship of Nature ; his love of
evening, moonlight, and starlight. For instance,
L'Isolement :

> Ici gronde le fleuve aux vagues écumantes,
> Il serpente et s'enfonce en un lointain obscur :
> Là le lac immobile étend ses eaux dormantes
> Où l'étoile du soir se lève dans l'azur.
> An sommet de ces monts couronnés de bois sombres,

Le crépuscule encore jette un dernier rayon ;
Et le char vaporeux de la reine des ombres
Monte et blanchit déjà les bords de l'horizon.

Le Soir :

Le soir ramène le silence . . . .
Venus se lève à l'horizon ;
A mes pieds l'étoile amoureuse
De sa lueur mystérieuse
Blanchit les tapis de gazon.
De ce hêtre au feuillage sombre
J'entends frissonner les rameaux ;
On dirait autour des tombeaux
Qu'on entend voltiger une ombre.
Tout-à-coup, détaché des cieux,
Un rayon de l'astre nocturne,
Glissant sur mon front taciturne,
Vient mollement toucher mes yeux.
Doux reflet d'un globe de flamme
Charmant rayon, que me veux-tu ?
Viens-tu dans mon sein abattu
Porter la lumière à mon âme ?

Descends-tu pour me révéler
Des mondes le divin mystère,
Ces secrets cachés dans la sphère
Où le jour va te rappeler ?

In the thought of happy past hours, he questions the lake :

Un soir, t'en souvient-il, nous voguions en silence ;
On n'entendait au loin, sur l'onde et sous les cieux,
Que le bruit des rameurs qui frappaient en cadence
Tes flots harmonieux.
O lac ! rochers muets ! grottes ! forêt obscure !
Vous que le temps épargne ou qu'il peut rajeunir
Gardez de cette nuit, gardez, belle nature,
Au moins le souvenir ! . . .
Que le vent qui gémit, le roseau qui soupire
Que les parfums légers de ton air embaumé,
Que tout ce qu'on entend, l'on voit, ou l'on respire,
Tout dise : ' ils ont aimés !

La Prière has :

Le roi brillant du jour, se couchant dans sa gloire,
Descend avec lenteur de son char de victoire ;
Le nuage éclatant qui le cache à nos yeux
Conserve en sillons d'or sa trace dans les cieux,
Et d'un reflet de pourpre inonde l'étendue.

Comme une lampe d'or dans l'azur suspendue,
La lune se balance aux bords de l'horizon ;
Ses rayons affaiblis dorment sur le gazon,
Et le voile des nuits sur les monts se déplie.
C'est l'heure, où la nature, un moment recueillie,
Entre la nuit qui touche et le jour qui s'enfuit
S'élève au créateur du jour et de la nuit,
Et semble offrir à Dieu dans son brillant langage,
De la création le magnifique hommage.
Voilà le sacrifice immense, universelle !
L'univers est le temple, et la terre est l'autel ;
Les cieux en sont le dôme et ses astres sans nombre,
Ces feux demi-voilés, pâle ornement de l'ombre,
Dans la voûte d'azur avec ordre semés,
Sont les sacrés flambeaux pour ce temple allumés. . .
Mais ce temple est sans voix. . . .

. . . Mon cœur seul parle dans ce silence—
La voix de l'univers c'est mon intelligence.
Sur les rayons du soir, sur les ailes du vent,
Elle s'élève à Dieu. . . .

Le Golfe de Baia :

    Vois-tu comme le flot paisible
    Sur le rivage vient mourir ?
    Mais déjà l'ombre plus épaisse
    Tombe et brunit les vastes mers ;
    Le bord s'efface, le bruit cesse,
    Le silence occupe les airs.
    C'est l'heure où la Mélancholie
    S'assied pensive et recueillie
    Aux bords silencieux des mers.

The decay of autumn corresponds to his own dolorous feelings :

Oui, dans ces jours d'automne où la nature expire,
A ses regards voilés je trouve plus d'attraits ;
C'est l'adieu d'un ami, c'est le dernier sourire
Des lèvres que la mort va fermer pour jamais.

This is from *Ischia :*

Le Soleil va porter le jour à d'autres mondes ;
Dans l'horizon désert Phébé monte sans bruit,
Et jette, en pénétrant les ténébres profondes,
Un voile transparent sur le front de la nuit.
Voyez du haut des monts ses clartés ondoyantes
Comme un fleuve de flamme inonder les coteaux,
Dormir dans les vallons on glisser sur les pentes,

> Ou rejaillir au loin du sein brillant des eaux. . . .
> Doux comme le soupir d'un enfant qui sommeille,
> Un son vague et plaintif se répand dans les airs. . . .
> Mortel ! ouvre ton âme à ces torrents de vie,
> Reçois par tous les sens les charmes de la nuit. . . .

He sees the transitoriness of all earthly things reflected in Nature :

> L'onde qui baise ce rivage,
> De quoi se plaint-elle à ses bords ?
> Pourquoi le roseau sur la plage, pourquoi le ruisseau
>   sous l'ombrage,
> Rendent-ils de tristes accords ?
> De quoi gémit la tourterelle ?   Tout naist, tout paise.

Such a depth of sympathy and dreamy dolorous reverie was new to France, but Rousseau had broken the ice, and henceforward feeling flowed freely. To Lamartine the theist, as to the pantheists Goethe, Shelley, and Byron, Nature was a friend and lover.

Victor Hugo was of the same mind, but his poetry is clearer and more plastic than Lamartine's. We quote from his finest poems, the *Feuilles d'Automne*. He was a true lyrist, familiar both with the external life of Nature and the inner life of man. His beautiful 'Ce qu'on entend sur la montagne' has the spirit of *Faust*. He imagines himself upon a mountain top, with earth on one side, the sea on the other ; and there he hears two voices unlike any ever heard before :

> L'une venait des mers, chant de gloire ! hymne
>   heureux !
> C'était la voix des flots qui se parlaient entre eux. . . .
> Or, comme je l'ai dit, l'Océan magnifique
> Épandait une voix joyeuse et pacifique
> Chantant comme la harpe aux temples de Sion,
> Et louait la beauté de la création.

while from the other voice :

> Pleurs et cris !   L'injure, l'anathème. . . .
> C'était la terre et l'homme qui pleuraient ! . . .
> L'une disait, Nature ! et l'autre, Humanité !

The personifications in this poem are beautiful. He, too, like Lamartine, loves sea and stars most of all. These verses from *Les Orientales* remind one of St Augustine :

J'étais seul près des flots par une nuit d'étoiles,
Pas un nuage aux cieux ; sur les mers pas de voiles,
Et les bois et les monts et toute la nature
Semblaient interroger dans confus murmure
Les flots des mers, les feux du ciel.
Et les étoiles d'or, légions infinies,
A voix haute, à voix basse, avec mille harmonies
Disaient en inclinant leurs couronnes de feu,
Et les flots bleus, que rien gouverne et n'arrête,
Disaient en recourbant l'écume de leur crête :
C'est le Seigneur Dieu, le Seigneur Dieu !

Parfois lorsque tout dort, je m'assieds plein de joie
Sous le dôme étoilé qui sur nos fronts flamboie ;
J'écoute si d'en haut il tombe quelque bruit ;
Et l'heure vainement me frappe de son aile
Quand je contemple ému cette fête eternelle
Que le ciel rayonnant donne au monde la nuit !
Souvent alors j'ai cru que ces soleils de flamme
Dans ce monde endormi n'échauffaient que mon âme ;
Qu'à les comprendre seul j'étais prédestiné ;
Que j'étais, moi, vaine ombre obscure et taciturne,
Le roi mystérieuse de la pompe nocturne ;
Que le ciel pour moi seul s'était illuminé !

The necessary condition of delight in Nature is very strikingly given :

Si vous avez en vous, vivantes et pressées,
Un monde intérieur d'images, de pensées,
De sentimens, d'amour, d'ardente passion
Pour féconder ce monde, échangez-le sans cesse
Avec l'autre univers visible qui vous presse !
Mêlez toute votre âme à la création. . . .
Que sous nos doigts puissans exhale la nature,
Cette immense clavier !

His lyrics are rich in fine scenes from Nature, unrolled in cold but stately periods, and the poetic intuition which always divines the spirit life brought him near to that pantheism which we find in all the greatest English and German poets of his time,[16] and which lay, too, at the root of German romanticism.

THE GERMAN ROMANTICISTS

Schiller did not possess the intrinsically lyrical genius of Goethe; his strength lay, not in song, but drama, and in a didactic form of epic—the song not of feeling, but of thought.

Descriptions of Nature occur here and there in his epics and dramas; but his feeling for her was chiefly theoretic. Like his contemporaries, he passed through a sentimental period; *Evening* shews this, and *Melancholy, to Laura*:

> Laura, a sunrise seems to break
> Where'er thy happy looks may glow. . . .
> Thy soul—a crystal river passing,
> Silver clear and sunbeam glassing,
> Mays into blossom sad autumn by thee:
> Night and desert, if they spy thee,
> To gardens laugh—with daylight shine,
> Lit by those happy smiles of thine !

With such ecstatic extravagances contrast the excellent descriptions of Nature full of objective life in his longer poems—for instance, the tumult of Charybdis and the unceasing rain in *The Diver*, evening in *The Hostage*, and landscape in *William Tell* and *The Walk*. In the last, as Julian Schmidt says, the ever varying scenery is made a ' frame for a kind of phenomenology of mankind.'

> Flowers of all hue are struggling into glow
> Along the blooming fields ; yet their sweet strife
> Melts into one harmonious concord. Lo !
> The path allures me through the pastoral green
> And the wide world of fields ! The labouring bee
> Hums round me, and on hesitating wing
> O'er beds of purple clover, quiveringly
> Hovers the butterfly. Save these, all life
> Sleeps in the glowing sunlight's steady sheen—
> E'en from the west no breeze the lull'd airs bring.
> Hark ! in the calm aloft I hear the skylark sing.
> The thicket rustles near, the alders bow
> Down their green coronals, and as I pass,
> Waves in the rising wind the silvering grass ;

Come ! day's ambrosial night ! receive me now
Beneath the roof by shadowy beeches made
Cool-breathing, etc.

Schiller's interest in Nature was more a matter
of reflection than direct observation; its real tend-
ency was philosophical and ethical. He called
Nature naive (he included naturalness in Nature);
those who seek her, sentimental ; but he overlooked
(as we saw in an earlier chapter) the fact that
antiquity did not always remain naive, and that
not all moderns are sentimental.

As Rousseau's pupil he drew a sharp distinction
between Nature and Art, and felt happy in solitude
where ' man with his torment does not come,' lying,
as he says in *The Bride of Messina*, like a child on
the bosom of Nature.

In Schiller's sense of the word, perhaps no poet
has been more sentimental about Nature than
Jean Paul.

He was the humorous and satirical idyllist *par
excellence*, and laid the scenes of his romances in
idyllic surroundings, using the trifling events of
daily life to wonderful purpose. There is an almost
oriental splendour in his pages, with their audacious
metaphors and mixture of ideas. With the excep-
tion of Lake Maggiore in *Titan*, he gives no set
descriptions of landscape ; but all his references to
it, all his sunrises and sunsets, are saturated with
the temperament of his characters, and they revel
in feeling. They all love Nature, and wander in-
defatigably about their own countryside, finding the
reflection of their feelings in her. There is a
constant interweaving of the human soul and the
universe ; therein lies his pantheistic trait. ' To
each man,' he said,[17] ' Nature appears different, and
the only question is, which is the most beautiful ?
Nature is for ever becoming flesh for mankind ;
outer Nature takes a different form in each mind.'
Certainly the nature of Jean Paul was different

from the Nature of other mortals. Was she more beautiful ? He wrote of her in his usual baroque style, with a wealth of thought and feeling, and everywhere the sparkle of genius ; but it is all presented in the strangest motley, as exaggerated and unenjoyable as can be. For example, from *Siebenkäs* :

> I appeared again then on the last evening of the year 1794, on the red waves of which so many bodies, bled to death, were borne away to the ocean of eternity.

> To the butterfly - proboscis of Siebenkäs, enough honey - cells were still open in every blue thistle-blossom of destiny.

> When they had passed the gate—that is to say, the un-Palmyra-like ruins of it — the crystal reflecting grotto of the August night stood open and shining above the dark green earth, and the ocean-calm of Nature stayed the wild storm of the human heart. Night was drawing and closing her curtain (a sky full of silent suns, not a breath of breeze moving in it) up above the world, and down beneath it the reaped corn stood in the sheaves without a rustle. The cricket with his one constant song, and a poor old man gathering snails for the snail pits, seemed to be the only things that dwelt in the far-reaching darkness.

When it was autumn in his heart :

> Above the meadows, where all the flowers were withered and dead ; above the fields, where the corn ears waved no more, floated dim phantom forms, all pale and wan, faint pictures of the past. Over the grand eternal woods and hills a biting mist was draped in clinging folds, as if all Nature, trembling into dust, must vanish in its wreaths. . . . But one bright thought pierced these dark fogs of Nature and the soul, turning them to a white gleaming mist, a dew all glittering with rainbow colours, and gently lighting upon flowers.

When his married life grew more unhappy, in December :

> The heart of our sorrowful Firmian grew sadder yet, as he stood upon this cold, burnt-out hearth-place of Nature.

and in spring

> it seemed to him as if his life dwelt, not in a bodily heart, but in some warm and tender tear, as if his heavy-laden soul were expanding and breaking away through some chink in its prison, and melting into a tone of music, a blue ether wave.

And *Titan* expresses that inner enfranchisement which Nature bestows upon us:

> Exalted Nature! when we see and love thee, we love our fellow-men more warmly, and when we must pity or forget them, thou still remainest with us, reposing before the moist eye like a verdant chain of mountains in the evening red. Ah! before the soul in whose sight the morning dew of its ideals has faded to a cold, grey drizzle . . . thou remainest, quickening Nature, with thy flowers and mountains and cataracts, a faithful comforter; and the bleeding son of the gods, cold and speechless, dashes the drop of anguish from his eyes, that they may rest, far and clear, on thy volcanoes, and on thy springs and on thy suns.

This is sunset in his abstruse artistic handling:

> The sun sinks, and the earth closes her great eye like that of a dying god. Then smoke the hills like altars; out of every wood ascends a chorus; the veils of day, the shadows, float around the enkindled transparent tree-tops, and fall upon the gay, gem-like flowers. And the burnished gold of the west throws back a dead gold on the east, and tinges with rosy light the hovering breast of the tremulous lark—the evening bell of Nature.

And this sunrise:

> The flame of the sun now shot up ever nearer to the kindled morning clouds; at length in the heavens, in the brooks and ponds, and in the blooming cups of dew, a hundred suns rose together, while a thousand colours floated over the earth, and one pure dazzling white broke from the sky. It seemed as if an almighty earthquake had forced up from the ocean, yet dripping, a new-created blooming plain, stretching out beyond the bounds of vision, with all its young instincts and powers; the fire of earth glowed beneath the roots of the immense hanging garden, and the fire of heaven poured down its flames and burnt the colours into

the mountain summits and the flowers. Between the porcelain towers of white mountains the coloured blooming heights stood as thrones of the Fruit-Goddess; over the far-spread camp of pleasure blossom-cups and sultry drops were pitched here and there like peopled tents ; the ground was inlaid with swarming nurseries of grasses and little hearts, and one heart detached itself after another with wings, or fins, or feelers, from the hot breeding - cell of Nature, and hummed and sucked and smacked its little lips, and sung : and for every little proboscis some blossom-cup of joy was already open. The darling child of the infinite mother, man, alone stood with bright joyful eyes upon the market-place of the living city of the sun, full of brilliance and noise, and gazed, delighted, around him into all its countless streets ; but his eternal mother rested veiled in immensity, and only by the warmth which went to his heart did he feel that he was lying upon hers.

For very overflow of thought and imagery and ecstasy of feeling, Jean Paul never achieved a balanced beauty of expression.

The ideal classic standard which Winckelmann and Lessing had laid down — simple and plastic, calm because objective, crystal-clear in thought and expression — and which Goethe and Schiller had sought to realize and imbue with modern ideas, was too strictly limited for the Romanticists. Hyperion's words expressed their taste more accurately : ' O, man is a god when he dreams, a beggar when he thinks ! ' and they laid stress upon restless movement, fantastic, highly-coloured effects, a crass subjectivity, a reckless licence of the imagination.

Actual and visible things were disregarded ; they did not accord with this claim for infinity and the nebulous, for exploring the secret depths of the soul.

It was perhaps a necessary reaction from Goethe's classicism ; but it passed like a bad dream, after tending, thanks to its heterogeneous elements, now to the mediæval period, now to that of Storm and Stress, and now to Goethe, Herder, and Winckel-

mann.   It certainly contained germs of good, which
have grown and flourished in our own day.

In keeping with its whole character, the Romantic
feeling for Nature was subjective and fantastic to
excess, mystically enthusiastic, often with a dreamy
symbolism at once deep and naive ;   its inmost
core was pantheistic, with a pantheism shading off
imperceptibly into mysticism.

After *Werther*, there is perhaps no work of modern
fiction in which Nature plays so artistic a part as in
Holderlin's *Hyperion*.

Embittered by life's failure to realize his ideals,
he cries : ' But thou art still visible, sun in the sky !
Thou art still green, sacred earth !   The streams
still rush to the sea, and shady trees rustle at noon.
The spring's song of joy sings my mortal thoughts
to sleep.   The abundance of the universe nourishes
and satiates my famished being to intoxication.'

This mystical pantheism could not be more clearly
expressed than here :

> O blessed Nature ! I know not how it happens
> when I lift my eyes to your beauty ; but all the joy
> of the sky is in the tears which I shed before you—a
> lover before the lady of his love.   When the soft waves
> of the air play round my breast, my whole being is
> speechless and listens.   Absorbed in the blue expanse,
> I often look up to the ether and down to the holy sea ;
> and it seems as if a kindred spirit opened its arms to
> me, as if the pain of loneliness were lost in the divine
> life.   To be one with all that lives, in blessed self-
> forgetfulness to return to the All of Nature, that is
> the height of thought and bliss—the sacred mountain
> height, the place of eternal rest, where noon loses its
> sultriness and thunder its voice, and the rough sea is
> like the waves in a field of wheat.

To such feeling as this the actualities are but
fetters, hindering aspiration.

'O, if great Nature be the daughter of a father,
is the daughter's heart not his heart ?   Is not he
her deepest feeling ?   But have I found it ?   Do I
know it ? '

He tries to discern the 'soul of Nature,' hears 'the melody of morning light begin with soft notes.' He says to the flower, 'You are my sister,' and to the springs, 'We are of one race': he finds symbolic resemblance between his heart and all the days and seasons: he feels the beauty of the 'land like paradise,' while scarcely ever, except in the poem *Heidelberg*, giving a clear sketch of scenery. A number of fine comparisons from Nature are scattered through his writings [18]:

> The caresses of the charming breezes.
>
> The light, clear, flattering sea.
>
> Sacred air, the sister of the mind which moves and lives in us with fiery force, present everywhere immortal.
>
> Earth, 'one of the flowers of the sky.'
>
> Heaven, 'the unending garden of life.'
>
> Beauty, that 'which is one and all.'

He describes his love in a mystical form :

> We were but one flower, and our souls lived in each other as flowers do, when they love and hide their joy within a closed calyx. . . . The clear starry night had now become my element, for the beautiful life of my love grew in the stillness as in the depths of earth gold grows mysteriously.

He delights 'thus to drink the joy of the world out of one cup with the lady of his love.'

'Yea, man is a sun, seeing all and transfiguring all when he loves; and when he does not love, he is like a dark dwelling in which a little smelly lamp is burning.' All this is soft and feminine, but it has real poetic charm.

Beautiful too, though sad and gloomy, is his *Song of Fate* :

> Nowhere may man abide,
> But painfully from hour to hour
> He stumbles blindly on to the unknown,
> As water falls from rock to rock
> The long year through.

His pantheism finds expression in the odes—in *To Nature*, for instance :

> Since my heart turneth upward to the sun
>   As one that hears her voice,
> Hailing the stars as brothers, and the spring
>   As melody divine;
> Since in the breath that stirs the wood thy soul,
>   The soul of joy, doth move
> On the still waters of my heart—therefore,
>   O Nature! these are golden days to me!

Tieck, too, was keenly alive to Nature. Spring[19]:

> Look all around thee how the spring advances!
> New life is playing through the gay green trees!
> See how in yonder bower the light leaf dances
> To the bird's tread and to the quivering breeze!
> How every blossom in the sunlight glances!
> The winter frost to his dark cavern flees,
> And earth, warm wakened, feels through every vein
> The kindling influence of the vernal rain.
> Now silvery streamlets, from the mountain stealing,
> Dance joyously the verdant vales along;
> Cold fear no more the songster's tongue is sealing,
> Down in the thick dark grove is heard his song.
> And all their bright and lovely hues revealing,
> A thousand plants the field and forest throng;
> Light comes upon the earth in radiant showers,
> And mingling rainbows play among the flowers.

All his writings seem intoxicated with Nature. The hero of his novel *William Lovell*, scamp though he is, a man of criminal egotism whose only law is licence, is deeply in love with Nature.

He wrote from Florence :

> Nature refreshes my soul with her endless beauty. I am often full of enthusiasm at the thousand charms of Nature and Art . . . at last my longing to travel to wonderful distant places is satisfied. Even as a child, when I stood outside my father's country-house, and gazed at the distant mountains and discovered a windmill on the very line of the horizon, it seemed to beckon me as it turned, my blood pulsed more quickly, my mind flew to distant regions, a strange longing often filled my eyes with tears.

> Often it seems to me as if the enigma in ourselves were about to be unriddled, as if we were suddenly to see the transformation of all our feelings and strange experiences. Night surrounded me with a hundred terrors, the transparent moonlight sky was like a crystal dome overhead—in this world the most unusual feelings were as shadows.

' Franz Sternbald ' had the same intoxicated feeling for Nature :

> I should like to fill the whole world with songs of love, to move moonrise and sunrise to echo back my joys and sorrows ; and trees, twigs, leaves, grasses to catch the melody and all repeat my music with a thousand tongues.[2]

To the Romantic School, Music and Nature were a passion ; they longed to resolve all their feelings, like Byron, at one flash, into music. ' For thought is too distant.' Night and the forest, moonlight and starlight, were in all their songs.

There is a background of landscape all through *Franz Sternbald's Wanderings.*

In the novels of the eighteenth century landscape had had no place ; Hermes once gave a few lines to sunset, but excused it as an extravagance, and begged readers and critics not to think that he only wanted to fill up the page.

Rousseau altered this ; Sophie la Roche, in her *Freundschaftlichen Frauenzimmerbriefen,* introduced ruins, moonlight scenery, hills, vales, and flowering hedges, etc., into scenes of thought and feeling ; and most of all, Goethe in *Werther* tunes scenery and soul to one key. In his later romances he avoided descriptions of scenery. Jean Paul, like Tieck in *Franz Sternbald,* never spares us one sunset or sunrise. Some of Tieck's concise descriptions are very telling, like Theodore Storm's at the present day :

> Rosy light quivered on the blades of grass, and morning moved in waves along them.

> The redder the evening grew, the heavier became his dreams ; the darkened trees, the shadows lengthening

across the fields, the smoke from the roofs of a little
village, and the stars coming into view one by one in
the sky—all this moved him deeply, moved him to a
wistful compassion for himself.

As Franz wanders about the wood :

He observes the trees reflected in a neighbouring
pond. He had never looked at landscape with this
pleasure, it had never been given to him to discern the
various colours and their shadows, the charm of the
stillness, the effect of the foliage, as now in the clear
water. Till now he had never drawn a landscape,
only looked at it as a necessary adjunct to many
historical pictures, had never felt that lifeless Nature
could herself compose something whole and complete
in itself, and so worthy to be represented.

Tieck's shorter stories, fairy tales and others,
shew taste for the mysterious and indefinite
aspects of Nature — reflections in water, rays of
light, cloud forms :

They became to him the most fitting characters in
which to record that indefinite inexpressible feeling
which gave its special colour to his spiritual life.[21]

The pantheism of Boehme, with whom he was
closely associated, always attracted him, and in
Jena he came under the influence of Steffens, and
also of Schelling, whose philosophy of Nature called
Nature a mysterious poem, a dreaming mind. This
mind it became the chief aim of Novalis, as well as
Tieck, to decipher.

From simple descriptions of Nature he went on
to read mystic meanings into her, seeking, psycho-
logically in his novels and mystically in his fairy
tales, to fathom the connection between natural
phenomena and elementary human feeling. *Blond
Egbert* was the earliest example of this :

Night looked sullenly through the windows, and the
trees without rustled in the wet cold . . . the moon
looked fitfully through breaks in the driving clouds.[22]

In the same book Bertha describes the horror of

loneliness, the vague longings, and then the over-whelming delight in new impressions, which seized her when she fled from home as a child and lost herself among the mountains.

The Runenberg gives in a very powerful way the idea of the weird fascination which the subterranean powers were supposed to exert over men, alluring and befooling them, and rousing their thirst for gold.

The demoniacal elements in mountain scenery, its crags and abysses, are contrasted with idyllic plains. The tale is sprinkled over with descriptions of Nature, which give it a fairy-like effect.[25]

The most extraordinary product of this School was Novalis. With him everything resolved itself into presentiment, twilight, night, into vague long-ings for a vague distant goal, which he expressed by the search for ' the blue flower.' This is from *Heinrich von Ofterdingen* :

' The cheerful pageant of the glorious evening rocked him in soft imaginings; the flower of his heart was visible now and then as by sheet light-ning.' He looked at Nature with the mystic's eye, and described her fantastically :

> I am never tired of looking minutely at the different plants. Growing plants are the direct language of the earth ; each new leaf, each remarkable flower, is a mystery which projects itself, and because it cannot move with love and longing, nor attain to words, is a dumb, quiet plant. When in solitude one finds such a flower, does it not seem as if all around it were brightened, and, best of all, do not the little feathered notes around it remain near ? One could weep for joy, and there, far from the world, stick hands and feet into the earth, to take root, and never more leave so delightful a spot. This green mysterious carpet of love is drawn over the whole earth.

It is not surprising that night should attract this unnaturally excited imagination most of all :

> Sacred, inexpressible, mysterious Night, delicious

> balsam drops from thy hands, from the poppy sheaf ;
> thou upliftest the heavy wings of the Spirit."

Night and death are delight and bliss.

The fairy - like tale of *Hyacinth and Little Rose*, with its charming personifications, is refreshing after all this :

> The violet told the strawberry in confidence, she told her friend the gooseberry, who never ceased to jeer when Hyacinth went, so the whole garden and wood soon knew it, and when Hyacinth went out, voices from all sides cried out, ' Little Rose is my favourite.' When he goes into the wide world to find the land of Isis, he asks the way of the animals, and of springs, rocks, and trees, and the flowers smile at him, the springs offer him a fresh drink, and there is wonderful music when he comes home. ' O that men could understand the music of Nature ! ' cries the listener in the tale. Then follows a description of ' the sweet passion for the being of Nature and her enchanting raptures,' and the charm of the poetic imagination which finds ' a great sympathy with man's heart ' in all the external world. For example, in the breath of wind, which ' with a thousand dark and dolorous notes seems to dissolve one's quiet grief into one deep melodious sigh of all Nature.'
>
> ' And am I myself other than the stream when I gaze gloomily down into its waters and lose my thoughts in its flow ? ' And in ecstasy the youth exclaims : ' Whose heart does not leap for joy, when he feels Nature's innermost life in its fulness, when that powerful feeling, for which language has no other name than love and bliss, spreads like a vapour through his being, and he sinks, palpitating, on the dark alluring breast of Nature, and his poor self is lost in the overwhelming waves of joy ? '

Here we have the key to the romantic feeling for Nature—communion of the soul with Nature in a twilight mood of dreamy absorption.

Yet amidst all this, real delight in romantic scenery was not quite lacking : witness Hulsen's [26] *Observations on Nature on a Journey through Switzerland* ; and the genuine lyric of Nature, untainted by mystic and sickly influences, was still to be heard, as in Eichendorff's beautiful songs and his *Tauge-nichts*.

The Romantic School, in fact, far as it erred from the path, did enlarge the life of feeling generally, and with that, feeling for Nature, and modern literature is still bound to it by a thousand threads.

Our modern rapture has thus been reached by a path which, with many deviations in its course, has come to us from a remote past, and is still carrying us farther forward.

Its present intensity is due to the growth of science, for although feeling has become more realistic and matter-of-fact in these days of electricity and the microscope, love for Nature has increased with knowledge. Science has even become the investigator of religion, and the pantheistic tendency of the great poets has passed into us, either in the idea of an all - present God, or in that of organic force working through matter — the indestructible active principle of life in the region of the visible. Our explorers combine enthusiasm for Nature with their tireless search for truth—for example, Humboldt, Haeckel, and Paul Güssfeldt ; and though, as the shadow side to this light, travelling and admiration of Nature have become a fashion, yet who nowadays can watch a great sunset or a storm over the sea, and remain insensible to the impression ?

Landscape painting and poetry shew the same deviations from the straight line of development as in earlier times. Our garden craft, like our architecture, is eclectic ; but the English park style is still the most adequate expression of prevalent taste : spaces of turf with tree groups, a view over land or sea, gradual change from garden to field ; to which has been added a wider cultivation of foreign plants. In landscape painting the zigzag course is very marked : landscapes such as Bocklin's, entirely projected by the imagination and corresponding to nothing on earth, hang together in our galleries with the most faithful studies from Nature. It is the same with literature. In fiction, novels which perpetuate the sentimental rhapsodies of an early period, and open their chapters with forced descriptions of landscape, stand side by side with the masterly work of great writers—for example, Spielhagen, Wilhelmine von Hillern, and Theodore Storm.

In poetry, the lyric of Nature is inexhaustible. Heine, the greatest lyrist after Goethe, though his poetry has, like the Nixie, an enchantingly fair body with a fish's tail, wrote in the *Travels in the Harz*: ' How infinitely blissful is the feeling when the outer world of phenomena blends and harmonizes with the inner world of feeling ;   when green trees, thoughts, birds' songs, sweet melancholy, the azure of heaven, memory, and the perfume of flowers, run together and form the loveliest of arabesques.'

But his delight in Nature was spoilt by irony and straining after effect—for example, in *The Fig Tree*; and although *The Lotos Flower* is a gem, and the *North Sea Pictures* shew the fine eye of a poet who, like Byron and Shelley, can create myths, his personifications as a whole are affected, and his personal feeling is forced upon Nature for the sake of a witty effect.

Every element of Nature has found skilled interpreters both in poetry and painting, and technical facility and truth of representation now stand on one level with the appreciation of her charms.

NOTES

INTRODUCTION

1. *Kritische Gänge.* Comp. Vischer, *Ueber den optischen Formsinn,* and Carl du Prel, *Psychologie der Lyrik.*
2. As in elegy *Ghatarkarparam.*
3. Comp. Humboldt, *Cosmos.* Schnaase, *Geschichte der bildenden Künste.*
4. See *Die Entwickelung des Naturgefühls bei den Griechen und Römern,* Biese.

CHAPTER I

1. Lucos ac nemora consecrant deorumque nominibus adpellant secretum illud, quod sola reverentia vident, Tac. Germ. Comp. Grimm, *Deutsche Mythologie.*
2. Grimm. Simrock, *Handbuch der Mythologie.*
3, 4, 5. Grimm.
6. *Geschichte der bildenden Künste.* Comp. Grimm, *Deutsche Rechtsaltertümer.*
7. Grimm.
8. Carrière, *Die Poesie.*

CHAPTER II

1. Clement of Rome. 1 *Cor.* 19, 20. Zoeckler, *Geschichte der Beziehungen zwischen Theologie und Naturwissenschaft.*
2. Comp. *Vita S. Basilii.*
3. *Basilii opera omnia.* Parisus, 1730.
4. *Cosmos.*
5. Biese, *Die Entwickelung des Naturgefühls bei den Griechen und Römern.*
6. *Mélanges philosophiques, historiques, et littéraires.*
7. *Homily* 4.   8. *Homily* 6.
9. Biese, *Die Entwickelung des Naturgefühls bei den Griechen und Römern.*
   ' In spring the Cydmian apple trees give blossom watered by river streams in the hallowed garden of the nymphs ; in spring the buds grow and swell beneath the leafy shadow of the vine branch. But my heart knoweth no season of respite; nay, like the Thracian blast that rageth with its lightning, so doth it bear down from Aphrodite's side, dark and fearless, with scorching frenzy in its train, and from its depths shaketh my heart with might.'
10. Comp. Biese, *op. cit.*
11. *Deutsche Rundschau,* 1879.

12. Comp. Biese, *op. cit.*

13. Chrysostom was not only utilitarian, but praised and enjoyed the world's beauty. From the fifth to third century, Greek progress in feeling for Nature can be traced from unconscious to conscious pleasure in her beauty.

14. *De Mortalitate*, cap. 4.

15. *Geschichte der christlich-lateinischen Literatur*.

16. When one thinks of Sappho, Simonides, Theocritus, Meleager, Catullus, Ovid, and Horace, it cannot be denied that this is true of Greek and Roman lyric.

17. As in the Homeric time, when each sphere of Nature was held to be subject to and under the influence of its special deity. But it cannot be admitted that metaphor was freer and bolder in the hymns ; on the contrary, it was very limited and monotonous.

18. In *Cathemerinon*.

19. Comp. fragrant gardens of Paradise, Hymn 3.

In Hamartigenia he says that the evil and ugly in Nature originates in the devil.

20. Ebert.

21. The Robinsonade of the hermit Bonosus upon a rocky island is interesting.

22. Comp. Biese, *op. cit.*

23. Comp. *ad Paulinum*, epist. 19, *Monum. German.* v. 2.

24. *Carm. nat.* 7.   25. *Ep.* xi.

26. *Migne Patrol* 60.   27. *Migne Patrol* 59.

28. Ebert.   29 and 30. Comp. Biese, *op. cit.*

31. *Migne Patrol* 58.   32. *Carm. lib.* i.

33. *Amœnitas loci* : Variorum libri Lugduni, 1677.

34. *Monum. Germ.*, 4th ed., Leo, lib. viii.

35. *Deutsche Rundschau*, 1882.

36. *Monum. German Histor.*, *poet. lat. medii ævi*, I. Berlin 1881, ed. Dümmler. Alcuin, *Carmen* 23.

37. Zoeckler, *Geschichte der Beziehungen zwischen Theologie und Naturwissenschaft*. ' On rocky crags by the sea, on shores fringed by oak or beech woods, in the shady depths of forests, on towering mountain tops, or on the banks of great rivers, one sees the ruins or the still inhabited buildings which once served as the dwellings of the monks who, with the cross as their only weapon, were the pioneers of our modern culture. Their flight from the life of traffic and bustle in the larger towns was by no means a flight from the beauties of Nature.' The last statement is only partly true. In the prime of the monastic era the beauties of Nature were held to be a snare of the devil. Still, in choosing a site, beauty of position was constantly referred to as an auxiliary motive. ' Bernhard loved the valley,' ' but Bernhard chose mountains,' are significant phrases,

38. Comp. Grimm, *Deutsche Mythologie*, on the old Germanic idea of a conflict between winter and spring.

39. Dümmler, vi. *Carolus et Leo papa*.

40. Walahfridi Strabi, *De cultura hortorum*.

41. Comp. H. von Eichen, *Geschichte und System der mittelalterlichen Weltanschauung*. Stuttg. Cotta, 1887.

CHAPTER III

1. Prutz, *Geschichte der Kreuzzuge*. Berlin, 1883.

2. Allatius, *Symmicta*. Coeln, 1653.

3. *Deutsche Pilgerreisen nach dem heiligen Lande*, Roehricht und Meissner. Berlin, 1880.

4. For excellent bibliographical evidence see *Die geographische Kenntnis der Alpen im Mittelalter* in supplement to *Münchner Allgem. Zeitung*, January 1885.

5. Comp. Oehlmann, *Die Alpenpässe im Mittelalter*, *Jahrbuch für Schweizer.*

6. Biese, *op. cit.*

7. Fr. Diez, *Leben und Werke der Troubadours*. Zwickau, 1829.

8. *Des Minnesangs Frühling*, von Lachmann-Haupt.

9. *Geschichte der Malerei*. Woermann und Wottmann.

10. 'Detailed study of Nature had begun ; but the attempt to blend the separate elements into a background landscape in perspective betrayed the insecurity and constraint of dilettante work at every point.' Ludwig Kämmerer on the period before Van Eyck in *Die Landschaft in der deutschen Kunst bis zum Tode Albrecht Dürers*. Leipzig, 1880.

CHAPTER IV

1. *Die Kultur der Renaissance in Italien*.

2. *Untersuchungen über die kampanische Wandmalerei*. Leipzig, 1873.

3. Comp. Schnaase, *op. cit.*

4. *Argon*, ii. 219 ; iii. 260, 298. Comp. Cic. *ad Att.*, iv. 18, 3.

5. *Renaissance und Humanismus in Italien und Deutschland*. Berlin, 1882. (Oncken, *Allgemeine Geschichte in Einzeldarstellungen*, ii. 8.)

6. *Itinerar. syr.*, Burckhardt ii.

7. *Loci specie percussus*, Burckhardt i.

8. In his paper 'Kulturgeschichte und Naturwissenschaft' (*Deutsche Rundschau*, vol. xiii.), which is full both of original ideas and of exaggerated summary opinions, Du Bois Reymond fails to do justice to this, and altogether misjudges Petrarch's feeling for Nature. After giving this letter in proof of mediæval feeling, he goes on to say : ' Full

of shame and remorse, he descends the mountain without another word. The poor fellow had given himself up to innocent enjoyment for a moment, without thinking of the welfare of his soul, and instead of gloomy introspection, had looked into the enticing outer world. Western humanity was so morbid at that time, that the consciousness of having done this was enough to cause painful inner conflict to a man like Petrarch—a man of refined feeling, and scientific, though not a deep thinker.' Even granting this, which is too tragically put, the world was on the very eve of freeing itself from this position, and Petrarch serves as a witness to the change.

9. Comp., too, *De Genealogia Deorum*, xv., in which he says of trees, meadows, brooks, flocks and herds, cottages, etc., that these things 'animum mulcent,' their effect is 'mentem in se colligere.'

10. Comp. Voigt, *Enea Silvio de' Piccolomini als Papst Pius II. und sein Zeitalter.*

11. Comp. Geiger and Ad. Wolff, *Die Klassiker aller Zeiten und Nationen.*

12. Quando mira la terra ornata e bella. Rime di V. Colonna.

13. Ombrosa selva che il mio duolo ascolti.

CHAPTER V

1. Ruge, *Geschichte des Zeitalters der Entdeckungen.* Berlin, 1881. (*Allgem. Geschichte in Einzeldarstellungen*, von Oncken.) *Die neu Welt der Landschaften*, etc. Strasburg, 1534.

2. *De rebus oceanicis et novo orbi Decades tres Petri Martyris at Angleria Mediolanensis. Coloniæ*, 1574.

3. *Il viaggio di Giovan Leone e Le Navagazioni, di Aloise da Mosto. di Pietro, di Cintra, di Anxone, di un Piloto Portuguese e di Vasco di Gama quali si leggono nella raccolta di Giovambattista Ramusio.* Venezia, 1837.

4. For example, this from Ramusio: 'And the coast is all low land, full of most beautiful and very tall trees, which are evergreen, as the leaves do not wither as do those in our country, but a new leaf appears before the other is cast off: the trees extend right down into the marshy tract of shore, and look as if flourishing on the sea. The coast is a most glorious sight, and in my opinion, though I have cruised about in many parts both in the East and in the West, I have never seen any coast which surpassed this in beauty. It is everywhere washed by many rivers, and small streams of little importance, as big ships will not be able to enter them.

5. Ideler, *Examen critique.* Cosmos.

6. *Coleccion de los viajes y decubrimientos que hicieron por mar los espanoles desde fines del siglo XV. con varios documentos ineditos . . . co-ordinata e illustrada por Don Martin Fernandez de Navarrete.* Madrid, 1858.

7. *Geschichte des Zeitalters der Entdeckungen.*

8. As he lay sick and despairing off Belem, an unknown voice said to him compassionately: 'O fool! and slow to believe and serve thy God. . . . He gave thee the keys of those barriers of the ocean sea which were closed with such mighty chains, and thou wast obeyed through many lands, and hast gained an honourable fame throughout Christendom.' In a letter to the King and Queen of Spain in fourth voyage.

9. Humboldt.   10. Biese, *op. cit.*

11. Zoeckler, *Geschichte der Beziehungen zwischen Theologie und Naturwissenschaft.*

12. F. Hammerich, *St Birgitta.*

13. Zoeckler, *op. cit.*

14, 15, 16, 17. Comp. Wilkens' *Fray Luis de Leon.* Halle, 1866.

18. Humboldt.

19. Comp. Carrière, *Die Poesie.*

20. Zoeckler, in Herzog's *Real - Encykl.*, xxi., refers to ' Le Solitaire des Indes ou la Vie de Gregoire Lopez.' Goerres, *Die christliche Mystik*; S. Arnold, *Leben der Gläubigen*; French, *Life of St Teresa.*

CHAPTER VI

1. In *Shakespeare Studien*, chap. 4, Hense treats Shakespeare's attitude towards Nature very suggestively; but I have gone my own way.

2. *Hamlet*, i. 3: 'The canker galls the infants of the spring too oft before their buttons be disclosed.' Comp. i. 1; *Romeo and Juliet*, i. 1; *Henry VI.*, part 2, iii. 1; *Tempest*, i. 2.

3. Comp. Henkel, *Das Goethe'sche Gleichnis*; *Henry IV.*, 2nd pt., iv. 4; *Richard II.*, i. 1; *Othello*, iii. 3, and v. 2; *Cymbeline*, ii. 4; *King John*, ii. 2; *Hamlet*, iii. 1; *Tempest*, iv. 2.

4. See Hense for bucolic idyllic traits.

5. *Poetische Personifikation in griechischen Dichtungen.*

CHAPTER VII

1. Comp. Woermann, *Ueber den landschaftlichen Natursinn der Griechen und Romer, Vorstudien zu einer Archäologie der Landschaftsmalerei.* München, 1871.

2. Comp. Schnaase, *Geschichte der bildenden Künste im 15 Jahrhundert*, edited by Lübke. Stuttgart, 1879.

3. Falke, *Geschichte des modernen Geschmacks.* Leipzig, 1880.

4. *Geschichte der deutschen Renaissance.* Stuttgart, 1873.

5. Comp. also Kaemmerer, *op. cit.*   6. Lübke, *op. cit.*

7. Lübke refers to A. von Zahn's searching work, *Dürer's Kunstlehre und sein Verhältnis zur Renaissance.* Leipzig, 1866.

8. Proportion III., B. T., iii. b.   Nuremberg, 1528.

9. *Op. cit.*

10. In what follows, I have borrowed largely from Rosenberg's interesting writings (*Greuzboten*, Nos. 43 and 44, 1884-85), and still more from Schnaase, Falke, and Carrière, as I myself only know the masters represented at Berlin and Munich.

11.
12. } Kaemmerer, *op. cit.*

CHAPTER VIII

1 and 2. *Renaissance und Humanismus in Italien und Deutschland.*

3. Zoeckler.

4. Comp. Hase, *Sebastian Frank von Woerd der Schwarmgeist.*

5. Comp. Hubert, *Kleine Schriften.*

6. Zoeckler, etc.

7. Comp. Uhland, *Schriften zur Geschichte der Dichtung und Sage.*   Alte hoch und nieder deutsche Volkslieder, where plants, ivy, holly, box, and willow, represent summer and winter.

8 and 9. Uhland.   10. Wunderhorn.   11. Biese, *op. cit.*

12. Fred Cohn, ' *Die Gärten in alter und neuer Zeit,*' *D. Rundschau* 18, 1879.   In Italy in the sixteenth century there was a change to this extent, that greenery was no longer clipt, but allowed to grow naturally, and the garden represented the transition from palace to landscape, from bare architectural forms to the free creations of Nature. The passion for flowers — the art of the pleasure garden, flourished in Holland and Germany.   (Falke.)

13. W. H. Riehl states (*Kulturstudien aus drei Jahrhunderten*) that Berlin, Augsburg, Leipzig, Darmstadt, and Mannheim were described in the seventeenth century as having ' very fine and delightful positions '; and the finest parts of the Black Forest, Harz and Thuringian mountains as ' very desolate,' deserted, and monotonous, or, at best, as not particularly pleasant scenery.   If only a region were flat and treeless, a delicious landscape could be charmed out of it.   Welcker, Court physician at Hesse Cassel, describing Schlangenbad in 1721, said that it lay in a desolate, unpleasing district, where nothing grew but foliage and grass,

but that through ingenious planting of clipt trees in lines and cross lines, some sort of artistic effect had been produced. Clearly the principles of French garden-craft had become a widely accepted dogma of taste. Riehl contrasts the periwig period with the mediæval, and concludes that the mediæval backgrounds of pictures implied feeling for the wild and romantic. He says: 'In the Middle Ages the painters chose romantic jagged forms of mountains and rocks for backgrounds, hence the wild, bare, and arid counted as a prototype of beautiful scenery, while some centuries later such forms were held to be too rustic and irregular for beauty.' One cannot entirely agree with this. He weakens it himself in what follows. 'It was not a real scene which rose Alp-like before their mind's eye, but an imaginary and sacred one ; their fantastic, romantic ideal called for rough and rugged environment': and adds, arguing in a circle, 'Their minds passed then to real portraiture of Nature, and decided the landscape eye of the period.' My own opinion is that the loftiness of the 'heroic' mountain backgrounds seemed suitable for the sacred subjects which loomed so large and sublime in their own minds, and that these backgrounds did not reveal their ideal of landscape beauty, nor 'a romantic feeling for Nature,' nor 'a taste for the romantic,' nor yet a wondrous change of view in the periwig period.

14. In his *Harburg Program* of 1883 (*Beiträge zur Geschichte des Naturgefühls*), after an incomplete survey of ancient and modern writings on the subject, Winter sketches the development of modern feeling for Nature in Germany from Opitz to 1770, as shewn in the literature of that period, basing his information chiefly upon Goedeke's *Deutsche Dichtung*.

15. Comp. Chovelius *Die bedeutendsten deutschen Romane des 17 Jahrhunderts*. Leipzig, 1866.

16. Chovelius.

17. Daniel Lohenstein's *Blumen*. Breslau, 1689.

CHAPTER IX

1. Freiherr von Ditfurth, *Deutsche Volks und Gesellschafts-lieder des 17 und 18 Jahrhunderts*, 1872.

2. Goedeke - Tittmannschen Sammlung, xiii., *Truts-Nachtigall*.

3. *Geschichte der deutschen Litteratur.*

4. Tittmann's *Deutsche Dichter des 17 Jahrhunderts*, vol. vi.

5. Comp., too, iv. 5 : 'Die ihr alles hört und saget, Luft und Forst und Meer durchjaget ; Echo, Sonne, Mond, und Wind, Sagt mir doch, wo steckt mein Kind ? '

21. 'Den sanften West bewegt mein Klagen, Es rauscht

der Bach den Seufzern nach Aus Mitleid meiner Plagen; Die Vögel schweigen, Um nur zu zeigen Dass diese schöne Tyrannei Auch Tieren überlegen sei.' *Abendlied* contains beautiful personifications: 'Der Feierabend ist gemacht, Die Arbeit schläft, der Traum erwacht, Die Sonne führt die Pferde trinken; Der Erdkreis wandert zu der Ruh, Die Nacht drückt ihm die Augen zu, Die schon dem süssen Schlafe winken.'

6. Hettner, *Litteraturgeschichte des 18 Jahrhunderts.*

7. Lappenberg in *Zeitschrift für Hamburgische Geschichte,* ii. Hettner, *op. cit.*

8. 'Ye fields and woods, my refuge from the toilsome world of business, receive me in your quiet sanctuaries and favour my Retreat and thoughtful Solitude. Ye verdant plains, how gladly I salute ye! Hail all ye blissful Mansions! Known Seats! Delightful Prospects! Majestick Beautys of this earth, and all ye rural Powers and Graces! Bless'd be ye chaste Abodes of happiest Mortals who here in peaceful Innocence enjoy a Life unenvy'd, the Divine, whilst with its bless'd Tranquility it affords a happy Leisure and Retreat for Man, who, made for contemplation and to search his own and other natures, may here best meditate the cause of Things, and, plac'd amidst the various scenes of Nature, may nearer view her Works. O glorious Nature! supremely fair and sovereignly good! All-loving and All-lovely All-Divine! Whose looks are so becoming, and of such infinite grace, whose study brings such Wisdom, and whose contemplation such Delight. . . . Since by thee (O Sovereign mind!) I have been form'd such as I am, intelligent and rational; since the peculiar Dignity of my Nature is to know and contemplate Thee; permit that with due freedom I exert those Facultys with which thou hast adorn'd me. Bear with my ventrous and bold approach. And since not vain Curiosity, nor fond Conceit, nor Love of aught save Thee alone, inspires me with such thoughts as these, be thou my Assistant, and guide me in this Pursuit; whilst I venture thus to tread the Labyrinth of wide Nature, and endeavour to trace thee in thy Works.'

9. Comp. Jacob von Falke, '*Der englische Garten*' (*Nord und Süd*, Nov. 1884), and his *Geschichte des modernen Geschmacks.*

10. *Dessins des édifices, meubles, habits, machines, et utensils des Chinois,* 1757.

CHAPTER X

1. '*Die Alpen im Lichte verschiedener Zeitalter,*' *Sammlung wissenschaftlicher Vorträge*, Virchow und Holtzendorff. Berlin, 1877.

2. Geschäfte Zwang und Grillen Entweihn nicht diese
    Trift ;
Ich finde hier im Stillen Des Unmuts Gegengift.
Es webet, wallt, und spielet, Das Laub um jeden
    Strauch,
Und jede Staude fühlet Des lauen Zephyrs Hauch.
Was mir vor Augen schwebet Gefällt und hüpft und
    sing ,
Und alles, alles lebet, Und alles scheint verjüngt.
Ihr Thäler und ihr Höhen Die Lust und Sommer
    schmückt l
Euch ungestört zu sehen, Ist, was mein Herz erquickt.
Die Reizung freier Felder Beschämt der Gärten Pracht,
Und in die offnen Wälder Wird ohne Zwang gelacht ....
In jährlich neuen Schätzen zeigt sich des Landmanns
    Glück,
Und Freiheit und Ergötzen Erheitern seinen Blick ....
Ihm prangt die fette Weide Und die betante Flur ;
Ihm grünet Lust und Freude Ihm malet die Natur.'

3. *Litteratur geschichte.*
4. *Sämtliche poetische Werke*, J. P. Uz. Leipzig, 1786.
5. *Samtliche Werke.* Berlin, 1803.
6. *Sämtliche Werke*, J. G. Jacobi, vol. viii. Zurich, 1882.
7. He said of his garden at Freiburg, which was laid out in terraces on a slope, that all that Flora and Pomona could offer was gathered there. It had a special Poet's Corner on a hillock under a poplar, where a moss-covered seat was laid for him upon some limestone rock-work ; white and yellow jasmine grew round, and laurels and myrtles hung down over his head. Here he would rest when he walked in the sun ; on his left was a mossy Ara, a little artificial stone altar on which he laid his book, and from here he could gaze across the visible bit of the distant Rhine to the Vosges, and give himself up undisturbed to his thoughts.
8. Gessner's *Schriften.* Zurich, 1770.
9. Spalding, *Die Bestimmung des Menschen.* Leipzig, 1768.
10. Klopstock's *Briefe.* Brunswick, 1867.
11. Comp. *Odes*, 'Die Kunst Tialfs ' and 'Winterfreuden.'
12. *Briefe.*
13. Julian Schmidt.
14. Comp. his letters from Switzerland, which contain nothing particular about the scenery. although he crossed the Lake of Zurich, and ' a wicked mountain,' to the Lake of Zug and Lucerne.
15. Claudius, who, at a time when the lyric both of poetry and music was lost in Germany in conventional tea and coffee songs, was the first to rediscover the direct expression of feeling—that is, Nature feeling. (Storm's *Hausbuch.*)

Chapter XI

1. I have obtained much information and suggestion from ' *Ueber die geographische Kenntnis der Alpen im Mittelalter,*' and ' *Ueber die Alpine Reiselitteratur in fruherer Zeit,*' in *Allgem. Zeitung,* Jan. 11, 1885, and Sept. 1885, respectively.

2. *Evagatorium* 3, *Bibliothek d. litterar. Vereins.* Stuttgart, 1849.

3. *Bibliothek des litterar. Vereins.* Stuttgart, 1886.

4. *Descriptio Larii lacus.* Milan, 1558.

5. *Itinerarium Basil.* 1624.

6. Osenbrüggen, *Wanderungen in der Schweiz,* 1867; *Entwickelungsgeschichte des Schweizreisens;* Friedländer, *Ueber die Entstehung und Entwickelung.*

7. Comp. Erich Schmidt, *Richardson, Rousseau, and Goethe.* Jena, 1875.

8. Remarks on several parts of Italy. London, 1761.

9. Letters of Lady M. Wortley Montagu, Sept. 25, 1718.

10. Friedländer, *op. cit.*

11. Schmidt. Moser's description of a sensitive soul in *Patriotischen Phantasien* is most amusing.

12. Laprade adduces little of importance in his book *Le Sentiment de la Nature* (2nd edition), the first volume of which I have dealt with elsewhere. I have little in common with Laprade, although he is the only writer who has treated the subject comprehensively and historically. His standpoint is that of Catholic theology; he never separates feeling for Nature from religion, and is severe upon unbelievers. The book is well written, and in parts clever, but only touches the surface and misses much. His position is thus laid down : ' Le vrai sentiment de la Nature, le seul poétique, le seul fécond et puissant, le seul innocent de tout danger, est celui qui ne sépare jamais l'idée des choses visibles de la pensée de Dieu.' He accounts for the lack of any important expressions of feeling for Nature in French classics with : ' Le génie de la France est le génie de l'action,' and ' L'âme humaine est le but de la poésie.' He recognizes that even with Fénélon ' la Nature reste à ses yeux comme une simple décoration du drame que l'homme y joue, le poete en lui ne la regarde jamais à travers les yeux du mystique.' Of the treatment of Nature in La Fontaine's Fables, he says : ' Ce n'est pas peindre la Nature, c'est l'abolir ' ; and draws this conclusion : ' Le sentiment de l'infini est absent de la poésie du dix-septième siècle aussi bien que le sentiment de la Nature ' ; and again : ' L'esprit général du dix-huitième siècle est la négation même de la poésie. . . . l'amour de la Nature n'était guerre autre

chose qu'une haine déguisée et une déclaration de guerre
à la société et à la réligion. Il n'y a pas trace du sentiment
légitime et profond qui attire l'artiste et le poete vers les
splendeurs de la création, révélatrices du monde invisible.
Ne demandez pas au dix-huitième siècle la poésie de la
Nature, pas plus que celle du cœur.' Buffon shews 'l'état
poétique des sciences de la Nature,' but his brilliant prose
painting lacks ' la présence de Dieu, la révélation de l'infini
les harmonies de l'âme et de la Nature n'existent pas pour
Buffon . . . . plus de la rhétorique que de vrai sentiment
de la Nature.'

13. Comp. the garden of Elysium in *La Nouvelle Héloïse*:
' Where the gardener's hand is nowhere to be discerned,
nothing contradicts the idea of a desert island, and I cannot
perceive any footsteps of men . . . you see nothing here
in an exact row, nothing level, Nature plants nothing by
the ruler.'

14. *Œuvres de Jacques Bernardin Henri de Saint Pierre.*

15. 'B. de S. Pierre a plus que Rousseau les facultés
propres du paysagiste, l'amour même du pittoresque, la
vive curiosité des sites, des animaux, et des plantes, la
couleur et une certaine magie spéciale du pinceau.' Laprade
adds the reproof: ' Sa pensée réligieuse est au-dessous de son
talent d'artiste et en abaisse le niveau.'

16. *Voyage round the World*, 1772–1775.

17. Paul Lemnius, 1597, *Landes Rugiae*; Kosegarten,
1777–1779; Rellstab, 1799, *Ausflucht nach der Insel Rugen*;
Navest, 1800, *Wanderungen durch die Insel Rugen*; Grumbke,
1805; *Indigena, Streifzuge durch das Rugenland*. J. P.
Hackert in 1762, and K. D. Friedrichs in 1792, painted the
scenery. Comp. E. Boll, *Die Insel Rügen*, 1858.

CHAPTER XII

1. Comp. Gottschall, *Poetik*. Breslau, 1853.

2. *Ueber Ossian und die Lieder alter Volker*, Sämtliche
Werke, Teil 7.

3. *Op. cit.*, Teil 15.

4. *Zur Philosophie und Geschichte*, 2 Teil.

5. J. G. Sulzer's *Unterredungen uber die Schonheit der
Natur nebst desselben moralischen Betrachtungen uber besondere
Gegenstande der Naturlehre* is typical. Charites describes
his conversion to the love of Nature by his friend Eukrates.
Eukrates woke him at dawn and led him to a hill close by,
as the sun rose. The fresh air, the birds' songs, and the
wide landscape move him, and Eukrates points out that
the love of Nature is the ' most natural of pleasures,' making

the labourer so happy that he forgets servitude and misery, and sings at his work. 'This pleasure is always new to us, and the heart, provided it be not possessed by vanity or stormy passions, lies always open to it. Do you not know that they who are in trouble, and, above all, they who are in love, find their chief relief here? Is not a sick man better cheered by sunshine than by any other refreshment?' Then he points out Nature's harmonies and changes of colour, and warns Charites to avoid the storms of the passions. 'Yonder brook is a picture of our soul; so long as it runs quietly between its banks, the water is clear and grass and flowers border it; but when it swells and flows tumultuously, all this ornament is torn away, and it becomes turbid. To delight in Nature the mind must be free. . . . She is a sanctity only approached by pure souls. . . . As only the quiet stream shews the sky and the objects around, so it is only on quiet souls that Nature's pictures are painted; ruffled water reflects nothing' He waxes eloquent about birds' songs, flowers, and brooks, and wanders by the hour in the woods, 'all his senses open to Nature's impressions,' which are 'rays from that source of all beauty, the sight of which will one day bless the soul.' His friend is soon convinced that Nature cannot be overpraised, and that her art is endlessly great.

6. *Vom Gefühl des Schönen und Physiologie überhaupt.* Winter.

7. Comp. *Das Flüchtigste.* 'Tadle nicht der Nachtigallen, Bald verhallend süsses Lied,' oder 'Nichts verliert sich,' etc.

8. Herder's *Nachlass*, Düntzer und F. G. von Herder, 1857.

9. Bernay's *Der junge Goethe.*

10. *Die Spröde, Die Bekehrte, Marz, Lust und Qual, Luna, Gegenwart.*

11. Laprade is all admiration for the 'incomparable artiste et poète inspiré du sentiment de la Nature, c'est qu'il excelle à peindre le monde extérieur et le cœur humain l'un par l'autre, qu'il mêle les images de l'univers visible à l'expression des sentiments intimes, de manière à n'en former qu'un seul tissu. . . . Tous les éléments d'un objet d'une situation apparaissent à la fois, et dans leur harmonie, essentielle à cet incomparable esprit.' He is astonished at the symbolism in *Werther*: 'Chaque lettre répond à la saison où elle est écrite . . . l'idée et l'image s'identifient dans un fait suprême, dans un cri; il se fait entre l'émotion intime et l'impression du dehors une sorte de fusion.' And despite Goethe's Greek paganism and pantheism, he declares: 'Le nom de Goethe marque une de ces grandes dates, une de ces grandes révolutions de la poésie—la plus grande, nous le croyons, depuis Homer.'

. . . 'Goethe est la plus haute expression poétique des tendances de notre siècle vers le monde extérieur et la philosophie de la Nature.'

12. Comp. *Tagebücher und Briefe Goethe's aus Italien an Frau von Stein und Herder.* E. Schmidt, Weimar, 1886.

13. Julian Schmidt.

14. *The Lady of the Lake* breathes a delightful freshness, the very spirit of mountain and wood, free alike from the moral preaching of Wordsworth, and from the storms of passion.

15. Laprade.

16. 'Sa formule réligieuse, c'est une question ; sa pensée, c'est le doute . . . l'artiste divinise chaque détail. Son panthéisme ne s'applique pas seulement à l'ensemble des choses ; Dieu tout entier est réellement présent pour lui dans chaque fragment de matière dans le plus immonde animal . . . c'est une réligion aussi vieille que l'humanité décline ; cela s'appelle purement et simplement le fétichisme.' (Laprade.)

17. *Vorschule der Æsthetik.* Compare 'With every genius a new Nature is created for us in the further unveiling of the old.' 2 Aufl. *Berlin Reimer,* 1827.

18. 'Like a lily softly swaying in the hushed air, so my being moves in its elements, in the charming dream of her.' 'Our souls rush forward in colossal plans, like exulting streams rushing perpetually through mountain and forest.' 'If the old mute rock of Fate did not stand opposing them, the waves of the heart would never foam so beautifully and become mind.' 'There is a night in the soul which no gleam of starlight, not even dry wood, illuminates,' etc.

19. Comp. Tieck's *Biographie von Koepke.* Brandes.

20. *Franz Sternbald,* I. Berlin, 1798.

21. Haym, *Die romantische Schule.* Berlin, 1870.

22. *Phantasus,* i. Berlin, 1812.

23. 'A young hunter was sitting in the heart of the mountains in a thoughtful mood beside his fowling-piece, while the noise of the water and the woods was sounding through the solitude . . . it grew darker . . . the birds of night began to shoot with fitful wing along their mazy courses . . . unthinkingly he pulled a straggling root from the earth, and on the instant heard with affright a stifled moan underground, which winded downwards in doleful tones, and died plaintively away in the deep distance. The sound went through his inmost heart ; it seized him as if he had unwittingly touched the wound, of which the dying frame of Nature was expiring in its agony.' (Runenberg.)

24. *Hymnen an die Nacht.*

25. In *Die Lehrlinge von Sais.*

26. *Athenäum,* iii., 1800.

INDEX

The Immortal Stone

The Immortal
STONE

CHINESE JADES from the Neolithic period to the twentieth century

JAMES C. S. LIN

SCALA

Contents

Foreword

THIS PUBLICATION constitutes the first book about the Chinese jade collection in the Fitzwilliam Museum and provides a welcome opportunity to introduce a wider audience to the historical and artistic development of this much collected and admired category. The museum houses around two hundred jades and other hardstones, covering the most important periods when jade was used in Chinese history. The book discusses 105 of these works in detail, the remainder being dealt with more briefly in the appendix. Each chapter provides an up-to-date assessment of a key aspect of the history of jade carving and use: the Chinese concept of jade and its geological sources; the archaeological and textual evidence for the value and significance of jade in Chinese society; the use of jade for funerary offerings in tombs before and during the Han periods; the exploitation of jade for objects of daily use in later periods, especially the Ming and Qing dynasties; the Qing dynasty jades that form the major part of the Fitzwilliam's collection, particularly works from the imperial collection; the market for jade, including the problem of fakes; and the history of jade collecting at the Fitzwilliam Museum.

The exploitation of jade for decorative and utilitarian objects in Chinese art, for use by the living or for the provision of the dead, varied considerably from period to period, and these fluctuations are reflected in the Fitzwilliam's collection. The prominent use of jade in the Neolithic cultures of the second and first millennia BC declined after the collapse of the Han empire, and it was not until the Ming and Qing periods that jades began to circulate again among affluent members of Chinese society. Among the highlights of the Fitzwilliam's collection from this later flourishing of jade carving are fifteen pieces that were made for the Qing imperial court. Some of these highly important works have labels that indicate their original locations within the palace or are inscribed with Emperor Qianlong's poems. Also strongly represented in the Fitzwilliam's collection are jade animal sculptures and vessels of various periods.

As with so much of our collections, the Fitzwilliam's jades were overwhelmingly acquired by gift or bequest. The principal benefactor was Oscar Raphael (d. 1941), a former student of Pembroke College, Cambridge, whose collection entered the museum in 1946 and constitutes more than half of the museum's current holdings. Raphael also assembled extensive collections of Asian art, including Islamic and Oriental ceramics, which his bequest split between the Fitzwilliam and the British Museum.

This publication is the outcome of extensive research on the museum's collection by Dr James Lin, Assistant Keeper of Applied Arts in the Fitzwilliam Museum, undertaken in Britain, China and Taiwan, sponsored by the British Academy. Publication of the book was made possible by the financial support of Daniel Eskenazi, Roger Keverne, the Mellon Fund and the Marlay Group of the Fitzwilliam Museum. It is our hope that this study will inspire further work on this material and that it will also encourage visitors to the museum, where the symbiotic beauty of form and material that Chinese jade carving achieves may be enjoyed to best effect.

TIMOTHY POTTS
DIRECTOR

1. What is jade?

THE CHINESE TERM for jade, *yu*, can be used to refer to any stone of beauty or value, such as agate, turquoise and quartz, or even to crystal or glass, all of which have been commonly found in tombs dating from the Neolithic to the Han. The *Shuowen jiezi* dictionary ('Explaining Simple and Analysing Compound Characters'), compiled by Xu Shen in AD 100, records: '*yu* are beautiful stones possessing five virtues'.[1] However, we do not know exactly what was meant by *yu* at that time, and even today, when Chinese scholars and curators compile catalogues, they tend to include agate, crystal and other such stones within the category of jades.

In the modern sciences of mineralogy and gemmology jade refers to two different mineral groups: nephrite and jadeite. According to S. Howard Hansford:

> Jadeite is a silicate of sodium and aluminium and is classed as a pyroxene. It is a cryptocrystalline mineral, the minute crystals being interlocked to form a compact aggregate. It ranks as 6.75 to 7 on Mohs's scale of hardness, and has a constant specific gravity close to 3.33 and a refractive index of 1.65 to 1.68. Nephrite, on the other hand, is a silicate of calcium and magnesium belonging to the amphibole group of minerals. … The hardness of nephrite is 6 to 6.5 on Mohs's scale and the specific gravity has limits in the range of 2.90 and 3.1, and the refractive index varies between 1.60 and 1.65.[2]

However, Andrew Middleton and Ian Freestone have pointed out that this definition excludes many objects that are traditionally regarded as being carved from jade, for much jade is a mixture of minerals rather than being pure nephrite or pure jadeite.[3] The jade used in China appears to have been almost entirely nephrite or nephrite-related until the eighteenth century AD, when jadeite from Burma began to be imported. Although other minerals were also employed, those that resembled nephrite were preferred. Wen Guang and Jing Zhichun state that 'Both nephrite and jadeite are true jade, whereas those minerals or mineral aggregates resembling true jade in appearance are termed "pseudojade" or "near jade".'[4]

According to Wen Guang and Jing Zhichun, nephrite jade deposits have two kinds of source. The first is associated with magnesian marbles and is exemplified by deposits from Kunlun in the Xinjiang autonomous region, Kuandian in Liaoning province, Wenchuan in Sichuan province and Chunchon in South Korea. The other source, within rocks containing serpentine minerals, has examples from Tianshan in Xinjiang, Xichuan in Henan province, and Hualien, Fengtien in Taiwan. These jades were mined from mountains or found in rivers.

As Middleton and Freestone note, 'it seems unlikely that the quarries in the far west were the source of the material used for the artefacts found at the earliest sites, some 3,000 km to the east'.[5] The nephrite deposits at Kuandian, Liaoning and Liyang county, Jiangsu, have therefore been regarded as the likely sources of some of the Neolithic jades.

In fact, archaeological finds have revealed that the jade materials used at that time varied from area to area. These variations may relate to the deposits

Map of China

themselves or to different workshops, personal preference, trading markets and status, not simply to hierarchical ranking, such as that later recorded in the *Zhou li* ('Rites of Zhou'), compiled between the fourth and second century BC. In addition, as many craftsmen reused ancient jade, the discovery of jade from ancient tombs, either deliberately or by chance, may have been another source of jade artefacts made in the later dynasties.

With the expansion of Chinese territory and foreign contact during the Qing dynasty (1644–1911), nephrite from Hetian (Khotan), Xinjiang, jadeite from Burma, agate and crystal from the Yangzi river regions, lapis lazuli from central Asia and Mughal-style jade from India were largely used from the eighteenth century onwards. Jade from Khotan was particularly appreciated by the Qianlong emperor (r. 1736–1795) and is valued by modern Chinese. In part this is because it is denser than other forms of nephrite, giving it a smooth, warm feeling that cannot be emulated. Further Khotan sites have been a major source of jade for several centuries. With the large demand for the market and uncontrolled digging, the jade mines in Khotan were gradually exhausted. This phenomenon has caused the price of genuine Khotan jade to reach exceptional levels today. Many inferior jades from other regions claim to be from Khotan in order to achieve a high price.

2. The value and significance of jade

PREHISTORIC JADE-CARVING techniques have been inferred from an examination of artefacts and from records of methods employed by Maori craftsmen in the nineteenth century. The stone was cut using sandstone or slate, in conjunction with quartz sand and water, and then shaped with sandstone rubbers. Holes were made using wood, bone or bamboo drills and wet sand as an abrasive. The holes were conical in shape, as the drill bits rapidly wore away. Metal tools were used in the Bronze and Iron ages.[6]

The complicated process of jade carving must always have involved a large workforce in a workshop environment and was consequently expensive. The ownership of jades was therefore confined in early times to the highest level of Chinese hierarchical society. The value of jade can be established from the various stories and legends, the most famous of which is 'Returning the Jade Disc Intact to Zhao State'. *Han Fei zi* (by Han Fei, d. 233 BC) records that:

> A piece of jade was discovered in the hills of Chu state by Bian He during the Warring States period [475–221 BC]. He was so excited about his discovery that he hastened to show it to the ruler, King Li of Chu. However, King Li didn't believe him and had one of his legs cut off for deceiving the ruler. When King Li died, the throne was passed on to King Wu, and Bian He presented the stone again; King Wu, again, did not believe him and had his other leg amputated as well. It was not until the next ruler, King Wen, ascended the throne that he had his craftsman work

on the stone. To their astonishment, they found a piece of incomparable white jade, which was made into a jade disc that was named as *He Shi Bi* [literally 'The Jade Disc of He'] in honour of its discoverer.[7]

In *Shi ji* ('Records of the Grand Historian'), compiled by the Han historian Sima Qian (145–86 BC), the story continues that the jade disc was stolen from Chu and eventually sold to the Zhao state. In 283 BC King Zhaoxiang of the Qin state offered fifteen cities to Zhao in exchange for the jade disc. This is the origin of the famous Chinese phrase *jia zhi lian cheng* ('valued in many cities'). The Zhao minister Lin Xiangru was dispatched to take the jade disc to Qin, but it became clear that Qin would not uphold its side of the bargain. Lin threatened to smash the jade disc but subsequently escaped back to Zhao with the disc intact.[8] The story continues with the Qin conquering the Zhao in 228 BC; when the king of Zhao submitted, he presented the disc. The disc vanished from the records soon after it came into the Qin's possession.

Some particular shapes of jades, such as *bi* (discs) and *gui* (sceptres), were used in ritual performances. Over 600 jade and stone covenant tablets, for example, were excavated at Houma in Shanxi province, and similar tablets have been excavated in Wenxian county, Henan province.[9] These covenant tablets from Houma were written with brush and ink and record the alliances entered into by the Zhao state clan with non-Zhao counties or city officials when feudal states fought to annex each other during the Eastern Zhou period (770–221 BC).

Two sets of jades, each comprising a jade disc, a *gui* sceptre and two *xi* (pointed jade pendants), were excavated at a temple site at Zhifu island, Yantai, Shandong province.[10] These were arranged in a particular order one metre below the ground, with the disc in the middle, the *gui* placed in the hole of the disc and the *xi* at either side, one metre apart. Both the *gui* and *xi* are plain, and the discs were incised with spirals in relief and covered with cinnabar. Archaeologists and scholars, relying on the records in *Shi ji*, believe that these jades were used as an offering to the Sun God, either by the First Emperor of Qin (259–210 BC) or by the Han Emperor Wudi (r. 140–87 BC).[11] Another two sets of jades comprising a jade disc, two *gui* and a *huang* pendant were found in Wolong village, Longxu Island, Shandong province, in 1979 and 1982 respectively and may also have been offerings to the Sun. The *Shi ji* notes several times that jade discs and sceptres were used in sacrifices to the water spirits of the Yellow River, Han Water and so on.[12]

Apart from its physical qualities and ritual significance, jade also has metaphorical associations. Confucius is said to have used jade as a metaphor for a gentleman, based on its physical characteristics. A famous text from the *Li ji* describes jade in virtuous terms:

> Soft, smooth and glossy, it appeared to them like benevolence; fine, compact and strong, like intelligence; angular, but not sharp and cutting, like righteousness; hanging down (in beads) as if it would fall to the ground, like (the humility of) propriety; when struck, yielding a note, clear and prolonged, yet terminating abruptly, like music; its flaws not concealing its beauty, nor its beauty concealing its flaws, like loyalty; with an internal radiance issuing from it on every side, like good faith; bright as a brilliant rainbow, like heaven; exquisite and mysterious, appearing in the hills and streams, like the earth; standing out conspicuous in the symbols of rank, like virtue; esteemed by all under the sky, like the path of truth and duty.[13]

In burial, bronze ritual vessels were placed in a specific order outside the coffin, but it was jade that was placed close to the body. In the Han period (206 BC–AD 220) jades were almost always used in burials. From tombs of the imperial family that have been excavated in the past two decades we can see that jade discs were placed on and underneath the body and that jade plugs were inserted into the body's orifices before the body was encased in a 'jade suit', made from more than 2,000 small jade plaques with holes at the corners. Gold, silver or copper threads were strung through these to form a suit in the shape of the human body (fig.1).

In the Han period the *Huainan wanbishu* ('The Ten Thousand Infallible Arts of the Prince of Huainan') of Liu An (*c.*180–122 BC) mentions that burying stones at the four corners of the house is a way of preventing it from being disturbed by ghosts.[14] Bamboo slips, entitled *rishu,* that were excavated from Shuihudi mentioned that peach wood and white stones could ward off evil.[15] The magical power of white stones and their use as a defence was also alluded to by an early fourth-century Daoist work, the *Baopuzi* ('The Master Embracing Simplicity', *c.* AD 320):

> If you encounter an official in the mountains, but only hear his voice without seeing any shape as it keeps shouting to you, throw a white stone at it, and it will stop.[16]

Stones, white stone and jades are commonly seen in Han burials. In *Shuowen jiezi* jade is described as 'the finest among stones' (*shi zhi mei zhe*) or 'the hardest among stones' (*shi zhi jian zhe*)[17]; these jades should therefore be regarded as analogous and possessed of the same or even stronger magical power. Jades were consequently employed in various forms, including as suits, discs, orifice plugs and weapons, in order to ward off demons and protect the tomb occupant from attack in the afterlife.

Jade is a durable material that can survive burial for thousands of years, and it is therefore linked in Chinese belief to immortality. In the records of *Shi ji* the Han emperor Wudi believed that drinking dew and jade powder from a jade cup conferred longevity. He therefore built a device for collecting dewdrops in the Jian Zhang Palace.[18] The *Baopuzi* records that 'When gold and jade are inserted into the nine orifices, corpses do not decay.'[19] The famous dictionary of Chinese herbs, *Ben Cao Gang Mu*, written by Li Shizhen (1518–1593), lists jade and other materials such as agate, crystal and mica, as having magical powers that could cure diseases and extend life.[20] The presence of such materials in tombs seems to confirm this belief.[21]

For more than seven millennia the value of jade in Chinese society has remained high. Because of this and its rarity, jade carvers have always made careful use of the available material. In the case of the tomb of Fu Hao (*c.*1200 BC), the consort of King Wu Ding of the Shang, a jade disc was fashioned into three arc-shaped tiger pendants (fig. 2), whose curved backs still retain the outline of the inner hole of the original disc. Even the waste from drilling was not discarded but was recycled into small ornaments such as beads, and in some cases early jades were later reused in completely new ways or different contexts.[22] In the tomb of Marquis Yi of Zeng in Sui county, Hubei, dating to 433 BC, for example, jade debris was even scattered around the body.[23] A masterpiece dating to the Qianlong period (r. 1736–95) was carved out of jade waste from a boulder. It depicts two ladies at a Moon Gate in a south Chinese garden and was possibly carved in

Fig. 1
Drawing of twelve parts of a jade suit
After Beijing 1980, vol. 1, p. 348 (fig. 227)

Fig. 2
Drawing of a jade disc converted into three arc-shaped tiger pendants
After *Kaogu*, October 1993, p. 946, pl. 65

Suzhou (fig. 3).²⁴ From the poem incised on this piece we know that the Qianlong emperor was highly pleased with the craftsman's skilful design.

Broken pieces of jade were often re-carved and reused in later periods. This jade ear-pick (Cat. 1) from the Museum's collection was re-cut from a fish pendant, which would have been part of a long pendant set placed around the neck and chest of a body buried during the Western Zhou period (c.1050–771 BC). Other similar examples have been excavated from Fu Hao's tomb at Anyang, Henan,²⁵ and from a Western Zhou tomb at Fufeng, Shaanxi.²⁶

Aesthetically and spiritually, jades have played an important role throughout Chinese history, although in some periods they were less commonly used, owing to a scarcity of resources. Some scholars have therefore proposed a 'Jade Age', to recognize the unique aspect of Chinese culture, and a 'Jade Road' as a parallel term for the Silk Road, emphasizing the importance of Hetian jade in Chinese culture and history.²⁷ The Chinese love of jade is demonstrated by the fact that most Chinese invest in it, rather than in gold and diamonds, and by the inclusion of a jade ring in the medals for the 2008 Olympic Games in Beijing.

Fig. 3
Two Ladies at the Moon Gate
18th century
H: 15.5 cm; L: 25 cm;
W: 10.8 cm
Palace Museum, Beijing

Cat. 1
Jade ear-pick re-carved from a damaged fish pendant
Western Zhou
(c.1050–771 BC)
L: 6.4 cm; W: 0.7 cm
O.24-1946

3. Jades from tombs

The dating of jades has always posed problems, since there are no scientific tests to establish the age of a particular carving. However, systematic excavations in China and comparison with archaeological finds can now help us to date these objects more precisely and to understand their function in ancient times.

Although jade has been prized in China since prehistory, some periods have made much greater use of it than others. Jade is rare in archaeological finds from the post-Han to Ming dynasties, for example, and this rarity is reflected in the collection at the Fitzwilliam Museum.

This chapter mainly discusses early jades in the collection, relating them to excavated pieces from tombs of different periods. They can be arranged by reference to the major sites and cultures when jades were primarily used: Hongshan culture (*c.*3500–*c.*2500 BC), Liangzhu culture (*c.*3000–*c.*2000 BC), Qijia culture (*c.*2100–*c.*1600 BC), the Shang dynasty (*c.*1600–*c.*1050 BC), Western Zhou period (*c.*1050–771 BC), Eastern Zhou period (770–221 BC) and the Han dynasty (206 BC–AD 220).

Most of the jades were ornaments used during their owner's life and buried with him or her for use in the afterlife. Some were used for ritual purposes, such as examples of *cong* ('tube'), and others were specifically made for burial, such as jade veils and jade suits. This chapter describes how these jades were used in different periods.

Hongshan culture

The people of the Hongshan culture (*c.*3500–*c.*2500 BC) comprised a major Neolithic society in north-east China. Hongshan sites are widespread, ranging from north of the Xilamulun river in Inner Mongolia to the southern part of western Liaoning province. Major burial and sacrificial sites have been excavated at Hutougou in Fuxin and at Niuheliang in Lingyuan-Jianping.[28] At the latter site archaeologists have discovered an underground temple complex, including an altar and cairns. The complex was constructed of stone platforms with painted walls. Fragments of clay figures, including a life-size female face with green jade eyes, were found in the temple. More than sixty tombs constructed of stone and covered with stone mounds have been excavated near by. Jade was the principal, and often the only, type of burial goods.

The Hongshan people carved jades in the shapes of massive, strange, coiled monsters, sometimes referred to as dragons, and also bracelets and head ornaments. The colours of these jades ranged from dark grass-green and opaque lemon-green to translucent greyish-white, and the motifs include pig-dragons (*zhulong*), objects shaped like horses' hoofs (*matixingshi*), dragons, rounded-square discs, hooked-cloud-shaped ornaments (*gouyunxingshi*), joined *bi*-shaped discs, and animal shapes such as birds, fish, tortoises, silkworms and cicadas. All of the jades found in Hongshan are in some sense ornaments, as they seem to have been attached to garments or to the body.

The design and style of carving of one seated humanoid figure (Cat. 2a & b) match the Hongshan-type criteria, although no parallel has yet been recorded in any excavation. The figure is of green jade with areas altered to brown, carved in the form of a human head, on which there are an elaborate animal-form head-dress and two

Cat. 2a & b
Jade humanoid figure from the Fitzwilliam Museum, front and back
Hongshan type
(*c.*3500–*c.*2500 BC)
H: 12.2 cm; W: 5.9 cm; D: 2.8 cm
O.55-1961

nub-like protrusions. The face is distinguished by prominent arch-shaped eyebrows joined in the middle of the forehead, two tear-shaped eyes and an elongated, pyramidal nose. A bi-conically bored hole, found in Hongshan jades only, was drilled horizontally through the neck. The carving is 12.2 cm high and 5.9 cm wide, and was bequeathed by Louis C.G. Clarke, a former director of the Museum, in 1960. It has been in the collection since long before the discovery of the Hongshan culture and is therefore likely to be genuine.

This figure can be compared to similar pieces from other museums. An example in Ostasiatiska Museum, Stockholm, has two pairs of long tines and two prominent ears (one of which seems to have been damaged) and is green in colour, with some brown areas (fig. 4). It is 10.5 cm high and was owned by the late Ernest Erickson before it entered the museum. Another similar piece is in the Palace Museum, Beijing (fig. 5). Its shape is similar to the one in Stockholm, but it is light green with a brown skin, closer in colour to the one at the Fitzwilliam Museum. It is 14.6 cm high and was acquired from a Mongolian collector in 1983. It was exhibited at the Art Gallery of New South Wales, Sydney, in 2007 and dated as a Hongshan piece.[29]

Before the excavation of the Hongshan culture in the 1980s, these humanoid figures were dated to the Zhou or Han periods.[30] Although nothing similar has been discovered during archaeological excavations so far, most scholars who have seen it agree that from the subject matter, and the way it was carved and drilled, the Fitzwilliam's piece is of Hongshan type, although the colour of the

material is perplexing, as it is not a typical Hongshan jade colour from north-east China.

Liangzhu culture

About one thousand years after the Hongshan culture, and more than 1,500 km away in the present-day southern Jiangsu and northern Zhejiang, large quantities of jades, including *cong* (tubes), *bi* (discs) and *yue* (axes), were put in tombs around and on the bodies of high-ranking individuals. These jades have been identified as belonging to what is now known as the Liangzhu culture (c.3000–c.2000 BC). Major Liangzhu tombs have been excavated at Zhanglingshan in Wu xian, Yaoshan in Yuhang, Fuquanshan at Qingpu and Wujin Sidun, Jiangsu province.[31]

Twenty-four jade discs and thirty-three jade *cong* were found at tomb M3 at Sidun, Jiangsu. To judge from the scorch marks on the occupant's thigh bones and some of the jades, a ritual involving the use of fire was practised at the burial. Archaeologists have suggested that ten jade discs would have been placed at the positions of the head and feet before a fire was set. The body of the occupant was then put into position before the fire was extinguished. A large number of jade *cong* were arranged around the body, and other pottery and jades near the head and feet. Two of the best-quality jade discs were finally placed on the chest and stomach before the tomb was covered with soil.[32]

Cong are objects with a square cross-section and pierced with an axial circular hole. The jade discs normally have plain surfaces, but the *cong* are usually decorated with a proto-monster mask design at the four corners, indicated by eyes and

Fig. 4
Humanoid figure
Hongshan period
(c.3500–2500 BC)
H: 10.5 cm
Museum of Far Eastern Antiquities, Stockholm, Gift of the Ernest Erickson Collection

Fig. 5
Humanoid figure
Hongshan period
(c.3500–2500 BC)
H: 14.6 cm; W: 6 cm;
D: 4.7 cm
Palace Museum, Beijing

Cat. 3
Jade *cong*
Neolithic period, Liangzhu
culture (*c.*3000–2000 BC)
H: 11 cm; W: 6.1 × 6.2 cm;
D: 6.7 cm
O.2-1946

The large, neatly cut discs were usually found on prominent parts of the body, such as the face and chest, while discs with jagged and uneven surfaces, such as this one from the Fitzwilliam (Cat. 4), were found in large numbers near the feet.[33] Neither jade discs nor *cong* could have been worn as ornaments. The placement of discs and *cong* in tombs suggests that these jades were important components of the ritual ceremony, as well as indications of social status.

There are clear regional and chronological differences between the jades of the Liangzhu culture. Large, tall *cong* are found in Jiangsu province but not in the tombs of Zhejiang. The length of the *cong* may also have depended on the rank of the individuals who owned them. The larger *cong* in Jiangsu province are less carefully worked than the smaller *cong* used in Zhejiang.[34] The debris from the drilling of the central hole of the *cong* was used to produce small beads for pendants that were also found in the tombs.

Although jades were essential to both the Hongshan and Liangzhu societies, the manner in which they were made suggests that they were differently deployed. The different categories of objects and their contexts in these two cultures also indicate differences in use, and presumably also in beliefs, between the two societies.[35]

Liangzhu jades have been collected and used differently in later periods. Several archaeological finds show that, during the Western Zhou, Liangzhu *cong* were occasionally placed between the legs of bodies in male tombs.[36] It was not until the first jade suit had been excavated from the tomb of Liu Sheng, king of Zhongshan (d. 113 BC), at Mancheng that it was realized that the

parallel bars (Cat. 3). These would have been time-consuming to produce, so ownership of such objects would connote an elevated social position. Liangzhu *bi* discs are of variable size, colour and thickness; the quality is also variable.

Cat. 4
Jade disc
Neolithic period, Liangzhu
culture (*c*.3000–2000 BC)
D: 18.9 cm;
D (middle hole): 4.5 cm
O.16-1946

Liangzhu jade *cong* was used as a genital box, a component of the jade suit.

Obviously the Zhou and Han people did not know how the Liangzhu people used jade *cong* in burial; nor did those who edited *Zhou li*, in which it was claimed that different *cong* were used as offerings to the earth. Emperor Qianlong in the eighteenth century even added stands so that they could be used as brush holders.

Qijia culture

The Qijia culture (*c*.2100–*c*.1600 BC) was first discovered at Qijiaping in 1924. The peoples of this culture lived across a wide geographical area in the upper and middle Yellow River region, including present-day Gansu, Qinghai province and Ningxia autonomous region. Their culture lasted from the Neolithic through to the Bronze Age in Mongolia (*c*.2050–1700 BC). It overlapped

Cat. 5
Unfinished jade disc
Qijia culture
(2100–1600 BC)
L: 21.5 cm; D: 6.1 cm
O.49-1946

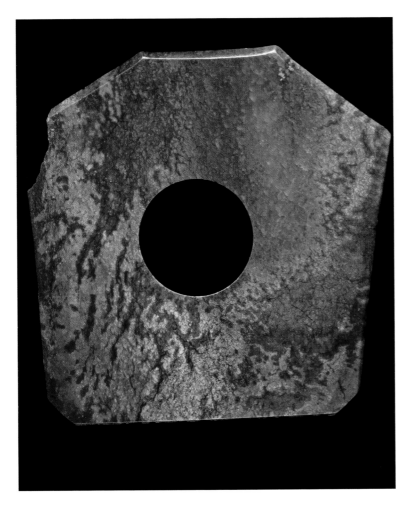

includes *cong* tubes, *bi* discs, *huang* arc-shaped pendants, ceremonial blades and beads. It is likely that the Qijia developed some of these shapes by imitating items from Liangzhu and Longshan.

As in the Liangzhu culture, jade discs were highly valued in the Qijia. In the fourth excavation at the site of Huangniangniangtai at Wuwei, dating to the late Qijia culture, 264 discs made of jade and stone were excavated from 62 tombs. The largest tomb contained 85 discs.[37] These discs were found near the body, either on top of or underneath the corpse. These discs were cut into slices from a block. A hole was drilled in the middle from one side, so the diameter of the hole is not even. The edges of the jade slices were cut to form a round disc shape and were then ground. As a result, discs in this area are of various shapes, including circular, oval and unfinished pieces with slightly square outer edges, such as the one in the Fitzwilliam Museum (Cat. 5).[38]

Cong in the Qijia culture were less important than discs in both Liangzhu and Qijia cultures, although they are occasionally found in tombs. Excavation reports do not give the location of *cong* in tombs in this area, but the ways of making a *cong* are very similar between Liangzhu and Qijia. After a lump of jade was cut from a block, a large hole was drilled through opposite faces, and triangular shapes were cut away at the four corners (Cat. 6). Qijia *cong* range from 2.5 cm to more than 26 cm in height.[39] Like the Liangzhu jade discs and *cong*, Qijia *cong* were also collected in the later periods. A few Qijia *cong* were found between legs of the male occupants in the Western Zhou tombs, and another Qijia-type *cong* on an inlaid bronze stand from the Eastern Zhou

with the Longshan culture (*c.* 2500–2000 BC), a Neolithic culture that was widespread in the central plains in the middle lower areas of the Yellow River.

Although jades played an important role in the Qijia culture, the material that was used seems to be very different from that found in eastern China. Jades from this area are brightly coloured, white, green, yellow or even black. Their typology

certain types of jades may have similar shapes to those from the Liangzhu, their functions in these two cultures were not the same. Therefore, the view that jades of the Qijia culture developed directly from the Liangzhu culture lacks evidence, particularly as the Qijia culture emphasized the *bi* and paid less attention to the *cong*.[42] One of the features of jade from Qijia culture is their plain, mostly unpolished, surfaces. In addition, one type of *cong* from the Gansu area has a long body and short neck, with sharp edges, and is of uneven length on its four sides; it is thus very different from the Liangzhu *cong*.[43]

Ceremonial blades form another category of jade that was very popular in the Qijia culture. These blades are thought to have developed from reaping knives.[44] This black jade (Cat. 7), with grey veining and three holes bored through it, is a typical ceremonial blade. It is smoothly polished, with a straight upper horizontal edge and a long cutting edge that is gracefully curved and bevelled on both sides. The two short sides, rounded at the edges, slope outwards slightly. The holes along the upper edge were drilled from one side (the two bigger holes at the ends and the smaller one in the middle were drilled from different sides).

period has been found in a Han tomb at Sanlidun, Lianshui, Jiangsu province, adapted for use as an incense burner (fig. 6).[40]

From a comparison of the shapes and functions of jade discs and *cong* from both periods, Huang Xuanpei has suggested that the jades from the Qijia culture may have developed from the Liangzhu or under the Liangzhu's influence. The use of jade discs and *cong* in the Qijia culture is much later than in Liangzhu. Since discs and *cong* were not found in pre-Qijia cultures such as the Majiayao and Yangshao, it can be inferred that the practice did not come from them.[41] Although

Much thicker blades in different colours are also found in the Qijia culture. Cat. 8 combines the forms of a knife and a tablet and is mottled green, with light brown areas. It is long and comparatively narrow, with a straight upper edge and a curved lower one. A hole was drilled from one side near the short end. The stone is quite thick and substantial, and is softly polished.

These blades puzzled scholars until some excavated evidence was available. Among the first to investigate the subject was Wu Dacheng (1835–1902). Wu's catalogue *Guyu tukao* ('Illustrated Study of Ancient Jades'), published in 1889, included some 228 illustrations. At least four discs, two *cong*, three blades and one spade have been identified as coming from the Qijia culture and are now in the collection of the Shanghai Museum.[45]

The interest in *kaoju xue* (evidential scholarship) and *jinshi xue* (studies in metal and stone) in the early Qing period led to sustained scholarly interest in ancient China, but it was not until the late Qing period that more and more scholars became engaged in the study of jade. Wu's study followed the methodology developed during the Song dynasty (960–1279), based on the *Sanli tu* ('Illustrated Catalogue of *Zhou li*, *Li ji* and *Yi li*', preface dated AD 954–9). Wu further refined the study of ancient jades by identifying and cataloguing a large quantity and variety of examples. Unfortunately, although his catalogue illustrates contour and ornament in the traditional manner of a Chinese encyclopaedia, it does not consider relief in any detail. Moreover, data for the reliable explanation of use and for exact dating were lacking in Wu's time. However, his catalogue unfortunately provided illustrations that facilitated the production of fake jades during the early twentieth century.

Shang dynasty

The Shang dynasty (*c.*1600–*c.*1050 BC) ruled in the north-eastern region of China, in the Yellow River valley. The history of this period has been gradually revealed by inscriptions on oracle bones and later by historical texts such as *Shi ji* and also by archaeological excavations in the past century. Large walled cities with palaces and temples, as well as royal and elite tombs, were found in two capitals at present-day Zhengzhou and Anyang.

Between one and thirty jades and anything from three to twenty-five bronze ritual vessels are commonly found in the tomb of an average member of the Shang elite from the Erligang period (*c.*1500–1300 BC) to the Anyang period (*c.*1300–1000 BC).[46] Large quantities of bronze and jade, made with a high level of craftsmanship, were excavated in 1976 from the intact tomb of the Shang queen Fu Hao (*c.*1200 BC), consort of King Wu Ding, revealing her great personal interest in jades. These late Shang jades encompass traditional pieces such as blades as well as

Cat. 8
Jade ceremonial blade
Qijia culture
(*c.*2100–1600 BC)
L: 33.7 cm; W: 5.9 cm
O.50-1946

completely new types such as animal figures and even some exotic pieces whose design may have been inspired by earlier works or which were perhaps collected through warfare.[47] Many of Fu Hao's jades were adapted from ancient pieces, probably because of a shortage of raw material.

The Shang may have been the only people of their day to have a written language, but they were certainly not alone in exerting power in the great landmass of China. In contrast with Anyang, two major finds from the middle and lower Yangzi river region, including the sacrificial pits of Guanghan Sanxingdui in Sichuan and the tomb at Xin'gan Dayangzhou in Jiangxi, reveal a great interest in different jade categories.[48] Among the 750 jades from Fu Hao's tomb, more than 500 are probably personal ornaments. In contrast, jades found in Pit 2 at Sanxingdui are primarily large blades. These were sometimes found in the pre-Anyang sites of Erlitou (c. nineteenth–sixteenth century BC) and Zhengzhou (c. fifteenth–fourteenth century BC) but were less common in Anyang. Furthermore, the majority of jade rings and discs from Pit 2 at Sanxingdui were found inside bronze vessels, which suggests that the jades were made for ritual rather than burial purposes.

In the case of Xin'gan Dayangzhou, most of the jades (in total 150 jades and almost 1,000 jade beads, along with a few pieces of turquoise and crystal) and a few bronze blades were found inside the coffin. Although only a few of them have been illustrated, the large quantity of beads and jade from the coffin are possibly from pendants or tassels that may have served a ceremonial function.

A comparison of the bronze and jade

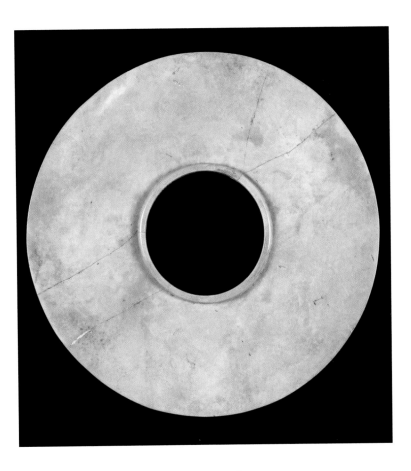

repertories of these three areas during the Shang period indicates that their material cultures and hence, perhaps, religious beliefs differed. Even so, a certain degree of exchange of material may have taken place.[49]

The Shang-dynasty jades in the Fitzwilliam's collection belong to the Lower Yellow River region category, as they resemble many similar items owned by Fu Hao. Cat. 9 is an opaque creamy white and grey jade collared (i.e., rimmed) disc with intense speckling and a few cracks in the surface. Many discs of this type have been found in Fu

Cat. 9
Jade collared disc
Shang dynasty
(c. 1600–c. 1050 BC)
D: 16.4 cm
O.6-1946

Hao's tomb, and the unusually large quantity of col-
lared discs found here and in other Anyang tombs
indicates that they were especially popular in Henan
at that time. Judging from the archaeological exca-
vations, this type of disc gradually disappeared at
the beginning of the Western Zhou. However, it
was later widely distributed in southern China and
South-East Asia,[50] and was also found in later
tombs: there are two examples from the seventh-
century tombs of the Huang state at Guangshan
Baoxiangsi.[51] Another similar example with an
inscription by the Qianlong emperor forms part of
the British Museum collection (1937.4-16.140). It
was thought by the Qianlong emperor to be a cup
stand.[52]

Jade copies of weapons appear in some Shang
tombs. The most popular is the dagger, known in
Chinese as a *ge*. Occasionally bronze weapons are
inlaid with turquoise. The interest in turquoise
seems to have resulted from the importation of
the material from inner Asia, where it was
extensively used at an earlier stage. This jade
dagger (Cat. 10a & b) has a relatively small blade
and handle. The blade tapers quickly to a sharp
tip. The bronze tang is decorated with a typical
Shang bronze monster face and inlaid with
turquoise.

Pendants in the shape of fish, tigers, deer,
cicadas, silkworms and various birds were very
common burial objects during the Shang. Some
of these shapes, such as fish and birds, were
continuously produced or reused throughout the
following Western Zhou period. Because of the
difficulty of dating these jades precisely, some of
these jade ornaments are discussed in the next
section.

Western Zhou period

In about 1050 BC the Zhou defeated the Shang,
whose language and culture they shared, and
established a capital at Hao (near the present-day
city of Xi'an). The early Zhou rulers, through
conquest and colonization, created a large empire
that lasted longer than any other in Chinese
history, although the dynasty retained political
and military control only during the Western
Zhou period (*c*.1050–771 BC).

From the middle Western Zhou onwards a
major change in ritual seems to have occurred,
leading to a different range of bronze vessels and
a great increase in the quantity of jade objects
found in tombs.[53] New categories of jade objects,
such as veils and long pendants, were found in
high-ranking tombs from Baoji, Tianma Qucun
and Sanmenxia. These jades were left on the body
of the deceased and must therefore have had an
important purpose.

The tombs of the lords of Yu at Baoji Zhuyuan-
gou and Rujiazhuang are especially important as
they pre-date all the tombs in the metropolitan
Western Zhou area that contained large quantities
of jade.[54] The occupants' heads, necks, chests and
abdomens were covered with numerous jades in
the shapes of fish (Cats. 11, 12, 13), birds (Cat. 14)
and deer, and also with carnelian and faience tubes
and beads, which may have been components of
complicated jade pendants. A large quantity of
cinnabar powder was placed around the head and
chest, perhaps for protection.[55]

No jade veils as such were found – that is to
say, jades covering the features of the face (eyes,
brows, nose and even teeth) and sewn on to a
textile – but the profusion of jades and beads

Cat. 11
Jade fish pendant
Western Zhou
(c.1050–771 BC)
L: 4.3 cm; W: 1.85 cm
O.19-1946

Cat. 12
Jade fish pendant
Western Zhou
(c.1050–771 BC)
L: 4.4 cm; W: 0.8 cm
O.5-1946

Cat. 13
Jade fish pendant
Western Zhou
(c.1050–771 BC)
L: 11.5 cm; W: 1.4 cm
O.9-1946

Cat. 14
Jade bird pendant
Late Shang
(c.14th–11th century BC)
L: 2.95 cm; W: 1.75 cm
O.45-1946

suggests that they may have been precursors to the use of veils and body coverings.

Between 1992 and 1995 seventeen tombs of marquises and their consorts were found at Tianma Qucun, Shanxi province, dating from the reign of King Mu (r. 947–928 BC) to the beginning of the Spring and Autumn period (770–480 BC).[56] Most are vertical pit tombs, with sloping access passages. Five of the seventeen tombs had been thoroughly looted (M1, M2, M6, M7, M32); another two (M8, M33) had been severely plundered but still retained a considerable number of objects; and ten were found intact. Xu Jay has pointed out, in his comparison of tombs M8 and M31, of a lord and his consort, that there was no great difference between the veils for men and those for women, although the women's graves tended to be richer in jades.[57]

Although the dates and the chronological order of the tombs from Qucun are still being debated, they reveal some gender-specific burial features and personal interests. For example, jade veils and slit ear-rings, as well as the giant dagger (*ge*; Cat. 15), which was placed on the chest, were all commonly found in both male and female tombs, but the occasional jade *cong* placed between the legs (Cat. 16) and later sets of gold ornaments around the waist and ritual bells are found only in male tombs. Jade implements such as axes, adzes and chisels were also found only in the male tombs. On the other hand, long ornaments found near the right side of the chest of the deceased and consisting of a nephrite plaque with dragon pattern and six strings of jade, agate and green faience beads are found only in the tombs of elite females.[58]

Cat. 15
Jade dagger
Western Zhou
(c.1050–771 BC)
L: 24.5 cm; W: 5.5 cm
O.29-1946

Cat. 16
Jade *cong*
Western Zhou
(c.1050–771 BC)
L: 5.9 cm; W: 5.7 cm;
H: 3.3 cm
O.48-1946

Fig. 7
Drawings of jade veil and body coverings from Henan Sanmenxia (late Western to early Eastern Zhou)
After Rawson 1995, p. 315, fig. 3

Similar characteristics were also observed in a high-ranking male tomb at Sanmenxia M2001, Henan province. The face veil included jades displaying facial features, with additional jades on the forehead, cheeks and chin (fig. 7). The body coverings were numerous necklaces and pendants, which were composed of six *huang* (arc-shaped pendants; Cat. 17), faience and agate beads, and were arranged over the upper part of the body.[59] In addition, jade *ge* (see Cat. 15) were placed near both hands or on the chest, and the tip of the *gui* (sceptre) always pointed towards the face.

These ornaments, rings (*huan*) and ceremonial *ge* and *gui* (blades or sceptres) may have been part of the ceremonial dress worn in life, but the placing of them in special positions on the body implies a religious function in death, such as to protect the body, rather than their being mere symbols of status. This was a relatively new practice and seems to be limited to this area. We shall see in the next section that, after the Zhou king and his nobles fled eastwards, reduced versions of jade carving became widespread in the Luoyang area of the new Eastern capital.

Eastern Zhou period

In 771 BC there was a political upheaval: a new dynasty, the Eastern Zhou, was established, and the capital was moved to Luoyi (present-day Luoyang, Henan province). This dynasty is divided into two periods: the Spring and Autumn period (770–476 BC) and the Warring States period (476–221 BC). During the Spring and Autumn period the Zhou domain gradually fragmented into over 140 separate states. Some of the powerful states began to annex weaker ones, so that by the Warring States period seven powerful states had formed: the Qin, Chu, Qi, Yan, Han, Zhao and Wei, known as 'the Seven Overlords of the Warring States period'.

As a result, regional variations in burial characteristics became more prominent, and this is reflected in the materials excavated from different areas.[60] Important tombs include the sixth-century northern tomb M251 of the Jin state at Taiyuan,[61] the southern tomb of the Marquis Yi of Zeng at Leigudun,[62] a fourth-century northern tomb of the Zhongshan state at Lingshou, Hebei,[63] third-century eastern tombs at Qufu and Linzi Shangwangcun,[64] and southern tombs such as Tianxingguan, Baoshan and Wangshan in Hubei.[65] Further south, particularly in the Chu domain, the interest in jades was less notable, perhaps owing to a shortage of material.

During the Eastern Zhou period personal ornaments such as *jue* (slit rings) and *guan* and *zhu* (tubular and round beads: Cats. 18, 19, 20) and tiger and dragon pendants (Cats. 21a & b) increased in number, while three-dimensional animal sculptures declined. New items such as *she* (archer's rings), sword fittings, *dai gou* (belt hooks; Cat. 22) and plaques with small holes at the corners appeared in many Eastern Zhou tombs. These are signs of increased contact with the adjacent countries. Although jade veils were still

Cat. 17
Jade tiger pendant
Western Zhou
(c.1050–771 BC)
L: 6.1 cm; W: 1.6 cm
O.40-1946

Cat. 18
Jade tubular bead
Spring and Autumn period
(6th–5th century BC)
L: 8.2 cm; W: 2.3 cm
O.13-1946

found in Eastern Zhou tombs, these were confined to the Luoyang area.

The custom of placing a long pendant on the body of the tomb owner may have still been practised in some high-ranking tombs during the Eastern Zhou. However, as the number of jades was smaller and the components more limited, they may have been less important than in the late Western Zhou.

A painted wooden figurine from Xinyang M2, Henan, wearing pendants that include jade *huang*, beads and rings with grooved designs (fig. 8), provides some illustrations of the composition of pendants, which may have varied with the region and the status of the tomb owners.[66] A simple jade ring decorated with small spirals in relief hung from the waist of a terracotta warrior (fig. 9) who was a chariot driver and buried outside the mausoleum of the First Emperor (d. 210 BC). A similar piece is in the Fitzwilliam's collection (Cat. 23).

Of some 10,000 Chu tombs that have been excavated, only about 300 contained jade or stone objects. After analysing and classifying these Chu tombs, the scholar Zuo Peng pointed out that central and southern Chu people, from the

Jiangling, Dangyang and Hunan areas, seem to have been more interested in glass beads than in jades. It is possible that jade was scarce in these areas and that glass was used as a substitute.

Most of the pendants found in this area are much simpler than those from the Yellow River basin areas, which are usually composed of rings, beads and tubes, the materials used for the rings being jade, stone and glass, while the beads are mostly of glass.[67] Cats. 19 and 20 are very typical

Cat. 19
Glass bead
Warring States period
(477–221 BC)
L: 2.5 cm
OC.137-1946

Cat. 20
Glass bead
Warring States period
(477–221 BC)
D: 2.1 cm
OC.138-1946

Fig. 8
Drawings of lacquer-painted figures wearing pendants that include jade rings with grooved designs. From a Chu tomb at Henen, Xinyang Eastern Zhou period, 4th century BC After Beijing 1986, fig. 79: 1, 2

Cat. 21a & b
A pair of jade dragon pendants
Warring States period,
4th–3rd century BC
L: 15.5 cm; W: 7.9 cm
O.11 A & B-1946

glass beads buried in the southern Chu areas during the fourth–third century BC. The former is a blue cylindrical bead with protuberances and inlaid with turquoise; the latter is a dark brown, kernel-shaped bead with three sets of concentric circles on the surface, which Chinese archaeologists have called *qing ting yan* ('dragonfly's eye'). These were used together with other beads made of jade, agate and turquoise, as parts of pendants and placed on the chest of the deceased.

In order to produce identical paired jade animal pendants, particularly dragons during the Warring States period, and to make the best use of material, vertical slices were cut through pre-carved objects, often leading to corresponding tool marks on the pendants (see Cats. 21a & b). These dragon shapes feature abstract designs, a powerful arched body, scrolling fins and claws, while the tail and the body are usually decorated with incised interlinking spirals.

Belt hooks of different sizes and materials were commonly found in tombs dating from the Warring States period through to the Han dynasty. To judge from their location near the waists of the deceased, the belt hooks normally functioned as part of the costume, for hanging ornaments. Surprisingly, some belt hooks were found near the neck, head, chest, legs, feet and even inside the mouth, and thus were probably talismans.[68] In several instances the archaeological finds show that belt hooks were found together with jade rings near the waist, so they may have functioned as buckles. With the change of costume in later periods, belt hooks were produced simply as trinkets or ornaments for the scholar's studio.

Cat. 23 (opposite)
Jade ring
Warring States period,
5th–4th century BC
D: 6.5 cm
O.10-1946

Fig. 9
A jade ring decorated with small spirals in relief, hung from the waist of a terracotta warrior
After Beijing 1998, p. 59, fig. 39

Cat. 22
Jade belt hook
Eastern Zhou,
4th–3rd century BC
L: 2.9 cm; H: 1.8 cm
O.70-1946

Han dynasty

The political chaos of the Warring States period was ended by Ying Zheng, the king of Qin state, in 221 BC, when he unified China, proclaiming himself the First Emperor of the Qin dynasty, or Qin Shihuangdi. Unfortunately, this first dynasty ruling the whole of China lasted for only fifteen years. The death of Qin Shihuangdi in 210 BC led to peasant uprisings, which continued throughout the reign of his son. In 206 BC, however, Liu Bang came to power and was proclaimed the first emperor of the Han dynasty, which survived for over 400 years. The period from 206 BC to AD 8 is known historically as the Western Han. Then, after a short interregnum under Wang Mang (AD 9–25), the Han dynasty re-established itself at Luoyang, and the subsequent period AD 25–220 is known as the Eastern Han.

Many tombs of imperial Liu family members have been found in eastern China, including the rulers of the Chu kingdom at Xuzhou, Jiangsu, the Lu kingdom at Qufu, Shandong, the Liang kingdom at Yongcheng, Henan, and the Zhongshan kingdom at Mancheng and Dingxian, Hebei, and the non-Liu king of Nanyue at Guangdong. The excavations in the Chu kingdom at Xuzhou, in particular, revealed an important phenomenon of the Han burials, namely a hierarchical system from the highest levels of the elite down to the lower levels in the tomb plans and their contents. The principal tombs at Xuzhou include those of the kings of Chu from different generations, who were buried at Beidongshan, Shizishan, Guishan, Tushan and Tuolanshan, and of their relatives at Jiulishan (Liu He, c.179–141 BC), Bojishan (Liu Yi, early Western Han) and Hanshan (Liu Zai, early Western Han), together with possible high-ranking but unknown officers at Houloushan and Zifangshan. The main differences between the social levels are that the kings' tomb passages were dug horizontally into a hill and connected with several chambers, while those of the relatives were dug vertically into the ground. In addition, the former were buried with real objects besides models and tomb figures, while the latter were generally equipped with models only.

The reason for our lack of knowledge of other major tombs is that no comparable excavations have yet been carried out at the two Han capitals,

Fig. 10
Jade suit from Shizishan, Xuzhou
c.178–154 BC
L: 175 cm
Xuzhou Museum, Jiangsu

Cat. 24
Jade cicada mouth amulet
Han dynasty, 2nd–1st
century BC
L: 5.9 cm; W: 3.3 cm
O.25-1946

Chang'an and Luoyang. Although most of these tombs were looted in antiquity, the discoveries of the intact tombs of the kings of Nanyue (Zhao Mei, d. 122 BC) at Guangzhou, Guangdong province, and of Zhongshan (Liu Sheng, d. 113 BC) and his consort Dou Wan (d. 104 BC) at Mancheng, Hebei province, have completely changed our perception of Han jades.

The unification of China under the Qin and Han brought together many regional burial features, including the use of jades, in the area represented by present-day eastern China. As a result, new varieties of jade object may have developed. We can find evidence of this development in the tombs of the Han imperial Liu family members in eastern China. These new categories included: a jade suit worn by the deceased (fig. 10); nine plugs, which were inserted into the orifices of the body; two hand grips (*wo*), usually jade pigs (animals possibly symbolic of wealth; Cat. 25), held in the hands; a mouth amulet (*han*, Cat. 24); a jade pillow; jade pendants and seals to represent the status of the deceased in the afterlife; discs (Cats. 26, 76), found on and beneath the body inside the jade suit; weapons for defence against intruders; and jade utensils for their use in the afterlife.

In fact, some of these categories had come into use long before the political unification of the Qin and Han,[69] but the Han saw a great expansion in the numbers of all of them. Jade and other stones were used almost obsessively near the bodies of the Liu princes. Stone was used for the chambers, coffins and some figures of miraculous animals, while jade was employed for suits, discs, pendants, seals, weapons and vessels. Stone

and jade seem to have played an important role in the Han imperial burial because they are permanent and unchanging. In addition, from contemporary texts and bamboo slips excavated from tombs we know that the ancient Chinese people regarded stones and jade as means of defence against demons and spirits. The preparation of these burial jades must have been very costly and time-consuming, so official workshops would have been established in the various kingdoms to supply objects for the imperial family members.

Orifice plugs

The jades for the nine orifices included two eye plaques, two ear plugs, two nose plugs, a mouth plug, anal plug and genital shroud. The eye plaques were usually almond-shaped and pierced at both ends, so that they could be sewn on to a cloth or silk mask that was placed over the face of the deceased. The ear, nose and anal plugs were hexagonal or cylindrical in shape and tapered slightly to a rounded end. A plug was also placed in the mouth of the deceased, usually in the form of a jade cicada (possibly a symbol of rebirth; Cat.

24), but in the case of the king of Zhongshan, Liu Sheng, and his consort Dou Wan, a crescent-shaped jade was used instead. The genital shroud of Liu Sheng was a cylinder reworked from a *cong*, which dated to the Liangzhu period.

Some of the nine orifice plugs, such as the eye plaques and nose plugs, were used in northern and eastern China before the Han unification.[70] The custom of using jade plugs for the orifices overlaps with the appearance of the jade suit. The number of jade plugs for the orifices seems to be unconnected with the status of the tomb occupant. For example, only seven orifice plugs were found in the tomb of Liu He (dating to 179–141 BC), although he did have a jade suit. The lower aristocratic tomb at Zifangshan M3, Xuzhou, dates to the very early Western Han but contained a jade veil and eight jade plugs. The complete nine orifice plugs were first found in the tombs of Liu Sheng and his consort, both of which also contained jade suits.

The term 'nine orifices' (*jiu qiao*) was mentioned as early as the two chapters titled 'Ten Questions' (*shi wen*) and 'Talks on the Loftiest Ways under Heaven' (*tianxia zhidao tan*) found on the bamboo-slip text from Mawangdui M3, dating to the second century BC.[71] In these texts the orifices were related to the vital essence, *qi*.[72] It has therefore been suggested that the purpose of inserting the jade plugs into them was to prevent the 'escape' of vital essence.[73]

However, an alternative view of the function of such plugs might be that they were believed to prevent evil spirits or ghosts taking up residence in the body and wreaking havoc there.[74] Evidence from texts shows that the Chinese in the Han

period were afraid that demons and spirits could cause bodily decay.[75] It is possible that Ge Hong had this in mind when he stated in the *Baopuzi* that 'When gold and jade are inserted into the nine orifices, corpses do not decay.'[76]

Discs

The use of jade discs had a long history and was revived in the Han. During the late Warring States period, especially in Qi, Lu and eastern Chu tombs, they became much more numerous and were placed on corpses (Cat. 26). For example, in tomb M2 at Changfeng Yanggongxiang, An'hui province, thirty-six jade discs were found on the body. In tombs M1 and M2 at Shangwang village, Linzi, Shandong province, eighteen and eleven jade discs respectively were found on the bodies of the tomb occupants. In tombs M52 and M58 at Qufu, Shandong, eighteen and sixteen jade discs respectively were placed on and under the corpses.[77] As Jessica Rawson has pointed out, this practice may have been copied from the Neolithic Liangzhu tombs that were found by chance at that time (see also the previous section).[78] The phenomenon was focused in eastern China and lasted into the Western Han, surface. In Shizishan, Xuzhou, although the tomb had been seriously looted, some jade discs were found and 1,800 jade tiles were inlaid in the lacquer coffin, creating a complete jade covering (fig. 11).[79]

In the case of Nanyue Wang fourteen discs were placed around his body, on his chest and under his back within the jade suit. All these discs were of finer material than that of the jade shroud. In addition, glass discs were found in the storage room of the tomb and glass discs in the main coffin chamber; these were substitutes for jade discs. Approximately 200 pottery discs were also found scattered on the top of the coffin in a tomb at Tongshan, Jiangsu province, of the Western Han.[80] Pottery was probably the least costly way to produce the large numbers of discs needed for funerary purposes.

In the lesser tombs, or where jade was less readily available, copies were made. For example, in Lady Dai's tomb at Mawangdui, thirty-two wooden discs were found in the southern and western compartments, which were identified as storerooms. A painted banner, with Lady Dai's portrait above a large *bi* intertwined with two rising dragons, was placed between the two innermost coffins.[81] In several areas, including Shandong, Jiangsu and Sichuan, discs with cross cords were common elements in tomb designs.[82] In Liu Sheng's case a large *bi*, decorated with a pair of dragons in ornate openwork patterns, was placed between the two coffins (fig. 12). A light green jade openwork pendant from the Fitzwilliam's collection (Cat. 27), decorated with a phoenix and covered with cinnabar, has fine lines carved on the surface to represent the eyes,

even after jade suits were first used.

In the Western Han discs were placed not only around the corpse, inside the jade suit, but were also found decorating the coffin or even placed on top of it. In Mancheng M1 thirteen discs were placed on Liu Sheng's chest and five under his back, inside his jade suit; in M2 eleven discs were placed on Dou Wan's chest and four under her back, also inside her jade suit. In addition, 192 jade tiles were found inside Dou Wan's lacquer coffin and twenty-six jade discs were inlaid on its outer

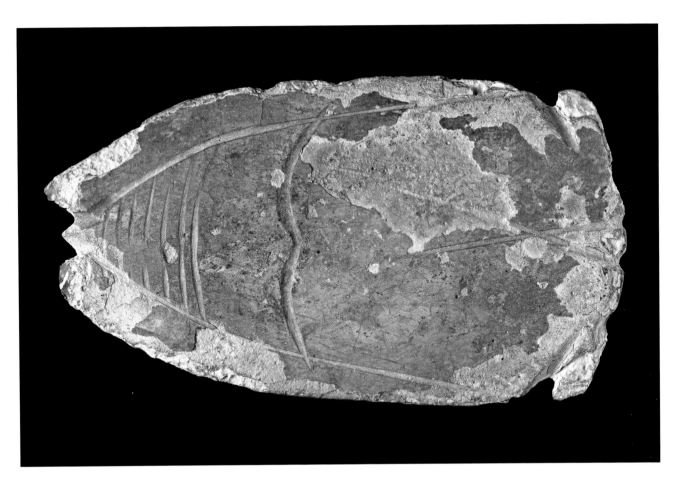

Cat. 28

Glass disc
Eastern Zhou to
Han period,
c.4th–1st century BC
D: 16 cm; H: 0.4 cm
O.1-1946

Cat. 29

Glass cicada used a
replacement for jade
Han dynasty,
1st century BC–
1st century AD
L: 5.7 cm; W: 3.15 cm
OC.134-1946

beak and feathers of the phoenix. It is 18 cm wide and 10 cm high. Judging from the damaged arch below the phoenix, this pendant may have been part of a large disc like the one found at Mancheng, Hebei province.

Glass

During the Han dynasty jade objects were largely used for burial, but in the tombs of females and lower-ranking aristocrats glass acted as a substitute for jade. These glass objects included discs (Cat. 28), which were placed on top of and underneath the body inside jade burial suits, and a cicada (Cat. 29), which was inserted into the mouth of the deceased. Sometimes glass was made into rectangular plaques to form part of a complete burial suit or discs to cover coffins. These glass plaques were made in a mould and were usually decorated with dragons, clouds, quatrefoils and tigers. Two special examples are those excavated from the tombs of unidentified kings' consorts from Guangling kingdom, Yangzhou, Jiangsu province. Some 600 glass plaques, some of them with decorations, were buried with a lady of noble rank named Mo Shu. About 4 km west of Mo Shu's tomb another nineteen glass plaques were found in a tomb at Baonudun.[83] Most of these plaques have the decoration described above. The traces of copper corrosion found on the plaques suggest that they were sewn together with copper thread, but, as these tombs have been looted, we do not know if they contained complete suits or just some of the components, such as a helmet, gloves and boots.[84]

A glass plaque from the Fitzwilliam Museum collection is moulded and decorated with a quatrefoil and inlaid with a turquoise in the middle. A dragon surrounds the quatrefoil, and a small hole has been drilled in each of the four corners. Fragments of gold foil are still visible on the surface (Cat. 30). Archaeological evidence suggests that it is part of a jade suit from the tomb of an elite female or a lower-ranking member of the imperial family. Given the large population of imperial family members from different kingdoms, it would seem that glass was often used as an alternative to jade, as its superficial appearance is almost identical. Glass burial objects in the Han period were usually found in south-east China, particularly in Yangzhou, Jiangsu province;

presumably there was a workshop dedicated to their production.

Sword fittings

Weapons made of jade were also buried in Han tombs but were still unusual at this period and were found only in powerful kingdoms. A jade halberd blade carved in the shape of a bronze weapon *ge*, along with a jade suit and many other jades, was found in a Chu king's tomb at Shizishan, Xuzhou, dating to the early Western Han. The same burial practice was also found at Liang king's tomb at Yongcheng, Henan province, and at Lu king's tomb at Qufu, Shandong province.

Much more common during this period was the burial of bronze or iron swords with jade

Cat. 30
Glass plaque used as part of a suit in the burial
Han period,
c. 1st century BC–
1st century AD
L: 6.1 cm; W: 3.9 cm;
H: 0.5 cm
OC.133-1946

Cat. 31
Jade sword pommel
Warring States period,
c.4th century BC
D: 1.9 cm
O.203-1946

Cat. 32
Jade guard
Han dynasty
(206 BC–AD 220)
L: 5.1 cm; W: 1.9 cm
O.28-1946

fittings. These fittings included a round pommel ornament attached to the end of the hilt (Cat. 31), a guard (Cat. 32), which is approximately triangular in shape to protect the hand from the blade, one or occasionally two scabbard slides (Cat. 33) to attach the sword to a belt, and a scabbard chape (Cat. 34), usually trapezoidal in shape, which formed the end of a scabbard.

Fig. 13 shows how the jade fittings were attached to a sword. The use of jade, rather than bronze or iron, suggests that the sword was not designed as a weapon for the living. The use of jade fittings with bronze or iron swords, as Rawson has suggested, reflects the desire to combine the material strength of the metal with the spiritual power of jade, and thereby to enhance the force and protection afforded by the weapon.[85]

All of the jades mentioned above can be classified as protective jades. They were found close to the body, as in the case of the intact tomb

Fig. 13
Drawing of sword fittings, after *Exhibition of Ancient Chinese Jades*, Tainan: Taiwan National College of the Arts, 1999, p. 53

Cat. 33
Jade scabbard slide
Han dynasty,
2nd–1st century BC
L: 10.5 cm; W: 2.35 cm;
H: 1.3 cm
O.18-1946

Cat. 34
Jade scabbard chape
Eastern Zhou or Han,
4th–1st century BC
L: 5.2 cm; W: 2.45 cm;
H: 5.3 cm
O.23-1946

of Liu Sheng, where jade plugs were inserted into the nine orifices before the body was covered with jade discs and then encased in a jade suit. The whole body was completely covered with several layers of jades, indicating how important it was felt to be to protect the body in this way.

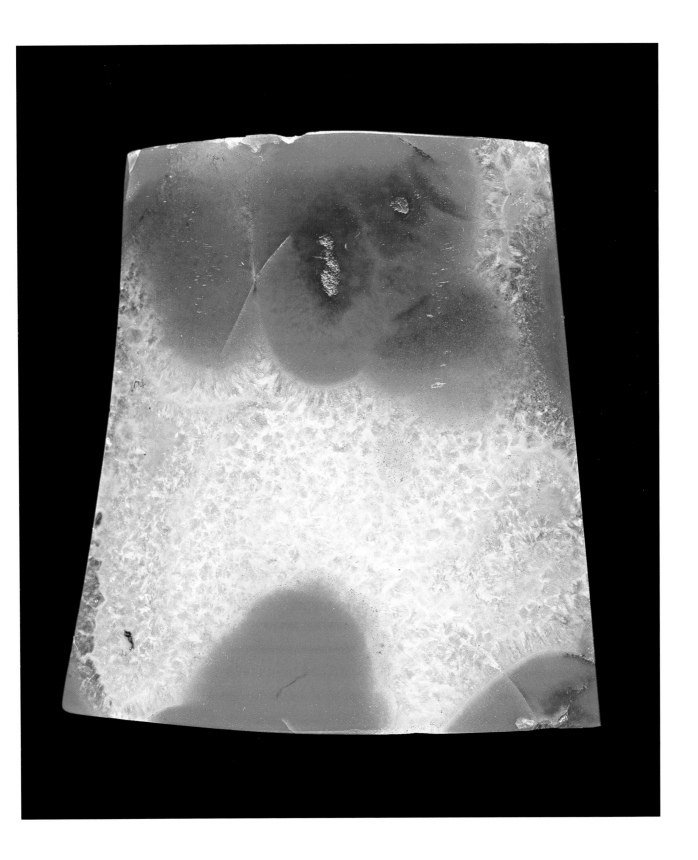

4. Jade for everyday life

I N LATER PERIODS jades were rarely made for burial purposes, as they had been in the Han dynasty. Instead, they were made into personal ornaments, trinkets, everyday utensils and ritual objects. This chapter mainly discusses jades from the later Ming (1368–1644) and Qing (1644– 1911) periods, based on the museum's collection. These jades can be divided into four categories: 1) animal sculptures that were made for display or as trinkets – most of them carrying auspicious connotations; 2) jades made for scholars' studios, such as paperweights and brush washers; 3) jade utensils, copied from contemporary porcelain, silver and ancient bronze utensils, and made to show off the owner's wealth and social status; 4) personal ornaments, such as hairpins, belt buckles and snuff bottles.

Most of these jades were passed down from generation to generation and are therefore very difficult to date precisely without reference to archaeological finds. This chapter will examine the textual records to explain why they were produced and to compare them with collections from other museums.

Animal sculptures: toys, trinkets and protection

Large numbers of small three-dimensional jade animal sculptures were found in the tomb of the Shang queen Fu Hao (c.1200 BC). These included figurines, dragons, birds, tigers, elephants, bears, owls, deer, monkeys, horses, cows, dogs, rams, rabbits, turtles, doves, frogs, cicadas and praying

Cat. 35
Jade buffalo said to have been brought to Peking by Emperor Yongle in AD 1422
H: 15 cm; L: 40 cm
O.31 & A-1946

mantis. All of these sculptures have strong and vivid decoration and are less than 5 cm long, so they are likely to have been trinkets of the owner during her life.[86]

In tomb M63 at Tianma Qucun, Shanxi province, a corroded bronze box containing jade animal sculptures was found in the north-west corner of the outer coffin within a vertical pit tomb dating to the Western Zhou period. The tomb owner was identified as one of the consorts of Marquis Bangfu of Jin (M64).[87]

Buffalo

Animal sculptures were popular soon after the unification of China in 221 BC. Stone buffaloes and horses were placed along the tomb passages as guardians in death of Huo Qubing, the favourite general of Emperor Wudi (r. 140–87 BC), and are now preserved in the Maoling museum. Small animal sculptures made of jade were found outside the mausoleum of Emperor Yuandi (r. 48–33 BC) and probably had a protective function.[88]

Clues to the functions of these animal sculptures may come from their sizes. A large bronze buffalo can be seen on the bank of the Summer Palace Lake outside Beijing. It was placed there in the belief that the sacred and powerful animal would repress any evil spirits that might disturb the lakes.[89] Large jade buffalo sculptures such as Cats. 35 and 36 may have been displayed in the houses of the rich or in the imperial household

Cat. 37
Jade buffalo
Late Ming to early Qing,
16th/17th century
H: 9 cm; L: 17 cm
O.1-1996

Cat. 38
Jade buffalo
Qing, Qianlong period,
18th century
L: 12.6 cm; H: 7 cm
O.14-1938

Fig. 14
Curio box
Qing dynasty (1644–1911)
National Palace Museum,
Taipei

to serve the same function, whereas smaller animal sculptures (Cats. 37, 38) may have been kept in a curio box (*duo bao ge*, fig. 14) as trinkets. Even smaller animal sculptures may have been used as paperweights in a scholar's studio.

The different nature of each type of animal may also have had its own symbolism. In China the ox, or water buffalo, has been invested with a variety of attributes. Because of its role in pulling ploughs, it became symbolic of spring and agriculture. Oxen are easy to identify by the swept-back and wide inward-curving horns, and were a favourite subject of jade carvers from the Ming onwards. In earlier periods, such as the Han or Northern Qi, oxen made of earthenware were depicted ploughing or pulling carriages. In later periods water buffalo were depicted at rest, lying on the ground with their heads turned almost 90 degrees, indicating that the world was at peace. Other buffalo hold rice grains in their mouths (Cat. 38), suggesting a good harvest.

Horse

The horse is another popular subject in Chinese decorative arts and first appeared on earthenware during the Han and Tang periods, when China had close contact with Central Asia. It has been suggested that the Han emperor Wudi was keen to conquer central Asia, not only because he wished to acquire drugs that would confer immortality, but also because he wanted a special breed of horse.[90] In the *Yi jing* ('Book of Changes') the dragon and horse represent *yang* and *yin* respectively, but in later mythology the horse became symbolic of *yang* and the ox of *yin*.[91]

Cat. 39 shows an elegant recumbent horse, carved with fine details from a black and dark grey jade boulder. When it first arrived in the Museum, this horse was dated to the Tang dynasty (AD 618–907) on the basis of the record in Zhu Derun's *Gu yu tu* ('Illustration of Ancient Jades') that five jade horses of various colours were made for the Tang emperor Xuanzong (r. AD 713–755).

Cat. 39
Jade horse said to have been brought to Peking by Emperor Yongle in AD 1422
H: 16.2 cm; L: 25.5 cm
O.34-1946

Cat. 40
Jade lion
Late Ming dynasty,
16th–17th century
L: 8.9 cm; H: 6.65 cm
O.58-1946

The same description can be found in the early seventeenth-century encyclopaedia *Sancai tuhui*, compiled by Wang Qi and Wang Siyi.[92] Since most of the larger-scale animal sculptures were produced in the Ming period or later, current opinion is that this jade horse is unlikely to be from earlier times.

Lion

The lion is not native to China and first became known there through the spread of Indian Buddhism. It is a temple guardian and also carries the Bodhisattva. In later periods the Chinese seem to have thought of the lion as a type of dog, depicting it with the features of a lion and the behaviour of a dog. These images were also commonly seen in porcelain, particularly *blanc de Chine*. It is worth noting that lions, whether they were made of stone and placed in front of sacred buildings or made of *blanc de Chine*, were either depicted with both forepaws on the ground or one raised in a menacing attitude, whereas jade lions are usually in a crouching position, with finely carved ridges along their backs, curled manes and sharp claws, as in Cat. 40, the design of which suggests that it was made as a trinket rather than as a guardian.

Elephant

The elephant is another animal that is closely linked to Buddhism, since Buddha descended from heaven on the back of an elephant. The pronunciation of the word for elephant, *xiang*, is similar in Mandarin to that of the word for auspicious (*xiang*), so the elephant is taken as a good omen. The phrase *Tai ping you xiang* means 'the elephant appears when the world is at peace'. 'Washing the white elephant' was a popular motif after the introduction of Buddhism into China and is often a subject of paintings. In the decorative arts the elephant is usually depicted with a vase on its back. In the case of the Fitzwilliam's example (Cat. 41) two monks or Buddhist figures, one holding a vase and the other an elephant tusk, sit on the back of an elephant. The pun of vase (*ping*) and elephant (*xiang*) forms the phrase *Tai ping jing xiang* ('The Scene of World at Peace').

Cat. 42 is possibly the largest jade elephant sculpture outside China. It is carved in a rather

Cat. 42
Jade elephant
Late 19th or
early 20th century
H: 19 cm; W: 43 cm
O.63-1946

Cat. 43
Jade *qilin*
Kangxi period
(1662–1722)
L: 18.4 cm; W: 13.95 cm;
H: 12.7 cm
O.64-1946

abstract way, with small eyes and giant ears rest-
ing on its front legs. Its material and carving
technique suggest that it was made either in the
late nineteenth or early twentieth century.

Qilin

The *qilin* – a mythical creature – rarely appears in
Chinese art. It was not until the Yuan dynasty and
onwards that *qilin* started to appear on blue and
white porcelain. During the Ming period the
appearance of a *qilin* underwent a marked change:
the head became that of a dragon, with its cus-
tomary two horns, and the tail became the flame-
like tail of the Buddhist lion.[93] This pale green
jade *qilin* (Cat. 43) is carved with vapour or clouds
issuing from its mouth. At its side is the book of

Cat. 44
Jade *qilin*
Late Ming or early Qing
dynasty, 17th–18th century
L: 8.25 cm; H: 7 cm
O.6-1938

knowledge, *Tian shu* ('Book from Heaven'). Flames emerge from its four legs, and clouds surround its body, suggesting that it is an auspicious creature. Fine striations also embellish the mane and tail.

The *qilin* is sometimes called the Dragon Horse (*long ma*), which is said to have emerged from the Yellow River and appeared to Fu Xi, the legendary First Emperor. It carried on its back a mystic map, from which the written language of China is said to have evolved.[94] Gradually the *qilin* bearing a book has come to signify best wishes to a scholar.

Cat. 44 is another *qilin*, carved from a piece of nephrite of two different colours. Such material was regularly used for snuff bottles in Suzhou. Judging from the material and the carving technique, this *qilin* is probably a masterpiece from the seventeenth or eighteenth century.

Crane

The crane is one of the commonest emblems of longevity in Chinese art, mainly because Chinese traditionally believed that cranes could live more than a thousand years. Furthermore, the pronunciation of the word for crane (*he*) is similar to that of the words for harmony (*he xie*).

This pale green jade with grey veining and inclusions (Cat. 45) is carved with two recumbent cranes, one holding a spray of fruiting peaches in its beak. Like cranes, peaches represent longevity in Chinese art, a topic that was particularly popular in the eighteenth century. The subject matter suggests that it could have been an auspicious gift for a birthday or marriage at that time.

It is important to note that all of the jade animal sculptures carved during the Ming and Qing periods, whether they were trinkets or studio objects, must have carried auspicious meanings and good wishes directed towards the viewer. However, some of the twelve zodiac animals, such as the rat, tiger, snake, dragon, chicken and pig, were not depicted. Some animal sculptures, such as monkeys, appear later in the Qing dynasty. Creatures such as the chicken seem to appear in paintings more regularly than in sculpture. In terms of aesthetics, most of these animals were depicted lying or crouching, a relaxed and elegant pose.

Objects for scholars' studios

Brush, ink, paper and inkstone are generally referred to as the 'Four Treasures of a Scholar's Studio', but there were in fact more studio objects than just these four, particularly during the periods when *literati* (scholar) artists were active in the Ming and Qing. Other items include brush rests, brush washers, brush pots, paperweights, water droppers and even seals and seal paste boxes. These objects were not necessarily all made of jade, and they were rarely buried in tombs. The earliest jade

Cat. 45
Jade recumbent cranes
Qing dynasty, 18th century
L: 10.3 cm; H: 5.4 cm
O.4-1938

Cat. 46
Jade water dropper in the
shape of a mythical animal
Qing dynasty, 18th century
L: 12.7 cm; H: 7.6 cm
O.8-1938

scholarly objects uncovered by archaeologists include a green jade brush rest, a crystal brush rest, a white jade lotus-leaf brush tester/water dropper, a white jade rabbit paperweight and a white jade seal with animal knob. The owner has been identified as Shi Shengzu, who died in AD 1274, five years before the collapse of the Southern Song dynasty.[95] He was a government officer, so the buried studio objects reflect his high social status.

Two jade inkstones and a jade brush washer were found buried in the tomb of Princess Chen of the Liao.[96] However, such objects were still rare during this period. It was not until the increase of wealth in the Ming and Qing dynasties that jades and related material made for scholars' studios increased. A crystal deer-shaped water dropper, a green jade inkstone, a jade flower-shaped water dropper, a jade brush rest, a jade brush holder and a crystal deer-shaped paperweight were excavated from the tomb of the Ming prince Zhu Tan (1370–1392) at Zou County, Shandong.[97] Large numbers of jade studio objects from the Qing dynasty survive in museums, but few were found in tombs.

Ming literature provides us with reliable information on the uses to which archaeological objects, discovered at that time, were put. Gao Lian's *Zun sheng ba jian* ('Eight Discourses on the Art of Living', with prefaces dated 1591) records that a pair of Han burial hand grips in the shape of pigs were used as paperweights. In addition, a white jade hunting dog, recumbent feline dragon, jade rabbit, buffalo, horse, deer, ram, toad, agate crouching tiger and crystal sleeping buffalo from the Song period were used as paperweights. A large jade scabbard slide was used as a wrist-rest. Shallow jade and crystal dishes were used as brush or ink testers. Round and square jade pots were used as water droppers. Gao Lian also describes a white jade *bi xie* (a mythical creature) made by Lu Zigang, an artisan from Suzhou. It was in an archaic design, with a hollow body to contain water and inlaid with turquoise.[98] Although we do not know exactly what this water dropper looked like, its description (apart from a lack of turquoise) fits that of a Qing dynasty water dropper from the Fitzwilliam collection (Cat. 46).

It is a pale green jade with areas of brownish

skin. The creature has a square, open jaw display-ing teeth and fangs. Wings extend from the four legs, and the horn is incised with the Chinese character *wang* ('king'). Wing-like extensions in relief are incised on the underside. A hole was drilled in the middle of its back, and a jade tube with a lid was installed. This water dropper was possibly copied from a bronze version that is illus-trated in the Qing imperial bronze catalogue *Xiqing gujian* ('Mirror of the Antiquity of the Xi Qing').[99]

Gao Lian's contemporary the scholar Wen Zhenheng (1585–1645) wrote *Zhang wu zhi* ('Treatise on Superfluous Things'), in which he described similar jade paperweights made in the form of rabbits, buffalo, horses, deer, rams, toads, crouching tigers, *bi xie* and feline dragons.[100] These records reflect the interest among Ming *literati* in collecting antiques for pleasure and for

use as studio objects. It also helps to explain why jade animal sculptures were produced in large numbers during those times. They may have been purchased as antiques, even though many were of recent manufacture. These records were referred to in the Qing dynasty in order to understand the Ming scholars' tastes and even to copy them.

Small jade animal sculptures are mostly carved in a kneeling or reclining position. This greyish green jade horse (Cat. 47) is a typical example. It has brown areas on the surface and is carved in a recumbent position, with its head turned over its back towards its tail. Its eyes look up attentively and are shown in incised lines. The legs are folded beneath the body. The mane and the tail are strongly striated. Another example is a greyish green jade carved with two nuzzling horses (Cat. 48). Their bodies are close together and their fea-tures well defined. Made for the *literati* and for

Cat. 47

Jade horse used as a paperweight
Late Ming or early Qing dynasty, 17th–18th century
L: 7 cm; H: 4.5 cm
O.2-1938

Cat. 48

Jade horses used as paperweight
Late Ming or early Qing dynasty, 17th–18th century
L: 7 cm; H: 4.5 cm
O.2-1938

Cat. 49

Glass paperweight
Qing dynasty, 18th–19th century
H: 6.5 cm; L: 12 cm
O.16-1951

those who wished to join their ranks, the horse is a symbol of rapid success.

The use of glass declined after the Han period but was reintroduced by Jesuit missionaries in the seventeenth century. Following the establishment of a glass workshop in the thirty-fifth year of Kangxi (1696), glass was widely used for imperial utensils and studio objects. This blue glass frog (Cat. 49) was probably used as a paperweight instead of a water dropper since, although there is a hole in its back, there is no corresponding hole in its mouth to release water drops. A similar piece made of crystal, but of much smaller size and without a hole in its back, is in the Palace Museum, Beijing.[101]

Apart from jade animals, other antiquities made of jade, or contemporary Ming pieces in an archaistic style, were also used as studio objects, such as paperweights, ink stick rests and scroll weights. A Han jade scabbard slide (fig. 15) was inset into a piece of sandalwood and used as a scroll weight, and a Ming one (fig. 16) was used as an ink stick rest. Both pieces are in the National Palace Museum, Taipei. These examples indicate how the jade sword slides (Cats. 50, 51, 52) in the Fitzwilliam Museum may have been used in the scholar's studio during the Ming period.

The use of jade antiquities as studio objects is confirmed by archaeological evidence. A sword guard decorated with interlinked scrolls, a scabbard slide with a feline dragon in relief, and a brush finial were found in the tomb at Hangzhou of Xian Yushu (1257–1302), a famous calligrapher in the Yuan dynasty.[102] There were no weapons in the tomb, so these objects are very likely to have been used as paperweights or ink stick rests or set in weighted rulers, as described in the texts.

Brush washers are the most common objects

Cat. 50
Jade scabbard slide
Late Ming dynasty,
16th–17th century
L: 7.65 cm; W: 1.9 cm;
H: 1.25 cm
O.2-1940

Cat. 51
Jade scabbard slide
Late Ming dynasty,
16th–17th century
L: 8.95 cm; W: 2.3 cm;
H: 1.6 cm
O.41-1946

Cat. 52
Jade scabbard slide
Ming dynasty (1368–1644)
L: 4.6 cm; W: 2.2 cm;
H: 1.45 cm,
O.42-1946

in the scholar's studio. Various designs are seen in the text records, from tombs and surviving objects in museums. Cat. 53 is a pale greyish-green jade brush washer of oval form in high relief and decorated with dragons emerging from the sea and chasing pearls among clouds. On the underside is a very finely worked whirlpool. A similar but much larger piece is in the Palace Museum, Beijing.[103] Cat. 54 is an opaque celadon jade, hollowed and carved with gnarled branches of prunus blossoms issuing from beneath a magnolia flower.

Belt hooks (*dai gou*) became popular again during the Song dynasty, but, although the shape was based on a Han belt hook, the patterns and function were altered. The body of this belt hook (Cat. 55) is decorated with rows of relief spirals and then narrows slightly to form the neck of a horned goat. The features of the goat – its eyes,

ears, mouth and horns – are simply shown in slight modelling and with incised lines. An almost identical one is in the Museum of East Asian Art at Bath.[104]

The reinterpretation of antique objects for a new purpose was often described in Ming texts. Belt hooks were used at that time, but not as part of clothing. Instead, Wen Zhenheng's *Zhang wu zhi* records that bronze *dai gou* were used to hang up scroll paintings, dusters and fans.[105] It is not known whether jade belt hooks were used in a similar way.

Seals were very common burial objects in the tombs of the high-ranking elite from the late Warring States period to the Han. They help archaeologists to identify the tomb owners and were probably intended as a method of identification in the underground world. Depending on the inscription, they could also be used as studio

Cat. 53

Jade brush washer
Late Ming dynasty,
16th–17th century
L: 17 cm; H: 9 cm
O.5-1934

Cat. 54
Jade brush washer
Late Ming dynasty,
16th–17th century
L: 17 cm; H: 9 cm
O.6-1951

Cat. 55
Jade belt hook
Song dynasty (960–1279)
L: 8.7 cm
O.35-1946

objects or to authenticate official documents.

Seals have always played an important role in Chinese society. Before the invention of the cash machine, people needed their personal seal when they withdrew money from the bank. Foreign businessmen, used to signing their names on contracts, found with astonishment that their Chinese counterparts preferred seals. All important documents need an official seal as a token of their authenticity.

Cat. 56a & b is a seal of dark brown jade, with a square base and a turtle-shaped knob. The inscription can be read as *Chun-nan Hou* ('Marquis of Chun-nan'). The design imitates a Han official seal, but the carving of the inscription suggests that it is a late Qing piece, and no record of a Marquis of Chun-nan has been found. As a result of railway construction work in the late nineteenth to early twentieth century in China, many antiques were unearthed from tombs, and

Cat. 56a & b
Jade seal
Qing dynasty, 19th century
Base: 2 x 1.9 cm; H: 1.95 cm
O.72-1946

the production of fakes such as this jade seal developed to satisfy the antique-collecting craze of that era.

Seal marks started to appear on paintings from the Song dynasty onwards. They vary in content, shape, size, material and calligraphy but can be distinguished by their inscriptions and categorized as artists' seals, leisure seals (known as *xian zhang*), studio seals, connoisseurs' seals (also known as *jian shang zhang*), collectors' seals (known as *shou cang zhang*), inspection seals and so on.

From the Song dynasty onwards, studio objects not only functioned as tools for writing and painting but have also been treated as 'works of art' that the *literati* might collect and discuss with friends and visitors. The intimate relationship between the *literati* and studio objects reached a peak during the late Ming period. Studio objects made of jade reflected the owner's social status, and the design reflected his personal tastes and connoisseurship. *Literati* scholars were in the mainstream of the society. Their interests in collecting antiquities as a medium for understanding the past influenced and stimulated the market and economy. As a result, many forgeries circulated in the market to meet the demand for antiquities.

Utensils

Jade vessels were rare in early China, partly because carving a vessel out of a jade boulder was wasteful. One jade vessel in the shape of a bronze basin was found in Fu Hao's tomb, and a similar Shang basin was recovered from a Western Zhou tomb. It was not until the Han dynasty that jade vessels in forms such as eared cups, beakers, a tubular cup on a narrow stem, and a rhyton appeared.[106] Even then, although jade vessels were still rare, the most numerous groups come from the tombs of the Xuzhou, who were at the top of the hierarchy of the Han dynasty. The appearance of these vessels and their location in tombs suggest that they served different functions.

As recorded in the *Shi ji*, Han Wudi believed that drinking dew and jade powder from a jade cup conferred longevity. He therefore built a device in the Jian Zhang Palace for collecting dewdrops.[107] In *Shan Hai Jing* ('The Classic of Mountains and Seas', some parts of which are thought to date from the Warring States period, although the bulk of the text dates from the Han) jades are associated with food offerings to the spirits on specific occasions.¹⁰⁸

The jade material itself represented durability and was regarded as possessing special powers when used for drinking and eating. The first Han emperor, Liu Bang, held up a jade cup and drank a toast to the longevity of the Grand Emperor.¹⁰⁹ A jade cup (*yu bei*) with the inscription 'Long Life to the Lord of Men' (*ren zhu yan shou*) was presented to Emperor Wen in 165 BC and led the emperor to order great feasting throughout the empire.¹¹⁰ The jade cup referred to in the text records may be similar to those found in the tombs of the king of Nanyue at Guangzhou and the king of Chu at Shizishan.

These vessels were modelled on pieces seen in lacquer, bronze and other materials but, being made of this precious material, were regarded as more potent and conferring additional special powers. Again the wish for potency that derived from the durable quality of jade may have been significant.¹¹¹

The design of jade utensils from the Tang dynasty onwards was naturally influenced by that of contemporary porcelain, gold and silver wares. This mottled grey jade bowl (Cat. 57) with scalloped flange and plain surface takes as its prototype a silver dish excavated from an eighth-century tomb in Inner Mongolia. Another similar

Cat. 58
Archaistic jade vase
Qing dynasty, late
18th–early 19th century
H: 30 cm; W: 23.4 cm;
D: 14.5 cm
O.52-1946

silver plate was found in a Yuan tomb outside Shanghai.[112] The bowl was carved, hollowed and highly polished. The scalloped flange suggests it was strongly influenced by contemporary silverware.

The use of jade utensils reached another peak in Chinese history during the Ming and Qing dynasties. Hundreds of jade plates were found in the house of Wang Zhen (active *c*.1442–6) after he fell from power,[113] and of the 857 jade vessels owned by the corrupt minister Yang Song (1480–1565) 311 were jade cups.[114] Similar sto-

ries were recorded in the Qing dynasty. He Shen (1750–1799) was a court official and a relative of Emperor Qianlong (r. 1736–95) who was found guilty of corruption by the Jiaqing emperor (r. 1796–1820). At least eighteen jade basins, thirty jade vases and thirteen tables of jade bowls and others were found in his possession.[115] Although we do not know exactly what the jade cups and utensils in Yang Song's and He Shen's collections looked like, more and more jade vessels excavated from tombs and hoards in the past two decades provide us with material to compare with surviving Ming and Qing vessels in museum collections, particularly those in the Palace Museum, Beijing.

After analysing the jade utensils from the tomb of the Wanli emperor (1573–1620) and others, Rawson has grouped the Ming vessels into four major categories: 1) archaic vessels based on ancient bronzes; 2) undecorated cups and bowls similar to equivalent pieces in porcelain; 3) vessels based on the forms of silver and gold objects; and 4) cups with flower-like handles.[116] These categories continued to be made into the Qing dynasty and can be seen in the collection of the Fitzwilliam Museum.

Archaic vessels based on ancient bronzes

The copying of bronze vessels in jade has a long history, from the Shang and Zhou periods (*c*.1500–500 BC), to the Song, Yuan, Ming and Qing dynasties, when archaism was in fashion. This large opaque grey-green jade *hu* ('vase'; Cat. 58) has brown inclusions and flecking; its shape was copied from a Han bronze *hu*, but it is decorated with a Shang and Zhou *taotie* ('monster face') motif. Each handle has a dragon head at the upper junction with the body of the vase. The stylized *taotie* in the middle shows characteristics from the late Qing period, possibly the late eighteenth to early nineteenth century, and was probably copied from a woodblock print. It must have been very difficult to hollow out the vase and polish it inside, which implies that there was a large market for archaistic style objects at that time.

Undecorated cups and bowls similar to equivalent pieces in porcelain

Jade cups (Cat. 59) with a pair of confronting feline dragons as handles seem to be a very popular design for Ming-period utensils. Other examples can be found in the Palace Museum, Beijing, and the Art Gallery at Tianjin,[117] and the tomb of Mu Rui at Jiangjunshan, Jiangning,

Jiangsu province.[118] This type of cup seems to have its origin in Song-dynasty *qingbai* cups (Cat. 60), although a late Ming jade cup (Cat. 61) bears an even closer resemblance to the *qingbai* cup as its foot-ring is much higher. Its surface was dyed and scorched to make it look older.

A pair of eighteenth-century slop jars, known as *zhadou* in Chinese, are in the Fitzwilliam Museum's collection (Cat. 62). One of the jars has brown areas on the rim, and both have been skilfully hollowed out with a bulbous bottom, which flares out to the wide trumpet mouth. They are based on porcelain versions that were popular before the Qing, such as this Jiajing-reign mark monochrome *zhadou* from the British Museum (fig. 17).

Another example is this eighteenth-century celadon jade dish (Cat. 63), which has a lifelike three-dimensional carving of two catfish at its

Cat. 59
Jade cup
Ming dynasty (1368–1644)
L: 14.5 cm; H: 8 cm
O.13-1951

Cat. 60
Qingbai cup
Song dynasty (960–1279)
H: 7.5 cm; L: 11 cm
C.71-1946

Cat. 61
Jade cup
Late Ming dynasty,
16th–17th century
W: 14.7 cm; H: 6 cm
O.54-1946

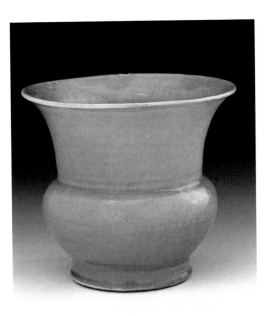

Cat. 62
Jade *zhadou*
Qing dynasty, 18th century
H: 8.5 cm
O.19A-1938

Fig. 17
Monochrome *zhadou*
Ming dynasty, Jiajing mark
and period (1522–66)
H: 12.7 cm
British Museum, London
OA 1947.7-12.283

centre. They swirl among a spray of reeds, which rises up the sides of the dish. The outer surface is decorated with egrets searching for fish in a lotus pond. The design of this dish was probably inspired by Longquan ceramics dating to the Southern Song dynasty (fig. 18). 'Catfish' in Chinese is *nian yu*, so that two catfish create the pun *nian nian you yu* ('a surplus every year'). Relief carving of this type can be found on bowls and dishes from the Qianlong period in private collections in the UK.[119]

Cat. 63
Jade dish with two fish
among reeds
Qing dynasty, 18th century
D: 18.8 cm; H: 6.1 cm
O.7-1951

Fig. 18
Longquan celadon bowl
decorated with two fish in
the centre
Southern Song dynasty
(1127–1279)
D: 21.8 cm; H: 4.5 cm
Private collection,
Cambridge

Vessels based on
the forms of silver and gold objects

This ewer of pale green jade (Cat. 64) has light
brown markings and veins. Iron oxide may have
been applied to the inner and outer surfaces to
give this piece the appearance of having been
buried and of great age. The handle is designed as
a feline dragon, and another small feline dragon
can be seen under the spout. The whole body is
incised with cloud patterns, the neck carved in
low relief. A similar piece dating to the mid–
Ming dynasty is in the Tianjin City Museum,[120]

and another is in the Hangzhou Historical
Museum.[121]

This basin is a further example of a metal uten-
sil rendered in jade (Cat. 65). It is an undecorated
green dish with a wide rim. The centre of the dish
is relatively flat, and there is no foot-ring; its sur-
face is softly polished. The jade dish is based on a
dish in a soft metal, either silver or gold. A similar
example but slightly larger in diameter (fig. 19)
was excavated from the underground palace at
Dingling, outside Beijing, which belonged to
Emperor Wanli.

Cat. 65
Jade basin
Ming dynasty, Wanli period
(r. 1573–1620)
D: 24.2 cm; H: 3.85 cm
O.112-1946

Fig. 19
Jade basin excavated from
Emperor Wanli's tomb at
Dingling, Beijing
1573–1621
D: 29 cm (mouth)
Dingling Museum, Beijing

Cups with flower-like handles

Another popular design during the Ming dynasty is exemplified by this cup with flower-like handles (Cat. 66). The pale white jade was hollowed and carved in openwork with gnarled branches of prunus blossoms issuing from underneath and two feline dragons hidden among them. Although it has a spout on one side, it seems unlikely to have been used as a drinking bowl as it is difficult to hold. Instead, it may have been a brush washer for the scholar's studio or simply an ornament.

The design of the earlier jade utensils appears to have been influenced by a search for immortality. During the medieval period in China jade utensils were rarely buried in tombs. We have no firm evidence that jade was ground into powder in order to cure diseases, as recorded in the texts. In the later Ming and Qing periods large numbers of jade utensils are mentioned in texts, and surviving objects can be seen in many museum collections. Their impractical designs (see Cats. 63, 64, 66) seem to suggest that they were intended to impress the viewers and to demonstrate their owner's wealth.

Cat. 66

Jade cup
Late Ming dynasty, 16th century
L: 16.5 cm; H: 6.2 cm
O.8-1951

Personal ornaments

Cat. 67
Jade hairpin
Late Ming dynasty,
16th century
L: 13.2 cm
O.77-1946

Cat. 68
Jade plaque as part of a
jade belt set
Possibly Liao period
(907–1125)
L: 5.4 cm; W: 2.65 cm;
H: 0.65 cm
O.43-1946

Jade personal ornaments have always formed a large proportion of archaeological finds. They include dress and hair ornaments, pendants, belts and small objects to hang about the body. In most cases they were treasured during life, then buried with their owners for the afterlife. They indicate the owner's gender, social rank and even, to some extent, religious background.

Hairpins have played an important role in Chinese costume since the Neolithic period. During the Shang period they were commonly made of bone, while gold and silver were popular in the Tang and Song periods. Hairpins made of jade became increasingly popular during the Ming period and have frequently been found in tombs. This opaque white jade hairpin (Cat. 67) has grey line inclusions. It tapers to a round tip, which is decorated with clouds. The underside is flat and undecorated. Hairpins such as this one can be identified as part of the Han Chinese costume and dated to the Ming dynasty, because of the distinctive hairstyles of that period. Some similarly shaped jade hairpins, but with different decoration, have been found in Ming tombs outside Shanghai.[122]

Belt plaques also played an essential role in Chinese costume and were marks of social status. This pale green jade plaque (Cat. 68), extensively altered to brown, has a smooth and undecorated surface, with four pairs of interconnected holes at the edges on the reverse for attachment. It was part of a belt set and may date from the Liao (907–1125) or Jin (1115–1234) periods, since plaques from the later Ming are usually larger in size and more decorated.

Fig. 20
Jade belt set excavated
from Emperor Wanli's
tomb at Dingling, Beijing
1573–1621
L: 146 cm
Dingling Museum, Beijing

Cat. 69a & b
Jade belt clasp
Ming dynasty (1368–1644)
L: 10.9 cm
O.33-1938

Belt sets were normally of between twelve and twenty-two plaques, but the number of plaques was not related to the official's rank.[123]

According to the Ming text *Ming hui yao* ('Assembling the Most Important of the Ming Dynasty'), belts of different types were restricted to particular ranks and jade belts could only be worn by first-rank officers.[124] Jade belt sets have been excavated widely from Ming tombs of various ranks, and in some cases several belt sets have been found. The plaques feature a variety of designs and shapes. Some corrupt officials, such as Yan Song (1480–1567) and Zhu Ning (*c.*1488–1505), were obsessed with jade belt sets. After both fell from power, 202 and 2,500 belt sets respectively were found in their possession,[125] while only twelve sets were found in the tomb of Emperor Wanli at Dingling (fig. 20).

Belt clasps were also used to fasten clothing, but Rawson has argued that they were likely to be for more personal use and so did not denote rank.[126] This white jade belt clasp (Cat. 69a & b) has brown staining and comprises two plaques: one with a curved hook in the form of an animal head, and the other with a shaped loop. Both plaques are decorated with openwork high-relief feline dragons confronting each other. Such clasps can be dated to the Ming dynasty, as several variations have been found in tombs.[127]

In later periods belt hooks served other

Cat. 70
Jade belt hook
Qing dynasty,
17th–18th century
L: 11.1 cm
O.36-1946

Cat. 71
Jade double-fish pomander
Qing dynasty, 18th century
L: 7.5 cm; W: 6.2 cm
O.90-1946

purposes in scholars' studios. This opaque grey jade belt hook (Cat. 70) is decorated with a cicada with a phoenix motif on each wing, and the hook terminates with a praying mantis with prominent eyes. This carving refers to a well-known proverb: when the praying mantis is trying to catch the cicada, it fails to notice that the yellow bird is behind (i.e., waiting to catch the praying mantis). The earliest record of a jade praying mantis belt hook is found in the preface to a panegyric in verse written by the Song poet Su Dongpo (1037–1101) on the jade collection of his friend Li Gonglin (1049–1106).[128] An almost identical piece in the Seattle Art Museum has been dated by James Watt to the Song dynasty or later, but it is very difficult to date jade objects precisely without comparing them with archaeological finds.

Judging from the symmetrical design on the wings and the unnatural colour of this cicada, this belt hook is likely to be an early Qing copy of an earlier piece. A similar hook, but carved from jadeite, is in the Hangzhou Historical Museum.[129]

Pomanders were originally made in silk or metal, but Qing-dynasty jade pomanders were mostly carved in the form of those made of silk.[130] This translucent pale green example (Cat. 71) is in the shape of two fish, with two pieces of red coral carved in the form of bats to act as stoppers at each end. It was used as a lady's ornament and could have hung from her belt, as shown from this eighteenth-century Chinese export glass painting (fig. 21). Fish symbolize fertility, abundance and a happy marriage. An identical jade double-fish pomander is in the Palace Museum, Beijing, which suggests that Cat. 71 might be from the Qing imperial collection.

Cat. 72a & b
Jade plaque signed by
Lu Zigang
Early Qing dynasty,
17th century
L: 5.6 cm; W: 3.6 cm
O.97-1946

Plaques

Apart from pomanders, white jade plaques carved in low relief with an image on one side and a narrative on the other were popular personal ornaments during the early eighteenth century. These plaques are bordered by relief frames that imitate wooden frames in furniture and architecture. The frame on each side is carved with confronting feline dragons.

Cat. 72a depicts a scholarly figure holding a walking-stick. The poem on the reverse, 'Collecting chrysanthemums near the eastern fences, I took a lazy look at the south Mountain' (Cat. 72b), indicates that this figure is Tao Yuanming (AD 365–427), who retired from government life and settled at the foot of Mount Zhongnan. Tao Yuanming was a lover of chrysanthemums.

This type of plaque is usually carved with a poem in running script (*xing shu*) and the signature of the famous Ming jade carver Lu Zigang (active during the second half of the sixteenth century), the only jade carver known to later generations. He was a native of Suzhou, and workshops in the city continued to produce carved white jade bearing his signature a century after he died. These plaques are therefore known to collectors as 'Zigang plaques'.

White jade eight-sided tubular beads are very rare, and there are few examples in modern collections. They are likely to have developed from the *Gang mao* of the Han dynasty in terms of shape and function. *Gang mao* were short, solid jade blocks that were inscribed with a curse that was intended to ward off evil spirits, and have a small axial hole for attachment. They were used as talismans for the afterlife but were not common burial objects even during the Han period.[131] The earliest reference to an eight-sided tubular bead was in Yang Boda's preface to *Introduction to Jades from Sui, Tang to Ming dynasties*. It is 5.9 cm long and 1.5 cm in diameter, with an axial hole. Two hundred and ninety-two characters were carved in sixteen lines on its surface in very fine double lines, the text being the famous Buddhist Heart Sutra. The bead, dated to AD 1120, was said to be from the imperial workshop (*xiu nei si*).[132]

Most of the tubular beads in museum collections are either six- or eight-sided but may have been carved as late as the nineteenth century.[133] This white jade bead (Cat. 73) in the Fitzwilliam Museum is incised with 210 characters in sixteen lines, a poem on 'Bai Zhu Dancing', a chapter from the Music section of the *Song Shu* ('History of the Song'). It is dated the eighth month, autumn, in the third year of the Zheng Zhi period, and it was a gift bestowed on Concubine Xia. However, neither the date nor any reference to Concubine Xia can be found in any text, so it is very likely that this bead is a fake produced in the late nineteenth or even early twentieth century for those interested in purchasing antiques.

Snuff bottles

The fashion of taking snuff began in China and Europe at almost the same time, around 1650, and was probably introduced to the imperial court by European priests. Because Chinese clothing had no pockets and the container had to be carried in the sleeve, the Chinese used bottles while Europeans used boxes.[134] Snuff-taking was a common practice in Qing society, from the emperor down to the common people, and mass production of

Cat. 73
Jade eight-sided tubular bead
Qing dynasty,
late 19th century
L: 6.2 cm; D: 1.6 cm
O.80-1946

snuff bottles took place at Suzhou and Yangzhou in order to meet the demands of the market. Indeed, images of officials and scholars holding snuff bottles are also seen in paintings, particularly those for export. The famous prime minister He Shen, who held office during the last third of emperor Qianlong's reign, had over 1,400 hard stone snuff bottles – of which at least 800 were of white jade – at the time he was forced by the emperor Jiaqing to commit suicide in 1799.[135]

The designs of snuff bottles, as with other contemporary decorative art, display layers of auspicious messages. The messages can be inferred from the form of the object, from the images depicted or from a rebus within the images. For example, Cat. 74 is a nephrite jade snuff bottle, carved in the form of a *bixi*, a mythical creature with the head of a fully fledged dragon, the tail of a *qilin*, the paws of a Buddhist lion and the body of a tortoise. Because this creature combines the features of various auspicious animals, it would be thought to possess all of their powers.

Cat. 75 is another well-known example, in the form of a goldfish with a branch of flowering lotus beneath the body. The material is a distinctive mixture of black and grey chalcedony, a mineral that was extremely popular in the Suzhou school. The combination of a goldfish and lotus is a well-known rebus, *Jinyu mantang*: 'May your hall be filled with gold and jade.'

5. Jade in the Qing dynasty

Jades from the Qing dynasty (1644–1911) represent a large portion of the Museum's collection. Among these we are proud to have some exquisite imperial pieces. Some of them bear the Qianlong emperor's poems, and some are incised with imperial reign marks. Details of the workmanship can be found in the *Neiwufu gezuo chengzuo huoji qingdang* ('Record of Activity in the Imperial Workshops', 1723–1911).

With the expansion of territory and of contact with neighbouring and foreign countries, jade carving in the Qing dynasty developed features that previous periods could not match. The sources of jade material were richer than ever. Large nephrite jade boulders were transferred from Xinjiang to Beijing, and some were shipped by canal to Yangzhou for carving if the imperial workshop in Beijing could not complete required objects in time; jadeite from Burma was imported and has played an important role in jade carving ever since; agate and crystal from the Yangzi River regions and lapis lazuli from Afghanistan were used for small ornaments or flower vases. Novel designs appeared, and carving skills improved because of competition in the market.

The Qianlong emperor is known to have been a jade lover. His tastes influenced jade designs in the market, but some of the jades produced in Suzhou and Yangzhou were beyond his control. The first part of this chapter will discuss the imperial jades in the Fitzwilliam Museum collection and how they were produced. The second part will discuss the major features of jade carving during this period, with reference to the collection.

The Qianlong emperor's jades in the Fitzwilliam Museum

The Qianlong emperor was a great collector and played an influential role in Chinese art history. The most impressive paintings and objects on view today in both the Palace Museum, Beijing, and the National Palace Museum, Taipei, were selected by him during his reign. He published catalogues for paintings and bronzes (*Shiqu baoji* and *Xiqing gujian* respectively). He also composed no fewer than 42,000 poems on different objects, and stamped his imperial seals all over the paintings he collected. A jade disc in the Fitzwilliam Museum (Cat. 76), which dates from the late Warring States period or the Han dynasty (*c.* third–first century BC), is incised with a poem on the edge that identifies it as part of his

Cat. 76
Jade disc
c. 3rd century BC, but
incised with a poem by
Emperor Qianlong in 1769
D: 16.3 cm; H: 0.55 cm
O.38-1946

Cat. 77a & b
Jade disc with imperial
mark and series number
Qing dynasty, Qianlong
period (1736–1795)
L: 12.8 cm; D: 7.3 cm
O.71-1946

collection. This greyish-green disc with brown speckling, decorated with a criss-cross pattern forming faceted bumps, was intended for burial. The poem is in *jin wen* style (the style usually cast on ancient bronzes) and is followed by two small seals, which can be read as *gu xiang* ('antique sense') and *tai pu* ('extremely primitive') and are dated to 1769. The poem is recorded in *Qing Gaozong yuzhi shiwen quanji* ('Poem Composed by the Emperor Gaozong, reign title of Qianlong') and can be read as:

> I read about *Liu rui* [the six auspicious ritual objects] in the text *Zhou li*
> The Han dynasty continued to follow the old practices
> I, of course, know how precious it is!
> The fact that I have composed a poem on this object is a complete coincidence.[136]

Like the scholars in the early Qing period, who were interested in *kaoju xue* ('studies in text evidence') and *jinshi xue* ('studies in metal and stone'), the Qianlong emperor's understanding of jades was based on the study of surviving texts. He therefore regarded this disc as one of the *liu rui* quoted from the *Zhou li*.[137] Similar examples can be seen in his poetry compilation about Han jade discs. A number of discs incised with Qianlong's poems on the edge have survived, and several examples are in the National Palace Museum, Taipei.[138]

A series of six jade pendants less than 20 cm in length, in the shape of discs and *gui* (sceptres),[139] was made at the beginning of the emperor

Qianlong's reign. The craftsmen numbered them according to the characters in the text *Qian zi wen* ('Thousand Characters Essay')[140] instead of figures. We do not know how many sets of jade pendants like these were made, but the *zaobanchu* (Manufacturing Department) was still producing them well after the fifteenth year of the emperor Qianlong's reign (1750).[141] Most of these jades are in the collection of the Palace Museum, Beijing, and the highest number found so far is 198, the piece marked with the 198th character from the *Qian zi wen*, *zan*. Some can also be found in the National Palace Museum, Taipei, and in private collections.

The one bequeathed to the museum by Oscar Raphael in 1941, which entered the collection in 1946 (Cat. 77a & b), is a small white disc in the Han style. Its prototype was found in Liu Sheng's tomb, as mentioned earlier (see fig. 12). The disc is surmounted by four dragons (the top pair confronting each other, the lower pair back to back) and with four characters in openwork. The four characters, *chang yi zi sun* ('benefit our sons and grandsons for ever'), in seal style, are incised on

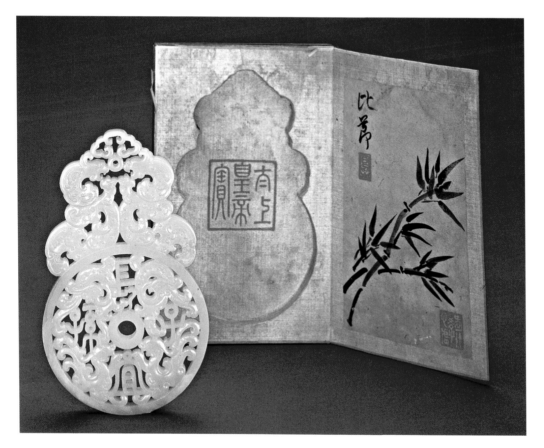

Fig. 22
Jade disc with series number '188'
Qianlong period
(1736–95)
L: 13.5 cm
Palace Museum, Beijing

Cat. 78
Jade rhyton
Qing dynasty, Qianlong
period, dated 1787
H: 15.5 cm
O.82-1946

the surface of the disc separated by a pair of confronting phoenixes on the top and a pair of confronting dragons on the bottom. On the edge of the disc, one side is incised with *Qianlong nian zhi* ('made in the Qianlong emperor's reign'), the other with *Liang zi yi bai liu shi ba hao* ('number 168, the character Liang') in *li shu* style. Three larger discs of the same design are in the Palace Museum, Beijing (fig. 22). The number of this disc and the character both match the order of *Qian zi wen*, so it seems likely that this disc was in the

emperor Qianlong's collection.[142]

From 1774 the emperor started to criticize the new styles (*xin yang*) and vulgar designs (*su yang*) produced by contemporary jade craftsmen. From 1781 he even used the term *yu er* ('jade nightmare') to describe their designs. These terms appeared regularly in his poems and on the jade rhyton in the Fitzwilliam's collection (Cat. 78), which is dated to the spring of 1787. The poem can be found in *Qing Gaozong yuzhi shiwen quanji* and translated as:

Cat. 79
Jade tripod (one of a pair),
copy from ancient bronze
drinking vessel with six
characters *Da Qing
Qianlong fangu* underneath

Qing dynasty,
Qianlong period
(1736–1795)
H: 14.4 cm
O.83-1946

Jade of Hetian [Khotan] was produced
    from the Jade River
The Mohammedans fished it out and paid
    it as tribute to the Court
There are places which cannot be
    reached;
They are secluded and muddy for years.
Jade by chance found there is like a
    precious gem
And even surpasses the Han jade in
    comparison.
Do not give it to a common workman to
    engrave a new design
But this is adapted from a dragon's tail and
    is well carved and polished
Which differs not from that on a Han
    piece in terms of material
High officials should write poems about it
    as on bowls and ink stones
It should not contain Ling Lu wine
But looks lovely holding flowers, which
    move to and fro as if dancing.
It has been carved so as to bring out the
    quality of the material.
It is the same way to choose a governor.[143]

The inscription is dated to the second moon of
the cyclical year Ding Wei (1787). The imperial
workshop diary *Neiwufu gezuo chengzuo huoji
qingdang* ('Record of Activity in the Imperial
Workshops') records that this rhyton was given
to the imperial Ruyi Guan workshop to reduce
the thickness of the rim and incise it with a *kai
shu* text written by the Qianlong emperor in
May of the fifty-second year of his reign
(1787).[144]

In this poem the emperor stressed that good-quality jade should not be given to a common workman to engrave a new design. Elsewhere he went further and suggested some methods to avoid this happening again. One of these methods was to encourage the craftsmen to copy images from ancient objects, particularly bronzes. A pair of white jade tripods (Cat. 79) is the best example in the museum's collection.

The design was copied from ancient bronze tripods (Cat. 80) but exhibited Qing features. Under the base of these vessels six characters *Da Qing Qianlong fangu* ('Imitating antiquity by Emperor Qianlong of the Great Qing dynasty', were incised. This pair of tripods was carved in Suzhou and incised with characters in the imperial workshop Ruyi Guan in January 1787.[145]

Apart from copying real objects from the imperial collection, woodblock prints such as *Xuanhe bogu tu* ('Illustrations of Xuanhe Antiquities'),[146] *Xiqing gujian* ('Mirror of the Antiquity of the Xi Qing')[147] and *Kaogu tu* ('Illustrations for the Study of Antiquity', by Lü Dalin, *c.*1092) also provided important sources for the craftsmen. For example, in the eighth year of Qianlong's reign two jade *bi xie*, a Han jade horse, a black jade horse, a jade tiger and an immortal figure from the *Kaogu tu* were transferred to the workshop so that copies could be made under his imperial order.[148]

Qianlong also promoted the use of paintings as a source of images for jade carving, and discouraged tribute objects that were perceived to feature vulgar designs such as openwork on daily used utensils. Under his influence the designs were deemed to have improved substantially by 1785.[149]

More importantly, most of these imperial

Fig. 23
Inventory numbers written in Chinese on labels accompanying the objects when they arrived at the Museum

objects in the Fitzwilliam's collection have inventory numbers written in Chinese on labels that identify their location in the imperial household (fig. 23). The jade rhyton has a paper label with the characters *Dong zi er bai er shi er hao* ('number 222 in the Dong, east category'), while the jade tripod has *Jia zi liu bai hao* ('number 600 in the Jia category').[150] The category title 'Dong' indicates that this jade rhyton was stored either in the eastern chamber of the imperial household or in a curiosity box as a trinket.

A pair of white bowls (Cat. 81), measuring 7.5 cm in height and 16.7 cm in diameter, carved from mutton jade, a material from Khotan in present-day Xinjiang autonomous region in western China, were loaned to the International Exhibition of Chinese Art at the Royal Academy of Arts between 1935 and 1936, before being bequeathed to the Museum by Oscar Raphael in 1941. They are large, carefully carved and polished. A paper label with the characters *Geng zi di si shi ba hao* ('forty-eighth number of the Gen character') accompanied the bowls when they arrived in the Museum in 1946 (see fig. 23).

Although the bowls lack the Qianlong emperor's inscription or any imperial mark, the quality of the jade, excellent carving and polishing, and the location label that accompanied them all indicate that they belonged to the imperial collection.

The difference between the labels from this pair of bowls and others is that some of the characters were printed instead of being written directly with a brush. Since the location label is

Cat. 81
Jade bowl (one of a pair)
Qianlong period
(1736–1795)
H: 7.4 cm; D: 16 cm
O.79a-1946

in a set format, an official could just fill in the title of chamber and number order, which would speed up the registration. This suggests that these objects were systematically catalogued and stored, and that jades were mass-produced in the imperial workshop during the emperor Qianlong's reign. One object may have had several labels to indicate where it was stored, by whom and to whom it was given and so on.[151] Since labels did not include descriptions of the objects, they would have to be kept with the objects at all times. It is likely that these jades were taken out

for the emperor to appreciate, then returned to the reserve afterwards.

Three imperial seals of a much later date (Cats. 82, 83, 84) are also in the Museum's collection. They are light green in colour, with small areas altered to white, and belong to the category of connoisseurs' seals. The handles represent two dragons back to back, and each handle has a yellow cord and tassels attached. They are made of the same material and belonged to two palaces, Yi-Kun and Li Jing Xuan, inside the Forbidden City. The seals read, in relief: 'Inspected by the

Cat. 82a, b & c
Jade seal
Qing dynasty, 19th century
L: 12.65 cm; W: 12.6 cm;
H: 9.5 cm
O.105-1946

Cat. 83a, b & c
Jade seal
Qing dynasty, 19th century
L: 14.5 cm; W: 6.75 cm;
H: 10.3 cm
O.106-1946

Cat. 84a, b & c
Jade seal
Qing dynasty, 19th century
L: 14.5 cm; W: 6.9 cm;
H: 9.8 cm
O.107-1946

Empress in the Yi-Kun Palace' (Cat. 82a & b); 'Inspected by the Emperor in the Li-Jing pavilion' (Cat. 83a & b), with the inscription surrounded by dragons; and 'Inspected and enjoyed in the Yi-Kun Palace' (Cat. 84a & b), with the inscription in intaglio and surrounded by phoenix and bamboo. Several similar seals are in the Forbidden City, Beijing.

Jade carving features in the Qing period

Emperor Qianlong's love of jade was a major influence in the development of jade craftsmanship, and the eighteenth century is recognized as one of the peaks in the history of Chinese jade carving. With the expansion of the empire during Qianlong's reign, sources of the material became more abundant than ever before.

Jade workshops outside the capital, particularly those from Suzhou and Yangzhou, competed to produce intricate novel designs that demonstrated their skills to the market, despite the disapproval of these designs by the emperor. Nevertheless, there was an ambivalence in Qianlong's poems, and some of the novel designs were actually being added to the imperial collection, as can now be seen in the National Palace Museum, Taipei, and the Palace Museum, Beijing. This section examines the major features of jade carving during the Qing period with reference to the Fitzwilliam Museum's collection and the text records.

Novel designs

This dark spinach-green jade pomander (Cat. 85) is carved and pierced with full-blown peony flowers and foliage; it appears to have been designed

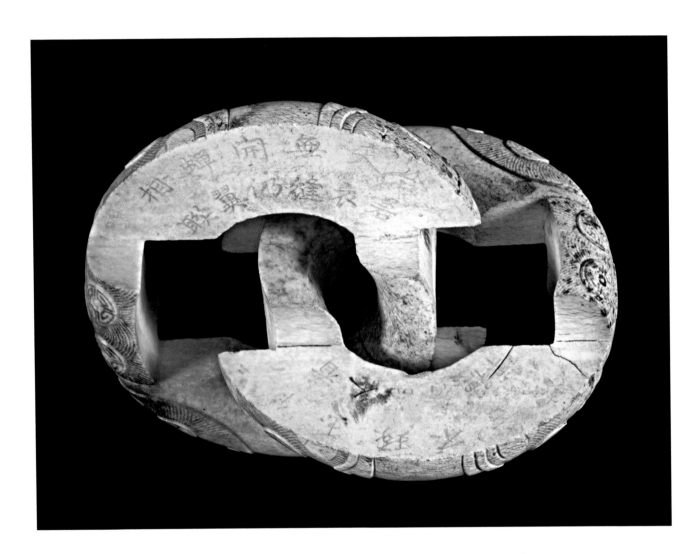

for non-burning incense or aromatic substances, such as dried flowers. Scholars have suggested that this design was influenced by the European Baroque style.[152] The elaborate openwork design, with its many tiny holes, would have made it very difficult to polish properly. In fact, this exaggerated design is thought to have been dictated by the need to cover flaws in the material. A similar piece carved in white jade is now in the Palace Museum, Beijing. In the fifty-ninth year of Qianlong's reign (1794) an imperial order was sent to Suzhou and Yangzhou to forbid this design.[153]

This opaque greyish white jade (Cat. 86), cut to form a double interlocking ring, is engraved with four Buddhist sayings. The motifs carved on the surface are copied from Liangzhu-period jade

Cat. 86
Jade interlocking ring
Qing dynasty, Qianlong
period (1736–95)
D: 7.2 cm
O.104-1946

Fig. 24
Jade interlocking ring
Qianlong period
(1736–95)
D: 7.2 cm
Palace Museum, Beijing

previous periods and became another feature of Qing-dynasty jade carving. From the poem by the emperor incised on the 'jade mountain' (*yu shan*), now in the Palace Museum, Beijing, we know that the choice to replicate paintings on a three-dimensional jade boulder was made simply because the material is durable and likely to last for ever.[154]

A painting from the imperial collection, *Great Yu Moving the Mountains* (*Da Yu kai shan tu*), was sent to the workshop as a model for the craftsmen to follow. Large and heavy jade carvings such as this one were usually sent to Yangzhou, as the imperial workshop was unable to complete the work in time. It became common for the jade workshops to use images from woodblock prints or famous paintings in order to produce carvings for studio display. In general, there are three major formats for these carvings: table screens, jade blocks and openwork sculptures. Owing to the limitation of the material, landscape scenes appear on jade boulders, and only openwork sculptures feature flowers and birds.

rings. This novel design had no practical function and was probably produced by a workshop in Suzhou or Yangzhou. Although Qianlong criticized this commercial phenomenon, some almost identical pieces, but carved from higher-quality jade, were in his collection catalogued as paperweights, and are now in the Palace Museum, Beijing (fig. 24).

Paintings as carvings on jades

The treatment of jade carving as a form of three-dimensional painting was not an invention of the Qing period but dates back to the Song dynasty, when landscape or flower-and-bird subjects were executed on jade pebbles. Nevertheless, the scale of production and the size of the jade boulders used during the Qing dynasty surpassed those of

Table screens

Ornamental table screens carved with figure and landscape scenes, mainly adopted from woodblock prints, became popular in the Qing dynasty. Cat. 87a & b depict a woman shaking mulberries from a tree with a long stick while her son stands near by, trying to catch them. To the right, a herd boy playing a flute sits astride a buffalo while crossing a bridge. On the other side are a fisherman on a boat and a woodcutter crossing a bridge. The whole composition is treated like a painting or printed image and was probably based

on a particular woodblock illustration.

The other type of table screen is based on the elaborate throne screens of the Qianlong period. This spinach jadeite screen (Cat. 88) has three sections on a hardwood stand, each of these panels being of a different size. The top and bottom panels of each section are carved in relief with flowers, including day lily, peony, hibiscus and lotus. The middle panels of each section depict children involved in different activities. On the left a child plays a *sheng* woodwind instrument; in the centre three children sit on the ground with a small bird on one of the children's sleeves; on the right a child plays a drum. The top of the frame of each section is decorated with a five-clawed gilt-metal dragon, and the base is carved with lotus petals and three *taotie* monster faces. The flowers, musical instrument and the baby boys all carry auspicious meanings connected with fertility.

Cat. 88
Imperial-style throne-back table screen
Qing dynasty, late 18th–early 19th century
H: 49 cm; W: 50 cm
O.20-1938

Cat. 89
Jade boulder carved with
Chinese landscape
Qing dynasty, 18th century
H: 12.2 cm; L: 15.8 cm
O.240-1936

Jade boulders

Spinach-coloured jade pebbles as boulders were found on riverbeds in the Xinjiang area and were carved with landscape scenes usually related to longevity. This jade boulder (Cat. 89) depicts a boy servant holding a branch from a peach tree and accompanying an elderly gentleman towards a pavilion in the mountains – a very common scene from Chinese landscape painting. The elderly man, pine tree, peach and the jade boulder itself all represent long life. The use of visual metaphors and puns was very popular among the decorative arts and paintings from the eighteenth century onwards, as was noted above.

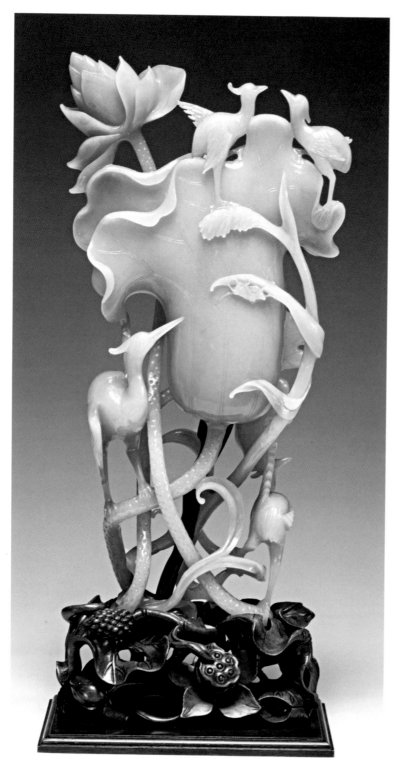

Openwork sculpture

Openwork sculptures are mainly carved with the theme of flowers and birds. This pale celadon jade (Cat. 90) carved in openwork depicts four egrets hunting among lotus flowers and leaves and reeds, a design associated with the notion of being academically on track and successful in the Imperial Civil Service examinations. The characters for 'egret' (*lu*, 鷺) and 'reed' (*lu*, 蘆) are homophones for the character for 'road' (*lu*, 路), and the character for 'lotus' (*lian*, 蓮) is a homophone for the character for 'continuous' (*lian*, 連). Together they form the phrase *lu lu lian ke* (路路連科), auguring well for a string of successes in exams.

Cat. 91 is a spinach-green jade carved as a vase of archaic form with openwork chains, at the foot of which stands a quail surrounded by rice grains. The word for 'rice grains' (*sui*, 穗) is a homophone of the word for 'annual' (*sui*, 歲), the word for 'vase' (*ping*, 瓶) a homophone for 'peace' (*ping*, 平), and the word for 'quail' (*an*, 鵪) a homophone for 'safe' (*an*, 安), so that together they form another auspicious phrase, *sui sui ping an* (歲歲平安, 'peaceful and safe every year').

Cat. 90
Jade openwork sculpture
Qing dynasty,
18th century
H: 30.5 cm
O.4-1951

Cat. 91
Jade vase
Qing dynasty,
late 18th century
H: 16.3 cm; W: 14.2 cm
O.18-1938

Calligraphy on jade

Besides the copying of paintings, calligraphy and sometimes emperor's seals were also incised on to jade. The Qianlong emperor was the first and only emperor to order that his own poems were incised on jade, porcelain and other objects, although the incision of calligraphy on stones has a long history in China. This jade block (Cat. 92) depicts the famous Indian Buddhist monk Damo (Bodhidharma), who spent nine years seeking enlightenment in a cave near the Shaolin Temple when he travelled to China. The artist cleverly arranged the composition of the figure, rock and mountain by using different tones in the material. A poem by the emperor with very fine carving, *kai shu*, is incised on the top of the block. Judging from the date of this poem (1766),[155] the block was probably carved in the same year.

Cat. 92
Jade boulder incised
with poem
Qing dynasty, 18th century
L: 16.8 cm; H: 7.8 cm
O.91-1946

Auspicious motifs

Ruyi sceptres were a symbol of blessings or well-satisfied wishes and were a popular decorative accessory and gift among aristocratic households during the Ming and Qing periods. According to *Zhuyeting za ji* ('Memoirs of the Bamboo Leaf Pavilion'), 'in important festivals and at New Year, the feudal lords and high officials would present *ruyi* sceptres to the court as a good omen of auspicious happenings'.[156] From the Yongzheng period a sceptre became a regular gift presented on the emperor's birthday. He Shen, the famously corrupt official during Qianlong's reign, possessed 1,200 jade *ruyi* at the time he was found guilty. Emperors also gave out *ruyi* sceptres as rewards to court officials and foreign diplomats. A famous jade *ruyi* in the collection of the Victoria & Albert Museum was an imperial gift to Sir George Leonard Staunton (1737–1801), who was second-in-command at the Peking embassy.[157]

This jade *ruyi* (Cat. 93) from the Fitzwilliam's collection is decorated with a peony between two catfish. Peonies are symbolic of prosperity, and the catfish (*nian yu*) create a pun for abundance year after year (*nian nian you yu*). The sceptre, which was said to have been looted from the Summer Palace in 1861, was bought from Sparks in January 1922 by Oscar Raphael.

Cat. 93
Jade *ruyi*
Qing dynasty,
late 18th century
L: 34.5 cm
OC.75-1946

Mughal style of jade

The Mughals were fierce Central Asian warriors earlier led by Genghis Khan (1162–1227) and Timur (1336–1405). They conquered northern India at the beginning of the sixteenth century to establish a powerful kingdom, and jade was imported into Mughal India from Central Asia towards the end of that century.[158] The first Mughal jade came into Emperor Qianlong's collection in 1756, when a tribe in Xinjiang paid a tribute to the court. After Qianlong defeated a rebellion by the Muslims in 1759, the number of Mughal jades reaching the court increased each year.

Although Qianlong criticized the Mughal jades in one of his poems, he wrote more than fifty poems about them, indicating that he was impassioned by their exotic designs.[159] He tried various ways to obtain them and even asked his workshop to imitate them. The high quality of these imitations has made it very difficult to identify which were the copies and which the originals. The main features of Mughal jades are their thin translucent bodies and high-relief floral designs.[160] Chrysanthemum petals and acanthus leaves are the most common plant motifs, as seen on the surface and base of this bowl (Cat. 94).

Cat. 94
Jade bowl in Mughal style
Qing dynasty, late 18th century/19th century
D: 10.25 cm; H: 5.2 cm
O.21-1938

Summary

Many high-quality jades were produced in the Qing period. They have provided us with considerable information. Jades of the Qing dynasty were used as utensils, personal ornaments, studio objects and religious objects, and were inlaid on furniture. As sources were abundant, large jade boulders carved with landscapes were produced, and this achievement demonstrates spectacular craftsmanship that surpassed that of previous dynasties.

Emperor Qianlong's tastes influenced jade production, but only to a limited extent. He was unable to control the private market for new designs and carving styles, and wrote about these as a 'jade nightmare', although ironically accepting some of these designs when they were presented to the court. His assertion that the imitation of antiquity was the way to avoid this 'nightmare' led to the production of many Qing-dynasty jades in archaic styles. On the other hand, new creations also met with the emperor's approval, such as the two ladies at a moon gate in a south Chinese garden (see fig. 3).

The use of puns to represent auspicious meanings was another feature of this period. What had started life as a pastime for the *literati* became an increasingly commercial practice and lasted until the twentieth century.

6. The market for jade

WE DO NOT KNOW WHEN the Chinese became interested in copying antiquities for commercial purposes, but the practice was already established by the Song dynasty (960–1279). Officials in the Song period looked to the past as an important source of general values for both the political and the social life of the time. After the Jin invasion of 1126–7 and the fall of the northern capital, both emperors and officials searched for sources of past values; antiquities were collected by the emperor and his highest officials in the expectation that they might transmit ancient values to their new owners.[161] Julia Murray has suggested that the rebuilding of the imperial collection would have been seen as a strengthening of the legitimacy of the Southern Song (1127–1279) and as demonstrating that the dynasty had not lost favour with heaven, despite the loss of the ancient homeland in the north.[162] Therefore during the Song the elite tended to collect ancient objects or copies of them, a fashion that stimulated the art market of the time.

In *Dong Jing Meng hua lu* the author (Meng Yuanlao, active 1126–47) records that selling antiques, including jades, in the street markets of the capital was common during the Northern Song (960–1127). Jade ornaments were part of a bride's dowry and a new-born baby's gift.[163] In the capital of Southern Song at Lin'an (present-day Hangzhou), an establishment called the Seven Treasures Shop (*qibao she*) sold jade belt plaques, bowls, vases and dishes.[164] These records indicate that possession of jade was no longer confined to rich or high-ranking individuals but had become more widespread.

With economic prosperity in southern China during the Ming period and the rise of a merchant class, collecting antiquities had become a way for merchants, as well as the nobility and scholars, to demonstrate their taste and wealth. Unfortunately the increasing demand for antiquities stimulated the rise of forgery. A famous Ming text, *Tian gong kai wu* ('Creations of Nature and Man'), states that workshops in Zhuan Zhu Alley (*zhuan zhu xiang*) in Suzhou had become a major jade-carving centre outside Beijing during the Ming dynasty. Although good craftsmen had always made their way to the capital, the most ingenious works actually came from Suzhou, and the craftsmen there were also very good at forging ancient jades, as mentioned in the Ming scholar Gao Lian's *Zun sheng ba jian*.

The great interest in antiquities led to the publication of at least seven editions between 1528 and 1603 of the catalogue *Xuanhe bogu tu* of the Song imperial bronze collection. A small version of the catalogue was produced as a guide for collectors during the late Ming period.[165] The widespread availability during the late Ming period of woodblock prints that recorded the dimensions and sometimes even the colours of archaic bronzes and jades from the imperial or famous *literati* collections provided the best reference for Ming artists when they depicted images of *wan gu tu* ('amusing oneself with appreciating and examining antiquities').[166] Some of these woodblock prints therefore became blueprints for the later spurious jade carvings and had a significant influence on the production of contemporary objects.[167] These items often combined features from different periods in one piece (Cat. 95); proportions were distorted (Cat. 96); unnatural

colours were produced by dyeing, or the jades were scorched to make them appear older in the expectation that they would fetch a higher price in the market (see Cat. 61).

This bracelet (Cat. 97) is made from a dark brown opaque stone with areas of russet, grey and yellow. Six relief semicircles embrace the eyes, perhaps representing cicadas, and enliven the surface. The prototype was a Liangzhu jade bracelet recorded in earlier woodblock printed books, such as *Gu yu tu* ('Illustrations of Ancient Jades') and *Sancai tuhui,* by Zhu Derun (*c.*1294–1365).

However, this particular bracelet was based on a late Qing print, *Tao zhai gu yu tu* ('Ancient Jade Illustrations from the Tao's Studio by Duan Fang', 1861–1911; fig. 25). Part of the surface has turned grey, and the motifs have slightly changed their shape owing to the application of heat. Before and during the early twentieth century acid, heat and artificial colours were used to make the surfaces of jades look older, usually damaging the objects themselves in the process (Cat. 98).

As fake jades became more widespread in the market during the late Qing period, scholars such

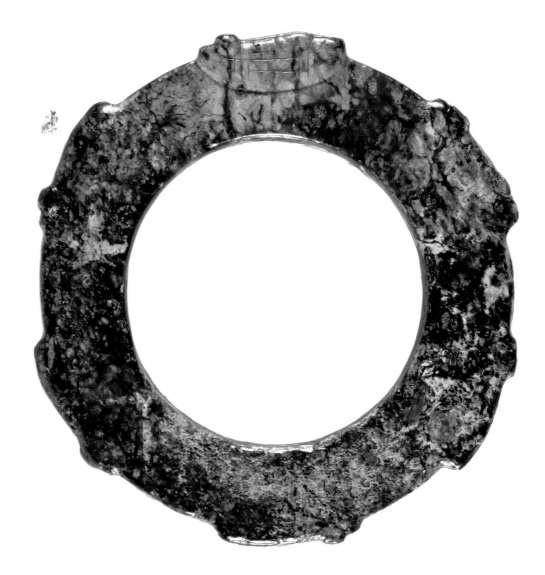

Cat. 97
Jade bracelet copied
from *Tao zhai gu yu tu* of
Dun Fang (1861–1911)
Qing dynasty, late 19th
century
D: 10.8 cm
O.7-1946

as Chen Xing concentrated on issues of interest to collectors. In his book *Yu Ji* ('Records of Jade', 1899) he described how to date jades by touching or even smelling objects. As jades age very little, they are particularly difficult to date.[168] This study of the appearance and touch of jades is still used by some connoisseurs today, particularly collectors in Taiwan and Hong Kong. However, there has been a change in approach, as there is now more archaeological evidence to consider.

Forgery techniques improved dramatically during the late nineteenth to early twentieth century. Objects found by chance during railway construction in different parts of China have provided opportunities for scholars to carry out research on antiquities, assisted curators to date objects more precisely, and given forgers further examples, particularly with the publication of images and detailed dimensions. This opaque greyish-green horse's head (Cat. 99) is faithfully copied from an excavation of a Han earthenware horse. Part of the body was scorched to give an appearance of age, but the dramatic contrast between areas makes its appearance very unnatural.

Another example of a jade copied from archaeological finds in the early twentieth century is this handle-shaped jade (Cat. 100). Handle-shaped jades commonly appeared in tombs dating from the late Shang to the early Western Zhou, but this pale green opaque jade has been altered extensively to creamy white and is decorated with a striated design; it is therefore unlike any examples from tombs. Furthermore, it is too thick, particularly the edge.

The copying of archaeological finds, but using different materials, is another feature of the early twentieth century. This jade figure (Cat. 101) is modelled on a Han burial figure made of pottery

Cat. 98
Jade scabbard chape
Early 20th century
L: 4.6 cm; W: 3.1 cm
O.26-1946

Cat. 99
Jade horse's head
Early 20th century
L: 12.8 cm; W: 10.5 cm
O.20-1946

Cat. 100
Handle-shaped jade
Early 20th century
L: 14.4 cm; W: 2.85 cm;
Thick: 0.65 cm
O.14-1946

Cat. 101
Jade standing figure
Early 20th century
H: 28.7 cm
O.32-1946

Fig. 26
Stone horse and female grooms
Early 20th century
H: 32 cm; L: 33.5 cm;
W: 12 cm
Courtesy of Norfolk Museums
and Archaeology Service

and painted with colours. Although the proportions match those of the original pottery figure, no such large jade figure has been found in any period of Chinese history. Another example is a set of three stone horses and female grooms (fig. 26) based on a Tang pottery horse. These are kept in Norwich Castle Museum.

Beyond simply producing a fake, it is more convincing to advertise images in respected magazines or even to produce a complete book of fakes. The publisher of a magazine does not necessarily know the subject matter well, so the decision to include advertisements is a financial matter and the publisher has no knowledge of or responsibility for the objects that dealers advertise in his magazine.

Faking a whole book

Chinese bookshops stock a wide range of publications that aim to help people to identify and collect Chinese antiques. As the Chinese economy booms, more and more people have become interested in collecting antiques as an investment, even travelling abroad to buy antiques from auctions and dealers. However, books of fake jades that have been professionally designed and printed can mislead collectors. In order to lend a note of authenticity, the authors often include a photograph of themselves with museum curators in the first few pages, followed by a section of genuine objects from the museums in the next few pages, whereas the rest of the jades in the book are all from private collections. No information about provenance is given, and they are all fakes. Publishing a book in China is easy and cheap; moreover, the publishers do not have to submit them for an independent book review.

Studying jade in the market helps us to understand the changes in the social, political and economic environment. The imitation of antiques could be a fashion, but it is almost impossible without the involvement of commerce. *Literati* during the late Ming period usually gathered to view paintings or antiques, and wrote down their comments on the colophon, in the case of paintings. It was partly because they were not confident enough about their collections that they needed second opinions from other scholars. History repeats itself, and with the high-quality fakes now circulating in the market, purchasing antiques is always a risk. Distinguishing a fake from a genuine piece requires a lot of handling experience of both genuine and fake objects, so the opinions of other scholars will help to reduce this risk. A good-quality fake could survive and become a research subject in the future, just as we are examining the history of Ming collecting today.

7. Chinese jades in the Fitzwilliam Museum

THE FIRST JADES to enter the collection of the Fitzwilliam Museum were two late eighteenth-century censers (Cat. 102) bequeathed by Frank McClean (1837–1904), an astronomer. He matriculated at Trinity College, Cambridge, in 1855 and became a scholar of the college and was a Wrangler in the mathematical Tripos of 1859. He collected ancient coins, manuscripts, early printed books, enamel and ivories in an ordered plan, but there is no record of how these two Chinese jade incense burners came to his collection. The early twentieth century was the period when Western connoisseurs and collectors started to take an interest in Chinese archaeology, owing to the discovery of many tombs during the construction of railways. Berthold Laufer's *Jade: A Study in Chinese Archaeology and Religion*, published in 1912, was the first serious investigation of the subject by a Western scholar.

Four major donors contributed to the museum's collection: A.W. Young in 1934, Cecil E. Byas in 1938, Oscar Raphael in 1946 and Mrs May Cippico, in accordance with the wishes of her aunt Mrs Constance Goetze, in 1951. She was a notable benefactor of the Museum during her lifetime. Unsurprisingly, each gift reflected its owner's tastes. The ten jades given by A.W. Young, a graduate of Trinity College, Cambridge, are utensils, including a jug (Cat. 103), a bowl, a brush washer, one incense burner, one pomander and five vases (one of which is made of crystal), whereas the twenty-six jades given by Cecil E.

Cat. 102
Jade censer
Qing dynasty, late 18th century
W: 21.7 cm; H: 14.2 cm
O.7-1904

Cat. 103
Jade jug
Qing dynasty, 19th century
H: 16.4 cm; W: 14.8 cm
O.7-1934

Byas in 1938 were mostly animal or figure sculptures (Cat. 104). Constance Goetze was interested in various materials: among the twenty-nine objects she bequeathed to the museum in 1951 were pieces in ivory, jasper, chalcedony, amethyst quartz, crystal, coral, rhinoceros horn, soapstone, jade and agate (Cat. 105). Oscar Raphael (fig. 27) is the most well known, not only because he was the major donor of oriental art to the Fitzwilliam Museum and one of the twelve founder members of the Oriental Ceramic Society but also because of his excellent taste.

Oscar Raphael was the fourth and youngest son of George Charles Raphael, a wealthy bullion merchant. He matriculated at Pembroke College, Cambridge, in October 1892 and was awarded an honorary degree by Cambridge University on 6 November 1939. He had impeccable

Cat. 105
Agate incense holder
Qing dynasty, 18th century
W: 15 cm; H: 13.8 cm
O.20-1951

and natural taste and was one of those deputed to visit China to select exhibits from the imperial collection for the great exhibition at Burlington House in 1935–6. He had close connections with various museums, particularly the British Museum and the Fitzwilliam Museum in Cambridge, to whom he jointly left his magnificent collection.

Raphael was best known as a collector of jade, and it was his wish that the Fitzwilliam Museum should receive the Chinese jades, except for such ritual burial jades as were needed to strengthen the British Museum collection.[169] The 115 jades he bequeathed to the Fitzwilliam in 1941 (which were received into the collection in 1946) were mainly objects for scholars' studios, luxury items for daily use and personal ornaments. Some of them originally formed part of the imperial col-

lection. Besides these, some important ritual objects and burial items also came to Cambridge: for example, a jade dagger (see Cat. 10b) inlaid with turquoise that was exhibited at Burlington House between 1935 and 1936 and at the Chinese exhibition in Manchester in 1936. It was lent to the San Francisco Golden Gate Exhibition in 1939, and then the Fogg Museum. Another important ritual jade is a ceremonial blade (see Cat. 7). Before the excavation of Neolithic tombs in the 1980s our understanding of Chinese history was limited to the text records, so ritual objects such as this blade, found before the early twentieth century, were usually categorized following Wu Dacheng's catalogue *Guyu tukao* ('Study and Illustration of Ancient Jades') and dated to the Zhou period.

The exquisite burial jades from Oscar

Raphael's collection include a Shang collared disc (see Cat. 9), an Eastern Zhou jade ring (see Cat. 23) and belt hook (see Cat. 22), as well as one large jade disc dating from Eastern Zhou to Han period (see Cat. 26) and a glass disc that was made to imitate jade (see Cat. 28). The Han dynasty jade disc and glass disc were purchased in 1935 and 1933 respectively from the dealer Ching Tsai Loo, who provided the information that the jade disc was found in Jin Cun, Henan province, and the glass disc at Tai Shou, Shandong. Loo was the pre-eminent dealer of Chinese art in the early twentieth century. He started his business in Paris, but his New York branch quickly gained in prominence. Loo was almost single-handedly responsible for introducing early Chinese art – bronzes, jades and paintings – to Western Europe and North America. Because of his connections in Asia he was able to obtain major pieces for such collectors as J.P. Morgan, Samuel Peters, Alfred Pillsbury and Henry Clay Frick, from eras never before represented in the West.

The other sources of Oscar Raphael's jade collection included such famous dealers as Orvar Karlbeck, John Sparks, Spink & Son, S.M. Franck, Bluett & Sons, Yamanaka and the Tonying Company. These dealers had a good knowledge of Chinese art and connections with China; they also provided works of art to other famous collectors. Orvar Karlbeck, a Swedish engineer, was working on the construction of the Tianjin and Pukou railway when archaeological material was unearthed; this formed the basis of his private collection. He later returned to China working on behalf of Western museums, and in 1957 published *Treasure Seeker in China*. Oscar Raphael bought some jades

from him in 1934 and 1937, all of which were from archaeological excavations, including a pair of Han handgrips (Cat. 25), a Qijia jade blade (Cat. 8), a Shang bronze dagger inlaid with turquoise (Cat. 10a & b) and a sword fitting (scabbard chape), dating from the Eastern Zhou to Han dynasty (4th–1st century BC; Cat. 34).

The 1920s and 1930s were a period of intense competition between collectors and museums for early Chinese art. Dealers such as John Sparks, Spink & Son, S.M. Franck and Bluetts in London and C.T. Loo, Yamanaka and the Tonying Company internationally specialized in this area and either had offices, or at least agents, working in and around Beijing and Shanghai who were supplying them directly. Oscar Raphael and other important and famous collectors in this period became their regular customers.

The Tonying (Tongyun) Company was established in Paris in 1902 by Zhang Renjie (1877–1950; also known as Zhang Jingjiang), from a wealthy family from Zhejiang province. Zhang gained an official appointment in 1902 as an attaché on the staff of the Qing government's ambassador to France, Sun Baoqi. While in Paris he established the Tonying Company for the importation and sale of works of art, tea and silk. The company remained a family business branching out to New York from its original base in Paris and its source in Shanghai. As well as dealing in its own right, the company supplied a number of British dealers, including John Sparks and Bluetts. Because of Zhang's position in China, the company was able to source high-quality works of art directly, including items from the old imperial collection.[170] The Han disc incised with the Qianlong emperor's poem from the Fitzwilliam's collection was bought from Bluetts in June 1930 by Raphael. The *ruyi* sceptre he bought from Sparks in January 1922 was said to have been looted from the Summer Palace in 1861 (see Cat. 93).

One cannot, however, always reply on dealers' information about provenance. To judge from the quality of this *ruyi*, it could be from the collection of any rich individual. Rumours about looted or excavated objects would have excited buyers, particularly as there was no law to control looting at that time.

Similar stories are attached to three jade animal sculptures: a buffalo, horse and *qilin* (Cats. 35, 39, 43). The buffalo and horse (it is said that a catalogue existed of the contents of the Palace, which stated that the buffalo and horse date from the Han dynasty) were brought to Beijing at the time of its foundation as the capital by the Emperor Yong Le (1403–1425), about AD 1420. Kangxi, inspecting the contents of the palace in the early years of his reign, was shown them and asked how it was that the Lung-ma (*qilin*) which brought the books of knowledge from over the waves of the Yellow River was not represented. This jade *qilin* was accordingly made.[171] Without a doubt these three animal sculptures are of imperial quality, but both the buffalo and the horse probably date to the late Ming or early Qing rather than the Han.

In fact, there are jades of much better quality and proper provenance that were originally from the imperial collection, in the form of five exquisite examples that were given by Oscar Raphael's friend and a member of the Oriental Ceramic Society, Sir Percival David, in 1931. They include

a jade rhyton incised with a poem by Emperor Qianlong on its edge, a pair of tripods with the imperial Qianlong mark and a pair of white jade plaques with the signature of the Ming-dynasty artist Lu Zigang, but these are obviously seventeenth-century pieces. They were part of the collection from the Forbidden City held in security for a loan made to the last Chinese Empress Dowager Cixi, and were purchased by Sir Percival David in 1924 from a bank in Beijing. Some of them still have yellow paper labels reading 'Eastern Hall No.344', 'No.1 category 600' or 'no.1 category *jia*', as discussed in Chapter 5 above.

Most of Oscar Raphael's collection of jades was exhibited in the first Chinese exhibition in Burlington House between 1935 and 1936 and at the Chinese exhibition in Manchester in 1936. Unfortunately, Raphael died in the late summer of 1941, a few months after becoming president of the Oriental Ceramic Society.

Collecting antiques requires not only a knowledge of art and history, but also luck and timing. Oscar Raphael formed his oriental collections thirty years before the outbreak of the First World War, a period when many tombs in China were being excavated, owing to construction work, and the antiquities exported. It was probably the first and last opportunity of its kind. Raphael's taste and knowledge of Chinese art can be witnessed from the objects on display in the museum, of which his bequest has formed the major part. The Fitzwilliam Museum is very privileged to have half of his collection for display, research and teaching. It is therefore very gratifying to have this opportunity to make the Museum's treasures in this area more accessible to the public.

Appendix

Given by A.W. Young MA, 25 January 1934:

Two-handled bowl, 19th century

Pale celadon jade, carved in relief in the centre of the interior with a medallion of lotus flowers with a long ribbed leaf and the exterior with peonies. The central floral design was possibly influenced by Mughal objects. A pair of loop handles formed by moths at the rim bearing loose rings.
L: 20.7 cm; D: 15.1 cm; H: 5 cm
O.4-1934

Vase, 19th century

Jasper vase in the shape of an archaic bronze *gu* wine container. Around the neck and base are handles bearing rings. The central body is decorated with Hindustani-like plant motifs. The areas around the handles are decorated with banana-leaf-like plants.
H: 16.3 cm
O.8-1934

Vase with cover, 18th century

Crystal, in the shape of an ancient bronze vessel resting on a short, spreading foot. The body is decorated with geometric *taotie* masks and the neck with tapering blades. A pair of monster-face handles from which loose rings are suspended and the domed cover surmounted by a lion.
H: 22 cm
O.13 & A-1934

Vase and cover, 19th century

White jade vase and cover, carved in high relief with a phoenix standing on top of a tree peony. The domed cover with a small phoenix standing on a square finial.
H: 20.5 cm (with lid); W: 10 cm
O.6 & A-1934

Vase with lid, late 18th century

Pale green flattened baluster jade vase, the body decorated with an archaistic *taotie* face between two cicadas. The neck set with phoenix handles and a band of roundels and beads decorated below.
H: 24.7 cm (with lid); W: 11 cm
O.10 & A-1934

Double box with a lid, 19th century

Pale green jadeite with splashes of apple green, carved as a double box and lid. The lid is decorated with three loose rings, the main body with three banana leaves between three loose ring handles, and the lower part with floral motifs.
H: 10.5 cm
O.12 & A-1934

Cecil C. Byas Bequest, 19 January 1938:

**Archaistic jadeite censer and cover,
19th century**
Apple-green jadeite censer in the form of a *ding*
cooking and ritual vessel, supported on four legs issuing
from animal masks. The main body is decorated with a
band of C-scrolls and a monster face on the broad
side. The dome is decorated with a band of C-scrolls
and surmounted by a beast with bifurcated tail. The
rims of both the censer and the cover are incised with
key-fret borders.
H: 19.5 cm (with lid); L: 13.3 cm; W: 9.3 cm
O.11 & A-1934

Vase with cover, 18th century
Crystal, in the shape of ancient bronze vessel resting
on a short, straight foot. The body is decorated with
floral sprays and the neck with plantain leaves. A pair
of *ruyi* handles from which loose rings are suspended
and the domed cover surmounted by a lion.
H: 20.5 cm
O.1 & A-1938

**Jade bowl with cover,
late 18th–19th century**
Pale greyish-green jade bowl standing on low foot-
ring and sloping outwards evenly to an out-turned
lip. Undecorated jade vessels carved in the shape of
porcelain objects probably represented the highest
quality of eating and drinking utensil.
D: 10.7cm; H: 7.5 cm
O.7 & A-1938

Carving of a horse, 17th–18th century
Greyish green jade with light brown veining. The
horse recumbent with its neck slightly arched as it
looks back towards its tail. Its eyes are cocked up
attentively and are shown in incised lines. The legs are
folded beneath the body. The mane and tail are
strongly striated.
L: 6.65 cm
O.3-1938

Water dropper, late 18th century
Pale grey jade water dropper in the shape of a cup.
The spout is designed as the head of a phoenix with
a perforation. The main body of this cup is designed
as a bird's wings and the base as bird's feet.
W: 10.2 cm; H: 5.1 cm
O.10-1938

Fisherman with a boy, late 19th century
Jade, pale celadon with brown skin, carved with an old fisherman wearing a hat and looking into a fish basket together with a boy holding a fish.
H: 10 cm
O.11-1938

Vase, 18th century
Pale celadon jade vase of flattened circular form supported on a splayed base. The body finely carved on each side with a panel enclosing prunus blossom and peony. The handles are decorated with three *ruyi* clouds in high relief.
H: 21.5 cm; W: 14 cm
O.13-1938

Naked boy kneeling, early 20th century
Greenish white jade figure of a naked boy, bent over and resting on his elbows with head slightly turned to one side. His arms are crossed on his chest, and he holds a bat, symbolic of good fortune, and a peach, for longevity. The boy wears bracelets on his ankles and wrists and is realistically carved.
L: 13 cm; H: 7.9 cm
O.16-1938

Pair of dogs, early 20th century
Apple-green jadeite with brown areas, carved with a pair of lion-dogs with heads raised looking alertly. On the head a long, striated mane runs between the ears down the back. The spine is indicated by a ridge of four small bumps, and the rest of the body is carved with fine lines to represent hairs.
L: 7.8 cm; H: 9 cm
O.12 A & B-1938

Cup, 16th century
Light grass-green jade cup with brown areas, carved with fluted and lobed sides with two handles, resting on a short, straight foot.
L: 15.9; H: 5.3 cm
O.15-1938

**Miniature vase with cover,
late 18th –19th century**
Pale greenish-white jade, decorated with a dragon in relief around the neck, and square-sectioned foot. A monster's face in the middle of a band below the neck and a band of chrysanthemum petals above the foot. The domed cover surmounted by a pearl finial.
H: 15.8 cm
O.17 & A-1938

Buddhist figure, 18th century
Soapstone, carved as a seated *luohan* (one who has achieved nirvana and freed himself from reincarnation), the chest incised with a Fo (Buddha) character. The collar, sleeves and hem of his robes incised with a design of scrolling lotus on a formalized wave ground.
H: 17.8 cm (including base)
O.22 & A -1938

Guanyin (Avalokiteshvara, Goddess of Mercy), 18th century
Soapstone, carved as a seated *guanyin* with fine carving for the hair and hem of her robes. Studded with pearls and semi-precious stones.
H: 10.3 cm; base W: 7.8 cm
O.24-1938

Figure of lions, 20th century
Soapstone carved with a large lioness and seven cubs surrounding her.
H: 7.8 cm; W: 4.2 cm
O.26-1938

Buddhist figure, 18th century
Soapstone, carved as a seated *luohan* with his eyes closed and his hands together in a respectful gesture. The collar, sleeves and hem of his robes incised with a design of scrolling lotus on a formalized wave ground.
H: 17.5 cm (including base)
O.23 & A-1938

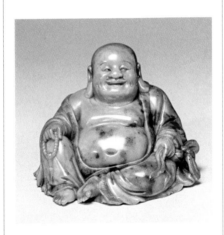

Seated Bu Dai, late 17th–18th century
Soapstone, carved as a seated *bu dai*, with a calico bag. The monk is supposed to have been the last incarnation of Maitreya and to have died in 917. He is usually represented seated with a large bare stomach, playing with children, and with a bag containing his belongings and food.
H: 9.2 cm; base W: 12 cm
O.25-1938

Buddha holding an open lotus blossom, 20th century
Lapis lazuli mounted on a jade stand. The Buddha is seated on a low lotus pedestal with legs crossed and hands resting one on the other, in the attitude of meditation. The face has a quiet expression with downcast eyes, and the hair is curled in small, shell-like knots over the entire head.
H: 11 cm, base W: 7.3 cm
O.27-1938

A pair of bowls, 18th century

Pale celadon jade bowls, the exteriors with four cartouches, gilded with long-tailed birds, pheasants and mandarin ducks among flowers, inside-gilded with dragons and foliage. The interior of the foot-ring decorated with acanthus leaves.

D: 14.9 cm; H: 6.1 cm
O.31A & B-1938

Cong **tube, Shang or Western Zhou, c.2000–1200 BC**

Dark to light grey jade with brown staining; a hole was drilled from both ends to meet in the middle. The four sides of this tube were decorated at a much later date, probably Ming or Qing period, with fine geometric intertwined birds and a striated band at each end of the tube.

H: 13.85 cm; D: 8 cm
O.3-1946

Dagger, Shang dynasty (c.1600–c.1050 BC)

Unusual large jade *ge* blade and a short but wide *tang* with traces of cinnabar. The edge and surface of this dagger have calcified. The tang with rows of parallel ridged grooves, a form of decoration derived from the pattern of metal sections seen on Erlitou bronze blades. A large hole on the blade and another, smaller one on the *tang* were drilled from the same side. The unfinished carved line, particularly the triangular shape in the middle, suggests that it was in the process of being altered into a different object. Large daggers such as this one are very unusual Shang tomb objects and may have appeared near the chest of the deceased.

L: 32 cm; W: 18.2 cm
O.21-1946

Black bear, Han dynasty (206 BC–AD 220)

Black jade, carved and polished, depicting a bear sitting up and eating with its paw. The reverse grooved, perhaps for attachment.

H: 5.1; L: 4.3; W: 1.5 cm
O.17-1946

Cong **tube, Neolithic (c.2500 BC) re-carved in the early 20th century**

Dark olive-green opaque jade with brown and reddish inclusions. Thick-walled, with a slightly raised collar around the central hole. The prism surfaces are covered by two bands of zoomorphic masks.

L: 12.65cm; W: 12.4 cm; H: 4.95 cm; D: 6.9 cm
O.4-1946

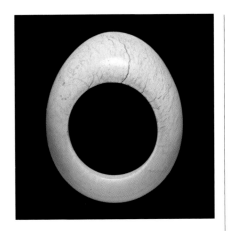

Archer's thumb ring, 19th century
Opaque white jade with plain surface
L: 4.2 cm
O.27-1946

Cicada, Ming dynasty (?)
Brown jade with altered areas, carved in the shape of
a cicada with simple lines. Two perforations drilled on
the top edge between the eyes.
L: 6.2 cm; W: 2.9 cm
O.37-1946

Plaque, Han dynasty, 2nd–1st century BC
Translucent pale green jade with brown flecks,
carved in the shape of a flower petal or eye and
decorated with a feline dragon (a motif seen in
imperial Liu family members' tombs in Xuzhou,
Jiangsu province).
L: 5 cm; W: 2.95 cm
O.44-1946

**Archer's thumb-ring-shaped pendant,
17th–18th century AD**
Green jade carved in openwork with a large central
hole, which suggests its design is based on a thumb
ring. The top of the ring is decorated with a dragon,
and there are feline dragons on both sides at the
bottom. This pendant was carved in the Ming or Qing
period, based on an image from a woodblock print.
L: 8 cm; W: 5.1 cm
O.30-1946

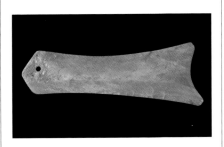

Blade, possibly Neolithic (c. 2000–1700 BC)
Light brown jade with some darker areas. It consists
of a slightly spreading blade with an asymmetrical
curved end. There is a curved raised rib on one side,
and it is flat on the back. A hole was drilled from one
side near the pointed end, which has been re-carved
in a later period.
L: 21.5 cm; W: 7.4 cm
O.39-1946

Bead, 19th century
Green jade tube with altered brown areas owing to
the application of heat. It was probably produced in
the 19th century in the earlier Shang style.
H: 4.85; D: 1.65 cm
O.46-1946

Box with lid carved in the shape of a duck, early 20th century
Soapstone carved in the form of a duck, unknown purpose.
L: 3.5 cm
O.47-1946

Vase, 20th century
Pale green jade with white spots all over, in the shape of a vase and carved with lotus flowers and leaves.
H: 28.8 cm; W: 9 cm
O.56-1946

Brush holder, 17th century
A brush holder of rock crystal cut in the form of a tree trunk.
H: 13 cm; W: 15.5 cm
O.61 & A-1946

Jade pendant, 19th century
White tinged with green and brown jade, decorated with a dragon in the Han style. A hole on it suggests it was possibly a dress clasp.
L: 6.5 cm
O.55-1946

Life-size figure of a duck, 19th century
Steatite figure of a duck on a lotus leaf; on the lid a lotus flower going to seed. Possibly used as an incense burner.
H: 25.4 cm
O.60 & A-1946

Shoulao immortal, 19th century
Turquoise green jadeite carved with the god of longevity standing holding a peach in his right hand and a stick in the other, accompanied by a crane at his feet that holds a _lingzhi_ fungus in its beak.
H: 27.9 cm
O.62-1946

Flute, 19th century
A celadon jade carved and hollowed to a tubular form with nine aligned oval apertures and two further apertures on the underside. Both ends capped with jadeite.
L: 54.5 cm
O.65-1946

Handle of a fan or fly whisk, 19th century
Brown and green jade
L: 14.8 cm; W: 6.3 cm
O.69-1946

Small vase, 19th century
Small vase in the shape of a Chinese cabbage, tinged with emerald green. Several small holes drilled in the petals suggest the work of insects. A ferric oxide mark is employed to represent a crumpled petal.
H: 7 cm; W: 6.6 cm
O.76-1946

Bowl, 18th century
Bowl of translucent chalcedony, with natural markings.
D: 12.6 cm; H: 6.8 cm
O.67-1946

Star God of Rank and Affluence, late 18th–19th century
Creamy yellow soapstone carved as a Star God of Rank and Affluence in the form of a long-bearded official, dressed in an elaborate hat and long, flowing robes. He is holding a *ruyi* sceptre in his left hand. The robes are intricately carved with elaborate floral designs.
H: 38 cm; W: 19.2 cm
O.73-1946

Fan, 19th century
White jade, incised design filled in with gold lacquer, a bird, plum tree and bamboo. On the reverse a poem. Red tassel with sacred knot at the end of the handle. Qianlong mark.
H: 27 cm
O.84-1946

Jade screen, 18th century
A screen, consisting of a flat slab of jade and framed in *zitan* wood with inlaid pearl design of vines. The slab shows signs of having been cut at a much earlier period. It is remarkable for its colouring: pale green and white with two bright orange spots, and marked all over with blotches varying from pale violet to deep amethyst.
H: 48.8 cm; W: 31.2 cm
O.85-1946

Saucer, 18th century
Transparent jadeite saucer almost entirely covered with brilliant emerald-green, moss-like markings.
D: 8.5 cm
O.87-1946

Bowl with lid, 19th century
Jadeite bowl and cover, pale apple green with splashes of emerald green, carved with rounded flared sides rising from a crisp foot to a slightly flaring rim, the domed cover with a shallow disc handle.
D: 11.7 cm
O.89 & A-1946

Brush washer, 19th century
Dark celadon jade with brown areas, well hollowed and boldly carved with gnarled branches of peach issuing from one side and extending over and around the irregular body. Two bats are carved around the rim and one underneath. The peach is symbolic of longevity, and the bat represents a pun on the word for 'luck'.
L: 13.8 cm; H: 6.9 cm; D: 8.8 cm
O.86-1946

A pair of saucers, 18th century
A pair of jadeite and smaragdite saucers, camphor-coloured with brilliant emerald-green and very dark green moss-like markings.
D: 12.9 cm
O.88 A & B-1946

Bowl, 18th century
Lapis lazuli bowl of trefoil form with raised moulded bands, a band of engraved key pattern and two other bands of engraved archaic ornamentation. After the style of early bronzes. Three pierced handles.
L: 8 cm; H: 6.5 cm
O.92-1946

Wall vase, 18th century
A wall vase of pale green jadeite with ferric oxide marks, very translucent. A branch of a tree in full flower cut in relief over the body of the vase; round the base and lip are key pattern bands. Pierced key-pattern handles.
H: 18.2 cm
O.94-1946

Pendant plaque, 17th–18th century
White jade carved in low relief. On one side a man directs a boy who is watering a plant; on the reverse a poem with the signature of the famous Ming jade carver Lu Zigang.
L: 6.5 cm; W: 4.2 cm
O.96-1946

Water dropper, 17th century
White jade, carved, drilled and engraved as a three-legged animal with the head of a *qilin* and body of a tortoise, hollowed out as a water dropper.
H: 7.2 cm
O.99-1946

Xi pendant, early 20th century
Small but relatively thick jade dagger-shaped pendant with pointed end and decorated with a distinctive Shang-dynasty feature, the monster's eye. This type of jade is interpreted as *xi*, which according to the texts was used to untie knots. However, judging from the thickness and the holes drilled on the top of this pendant, it is more likely to be an ornament.
L: 4.9 cm; W: 1.9 cm; Thickness: 1.1 cm
O.95-1946

Water pot, late 18th century
Water pot of yellow chalcedony in the form of a phoenix carrying a *lingzhi* fungus in its beak.
L: 9.3 cm; W: 7.6 cm; H: 3.7 cm
O.98-1946

Ring, possibly Neolithic, c. 2000–1700 BC
Black jade ring with plain surface.
D: 9.2 cm
O.100-1946

Scabbard chape, Eastern Zhou or Han, 4th–1st century BC
Dark brown jade with black staining, carved in approximately trapezoidal shape. Three joined holes on the top for attachment to the scabbard. Undecorated smooth surface.
L: 5.5 cm; W: 4.5 cm
O.101-1946

Bowl, 19th century
Chalcedony bowl, hollowed with plain surface
D: 11.2 cm; H: 7 cm
O.103-1946

Small pendant, late Western Zhou
Pale green pendant with a hole for suspension. It is likely to be a part of a complicated jade pendant set. A similar one was excavated from Xinzheng, Henan province.
L: 1.8 cm
O.109-1946

Three-legged toad, 19th century
Marble, carved in the shape of a three-legged toad, hollowed out for use as a water container.
H: 14.3 cm; L: 25 cm
O.102-1946

A pair of soapstone seals, 19th century
Red and grey, with handles carved as a lion and cub, emblematic of Emperor and Empress. The characters read: 'Nourish your mind and cultivate your nature.'
H: 21.4 cm; base: 8.6 x 8.6 cm
O.108 A & B-1946

Oblong bead, 19th century
Dark brown and white jade drilled with a central hole.
H: 2 cm; D: 1.8 cm
O.110-1946

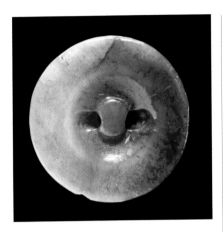

Button, uncertain date
Brown and white jade, with a pair of interconnected holes on the reverse for attachment. Buttons made of jade have never been found in any excavation.
D: 2.1 cm
O.111-1946

Dish, 18th century
Translucent milky white jade dish, supported on a short, straight foot rounding to broad shallow sides turned slightly outward at the rim.
D: 23.5 cm; H: 3.2 cm
O.114-1946

Ornament or sword pommel, Eastern Zhou, 4th–3rd century BC
Turquoise, uneven surface with a hole drilled in the centre from one side. Possibly used as an ornament or a sword pommel.
D: 2.85 cm
O.116-1946

Bowl, 18th century
Jadeite bowl of icy tone with dark green inclusions, rounded sides rising from a crisp foot to a flaring rim.
D: 17.2 cm; H: 7.5 cm
O.113-1946

Brush bath, 19th century
Pale white jade, semi-translucent, incised with four characters, *Qianlong nian zhi* ('Made in the reign of Emperor Qianlong'), underneath.
L: 13 cm; W: 7.5 cm
O.115-1946

Vase, 19th century
Green marble vase, carved in the shape of a magnolia flower.
H: 32 cm (without stand)
O.117-1946

Given by Mrs May Cippico in accordance with the
wishes of Mrs Constance Goetze, 19 April 1951:

Vase, 18th century
'Red carnelian, carved in the shape of an ancient
bronze vase, surrounded by a feline dragon and a
phoenix at either side among *ruyi* fungi clouds.
H: 12.8 cm; W: 12 cm
O.118-1946

Female immortal, 19th century
Opaque light green jade, carved as a standing female
immortal. Her hair is in a tight coiffure, and the robes
hang elegantly down the body with pendant sleeves,
some flying edges and heavily gathered around the
feet. A long branch of double gourd across her
shoulders and the other hand holding a peony/lotus
flower.
H: 24 cm; W: 8.5 cm
O.3-1951

Bowl, late 18th century
Lavender-green jadeite bowl resting on a short
straight foot, plain surface.
D: 13.1 cm; H: 4.4 cm
O.9-1951

Axe head or chisel, 20th century
A dark brown opaque diminutive axe head or chisel;
one end sharpened and the other hammer-shaped.
The hole was drilled from both sides.
L: 6.1 cm; W: 3.5 cm
O.120-1946

Phoenix on a rock, late 18th century
Celadon green jade carved and pierced with a
phoenix holding a large spray of peony and standing
on rockwork. It has a short crest and a long curling
tail.
H: 21 cm; W: 7 cm
O.5-1951

Jade vase and cover, 18th century
Pale celadon-green jade, carved in high relief with an
egret standing among lotus flowers and leaves which
emerge from the waves below. The neck decorated
with a band of roundels and two monkey heads.
H: 19.2 cm
O.10 & A-1951

Vase and cover, 19th century

Jadeite vase with lid, carved in the shape of a melon and decorated with a praying mantis on a leaf and a dragonfly on a smaller melon.

H: 16 cm; W: 8.5 cm

O.11 & A-1951

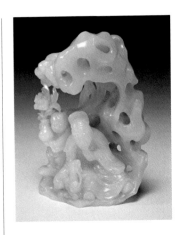

Jade boulder, 18th century

Pale celadon-green jade, carved and pierced with a seated elderly scholar taming a ram, which has a *lingzhi* fungus emerging from its mouth. A boy servant holding a vase stands near by in a cave.

H: 12.8 cm; W: 8.6 cm

O.14-1951

Octagonal bowl, 19th century

Octagonal bowl with eight ring ornaments on eight bracket feet. The rim is decorated with a band of lotus flowers and the handles as a pair of pierced lotuses with suspended rings.

L: 21 cm; H: 6 cm

O.16-1951

Miniature vase, 19th century

Pale celadon jade, hollowed and carved with a miniature vase with two *ruyi* cloud handles, from which loose rings are suspended. One side decorated with two high-relief feline dragons, one clambering over the rim and the other descending near the base; the other side decorated with a phoenix standing on a rock underneath a giant peony flower.

H: 11.5 cm

O.12-1951

Standing lady, 19th century

Apple-green jadeite with dark green inclusions, as a standing lady wearing a long flowing robe and holding a scroll in her hands.

H: 27.5 cm

O.15-1951

Liu Hai and three-legged toad, early 20th century

Jadeite figure of Liu Hai, depicted as a young man standing on a three-legged toad, with a coin in his right hand and another smaller three-legged toad on his left hand. Liu Hai is always regarded as a benevolent Daoist deity.

H: 15 cm

O.17-1951

Vase, 19th century
Jasper vase carved as an entwining pomegranate tree and two birds. Underneath incised with a seal *Qianlong nian zhi* ('Made in the reign of Emperor Qianlong [1736–95]').
H: 15.4 cm; W: 12 cm
O.18-1951

Dancing figure, late 19th century
Semi-translucent agate, carved as a dancing figure
H: 16.4 cm; W: 5.5 cm
O.21-1951

Liu Hai and three-legged toad, 19th century
Amethyst quartz, carved with the Immortal Liu Hai, holding a three-legged frog in his right hand and stepping on another larger one. There are all sorts of legends about Liu Hai, but he is usually depicted as a young man standing on a three-legged toad and swinging a string of coins.
H: 8.9 cm; W: 5.5 cm
O.23-1951

Vase and cover, 19th century
Chalcedony vase and cover, carved with three feline dragons surrounding the vase in high relief and another one on the lid.
H: 13.7 cm; W: 8.3 cm
O.19 & A-1951

Brush washer, 18th century
Dark green agate, carved in the shape of a lotus leaf, decorated with a frog outside.
W: 7 cm; H: 3.8 cm
O.22-1951

Vase, 19th century
Transparent and light green crystal worked in the form of an irregular section of *lingzhi* fungus, bamboo and banana tree. Two small uneven vases issue from the root of the *lingzhi* fungus. The design is very likely to have been adopted from the plants seen in Suzhou landscape gardens.
H: 14 cm; W: 9.9 cm
O.24-1951

Standing figure, 18th century
Soapstone, carved with a female figure standing on a
horned tortoise and playing a flute.
H: 22.8 cm; base W: 7.8 cm
O.29-1951

Glossary

an (quail)	鵪	*dai gou*	帶鉤
an (safe)	安	Damo (Bodhidharma)	達摩
An'hui	安徽	Dangyang	當陽
Anyang	安陽	*Da Qing Qianlong fangu*	大清乾隆仿古
Bai Zhu	白紵	Da Tong	大同
Bangfu	邦父	*Da Yu kai shan tu*	大禹開山圖
Baoji Zhuyuangou	寶雞竹園溝	*di*	狄
Baonudun	寶女墩	*ding*	鼎
Baopuzi (pao-p'u-tzu)	抱朴子	Dingling	定陵
Baoshan	包山	Ding Wei	丁未
Beidongshan	北洞山	Dingxian	定縣
Beijing	北京	*Dong Jing Meng hua lu*	東京夢華錄
Ben Cao Gang Mu	本草綱目	*Dong zi er bai er shi er hao*	東字二百二十二號
bi	璧	Dou Wan	竇綰
Bian He	汴和	Duan Fang	端方
bixi	贔屭	*duo bao ge*	多寶格
bi xie	避邪	Erligang	二里岡
bo (lord)	伯	Erlitou	二里頭
Bogu tu	博古圖	Fangshan Liulihe	房山琉璃河
Bojishan	簸箕山	Fanshan	反山
Bozhou	亳州	Fenghuangtai	鳳凰台
Bu dai	布袋	Fengtian	豐田
Chang'an	長安	Fo	佛
Changfeng Yanggongxiang	長豐楊公鄉	*fu* (axe)	斧
Chang Lituan	張麗端	Fufeng	扶風
Changshu	常熟	Fu Hao	婦好
chang yi zi sun	長宜子孫	Fuquanshan	福泉山
Chen Xing	陳性	Fu Xi	伏羲
Chu (state)	楚	Fuxin	阜新
Chunchon	春川	*Gang mao*	岡卯
Chun-nan Hou	渾南侯	Gansu	甘肅
Cixi	慈禧	Gao Lian	高廉
cong	琮	Gaozong (Song emperor)	高宗 (宋)
Congshu jicheng chubian	叢書集成初編	*ge*	戈
Dahamencun	大哈門村	Ge Hong	葛洪
Dai	駄	*Geng zi di si shi ba hao*	庚字第四十八號

gong (duke)	公	*He shi bi*	和氏璧
gong-gui	躬圭	Hetian (Khotan)	和田(闐)
gouyunxingshi	勾雲形飾	Hindustan	痕都斯坦
gu	瓠	Hongdong	洪洞
guan and *zhu*	管珠	Hongshan (culture)	紅山
Guangdong	廣東	*hou* (marquis)	侯
Guanghan Sanxingdui	廣漢三星堆	Houcun	後村
Guangling (kingdom)	廣陵	Houloushan	後樓山
Guangshan Baoxiangsi	光山寶相寺	Houma	侯馬
Guangzhou	廣州	Hou xin	後辛
guanyin	觀音	*hu*	壺
gu-bi	穀璧	Hua (Mount)	華山
gui	圭	*Huainan wanbishu*	淮南萬畢術
Guishan	龜山	Hualien	花蓮
Guiyang	貴陽	*huan* ('rings')	環
Guizhou	貴州	*huang* (arc-shaped pendant)	璜
Guo (state)	虢	Huang (state)	黃國
gu xiang	古香	Huangniangniangtai	皇娘娘臺
gu yu tu	古玉圖	Huang Tsui-mei	黃翠梅
Gu yu tu kao	古玉圖考	*huan-gui*	環圭
Gu yu tu pu	古玉圖譜	Huang Xuanpei	黃宣佩
han	琀	Hubei	湖北
han (water)	漢水	Hunan	湖南
Han (state)	韓	Hutougou	胡頭溝
Han Fei Zi	韓非子	Huo Qubing	霍去病
Han Gaozu	漢高祖	Jiangjunshan	將軍山
Hangzhou	杭州	Jiangling	江陵
Hanjiang	邗江	Jiangning	江寧
Hanshan	韓山	Jiangsu	江蘇
Hao	鎬	Jiang Tao	姜濤
he (crane)	鶴	Jiangxi	江西
he xie (harmony)	和諧	Jianping	建平
Hebei	河北	*jian shang zhang*	鑑賞章
Hejiacun	何家村	Jian Zhang Palace	建章宮
Henan	河南	Jiajing (emperor)	嘉靖
He Shen	和珅	Jiaqing (emperor)	嘉慶

Majiayao	馬家窯	Qingpu	青浦
Mancheng	滿城	*qing ting yan*	蜻蜓眼
Maoling	茂陵	Qin Shihuangdi	秦始皇帝
matixingshi	馬蹄形飾	Qinzong (Northern Song emperor)	(北宋) 欽宗
Mawangdui	馬王堆	Qufu	曲阜
Meng Yuanlao	孟元老	*ren zhu yan shou*	人主延壽
Ming hui yao	明會要	*ri shu*	日書
Mo Shu	莫書	Rujiazhuang	茹家莊
(King) Mu	穆王	*ruyi* sceptre	如意
Mu Rui	沐睿	Ruyi Guan	如意館
nan (baron)	男	*Sancai tuhui*	三才圖繪
Nanyue Wang	南越王	Sanlidun	三里墩
Neiwufu gezuo chengzuo	內務府各作成做	*Sanli tu*	三禮圖
huoji qingdang	活計清檔	Sanmenxia	三門峽
nian nian you yu	年年有餘	Shaanxi	陝西
nian yu	鯰魚	Shandong	山東
Ningxia	寧夏	Shang	商
Niuheliang	牛河梁	Shanghai	上海
ping (vase)	瓶	*Shan Hai Jing*	山海經
ping (safe)	平	Shanxi	山西
Pingshan	平山	Shaolin Temple	少林寺
Pingwu	平武	*she*	韘
Pu-bi	蒲璧	*sheng*	笙
Pu Yi	溥儀	*Shi ji*	史記
qi	氣	*Shiqu baoji*	石渠寶笈
Qi (state, kingdom)	齊國	Shi Shengzu	史繩祖
Qianlong (emperor)	乾隆	*shi wen*	十問
Qianlong nian zhi	乾隆年製	*shi zhi jian zhe*	石之堅者
Qian zi wen	千字文	*shi zhi mei zhe*	石之美者
qibao she	七寶社	Shizishan	獅子山
Qijia (culture)	齊家文化	*shou cang zhang*	收藏章
Qijiaping	齊家坪	Shuihudi	睡虎地
qilin	麒麟	*Shuowen jiezi*	說文解字
Qin (state)	秦國	Sichuan	四川
qingbai	青白	Sima Qian	司馬遷
Qing Gaozong yuzhi shiwen quanji	清高宗御製詩文全集	*Song shu*	宋書

Su Dongpo	蘇東坡	Wangshan	望山
sui (rice grains)	穗	Wang Siyi	王思義
sui (annual)	歲	Wanli (emperor)	萬曆
Sui (county)	隨縣	Wei (state)	魏國
sui sui ping an	歲歲平安	(Emperor) Wen	文帝
Sun Baoqi	孫寶琦	(king) Wen of Chu	楚文王
Sun Zhixin	孫志新	Wenchuan	汶川
su yang	俗樣	Wen Guang	聞廣
Suzhou	蘇州	Wenxi	聞喜
Taipei	台北	Wenxian	聞縣
Tai ping jing xiang	太平景象	Wen Zhenheng	文震亨
Tai ping you xiang	太平有象	wo	握
tai pu	太璞	Wolong village	臥龍村
Taiwan	台灣	(king) Wu of Chu	楚武王
Taiyuan	太原	Wu Dacheng	吳大澂
taotie	饕餮	(Han) Wudi	武帝
Tao Yuanming	陶淵明	(king) Wu Ding	武丁
Tao zhai gu yu tu	陶齋古玉图	Wujin Sidun	武進寺墩
Tian gong kai wu	天工開物	Wuwei	武威
Tianjin	天津	Wu xian	吳縣
Tianma Qucun	天馬曲村	xi	觿
Tianshan	天山	Xi'an	西安
Tian shu	天書	Xia Du	下都
Tianshui bingshan lu	天水冰山錄	Xia Fei (concubine)	夏妃
tianxia zhidao tan	天下至道談	Xia Nai	夏鼐
Tianxingguan	天星觀	xiang (auspicious)	祥
Tongshan	銅山	Xian Yushu	鮮于樞
Tsai Mei-fen	蔡玫芬	xian zhang	閒章
Tuolanshan	駝籃山	Xichuan	淅川
Tushan	土山	Xilamulun	西拉木倫
wang	王	Xin'gan Dayangzhou	新干大洋洲
Wang Mang	王莽	xin-gui	信圭
wan gu tu	玩古圖	xing shu	行書
Wang Zhen	王振	Xinjiang	新疆
Wang Zunguo	汪遵國	Xinyang	信陽
Wang Qi	王圻	xin yang	新樣

Xiqing gujian	西清古鑑	Zeng	曾
xiu nei si	修內司	*zhadou*	渣斗
Xuanhe bogu tu	宣和博古圖	Zhang Jingjiang	張靜江
(Tang) Xuan zong	唐宣宗	Zhanglingshan	張陵山
Xu Jay	許傑	Zhang Renjie	張人傑
Xu Shen	許慎	Zhangshu	樟樹
Xuzhou	徐州	*Zhang wu zhi*	長物志
Yan (state)	燕國	Zhao (state)	趙國
yang	陽	Zhao Mei	趙眛
Yang Boda	楊伯達	Zhaoxiang (king)	昭相王
Yangshao culture	仰韶文化	Zhejiang	浙江
Yang Song	嚴嵩	Zhengde (emperor)	正德
Yangzhou	揚州	*zhen-gui*	鎮圭
Yantai	煙台	Zheng Xuan	鄭玄
Yaoshan	瑤山	Zheng Zhi	政治
(Marquis) Yi of Zeng	曾侯乙	Zhengzhou	鄭州
Yi jing	易經	Zhenliucun	枕流村
Yi-Kun Palace	翊坤宮	Zhifangtou	紙坊頭
Yi li	儀禮	Zhifu	芝罘
yin	陰	*Zhi zi yi bai liu shi jiu hao*	知字一百六十九號
Ying Zheng	瀛政	Zhongnan (Mount)	鍾南山
Yongcheng (Henan province)	永城	Zhongshan (state)	中山國
Yongcheng (Shaanxi province)	雍城	*Zhou li*	周禮
Yong Le (Emperor)	永樂	Zhou Xingsi	周興嗣
Yongzheng	雍正	*zhulong*	豬龍
Yu (state)	強國	*zhuan zhu xiang*	專諸巷
yu	玉	Zhu Derun	朱德潤
Yuandi	元帝	Zhu Ning	朱寧
yu bei	玉杯	Zhu Tan	朱檀
yue	鉞	*Zhuyeting za ji*	竹葉亭雜記
yu er	玉厄	Zifangshan	子房山
Yuhang	余杭	*zitan*	紫檀
Yu Ji	玉紀	Zou (county)	鄒
yu shan	玉山	*Zun sheng ba jian*	遵生八箋
zan	贊	Zuo Peng	左鵬
Zaobanchu huo ji dang	造辦處活計檔		

Notes

1 Taipei 1955, p. 10.

2 Hansford 1969, pp. 8–9.

3 Middleton & Freestone 1995, p. 413.

4 Wen & Jing 1997, p. 109.

5 Middleton & Freestone 1995, pp. 416–7.

6 Hansford 1969, p. 17.

7 Shanghai 1940, pp. 330–31.

8 Beijing 1959, pp. 2439–41.

9 *Wenwu*, April 1972, pp. 27–37, 71; see also Allan 2005, p. 204.

10 *Wenwu*, August 1976, pp. 93–4.

11 *Wenwu*, January 1993, pp. 62–8; Lu Zhaoyin 1998, p.44.

12 Beijing 1959, p. 1413.

13 Legge 1967, vol. 2, p. 464.

14 Hunan 1939, preface.

15 Liu Lexian 1994, p. 257.

16 Wang Ming 1980, 17.278; Ware 1966, p. 288.

17 Taipei 1955, p.10.

18 Beijing 1959, p. 459.

19 Wang Ming 1980, p. 45.

20 Beijing 1975, pp. 614–23.

21 For cinnabar, amber and coral found in a Tang hoard at Hejiacun, Xi'an, see *Wenwu*, July1972, pp. 30–42; for mica found around the body from a Sui tomb, see *Wenwu*, October 1992, pp. 23–7; for jade suits found in Han tombs, see Lin 2002.

22 For example, fragment of a Hongshan period (*c.* 3500 BC) ornament found with Western Zhou jades in Western Zhou tombs at Beijing Fangshan Liulihe (*c.*950 BC); see Rawson 1997, p.171.

23 Beijing 1989, pp. 429–30.

24 See Hebei 1991–3, vol. 6, pl. 277; see also Rawski & Rawson 2005, pl. 223.

25 Beijing 1980a, pl. 127: 2.

26 *Wenwu*, April 2005, p. 22, pl. 45. For more discussion on reuse of ancient jades, see Rawson 1997.

27 This subject was discussed during the second international jade conference at Hetian, 22–5 August 2006.

28 For tombs at Hutougou see *Wenwu*, June 1984, pp. 1–5; for tombs from Niuheliang see *Wenwu*, August 1986, pp. 1–17, 18–24, and *Wenwu*, August 1997, pp. 4–14, 15–19.

29 Liu Yang 2007, pp. 72–85, fig.1.

30 Forsyth 1990, p. 61.

31 For tombs at Wujin Sidun see *Kaogu*, March 1981, pp. 193–9; and *Kaogu*, February 1984, pp. 109–29. For tombs at Zhanglingshan see *Wenwu ziliao congkan*, June 1982, pp. 25–35, and *Wenwu*, October 1986, pp. 26–35. For tombs at Fuquanshan see *Wenwu*, February 1984, pp. 1–5, and *Wenwu*, October 1986, pp. 1–25. For tombs at Fanshan, Yuhang, see *Wenwu*, October 1986, pp. 36–8. For tombs at Changshu, Jiangsu, see *Wenwu*, February 1984, pp. 12–16. For a discussion of the date of Liangzhu see Sun Zhixin 1993, pp. 1–40; and Huang Tsui-mei 1992. For a general discussion of the Liangzhu culture see Beijing & Hong Kong 1989 and Wang Zungou 1984, pp. 23–36.

32 Beijing & Hong Kong 1989; Tang Chung 1998, vol. 3, pls. 113–4; *Kaogu*, February 1984, pp. 113–4.

33 Similar discs are found at Liangzhu sites at Sidun, Wujin and Changshu, Jiangsu province; see *Wenwu*, February 1984, p. 15, fig. 4:3, and p. 20, fig. 16.

34 Rawson 1995, pp. 33–4.

35 A Hongshan tomb might have yielded between ten and twenty pieces of jade at most, while a Liangzhu tomb might contain between one and two hundred, including small jade beads. The Liangzhu jades also range widely in size and weight, such as the largest jade disc, *bi*, and tall tubes, *cong*. In addition, in the Liangzhu society there are also other goods buried in tombs, notably very fine ceramics. See Rawson 1995, p. 33; and Beijing & Hong Kong 1989.

36 For example, see M8 and M91 at Tianma Qucun, Shaanxi; *Wenwu*, July 1995, pp.4–39; and *Wenwu*, January 1994, pp. 4–28.

37 *Kaogu xuebao*, April 1978, pp. 421–48.

38 A similar one was found in the site of Huangniangniangtai; see Huang Xuanpei 1998, pp. 184–91, fig.19.1.

39 Yang Meili 2001, pp. 21–8.

40 *Kaogu*, February 1974, pp. 80–87, 89, fig. 3:2; see also Rawson 1995, p. 24, fig. 9.

41 Huang Xuanpei 1998, pp. 184–91, particularly p. 191.

42 Ye Maolin 2005, pp. 5–9.

43 For similar examples from the archaeological finds see Beijing 2005, vol.15, pls. 31, 35, 36, 37, 38.

44 Rawson 1995, pp. 184–5; Huang Xuanpei 1998, p. 190.

45 Xie Duanju 2001, p. 2; Huang Xuanpei 1998, pp. 184–91.

46 The Anyang period, corresponding to the reigns of the last twelve Shang kings, runs from about 1300 BC to 1000 BC. Hence the tomb of Fu Hao, consort of the fourth Anyang king, can be dated to around 1200 BC. The Erligang period, named after a typical site at modern Zhengzhou, precedes the Anyang period and can be taken as 1500 to 1300 BC. See Kaogu, April 1981, pp. 491–518; Rawson 1995, p. 40; Bagley 1991, p. 231, n. 1.

47 Coiled dragons from Fu Hao's tomb are an example that was borrowed from the Hongshan culture. For further discussion, see Rawson 1995, p. 43.

48 For a comparison of bronze and jade repertories between Fu Hao's tomb, Guanghan Sanxingdui and Xin'gan Dayangzhou, see Bagley 1990, pp. 52–67; and Bagley 1993.

49 While most scholars have argued that the sophistication of Shang bronzes and jades was copied by people on the periphery, Jessica Rawson suggests this exchange also took place in the other direction. She further pointed out that Shang may have traded, seized and copied both bronze and jades from their neighbours. See Rawson 1995, p. 40.

50 Rawson 1995, p. 165.

51 Kaogu, April 1984, pp. 302–32, figs. 16:10; 26:2.

52 Rawson 1995, fig. 100.

53 Rawson 1990, pp. 93–110.

54 The tombs of the lords of Yu state at Baoji area have a clear chronology, which helps us to understand the ritual revolution by comparing the burial objects. The chronology of the lords of Yu state has been suggested by archaeological finds as follows: M1 at Zhifangtou (c.1050 BC) / M13 at Zhuyuangou (c.1040–1025 BC) / M7 at Zhuyuangou (c.1025–1000 BC) / M1 at Rujiazhuang (c.970 BC). See Beijing 1988, p. 415. For a fuller discussion see Rawson 1995, especially pp. 47–50.

55 See Beijing 1988, p. 424; and Rawson 2009.

56 As Xu Jay pointed out, none of the names of the marquises from this cemetery matches those in the chronology of the Jin marquisate given in the Western Han period Shi ji. He also suggested that the ordering of the graves proposed by the excavators cannot be trusted. For details of the tomb occupants see Xu Jay 1996, pp. 193–231, especially p. 204, Table 2. The author of Shi ji, Sima Qian, was active during Wudi's reign (140–87 BC), approximately seven centuries after the Western Zhou. It is reasonable to assume that he may have made mistakes when he gathered information from a number of sources.

57 See Xu Jay 1996, p. 221.

58 Some further Jin tombs outside the Houma site, including tombs at Hongdong and Wenxi, appear to have many fewer jades. They were buried in much smaller-scale tombs and are of almost the same date as those at Qucun. This may indicate that the royal rank of tombs should definitely have jades.

59 Three large sets of pendants were excavated from tombs M2001, M2009 and M2012. The former two have been identified as the Lords of Guo state and the last one as that of a female aristocrat. The jade pendant from tomb M2012 is composed of five huang and beads – that is, similar to the one from tomb M91 at Tianma Qucun. Apart from tomb M2001, no jade veils were reported from tomb M2009 and M2012. See Jiang Tao and Li Xiuping 1998, p. 53; Tang Chung 1998, vol. 3, pls. 349–60; and Beijing 1999.

60 There had always been strong regional differences, but these had not always been conspicuous because in early times not all areas were wealthy enough to own jades and bronzes.

61 Beijing 1996a, pp. 138–56.

62 See Beijing 1989, pp. 399–431.

63 Beijing 1995, pp. 165–240.

64 For tombs at Qufu see Ji'nan 1982. For tombs at Linzi Shangwangcun see Ji'nan 1997.

65 For the tomb at Tianxingguan see Kaogu xuebao, January 1982, pp. 71–116. For the tomb at Baoshan see Beijing 1991b; for the tomb at Wangshan see Beijing 1996b.

66 Beijing 1986, figs. 79:1, 2. However, it should be noted that these figurines only represented the servants of the tomb occupants.

67 Zuo Peng 1998, pp. 55–66.

68 Wang Renxiang 1982, pp. 75–94.

69 For example, sword fittings with three-dimensional feline creatures on the surface from the third-century BC tomb at Shangwangcun, Shandong: see Ji'nan 1997, and *Wenwu*, June 1997, pp. 14–26. For a jade halberd from a Qin mausoleum at Yongcheng, Shaanxi, often considered to be the tomb of Jing Gong (*c.* 577–537 BC), see Tang Chung 1998, vol.3, pl. 372. As for a coffin inlaid with stone plaques from a fifth-century tomb at Xiadu, Hebei, see *Kaogu*, November 1965, pp. 548–61, 598; see also *Kaogu*, November 1965, pp. 562–70. The use of jade discs in eastern China has a long tradition: see Lin 2002, pp. 81–9.

70 Two eye plaques and a mouth amulet were found in Taiyuan, Shanxi, dating to 475–450 BC; see Beijing 1996b, pl. 105:3. Two eye plaques, nose plugs and a mouth amulet were found at Pingshan, Hebei, *c.*327–313 BC; see Beijing 1995, pl. 174:2. Two eye-shaped plaques were found in Zibo, Shandong, dating to the late Warring States period; see *Kaogu*, May 1988, pp. 467–71.

71 The bamboo-slip texts *Shi wen* and *Tianxia zhidao tan* from Mawangdui M3 provide theoretical and practical knowledge concerning macrobiotic hygiene in the form of interviews in which noble patrons seek instruction from esoteric masters. The 101 bamboo slips of *Shi wen* are approximately 23 cm long and 8 mm wide. They contain ten dialogues in which ten macrobiotic specialists respond to questions. The teachings include instructions for executing cultivation techniques, often describing the process in esoteric and metaphoric language. The 56 bamboo slips of *Tianxia zhidao tan* are approximately 28 cm long and 0.5 cm wide. They primarily concern sexual cultivation. See Hebei 1994. See also Harper 1998, pp. 385–411, 425–38.

72 In the text *shi wen* it records that 'He who is skilled at cultivating vapour lets the old vapour disperse at night and the new vapour gather at dawn, thereby penetrating the nine apertures (*jiu qiao*) and filling the six cavities'. See Hebei 1994, vol. 1, p. 17.

73 Xia Nai was the first scholar who suggested that the nine orifice plugs, which plug the orifices in the body of the dead, were designed to prevent the escape of vital essences. See Xia Nai 1983, p. 31. The notion of vital essence, *qi*, was combined with that of the *yin* and *yang* (the positive and negative forces) and accounted for all phenomena in the universe. It was widely discussed in the Han texts. See Graham 1989, part 4, and Harper 1999, pp. 813–84.

74 This was suggested in Yates 1994, p. 73.

75 The *Jie* (spellbinding) section of bamboo slips entitled 'daybooks' from the Shuihudi (a Qin tomb found in Hubei, dating to 217 BC) instructed people on how to protect themselves from demons. Similar records were also seen in bamboo slips found in Han tombs and reveal that during those centuries peoples in the south, and probably elsewhere, believed that demonic intrusion was a significant cause of illness. Therefore, special recipes (including magical, exorcizing recipes for compounding drugs and therapeutic treatments) were taken to cure the disease. See Harper 1985, pp. 471–83. It is almost certain that, instead of believing that decomposition was a natural process, the Han people may have thought that the body decomposed owing to attack by evil spirits. See Lin 2007, pp.188–9.

76 Ge Hong's comment may be the earliest explicit literary statement of this belief, but the evidence from Han archaeology substantiates such concepts and dates to several centuries earlier. It seems possible that he was recording an ancient tradition. See Wang Ming 1980, p. 45. However, no gold orifice plugs have ever been found in excavations.

77 For jade discs from tomb M2 at Changfeng Yanggongxiang, An'hui, see *Kaoguxue jikan*, February 1982, pp. 47–60, especially p. 59, fig. 12. For discs from tomb M1 and M2 at Shangwangcun, Linzi, Shangdong, see *Wenwu*, June 1997, pp. 14–26; also Ji'nan 1997, pp. 5–70. For discs from tomb M52 and M58 at Qufu, Shandong, see Ji'nan 1982, especially pp. 114–74.

78 See Rawson 1998b, p. 127, n. 270. In fact, ancient tombs found by accident or on purpose in the Han period

were recorded in some texts, such as *Hou Han shu*. See Beijing 1965, p. 1450.

79 *Wenwu*, August 1998, pp. 4–33; *Kaogu yu wenwu*, January 1999, pp. 55–71.

80 *Wenwu*, April 1973, pp. 21–34, especially p. 27.

81 Beijing 1973, pp. 119–20.

82 In Sichuan the discs were often replaced by coins. In many lesser tombs images of jade discs were incised on stone or brick, or painted on brick or lacquer. See Rawson 1998b.

83 *Wenwu*, October 1991, p. 54.

84 An incomplete jade suit, composed of a helmet, face veil, gloves and boots, was found in an intact catacomb tomb at Linyi, Shandong. See *Kaogu*, June 1980, pp. 493–5.

85 Rawson 1995, p. 290.

86 Apart from these small jade animal sculptures, a stone sculpture in the shape of a buffalo inscribed with Fu Hao's posthumous name *Hou Xin,* and two jade basins were found on the top of her outer coffin. As Rawson has suggested, these items may be part of the ritual of sealing the grave and not related to the smaller sculptures mentioned here. Rawson 1995, p. 386.

87 *Wenwu*, August 1994, pp. 4–21.

88 Four small animal sculptures – a bear, an eagle, a horse and rider and a *bixie* – were found outside Emperor Yuandi's mausoleum; see Hebei 1991–3, vol. 4, pls.147, 148, 150 and 151.

89 Williams 1932, pp. 299–301.

90 London 1968, 'Horse'.

91 Eberhard 1986, p.147.

92 The same phenomenon is also observed in *Gu yu tu pu* ('Illustrated Description of Ancient Jades'), which was attributed to Long Dayuan (*c.* 1176) of the Song dynasty. However, the drawings in *Gu yu tu pu* were compiled from *Sanli tu, Kaogu tu* and *Bogu tu* etc., and there is no evidence that the compilers worked from additional material known in the Song. In addition, most scholars argue that *gu yu tu pu* was compiled at a much later time, possibly in the Qing dynasty. See Shanghai 1948, preface.

93 London 1968, '*Qilin*'.

94 Williams 1932, pp. 409–11.

95 *Kaogu*, November 1983, pp. 1004–11, 1018.

96 Beijing 1993a, pp. 59–60.

97 *Wenwu,* May 1972, pp. 25–36.

98 Chengdu 1985, pp. 109–18; Clunas 1986.

99 Taipei 1965, vol. 6, p. 3241.

100 Jiangsu, 1984, p. 266.

101 Hebei 1991–3, vol. 6, pl. 309.

102 *Wenwu*, September 1990, pp. 22–5.

103 Hebei 1991–3, vol. 6, pl. 333.

104 Forsyth & McElney 1994, pl. 315.

105 Jiangsu, 1984, p. 275.

106 For a jade *gui* found in the tomb of Lady Fuhao, see Yang Boda 1991, pl. 59; for another Shang jade *gui* found in a Western Zhou tomb, see *Kaogu,* September 2000, pp. 9–24. Also Lin 2004, pp. 183–5.

107 Beijing 1959, p. 459, n. 14.

108 Birrell 1999, pp. 21–2.

109 Beijing 1959, p. 386; Beijing 1960, p. 66.

110 Beijing 1960, p. 128; Watson 1993, p. 23; Dubs 1938, pp. 259–60.

111 Rawson 1998b, pp. 125–36.

112 *Wenwu*, July 1982, pp.54–60, pl. 5:4. For another similar one from the archaeological find from a Jin tomb at Xuanhua, Hebei, see *Wenwu*, October 1990, p. 5, fig. 11.

113 Yang Boda 1993, p. 20.

114 Wilson 2004, p. 42.

115 Other items included 18 jade *ding* tripods, 28 imperial jade gongs, 22 jade statues representing Guanyin and Buddhist figures, 507 jade *ruyi* sceptres, 3,411 small jade sceptres and 154 large jade bowls. See Beurdeley 1966, p. 185.

116 Rawson 1995, p. 388.

117 Hebei 1991–3, vol. 5, pls. 233–4.

118 Beijing 2005, vol. 7, pl. 192.

119 For a lobed jade dish decorated with catfish and fungus, see Forsyth & McElney 1994, pl. 341; for a jade dish decorated with two fish among reeds, see Rawson 1995, pl. 29:9.

120 Hebei 1991–3, vol. 5, pl. 241.

121 Li Hai 2003, pl. 170.

122 See Huang Xuanpei 2001, p. 198, pl. 135. Another similar example has been found in Gong Mian's tomb at

Wuxi; see Hebei 1991–3, vol. 5, pl. 279. Another two with plain surfaces were excavated from Dahamencun, Datong, Qinghai province and a tomb at Zhenlincun, Pingwu, Sichuan province respectively; see Beijing 2005, vol. 13, pl. 196, and vol. 15, pl. 182.

123 Bai Ning & Wang Quan 2002, pp. 308–22; and Hua Cixiang 2002, pp. 323–32.

124 *Ming hui yao* was written much later in the Qing period by Long Wenbin (1824–1893), recording the most important official system of the previous dynasty.

125 Beijing 2002, pp. 160–61.

126 Rawson 1995, p. 340, pl. 25:19.

127 Similar jade belt clasps have been excavated from a construction site at Zhangshu, Jiangxi province, and a tomb in Guiyang, Guizhou province. See Beijing 2005, vol. 9, pl. 162; and vol. 12, pl. 223. See also Xu Lin 2002, p. 294, fig. 9.

128 Watt 1989, pp. 70–71.

129 Li Hai 2003, pl. 197.

130 Watt 1989, p. 103.

131 There are only a few examples of *Gang mao* found in tombs dating to the Eastern Han. One measures 2.3 cm in length and is carved with 34 characters and was excavated from a tomb at Houcun, Jingxian, Hebei province; one measures 2.25 cm in length and is carved with 66 characters and was excavated from Tomb No.1 at Fenghuangtai, Bozhou, An'hui province; the other measures 2.2 cm, carved with 32 characters and was excavated from Tomb No.2 at Ganquan, Hanjiang, Jiangsu province. See Beijing 2005, vol. 1, pl. 220; vol. 6, pl. 154; and vol. 7, pl. 154.

132 Yang Boda 1993, p. 9.

133 Jenny So's lecture at the Song conference in February 2007 discussed some of these tubular beads.

134 Perry 1960, p. 25.

135 Moss 1993, vol. 1, p. 41.

136 Beijing 1993b, vol. 5, p. 521.

137 *Liu rui* in *Zhou li* are categorized as follows: the *wang* (king) uses the *zhen-gui*; the *gong* (duke) uses the *huan-gui*; the *hou* (marquis) uses the *xin-gui*; the *bo* (lord) uses the *gong-gui*; the *zi* (noble) uses the *gu-bi*; and the *nan* (baron) uses the *pu-bi*. See Taipei 1972, pp. 192–3.

138 Thanks to Yang Meili and Cai Meifeng for kindly showing me their collection when I visited the National Palace Museum, Taipei, on 17 February 2006.

139 In the list from the Palace Museum, Beijing, the curator Zhang Guangwen recorded them as *fu* (axe); Zhang Guangwen 2002, pp. 355–67. However, Chang Li-tuan, the curator of the Antiquity Department, at the National Palace Museum, Taipei, suggests that they should be *gui* instead of *fu* axe; see Chang Li-tuan 2001, p. 88.

140 *Qian zi wen* was the first text used to educate young children in early China, written by an official, Zhou Xingsi, during the reign of Emperor Wu of the Liang dynasty (r. 503–15). The *Qian zi wen* is a four-character, 250-line long poem of 1,000 non-repeated characters introducing children to astronomy, nature, history, geography, agriculture, sacrifice to the ancestors, gardening and other everyday topics.

141 Zhang Guangwen 2002, pp. 355–67.

142 An identical one measuring 14.8 cm with the series number 169 (*Zhi zi yi bai liu shi jiu hao*) was sold at Sotheby's, Hong Kong, 27 April 2003; see catalogue lot 3. Another one, measuring 13.5 cm in length, with the series number 188, is now in the Palace Museum, Beijing; see Hong Kong 1995, vol. 3, pl. 127.

143 Beijing 1993b, vol. 8, p .682.

144 *Neiwufu gezuo chengzuo huoji qingdang*. This record record of activities in the imperial workshop began in the first year of Emperor Yongzheng's reign (1723) and ended in the third year of the last emperor, Pu Yi (1911). See Hou Haozhi 2006, pp. 74–84.

145 *Neiwufu gezuo chengzuo huoji qingdang*: fifty-second year of Qianlong's reign (1787).

146 *Xuanhe bogu tu* is also known as *Bogu tu*, which was a catalogue of the Northern Song imperial collection of archaic bronzes from the Shang to the Tang dynasty. It was compiled between 1107 and 1123, recording the shape, decoration, dimension, image and inscription of each object.

147 A 40-volume catalogue of Chinese bronzes in the collection of the Qianlong emperor, compiled between 1749 and 1755 and documenting 1,529 bronzes in the Imperial collection.

148 Li Jiufang 1993, p. 10.

149 Beijing 1993b, vol. 8, p. 449.

150 The categories 'Dong' and 'Jia' were very common inventory titles for cataloguing objects in China before the twentieth century and could be used by anyone, particularly businessmen.

151 For this information I thank Chang Li-tuan at the National Palace Museum, Taipei.

152 Li Jiufang 1993, p. 13.

153 Chang Li-tuan 2003, p. 40.

154 The poem incised on the scene of 'Great Yu Pacifying the Flood', from Yarkand's Mount Mirtagh, records the superior permanence of jade over ink on paper. See Beijing 1993b, vol. 8, p. 814.

155 Beijing 1993b, vol. 5, p. 150.

156 Hong Kong 2005, p. 359.

157 Wilson 2004, p. 90, pl. 91.

158 Markel 1990, pp. 22–3.

159 Li Jiufang 1993, p. 14.

160 Teng Shu-p'ing 2007.

161 Rawson 1995, p. 88.

162 Gaozong (r. 1127–1162) assumed the throne in June 1127 as the successor to his brother Qinzong (r. 1126–1127), who had been captured by the Jin in the north. In order to ensure the acceptance of his political programme and the survival of the dynasty, Gaozong had to win the allegiance of the scholar class, which was vital to successful civilian rule. Much of Gaozong's involvement with art was influenced by his need to confirm his legitimacy and enhance his authority. For example, he often copied ancient masterpieces of calligraphy and bestowed these writings on his ministers and generals to promote feelings of loyalty and devotion in the recipients, following a precedent that he associated with Northern Song emperors. See Murray 1989, pp. 27–36; Murray 1993, pp. 10–11.

163 Shanghai 1935–7.

164 Yang Boda 1993, p. 6.

165 Hsu Ya-hwei, 2004, p. 266.

166 Hsu Ya-hwei, 2004, pp. 264–75.

167 Rawson 1995, p. 94.

168 Some late Qing works on jade research, including Chen Xing's *Yu Ji*, are compiled and reprinted in *Guyu kaoshi jianshang congpian*; see Beijing 1992a, pp. 883–910.

169 Gray 1945, pp. 276–83.

170 A long-standing friend from his Paris days was Li Shizeng, who became chairman of the newly created Palace Museum in 1925 and was responsible for the inventory of the Imperial Collections. Zhang also oversaw the beginning of the removal of more than half of the Imperial Collections to Shanghai in 1933, following the Japanese invasion of Manchuria. It was during this period that many imperial works of art found their way into Western collections through dealers such as Zhang.

171 Gray 1945, p. 279.

Bibliography

Allan 2005
Allan, Sarah (ed.): *The Formation of Chinese Civilization: An Archaeological Perspective*, New Haven and London: Yale University Press, 2005

Bagley 1990
Bagley, R.W.: 'A Shang City in Sichuan Province', *Orientations,* November 1990, pp. 52–67

Bagley 1991
Bagley, R.W.: *Changjiang Bronzes and Shang Archaeology*, International Colloquium on Chinese Art History, *Proceedings: Antiquities,* 1, Taipei: National Palace Museum 1992, pp. 215–55

Bagley 1993
Bagley, R.W.: 'An Early Bronze Age Tomb in Jiangxi Province', *Orientations,* July 1993, pp. 20–35

Bai Ning & Wang Quan 2002
Bai Ning and Wang Quan (白寧、王泉): 'Cong Nanjingshi bowuguan cang Mingdai yudai lunji Mingdai yudai shiyong zhidu (從南京市博物館藏明代玉帶論及明代玉帶使用制度)', *Zhongguo Sui Tang zhi Qingdai yuqi xueshu yantaohui lunwenji* (中國隋唐至清代玉器學術研討會論文集), Shanghai: Guji Chubanshe, 2002, pp. 308–322

Beijing 1956
Ming hui yao (明會要), by Long Wenbin (龍文彬, 1824–1893), repr. Beijing: Zhonghua shuju, 1956

Beijing 1959
Shi ji (史記), by Sima Qian (司馬遷 *c.*145–*c.*86 BC), repr. Beijing: Zhonghua Shuju, 1959

Beijing 1960
Han shu (漢書), by Ban Gu (班固, AD 32–92), repr. Beijing: Zhonghua shuju, 1960

Beijing 1965
Hou Han shu (後漢書), by Fan Ye (范曄 398-446), Beijing: Zhonghua shuju, 1965

Beijing 1966
Huainanzi (淮南子), attributed to Liu An (劉安, *c.* 179–122 BC), in *Sibu beiyao*, repr. Beijing: Zhonghua shuju, 1966

Beijing 1973
Changsha Mawangdui yi hao Han mu (長沙馬王堆一號漢墓), 2 vols, Beijing: Wenwu Chubanshe, 1973

Beijing 1975
Ben Cao Gang Mu (本草綱目), by Li Shizhen (李時珍, *c.* 1518–1593), repr. Beijing: Renmin Weisheng Chubanshe, 1975

Beijing 1977
Song shi (宋史), by Tuo Tuo (托托, 1313–1355), repr. Beijing: Zhonghua Shuju, 1977

Beijing 1980a
Yinxu Fu Hao mu (殷墟婦好墓), Beijing: Wenwu Chubanshe, 1980

Beijing 1980b
Mancheng Han mu fajue baogao (滿城漢墓發掘報告), 2 vols, Beijing: Wenwu Chubanshe, 1980

Beijing 1980c
Sui xian Zeng Hou Yi mu (隨縣曾侯乙墓), Beijing: Wenwu Chubanshe, 1980

Beijing 1986
Xinyang Chu mu (信陽楚墓), Beijing: Wenwu Chubanshe, 1986

Beijing 1987
Kaogu tu (考古圖), by Lü Dalin (呂大臨, *c.* 1092), repr. in *Si ku quan shu* 四庫全書 in 1753. Beijing: Zhonghua Shuju, 1987

Beijing 1988
Baoji Yuguo mu di (寶雞魚國墓地), Beijing: Wenwu Chubanshe, 1988

Beijing 1989
Zeng Hou Yi mu (曾侯乙墓), 2 vols, Beijing: Wenwu Chubanshe, 1989

Beijing & Hong Kong 1989
Liangzhu Wenhua Yuqi (良渚文化玉器), Beijing: Wenwu Chubanshe, and Hong Kong: The Woods Publishing Company, 1989

Beijing 1990
Ding Ling (定陵), Beijing: Wenwu Chubanshe, 1990

Beijing 1991a
Xi Han Nan Yue Wang mu (西漢南越王墓), 2 vols, Beijing: Wenwu Chubanshe, 1991

Beijing 1991b
Baoshan Chumu (包山楚墓), 2 vols, Beijing: Wenwu Chubanshe, 1991

Beijing 1991c
Xichuan Xiasi Chunqiu Chu mu (淅川下寺春秋楚墓), Beijing: Wenwu Chubanshe, 1991

Beijing 1992a
Guyu kaoshi jianshang congbian
(古玉考釋鑑賞叢編), Beijing: Shumu
Wenxian Chubanshe, 1992

Beijing 1992b
Yu ji (玉紀), by Chen Xing (陳性, *c.* 1899),
repr. Beijing: Shumu Wenxian Chubanshe,
1992

Beijing 1993a
Liao Cheng guo gongzhu mu (遼陳國公主墓),
Beijing: Wenwu Chubanshe, 1993, pp. 59–60

Beijing 1993b
*Qing Gao-zong (Qian-long) yu zhi shi wen quan
ji* (清高宗御製詩文全集), Beijing: Zhongguo
Renmin Dauxue, 1993

Beijing 1995
Cuomu–Zhangguo zhongshanguo guowang zhi mu
(譽墓戰國中山國國王之墓), Beijing: Wenwu
Chubanshe, 1995

Beijing 1996a
Taiyuan Jinguo Zhaoqing mu
(太原晉國趙卿墓), Beijing: Wenwu
Chubanshe, 1996

Beijing 1996b
Jiangling Wangshan Shazhong Chu mu
(江陵望山沙冢楚墓), Beijing: Wenwu
Chubanshe, 1996

Beijing 1997
Xin'gan Shangdai damu (新干商代大墓),
Beijing: Wenwu Chubanshe, 1997

Beijing 1998
Qin Shihuangling tongchema fajue baogao
(秦始皇陵銅車馬發掘報告), Beijing: Wenwu
Chubanshe, 1998

Beijing 1999
Sanmenxia Guoguo mu (三門峽虢國墓), 2 vols,
Beijing: Wenwu Chubanshe, 1999

Beijing 2000
Qin Shihuangdi Lingyuan Kaogu baogao
(秦始皇帝陵園考古報告), Beijing: Kexue
Chubanshe, 2000

Beijing 2002
Tianshui bingshan lu (天水冰山錄), repr.
Beijing: Guji Chubanshe, 2002

Beijing 2005
Zhonguo chutu yuqi quanji
(中國出土玉器全集), vols 1–15, Beijing:
Science Press, 2005

Beurdeley 1966
Beurdeley, Michel: *The Chinese Collector through
the Centuries: From the Han to the 20th Century*,
Vermont and Tokyo: Charles E. Tuttle
Company, Inc., 1966

Birrell 1999
Birrell, Anne: *The Classic of Mountains and Seas*,
London: Penguin Classics, 1999

Chang Li-tuan 2001
Chang Li-tuan (張麗端): 'Cong yu Er' lun
Qing Qianlong zhongwanqi shengxing de
yuqi leixing yu diwang pinwei' 從玉厄論乾隆
中晚期盛行的玉器類型與帝王品味,
Gugong xueshu jikan (故宮學術季刊), Taipei:
The National Palace Museum Taipei, 2001,
pp. 61-116

Chang Li-tuan 2003
Chang Li-tuan (張麗端): 'Yu hua xun
(玉花薰)', *Gugong wenwu yuekan*
(故宮文物月刊), July 2003, p. 40

Chengdu 1985
Yan xian qing shang jian (燕閒清賞箋), by Gao
Lian (高濂), repr. Chengdu: Bashu Shushe,
1985, pp. 109–118

Clunas 1986
Clunas, Craig: 'Jade Carvers and their
Customers in Ming China', *Transactions of the
Oriental Ceramic Society*, vol. 50, 1985–6, pp.
69–85

Clunas 1997
Clunas, Craig: 'The Idea of Gu Yu', *Chinese
Jades: Colloquies on Art & Archaeology in Asia*,
18, 1997, pp. 205–14

Dubs 1938
Dubs, Homer H.: *The History of the Former
Han Dynasty*, Baltimore: Waverly Press, 1938

Eberhard 1986
Eberhard, Wolfram: *A Dictionary of Chinese
Symbols*, London and New York: Routledge &
Kegan Paul, 1986

Forsyth 1990
Forsyth, Angus: 'Five Chinese Jade Figures: A
Study of the Development of Sculptural Form
in Hongshan Neolithic Jade Working',
Orientations, May 1990, pp. 54–63

Forsyth & McElney 1994
Forsyth, Angus, and McElney, Brian: *Jades from
China*, Bath: The Museum of East Asian Art,
1994

Graham 1989
Graham, Angus Charles: *Disputers of the Tao:
Philosophical Argument in Ancient China*, La Salle:
Open Court Publishing Company, 1989

Gray 1945
Gray, Basil: 'The Oscar Raphael Collection for the Nation', *The Burlington Magazine*, 87/512, 1945, pp. 276–83

Hansford 1969
Hansford, S. Howard: *Jades: Essence of Hills and Streams*, London: Kegan Paul, 1969

Harper 1985
Harper, Donald: 'A Chinese Demonography of the Third Century B.C.', *Harvard Journal of Asiatic Studies*, 45/2, 1985, pp. 459–98

Harper 1998
Harper, Donald: *Early Chinese Medical Literature: The Mawangdui Medical Manuscripts*, London: Kegan Paul International, 1998

Harper 1999
Harper, Donald: 'Warring States Natural Philosophy and Occult Thought', *Cambridge History of China*, ed. Michael Loewe and Edward Shaughnessy, Cambridge: Cambridge University Press, 1999, pp. 223-252

Hebei 1991–3
Zhongguo yuqi quanji (中國玉器全集), vol. 6 (Qing), 1991; vol.1 (Neolithic), 1992; vol. 2 (Shang and W. Zhou), 1993; vol. 5 (Sui, Tang and Ming), 1993; vol. 3 (Spring and Autumn, Warring States period), 1993; vol. 4 (Qin, Han and Six Dynasties), 1993, Shijiazhuang: Hebei Chubanshe, 1991–3

Hebei 1994
Zhongguo fangnei miji (中國房內秘籍), Hebei: Kexue Chubanshe 1994

Hong Kong 1995
The Complete Collection of Treasures of the Palace Museum: Jadeware, Hong Kong, 1995

Hong Kong 2005
Auspicious Emblems – Chinese Culture Treasure: 45th Anniversary Exhibition of the Min Chiu Society, Hong Kong: Hong Kong Museum of Art, 2005

Hou Haozhi 2006
Hou Haozhi (侯皓之): 'Huojidang de youlai yu qizhong de manyu hanyi' '活計檔的由來與其中的滿語漢譯', *Gugong wenwu yuekan* (故宮文物月刊), December 2006, pp. 74–84

Hsu Ya-hwei 2004
Hsu Ya-hwei (徐雅惠): 'Wan Ming de gu tong zhishi yu fanggu tongqi (晚明的古銅知識與仿古銅器), *Through the Prism of the Past: Antiquarian Trends in Chinese Art of the 16th to 18th Century*, Taipei: National Palace Museum, 2004, pp. 264–75

Hua Cixiang 2002
Hua Cixiang (華慈祥): 'Ming dai yudai xingzhi ji xiangguan wenti chuyi (明代玉帶形制及相關問題芻議)', *Zhongguo Sui Tang zhi Qingdai yuqi xueshu yantaohui lunwenji* (中國隋唐至清代玉器學術研討會論文集), Shanghai: Guji Chubanshe, 2002, pp. 323–32

Huang Tsui-Mei 1992
Huang Tsui-Mei (黃翠梅): 'The Role of Jade in the Late Neolithic Culture of Ancient China: The Case of Liangzhu', PhD diss., University of Pittsburgh, 1992

Huang Xuanpei 1998
Huang Xuanpei (黃宣佩): 'Qijia wenhua yu liqi (齊家文化玉禮器)', *East Asian Jade: Symbol of Excellence*, Hong Kong: The Chinese University of Hong Kong 1998, vol. I, pp. 184–91

Huang Xuanpei 2001
Huang Xuanpei (ed.): *Shanghai chutu Tang, Song, Yuan, Ming, Qing yuqi* (上海出土唐、宋、元、明、清玉器), Shanghai: Renmin Chubanshe, 2001

Hunan 1939
Huainan wanbishu (淮南萬畢術), attributed to Liu An (*c*.179–122 BC), repr. in *Congshu jicheng chubian* (叢書集成初編), Hunan: Shangwu Yinshuguan, 1939

Jiangsu 1984
Zhang wu zhi jiao zhu 長物志校注, Jiangsu: Kexue jishu chubanshe, 1984

Jiang Tao & Li Xiuping 1998
Jiang Tao (江濤) and Li Xiuping (李秀萍): 'Guoguo mudi chutu yuqi de renshi yu yanjiu (虢國墓地出土玉器的認識與研究)', *East Asian Jade: Symbol of Excellence*, Hong Kong: The Chinese University of Hong Kong 1998, vol. 2, pp 47–65

Ji'nan 1982
Qufu Luguo gucheng (曲阜魯國故城), Ji'nan: Qilu Shushe, 1982

Ji'nan 1997
Linzi Shang wang mu di (臨淄商王墓地), Ji'nan: Qilu Shushe, 1997

Kaogu
Kaogu (考古; *Kaogu tongxun* 考古通訊, 1955–8), Beijing: Kexue Chubanshe, 1959–

Kaogu xuebao
Kaogu xuebao (考古學報), Beijing: Kexue Chubanshe, 1951–

Kaogu yu wenwu
Kaogu yu wenwu (考古與文物), Xi'an: Shaanxi Renmin Chubanshe, 1980–

Kaoguxue jikan
Kaoguxue jikan (考古學輯刊), Beijing: Zhongguo Shehui Kexue Chubanshe, 1981–

Karlbeck 1957
Karlbeck, Orvar: *Treasure Seeker in China*, London: The Cresset Press, 1957

Legge 1967
Legge, J. (edited with introduction and study guide by Ch'u Chai and Winberg Chai): *Li Chi, Book of Rite: An Encyclopedia of Ancient Ceremonial Usages, Religious Creeds, and Social Institutions*, 2 vols, New York: University Books, 1967

Li Hai 2003
Li Hai (李海) (ed.): *Hangzhou gu yu* (杭州古玉), Beijing: Wenwu Chubanshe, 2003

Li Jiufang 1993
Li Jiufang (李久芳): '*Qingdai zhuo yu gongyi gailun* (清代琢玉工藝概論)', *Zhongguo yuqi quanji* (中國玉器全集) (6), Shijiazhuang: Hebei Meishu Chubanshe, 1993 pp. 1–15

Lin 2002
Lin, James (林政昇): 'Han Burial Jades: The Role of Jade in the Han Dynasty Tombs (206 BC–AD 220)', DPhil. diss., University of Oxford, 2002

Lin 2004
Lin, James (林政昇): 'Han Dynasty Jade Utensils', *Art and Collection*, Taipei, April 2004, pp. 183–5

Lin 2007
Lin, James (林政昇): 'Armour for the Afterlife', in Jane Portal (ed.) *The First Emperor: China's Terracotta Army*, London: British Museum Press, 2007, pp. 180–191

Liu Lexian 1994
Liu Lexian (劉樂賢): *Shuihudi Qinjian Rishu Yanjiu* (睡虎地秦簡日書研究), Taipei: Wenjin Chubanshe, 1994

Liu Yang 2007
Liu Yang (柳揚): 'Translucent World: Representations of Nature in Chinese Jade', *Arts of Asia*, 37, 2007, pp. 72–85

London 1968
The Animal in Chinese Art, London: The Arts Council of Great Britain and The Oriental Ceramic Society, 1968

Lu Zhaoyin 1998
Lu Zhaoyin (盧兆蔭): 'Luelun Handai Liyi yong yu de jicheng yu fazhan (略論漢代禮儀用玉的繼承與發展)', *Wenwu*, March 1998, pp. 43–48

Markel 1990
Markel, Stephen: 'Fit for an Emperor: Inscribed Works of Decorative Art Acquired by the Great Mughals', *Orientations*, August 1990, pp. 22–36

Middleton & Freestone 1995
Middleton, Andrew, and Freestone, Ian: 'The Mineralogy and Occurrence of Jade', *Chinese Jade: From the Neolithic to the Qing*, London: British Museum Press, 1995, pp. 413–23

Moss 1993
Moss, Hugh (ed.): *The Art of the Chinese Snuff Bottle*, New York: Weatherhill, Inc., 1993

Murray 1989
Murray, Julia K.: 'Sung Kao-Tsung as Artist and Patron: The Theme of Dynastic Revival', *Artists and Patrons: Some Social and Economic Aspects of Chinese Painting*, Seattle: University of Washington Press 1989, pp. 27–36

Murray 1993
Murray, Julia K.: *Ma Hezhi and the Illustration of the Book of Odes*, Cambridge: Cambridge University Press, 1993

Neiwufu
Neiwufu gezuo chengzuo huoji qingdang (內務府各作成作活計清檔 Record of Activities in the Imperial Workshop), kept in the Palace Museum, Beijing, and National Palace Museum, Taipei

Perry 1960
Perry, Lilla S.: *Chinese Snuff Bottles: The Adventures and Studies of a Collector*, Rutland, VT, and Tokyo: Charles E. Tuttle, 1960

Rawski & Rawson 2005
Rawski, Evelyn S., and Rawson, Jessica: *China: The Three Emperors (1662–1795)*, London: Royal Academy of Arts, 2005

Rawson 1990
Rawson, Jessica M.: *Western Zhou Bronzes from the Arthur M. Sackler Collection*, Washington, DC, and Cambridge, MA: Arthur M. Sackler Foundation and Arthur M. Sackler Museum, Harvard University, 1990

Rawson 1993
Rawson, Jessica M.: 'Contact between Southern China and Henan during the Shang Period', *Transactions of the Oriental Ceramic Society*, 57, 1992–3, pp. 1–24

Rawson 1995
Rawson, Jessica M.: *Chinese Jade: From the Neolithic to the Qing*, London: British Museum Press, 1995

Rawson 1997
Rawson, Jessica M.: 'The Reuse of Ancient Jades', *Chinese Jades: Colloquies on Art & Archaeology in Asia,* 18, London: SOAS 1997, pp. 171–88

Rawson 1998a
Rawson, Jessica M.: 'Commanding the Spirits: Control through Bronze and Jade', *Orientations,* February 1998, pp. 33–45

Rawson 1998b
Rawson, Jessica M.: 'Transformed into Jade: Changes in Material in the Warring States, Qin and Han Periods', *East Asian Jade: Symbol of Excellence*, Hong Kong: The Chinese University of Hong Kong, 1998, vol. 2, pp. 125–36

Rawson 2009
Rawson, Jessica M.: *Carnelian Beads, Animal Figures and Exotic Vessels: Traces of Contact between the Chinese States and Inner Asia, c. 1000–650 BC* (forthcoming)

Shanghai 1930
Tian gong kai wu (天工開物), by Song Yingxing (宋應星), repr. Shanghai: Huatong Shuju, 1930

Shanghai 1935–7
Dong jing meng hua lu (東京夢華錄), by Meng Yuanlao (孟元老, *fl.*1126 - 1147), repr. in *Congshu jicheng chubian*, Shanghai: Shangwu Yinshu Guan, 1935–7

Shanghai 1936
Taozhai guyu tu (陶齋古玉圖), Shanghai: Sanmalu Laiqingge Shu Zhuang, 1936

Shanghai 1940
Han fei zi jiao yi (韓非子校譯), Shanghai: Zhonghua Shuju, 1940

Shanghai 1948
Gu yu tu kao (古玉圖考), by Wu Dacheng (吳大澂, 1835–1902), Shanghai: Zhonghua shuju, 1948

Shanghai 1988
Sanli tu (三禮圖, comp. by Nei Chongyi 聶崇義 in 954–959), repr. in *Sibu congkan sanbian* (四部叢刊三編), Shanghai: Guji Chubanshe, 1988

Sun Zhixin 1993
Sun Zhixin: 'The Liangzhu Culture', *Early China,* Society for the Study of Early China, Berkeley, 1993, pp. 1–40

Tainan 1999
Exhibition of Ancient Chinese Jades, Tainan: Taiwan National College of the Arts, 1999

Taipei 1955
Shuowen jiezi duan zhu (說文解字段註), Taipei: Yiwen Yinshuguan, 1955

Taipei 1965
Xi qing gu jian (西清古鑑), repr. Taipei: Daxin Shuju, 1965

Taipei 1970
Sancai tuhui (三才圖繪, comp. in 1609), repr. Taipei: Chengwen Chubanshe, 1970

Taipei 1972
Zhou li (周禮; comp. 4th–2nd century BC), repr. Taipei: Taiwan Shangwu Shuju, 1972

Taipei 1974
Zuo zhuan (左傳), attributed to a shadowy Zuo Qiuming (左丘明, probably 4th or 3rd century BC), repr. Taipei: Taiwan Shangwu Yinshuguan, 1974

Tang Chung 1998
Tang Chung (鄧聰) (ed.): *Dong Ya Yuqi* (東亞玉器), Hong Kong: The Chinese University of Hong Kong, 1998

Teng, Shu-p'ing 2007
Teng, Shu-p'ing (鄧淑蘋), Exquisite Beauty: Islamic Jades, Taipei: National Palace Museum, 2007

Wang Ming 1980
Wang Ming (王明): *Baopuzi neipian jiaoshi* (抱朴子內篇校釋), Beijing: Zhonghua Shuju, 1980

Wang Renxiang 1982
Wang Renxiang (王仁湘): 'Gu dai Daigou yongtu kaoshi (古代帶鉤用途考釋)', Wenwu, October 1982, pp. 75–94

Wang Zunguo 1984
Wang Zunguo (汪遵國): 'Liangzhu wenhua "yulianzang" shulue (良渚文化" 玉殮葬" 述略)', *Wenwu*, February 1984, pp. 23–36

Ware 1966
Ware, James R.: *Alchemy, Medicine and Religion in the China of AD 320: The Nei P'ien of Ko Hung (pao-p'u-tzu)*, Cambridge, MA: The MIT Press, 1966

Watson 1993
Burton, Watson: *Records of the Grand Historian: Qin*, Hong Kong and New York, Columbia University Press, 1993

Watt 1989
Watt, James: *Chinese Jades from the Collection of the Seattle Art Museum*, Seattle: Seattle Art Museum, 1989

Wen & Jing 1997
Wen Guang (聞廣) and Jing Zhichun (荊志淳): 'A Geoarchaeological Study', *Chinese Jades: Colloquies on Art & Archaeology in Asia*, 18, London: SOAS, 1997, pp. 105–31

Wenwu
Wenwu (文物; before 1959, *Wenwu cankao ziliao*), Beijing: Wenwu Chubanshe, 1950–

Wenwu jikan
Wenwu jikan (文物季刊), Beijing: Wenwu Chubanshe, 1980–

Wenwu ziliao congkan
Wenwu ziliao congkan (文物資料叢刊), Beijing: Wenwu Chubanshe, 1977–

Williams 1932
Williams, C. A. S.: *Outlines of Chinese Symbolism and Art Motives*, Shanghai: Kelly and Walsh Limited, 1932

Wilson 2004
Wilson, Ming: *Chinese Jades*, London: V & A Publications, 2004

Xia Nai 1983
Xia Nai (夏鼐): *Jade and Silk of Han China*, trans. and ed. Chu-tsing Li, Lawrence, KS: Helen Foresman Spencer Museum of Art, University of Kansas, 1983

Xie Duanju 2001
Xie Duanju (謝端琚): 'Huanghe shangyou shiqian wenhua yuqi yanjiu (黃河上游史前文化玉器研究)', *Gugong xueshu jikan* (故宮學術季刊), 19/2, 2001, pp. 1–34

Xu Jay 1996
Xu Jay (許傑): 'The Cemetery of the Western Zhou Lords of Jin', *Artibus Asiae*, 1996, pp. 193–231

Xu Lin 2002
Xu Lin (徐琳): 'Yuan Qianyu mu, Ming Gulin mu chutu bufen yuqi yanjiu (元錢裕墓、明顧林墓出土部分玉器研究)', *Zhongguo Sui Tang zhi Qingdai yuqi xueshu yantaohui lunwenji* (中國隋唐至清代玉器學術研討會論文集), Shanghai: Gu Ji Chubanshe, 2002, pp. 289-307

Yang Boda 1991
Yang Boda (楊伯達) (ed.): *Zhongguo meishu quanji-gongimeishu bian 9: yuqi* (中國美術全集—工藝美術編玉器), Beijing: Wenwu Chubanshe, 1991

Yang Boda 1993
Yang Boda (楊伯達): 'Sui, Tang, Ming dai yuqi shulue (隋、唐、明代玉器述略)', *Zhongguo yuqi quanji* (中國玉器全集) (5), Shijiazhuang: Hebei Meishu Chubanshe, 1993 pp. 1-29

Yang Meili 2001
Yang Meili (楊美莉): 'Yuan cang Huanghe shang, zhong you yu cong de yangjiu (院藏黃河上、中游玉琮的研究)', *Gugong xueshu jikan,* (故宮學術季刊) 2001, pp. 13–66

Yangzhou 1991
Gu yu tu pu (古玉圖譜), attributed to Long Dayuan (龍大淵, *c.* 1176), repr. Yangzhou: Jiangsu Guangling Guji Keyinshe, 1991

Yates 1994
Yates, Robin: 'Body, Space, Time and Bureaucracy: Boundary Creation and Control Mechanisma in Early China', *Boundaries in China*, London: Reaktion Books, 1994, pp. 56–80

Ye Maolin 2005
Ye Maolin (葉茂林): 'Gansu, Qinghai, Ningxia Xinjiang chutu yuqi gaishu (甘肅、青海、寧夏、新疆地區出土玉器概述)', *Zhongguo chutu yuqi quanji* (中國出土玉器全集), vol. 15, Beijing: Science Press, 2005

Zhang Guangwen 2002
Zhang Guangwen (張廣文): 'Daiyou Qinziwen xuhao de Qianlong kuan yuqi (帶有千字文序號的乾隆款玉器), *Zhongguo Sui Tang zhi Qingdai yuqi xueshu yantaohui lunwenji* (中國隋唐至清代玉器學術研討會論文集), Shanghai: Guji Chubanshe, 2002, pp. 355–67

Zuo Peng 1998
Zuo Peng (左鵬): 'Chu guo zhuyu peishi zhi yanjiu (楚國珠玉佩飾之研究)', *Jianhan Kaogu* (江漢考古), February 1998, pp. 55–66

Index

Note: page numbers in *italic* are for illustrations

First published in 2009 by
Scala Publishers Ltd
Northburgh House
10 Northburgh St
London EC1V 0AT
Telephone: +44 (0) 20 7490 9900
www.scalapublishers.com

USA Distributor: Art Media Resources, Inc.
www.artmediaresources.com

Hardback ISBN: 9781857595819
Paperback ISBN: 9781857595949

Project editor: Esme West
Copy editor: Matthew Taylor
Photographer: Michael Jones
Designer: Nigel Soper
Printed and bound in Singapore TBC

10 9 8 7 6 5 4 3 2 1

PAGE 2: Jade vase, late 18th century
PAGE 4: Jade table screen, late 18th century
PAGE 6: Jade snuff bottle, 18th century

Acknowledgements

I have been working on this catalogue since I arrived in Cambridge in September 2004. My imagination had been captured by my accidental discovery of a poem by Emperor Qianlong incised on the edge of a Han jade disc, a discovery that helped me to appreciate the quality of the Fitzwilliam collection and provided the inspiration for this catalogue.

The British Academy very kindly sponsored my field trips to China and Taiwan between 2006 and 2007, allowing me to see collections in other museums and to discuss the Fitzwilliam's collection with curators and archaeologists. I am very grateful also for the help provided by academic colleagues in Taiwan and China: Mrs Chang Lituan and Mrs Cheng Shu-fang, curators of the National Palace Museum, Taipei; Mrs Yang Meili, previous curator of the National Palace Museum, Taipei; Mr Li Yinde, the Director of Xuzhou Museum, Jiangsu; Mr Zhang Guangwen and Miss Xu Lin, curators of the Palace Museum, Beijing: and Mr Wang Zhengshu and Mr Lu Pengliang, curators of the Shanghai Museum. Professor Dame Jessica Rawson, Dr Julia Poole and my friends Peter Chare and Dr John Shakeshaft have been kind enough to read through the manuscript carefully and have made many useful suggestions. My colleague Dr Adam Stevens very kindly helped with proofreading.

This catalogue is a result of teamwork. I owe a debt to my colleagues, particularly the Director of The Fitzwilliam Museum, Dr Timothy Potts, and Assistant Directors David Scrase and Margaret Greeves, who have kindly supported this project. Dr John Brown, one of the Syndics, and Mrs Sue Rhodes have raised funds for the catalogue and exhibition. Miss J. S. Ringrose, Honorary Archivist at Pembroke College, Cambridge, along with Nicholas Robinson and Lewis Tiffany, librarians at the Fitzwilliam, have helped me to locate references to those important jade donors to our museum; my niece, Lin Yi-hui, has kindly helped me with ancient Chinese characters; the photographer, Michael Jones, has been very patient and produced many stunning images for the catalogue; and technicians Andrew Maloney, Nik Zolman, Amy Tufts and secretaries Anna Lloyd-Griffiths, Sandra O'Neill and Barbara Burstein have all given valuable assistance in the creation of both the exhibition and this catalogue. Last but not least, this catalogue could not have been published without the generous financial support provided by Daniel Eskenazi, Roger Keverne, The Mellon Fund and Marlay Group.

JAMES C. S. LIN
The Fitzwilliam Museum, Cambridge
January 2009